DEATH IN THE MODERN WORLD

D0218036

Sara Miller McCune founded SAGE Publishing in 1965 to support the dissemination of usable knowledge and educate a global community. SAGE publishes more than 1000 journals and over 800 new books each year, spanning a wide range of subject areas. Our growing selection of library products includes archives, data, case studies and video. SAGE remains majority owned by our founder and after her lifetime will become owned by a charitable trust that secures the company's continued independence.

Los Angeles | London | New Delhi | Singapore | Washington DC | Melbourne

DEATH IN THE MODERN WORLD

Tony Walter

Los Angeles | London | New Delhi
Singapore | Washington DC | Melbourne

Los Angeles | London | New Delhi
Singapore | Washington DC | Melbourne

SAGE Publications Ltd
1 Oliver's Yard
55 City Road
London EC1Y 1SP

SAGE Publications Inc.
2455 Teller Road
Thousand Oaks, California 91320

SAGE Publications India Pvt Ltd
B 1/I 1 Mohan Cooperative Industrial Area
Mathura Road
New Delhi 110 044

SAGE Publications Asia-Pacific Pte Ltd
3 Church Street
#10-04 Samsung Hub
Singapore 049483

Editor: Natalie Aguilera
Assistant editor: Eve Williams
Production editor: Katherine Haw
Copyeditor: Solveig Gardner Servian
Proofreader: Rebecca Storr
Indexer: Cathryn Pritchard
Marketing manager: George Kimble
Cover design: Francis Kenney
Typeset by: C&M Digitals (P) Ltd, Chennai, India
Printed in the UK

© Tony Walter 2020

First published 2020

Apart from any fair dealing for the purposes of research or private study, or criticism or review, as permitted under the Copyright, Designs and Patents Act, 1988, this publication may be reproduced, stored or transmitted in any form, or by any means, only with the prior permission in writing of the publishers, or in the case of reprographic reproduction, in accordance with the terms of licences issued by the Copyright Licensing Agency. Enquiries concerning reproduction outside those terms should be sent to the publishers.

Library of Congress Control Number: 2019949071

British Library Cataloguing in Publication data

A catalogue record for this book is available from the British Library

ISBN 978-1-5264-0293-6
ISBN 978-1-5264-0294-3 (pbk)

At SAGE we take sustainability seriously. Most of our products are printed in the UK using responsibly sourced papers and boards. When we print overseas we ensure sustainable papers are used as measured by the PREPS grading system. We undertake an annual audit to monitor our sustainability.

CONTENTS

ABOUT THE AUTHOR

Tony Walter is Emeritus Professor of Death Studies at the University of Bath, UK. His research into death and society has included end-of-life care, social networks and care, funeral practice, bereavement, spiritualism, belief in reincarnation, the idea that the dead become angels, mass media and social media, pilgrimage, and the use of human remains in exhibitions. He has lectured around the world, and has also trained clergy and funeral celebrants. His 17 books include *Funerals* (1990), *Pilgrimage in Popular Culture* (1993), *The Revival of Death* (1994), *The Eclipse of Eternity* (1996), *On Bereavement* (1999), and *What Death Means Now* (2017). Before 1994, he was freelance, writing books and articles on religion, landscape, social security reform, and basic income.

ACKNOWLEDGEMENTS

It would be impossible to acknowledge everyone who over thirty years has in one way or another influenced this book. Of course, none of them are responsible for the result.

Among the many who have stimulated and extended my sociological imagination, I am particularly indebted to David Clark, Grace Davie, Christie Davies, François Gauthier, Allan Kellehear, Linda Woodhead, Michael Young, and Shahaduz Zaman. I have also greatly benefitted from belonging to the University of Bath's *Centre for Death and Society*, not least its mind-stretching seminars and conferences and its academic visitors from around the world. The University library's extensive holdings and ever helpful staff have also been invaluable. Further afield, I have been sustained by regular meetings with kindred scholars in Alba Iulia (Romania), Dumfries (Scotland), Nijmegen (the Netherlands), Sigtuna (Sweden), Zurich and Fribourg (Switzerland); and I have valued feedback on public lectures given in Denmark, Germany, Romania, Japan and New Zealand where I outlined the framework which eventually became this book.

Many international students and kind hosts around the world have opened my eyes to how others 'do death', including Kumiko Hori and Hiroshi Yamazaki (Japan), See Mieng Tan (Singapore), Ruth McManus (New Zealand), Kingston Kajese and Jenny Hunt (Zimbabwe), and Renske Visser (the Netherlands). Practitioners in several countries have taken time to show me around their hospice, funeral parlour, crematorium, temple, or shrine. Friends and colleagues with no specialist knowledge have gone out of their way to help in one way or another; Maya van Trier (Belgium), Jan Otto Andersson (Finland), Bruce and Val Ayres-Wearne (Australia), Stephen Nickless, and Peter Cressey (UK) are just a few who come to mind. Thank you also to my Sociology students for permission to quote from their class memos.

And so to the book itself. Thank you to Joanna Wojtkowiak who back in 2009 suggested I write the book. SAGE's nine – yes nine – anonymous reviewers offered constructive comments on the original proposal, many of which I have incorporated, and the following have given helpful feedback on various chapters: Candi Cann, Chao Fang, Cynthia Goh, John Harris, Ida Marie Høeg, Christoph Jedan, Annika Jonsson, Anne Kjaersgaard, Rebekah Lee, and Nina Parish.

Finally, my sincere thanks to Mandy Robertson for providing a place and the time in which to write.

If I have forgotten anyone, please accept my apologies. And if the book has got anything wrong, which – given its breadth – is entirely possible, the responsibility is mine alone.

INTRODUCTION: DEATH'S JIGSAW

Death comes to all humans, but how death is managed, symbolized and experienced varies widely, not only between individuals but also between groups. What then shapes how a society manages death, dying and bereavement today? Are all modern countries similar? How important are culture, the physical environment, national histories, national laws and institutions, and globalization? This is the first book to look at how all these different factors shape death and dying in the modern world – in other words, the first book to attempt to complete the entire jigsaw.

Many writers contrast death in the modern world with previous eras. There is a heroic narrative of modern medicine and sanitation banishing infectious disease and radically increasing human longevity. And there is another narrative of increased psycho-social risk, as medicalization and professionalization detach dying and bereaved people from the community and religion that are nostalgically supposed to have supported them in past times. I do not peddle either narrative. I argue that what is distinctive about modern dying and grieving, and there is much that is distinctive, interacts with culture, environment, economic (in)security, and national history and institutions to create considerable variety.

Thirty years ago, as I was writing the book that comprised my first venture into this field (Walter, 1990), I felt my writing was slipping and sliding around. One paragraph was certainly true of England, but probably not Scotland or Northern Ireland; the next paragraph might be true of all English speaking societies; the next of all advanced industrial societies throughout the world; the next of northern western European countries but not of Eastern Europe, Mediterranean Europe or the USA, and certainly not of Japan or China; and so on, and so on. But it was not an academic book for which precision was essential, so I carried on writing regardless.

The unresolved issue of national differences in death practices has intrigued me ever since. When in the mid-1990s I began to teach the sociology of death at bachelors and then masters level and looked around for suitable textbooks, I found that most of them – especially those written by authors from powerful countries like the USA or once powerful countries like the UK – mix up modernity and their own national culture and institutions.[1] Worse still, I got the impression these authors did not even know they were mixing things up. Bryan Turner (1990: 343) has observed this in other areas of sociology: 'Since its formal inception in the first half of the nineteenth century, sociology has been, generally implicitly, located in a tension or contradiction between a science of particular nation-states and a science of global or universal processes.' Since comparing one group (such as a nation) and sub-group (such as men and women, or social classes) with another is the essence of sociological analysis, these death-related textbooks were not going to help my students understand whether various deathways were due to modernity, to national histories, to culture, to power relationships, or to what. So the present book is particularly concerned to identify national differences – even at a time when some consider the nation state to be withering in the face of globalization and transnational institutions.

So much depends on time and place – on when and where you were born. There are about 56 million deaths a year across the world, and most of these are in 'developing' societies (Clark et al., 2017). In terms of place, this book focuses on the minority of global deaths that occur in 'developed' countries – which is not to say that the rest of the world never appears in the periphery of my lens. In terms of time, my focus is the present day – how the present is shaped by the past, and how economy, society, history, geography, and culture interact in complex ways to shape people's experiences of dying and grief. People's economic position is central to my analysis, which draws more on the concept of economic insecurity (Inglehart, 1981; Standing, 2011) than on traditional concepts of social class. Examples come from many countries, though (reflecting my own reading, travels and contacts) not equally. I write more, for example, about the USA and the UK than any other countries; more about China than India, Japan than Korea, the Netherlands than France, Denmark than Norway, Serbia than Bulgaria.

Unlike many books on death and society, this one does not have chapters devoted to dying, to funerals, to burial and cremation, or to bereavement. Instead, each chapter discusses a key factor (such as money, communication technologies, economic in/security, risk, the family, religion, war) that shapes the organization and experience of dying and loss; I then invite you the reader to work out how each factor operates in your own country or society, and so to understand how your own society manages death. My aim is not to tell you about your own society but to provide sociological tools to help you understand it – each chapter ends with a question or questions inviting you to do just this. Please note that the book's division of chapters into social factors rather than aspects of death means that some substantive topics – such as hospice, compassionate community, funerals, or grief – appear in more than one chapter.

I hope you will find this an interesting journey. You may have heard of the Mexican Day of the Dead, or of Irish wakes, or you may know that euthanasia is permitted in certain countries. But apart from a few such practices, many people who are very aware of national differences in, say, cuisine may be totally unaware of the very many differences, big and little, in how modern nations handle death and dying. I don't believe this is because people don't want to think about death. I have taught health care and other practitioners who are passionate about their work with the dying and bereaved, yet whose eyes pop out of their heads when fellow students from elsewhere describe their country's deathways.

Many Britons, for example, have no idea that Britain is the only European country not to re-use graves every 10–20 years; most Americans have little idea how uniquely American are their funeral customs.

Parts I and V look at factors that profoundly affect the deaths of everyone who lives in an advanced industrial society. Parts II, III and IV look at differences, both within and across societies. Part I shows how certain economic and technological developments shape modern deathways in similar ways, whatever the society. Part II focuses on risk and insecurity. Modern societies generally create a more economically secure life for their populations, yet can also create considerable insecurity – especially in the early stages of modernization, and later when de-industrialization and globalization erode traditional heavy industry. Economic security/insecurity radically influences many aspects of death, dying and grieving. And as well as minimizing old risks, such as premature death through famine or cholera, modernity also creates new risks, not least environmental. So the effects of modernity are highly variable, depending on precisely where and when you live. Part III looks at culture, specifically individualism, family, and religion. Part IV on the nation state focuses on the key period in which each nation modernized, long-term consequences of war, and national institutions (plus the ideology and politics that always accompany formal institutions). Highlighted throughout is 'path dependency' – how institutions, policies and practices start, shapes how they continue. To give a simple example, a nation's idea of 'hospice' depends partly on whether hospices in that nation began with cancer sufferers (UK), the frail elderly (the Netherlands), or people with AIDS (Switzerland). Part V considers to what extent globalization may be erasing some of the differences between nations and within nations, and asks 'what is death's future?'.

Most social science writers on death and dying have focused on just a few factors, just a few pieces of the jigsaw. Allan Kellehear (2007), for example, has shown how economic structures have shaped dying across the millennia, which I consider in Part I; historian Philippe Ariès (1981) highlighted the power of ideas and culture, which I consider in Part III; and Ruth McManus (2013) has applied theories of globalization, which I introduce in Part V. As well as these pieces of the jigsaw, this book adds new pieces to the puzzle – risk and the environment (Part II), and the nation (Part IV). I also apply theories (such as post-materialism) and perspectives (such as comparative analysis) that have not hitherto been used to illuminate why we moderns deal as we do with the end of life.

Note

1. The exceptions emanate from countries that struggle to retain their identity vis-à-vis more powerful neighbours, such as Canada (Northcott and Wilson, 2008) or New Zealand (McManus, 2013).

PART I

MODERNITY

Modern societies are often thought of as affluent and urban, with skyscrapers rather than mud huts gracing the skyline, and there is some truth in this picture. But modernity's most profound impact on individuals, families, and society has been in reducing premature death. Plague, famine, and even arguably war have been controlled (Harari, 2015). As countries develop economically, death for most is postponed into old age, often into late old age, something that few humans throughout history and prehistory could have hoped for. Indeed, economic development from pre-industrial to post-industrial typically more than doubles life expectancy at birth. This extraordinary achievement results from economic and technological development, not least in food production and distribution, sanitation, and medicine – it is in extending human lives that modernity's domestication of nature most deeply affects the lives of individuals and families. As philosopher Stephen Cave (2012) puts it, civilization comprises a series of life-extension technologies: agriculture, engineering, public health, pharmaceuticals. Of course, worrying evidence of environmental damage, global warming and drug-resistant bacteria indicates limits to modernity's control of nature and hence of death – limits which Part II will consider.

For now, Part I examines how economic and technological developments have shaped not only life expectancy, but also the experience of dying, the organization of funerals, expectations of the bereaved, and relationships between the living and the dead. A study of Iran's capital city Tehran found that those with greater access to money and education not only benefit from improved life expectancy but are also 'more individualistic, more secular, more interested in consumerism, tend to show greater emotional restraint in the face of loss and grief, and are generally minimalistic in their death-related rituals' (Bayatrizi and Tehrani, 2017: 18). Modernity affects everything to do with death, dying and grief.

What, though, is modernity? Clearly it entails economic and technological development, urbanization, bureaucratic organization, and structural differentiation whereby health care, schooling, religion, family, and so on become separate social institutions. Even those who live in the countryside in modern societies have access to clean water, modern communications, expert health care, and most of modernity's other benefits. According to Elias (1978), modernity also increases cultural and personal control over the body and its emotions, both of which are challenged at the end of life when the body no longer responds to its owner's instructions and emotions may be out of control. It used also to be thought that modernity undermines religion, but this is becoming much less certain when we expand our gaze from twentieth-century Europe to the entire twenty-first century globe (Chapter 10).

Part I oscillates between economic and technological change. Chapter 1 looks at one of the major consequences of improved economic and material conditions, namely a doubling of the average human lifespan between pre-industrial and post-industrial times. Chapter 2 looks at 'techniques of health' that dominate how dying, the dead body and mourning are seen in modernity. Chapter 3 goes back to economics, exploring how modernity values and prices life, death and care. Chapter 4 returns to technology, discussing the new communication technologies that are re-shaping twenty-first century dying and grieving. Chapter 5 asks whether all this adds up to a modern 'denial' or 'sequestration' of death and dying.

1

LONGEVITY

Throughout prehistory and most of history, human life expectancy at birth has been 25–35 years and in unusually healthy societies 30–40 years; this includes many deaths in infancy. It is only since the second half of the nineteenth century that the adult death rate has come down significantly in modern western societies, and only since the early twentieth century has the infant mortality rate dramatically declined. Worldwide, average life expectancy has increased at almost three months per year since the mid-nineteenth century, amounting to a total increase in lifespan of around 40 years, though for most countries this increase has only been manifest since the Second World War. Globally, newborns can now expect to live to 72. For several of the most economically developed countries, the figure is 82–84 years and still growing, though longevity in highly industrialized countries with very unequal income distributions such as the USA has yet to reach 80. Between 1960 and 2016, longevity in most of the world's poorer countries, such as Nepal, Afghanistan, and Ethiopia, has risen dramatically – in Nepal doubling from 35 to 70 (Figure 1.1). In 2015, 55 per cent of deaths worldwide were at age 65 or over, up from 41 per cent in 1990 (United Nations, 2017). By historical standards, this is a quite extraordinary achievement.

Country	1960	2016
Afghanistan	32	64
Nepal	35	70
Somalia	37	56
Benin	37	61
Ethiopia	38	65
India	41	69
China	44	76
Iran	45	76
Algeria	46	76
Bangladesh	46	72

(Continued)

Figure 1.1   (Continued)

Country	1960	2016
Saudi Arabia	46	75
Morocco	48	76
Zimbabwe	52	61
South Africa	52	63
Brazil	54	75
Mexico	57	77
Cuba	64	80
Argentina	65	77
Russian Federation	66	72
Singapore	67	83
Ukraine	68	71
Japan	68	84
Germany	69	81
Italy	69	83
Spain	69	83
USA	70	79
France	70	82
Ireland	70	82
UK	71	81
Australia	71	83
Canada	71	82
Iceland	73	82
Sweden	73	82
Netherlands	74	82
World	**53**	**72**

Figure 1.1   Life expectancy at birth (the average number of years a newborn is expected to live if current mortality rates continue) (World Bank https://data.worldbank.org/indicator/ SP.DYN.LE00.IN – accessed 6 February 2018)

There are, however, exceptions to this trend (Seale, 2000). From 1975 to 1995, life expectancy at birth fell in 16 countries, mainly African countries engulfed by the AIDS epidemic and newly independent states that emerged out of the USSR where increases in cardiovascular disease, accidental poisoning, suicide, and homicide followed the fall of communism. In Uganda where AIDS was the main cause of death for young adults in Uganda, life expectancy at birth fell from 56 to 41. In Russia, male life expectancy fell dramatically with the fall of communism, from an average of 64 for the years 1985–1990 to 57 in 1994. Those countries which, by contrast, have had stable and continuing communist governments have fared much better; from 1960 to 2016, life expectancy at birth in China has risen from 44 to 76, and in Cuba (with a very low per capita income but the world's most egalitarian health care system) from 64 to a staggering 80 – a figure otherwise reached only by very affluent countries.

As shown by Russia, Ukraine, Zimbabwe, and Somalia (Figure 1.1), political turmoil that causes economic stagnation or decline can limit or even reverse gains in longevity. In Britain, where austerity measures have restricted health and welfare expenditure since the 2008 economic crash, life expectancy has stalled since 2010 and has gone down in several economically declining areas (Smyth, 2018), as it has in the USA where drug deaths are increasing (Tinker, 2017). Economic change and economic reform can cause people to die (Schrecker and Bambra, 2015), even while the overall global picture is of increasing longevity.

Economic development is therefore strongly associated with longevity, but it is not the only factor (Day et al., 2008). Longevity is undermined if a nation, however affluent overall, is economically very unequal. The greater the economic inequality within a nation, the bigger the social class difference in risk of death from almost all causes, and this affects everyone including the affluent (Wilkinson and Pickett, 2009). Why this should be is a matter of some debate, but one possibility is that inequality undermines social cohesion, which increases everyone's stress, fear, and insecurity (Figure 1.2). The beneficial health outcomes of economic equality are clearly demonstrated by Cuba.

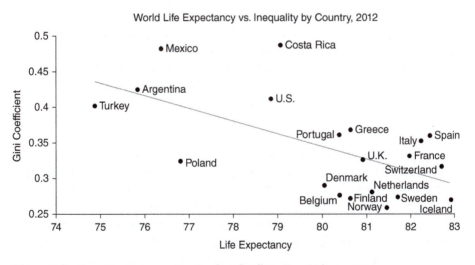

Figure 1.2 Inequality (measured by the Gini Coefficient) and life expectancy

The simple statistic of life expectancy at birth masks variations not only in gender, social class and ethnicity but also in how the chances of dying in any one year are spread over the lifespan. In pre-industrial societies, childhood and especially infancy were times of very real danger. This is illustrated from the records for 1813 of my local parish church in Widcombe, a village of labourers and small businesses servicing upper-class visitors to the nearby spa town of Bath. Taking 28 consecutive deaths at random, we find the following ages at death: 0.9, 1.7, 51, 0.9, 23, about 70, 70, 69, 15, 2, 17, about 80, 77, 9, 5, 4.7, 0.11, 6 weeks, 21, 60, 38, 28, 41, 0.6, 24, 1.8, 73, 10 days.

Several things are clear from this pattern. First, infancy was the most dangerous period; second, deaths in childhood after infancy were not uncommon; third, those who survived childhood had a fair chance of reaching 70; fourth, very few people lived much beyond 70. This is consistent with one analysis of longevity in hunter-gatherers for whom the most common age for adults to die is around 70, 'before which time humans remain vigorous producers, and after which senescence rapidly occurs and people die. We hypothesize that human bodies are designed to function well for about seven decades in the environment in which our species evolved' (Gurven and Kaplan, 2007: 322). This was alluded to 3,000 years ago by the writer of Psalm 90: 'The days of our years are threescore years and ten; and if by reason of strength they be fourscore years, yet is their strength labour and sorrow; for it is soon cut off, and we fly away.' Few lived much beyond 70, and for those who did it was not always a pleasure.

PREMATURE DEATH: CAUSES AND CURES

What then caused people to die before the three score and ten that God and/or evolution has allotted us as a species? The most common cause was infection, revealed also in the Widcombe church records. Thus from 1752-1764 there were 45 or so burials a year, but in 1766 there were 80 burials and in 1775 there were 93, of which 57 were of children. Clearly an epidemic – possibly cholera – struck the village in these two years, and children were the most susceptible. Kellehear (2007) argues that infectious diseases came to be the prime cause of death thousands of years ago in the Neolithic revolution when small bands of nomadic hunter-gatherers settled down to become agriculturalists. Settling in one place, they came to live cheek by jowl with a larger number of fellow humans, 150 perhaps in a village rather than 30 in a hunter-gatherer band. Early farmers also lived and slept close to their animals – good conditions for the spread of infectious disease not only from human to human but also from animal to human. Famine became more likely as communities came to depend on just one or two crops; crop failure benefitted those who could afford to keep a surplus from the previous year, in turn enhancing their power and further impoverishing those with no surplus – who in turn would have less strength to fight infections or not succumb to starvation. Settlement created inequalities of wealth, in turn causing differences in life expectancy.[1]

It has also been argued that, while egalitarian hunter-gatherer societies were relatively peaceable, permanent settlement increased the likelihood of violent death: people could not easily move away from conflict or natural disaster, more centralized power meant that people could be ordered to fight, territories were more defined and likely to be fought over, and crop productivity could increase population pressure and attendant conflict (Ferguson, 1997). Others, such as Pinker (2012), have strongly argued that there never was a violence-free hunter-gatherer paradise, and indeed that violence has steadily declined over the very long run through to the present day – though European colonialism and war-mongering over the past half millennium have proved particularly violent. State expansion, incorporating tribal groups into nation or empire, has both pacified local conflicts and incited new forms of inter-state violence.

Whatever the details of humankind's long history of plague, famine and war, it is clear that by the time humans start to urbanize and industrialize, the main killer, most of the time, is infectious disease. It is also clear that modernity has controlled such diseases not by high-tech medicine but by public health measures, particularly improvements in sanitation and nutrition. Clean water, flushing toilets, and efficient sewers as standard accoutrements of both urban and rural living have done wonders for human health. Immunization against some diseases has also helped. Twentieth-century developments such as penicillin, antibiotics, and other curative medical measures played a surprisingly small role in the battle against premature death.

LIVING BEYOND 70: CAUSES AND CONSEQUENCES

With premature death in advanced industrial societies now a relatively rare occurrence in peacetime (and hence particularly tragic when it does occur), what has surprised a wide range of scientists is that longevity in old age continues to increase. Not only are most people getting to 70, but more and more are living to 80, 90, and even 100. Why is this? Here it seems that curative medicine in the form of surgical operations and drugs have been somewhat successful in, for example, extending the lives of many with chronic heart disease. Immunization against influenza and antibiotic treatment for pneumonia is keeping alive some older people who otherwise would have succumbed to these infections. Old people in the twenty-first century are also reaping the benefits of improvements in the twentieth: a lifetime of good nutrition, the shift from body-crushing manual labour to office labour, fewer accidents at work, elimination of city smog, and (more recently) reductions in smoking means people enter old age in better shape. Members of advanced industrial societies today who get to 60 or 70, but not to 80 or 90, have often reaped the bitter rewards of cigarettes, asbestos or other products of modernity that, for them, were not controlled in time.

Whatever the causes, the chief consequence is that death now resides mainly within the province of old age. If getting to 70 was once a cause of thanks to God, today not getting to 70 is often seen as an offence against the natural order, a tragedy.

So if relatively few people in modern societies die prematurely of infectious disease, what does everyone else die of? In essence, the non-communicable diseases to which they are now vulnerable are caused by longer lives which allow time either for cells to grow abnormally (as in cancer) or for the body to deteriorate through old age (leading for example to heart attacks, stroke, lung disorders and dementia).

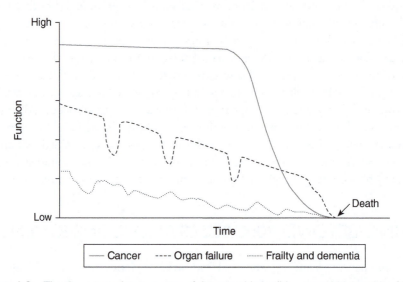

Figure 1.3   The three typical trajectories of dying in old age (Murray and McLoughlin, 2012)

This leads to new kinds of what sociologists call 'dying trajectories'. Whereas infections generally kill over a few days or a week or two, dying in older age often takes months or years. Figure 1.3 shows the main patterns of dying at older ages:

1. With cancers, functioning can often be maintained for months or years before a rapid decline a few weeks before the end.

2. Organ failure comprises a series of episodes (such as heart attack or stroke) each of which, though not fatal, reduces subsequent functioning until the final fatal episode. Living with such a condition, or conditions, can last years or decades, with decreasing functioning lowering quality of life and morale.

3. Frailty 'is the fragility of multiple body systems as their customary reserves diminish with age and disease' (Lynn and Adamson, 2003: 5). Often including dementia, it entails 'prolonged dwindling'; with few reserves, small setbacks easily escalate.

Trajectories 1, 2 and 3 each account for around 30 per cent of those who die in advanced industrial societies. In trajectories 2 and 3, predicting when death will come is not at all easy. In most advanced industrial countries, the proportion of people dying on trajectory 1 (cancer) is going down, while those dying on trajectory 3 (frailty) is going up.

The longer we live, the more likely we are to age and die with multiple conditions. The same person may develop arthritis in their fifties, have two heart attacks in their sixties, develop lung disease in their seventies, and then develop dementia in their eighties. Each condition impacts on the others – physiologically, pharmaceutically, and in terms of lifestyle. Each condition needs managing, primarily through drugs whose combination also needs managing because a drug that eases one condition may worsen another. What the person will eventually die of and when is difficult to predict, and it is quite likely that at no point will they be given a terminal diagnosis (Kellehear, 2016).

I now look at some social and spiritual consequences of so many people in the modern world living so long, and then experiencing slow, sometimes unrecognized, dying.

DYING

Allan Kellehear's ambitious *A Social History of Dying* (2007) covers all of history and much of prehistory. Though details of his analysis of hunter-gatherers have been disputed, his book clearly shows that each era's typical dying trajectory has profound social and spiritual consequences. He argues that adult death in hunter-gatherer societies often came quickly, for example in childbirth or in an accident. With little or no time to prepare for death, he argues that *dying* came mainly after physical death. This is evidenced by the concept, typical of such societies, of an otherworld journey, of the soul going on a journey from this world to, eventually, the next, mirrored in shamanistic trance journeys to other realities.

The shift to permanent settlement, whether village or ancient city, enlarged the scale of social organization and enabled a division of labour; one of the first specialized occupations, engaged in by people who did not have to grow their own food, was that of the priest. So dying came to be presided over by priests, and in time by the rites of what now have come to be called 'world religions'. This first 'professionalization' of dying therefore involved not doctors, who had little to offer at the deathbed, but religious professionals. Infections offered the dying person and their family a few days' notice that death was imminent, so preparations could be made *before* the physical death – which in the European Middle Ages were termed the *ars moriendi*, the art of dying. As well as discussions with the family about property and other practical matters, spiritual preparations could be made; after death, most religions also provide ongoing rituals to help the soul on its way. This is the kind of dying that modern people often think of as 'traditional' or 'pre-modern'.

The recent shift to prolonged dying after a long life, however, profoundly unpicks this 'traditional' dying. If the traditional *ars moriendi* took just a few days, what is someone today with metastatic cancer, heart disease, chronic lung disease or elderly frailty – perhaps compounded by dementia or crippling arthritis – to do with their remaining months or years? This question has been addressed in the case of cancer by the hospice and palliative care movement which encourages people to live their dying their own chosen way; 'the aim is to increase the quality not the quantity of however much time remains'(du Boulay, 1984). It dominates the debate about elderly frailty: what quality of life is possible for those who have survived all their peers and whose painful, unresponsive bodies dominate their every hour and every movement of hand, arm or leg? It is what drives calls for euthanasia and assisted dying; if there is little quality in a person's remaining years, then should they not have the choice to end their life now?

It can also lead to what Kellehear (2007) calls 'shameful dying'. If the new 'good death' of palliative care and euthanasia is where the person takes control of their life and dies as they would want, what about those who cannot take control: those with dementia, those who are mentally and/or communicatively incapacitated by stroke or coma, those whose lives are taken over by heroin or other life-threatening addictive drugs, those caught up in or fleeing war and civil war? Religious prayers and rites preparing them for heaven might make their deaths good enough, but the contemporary secular emphasis on control and choice condemns them to shameful dying.

All these profound shifts in how humans think about and try to manage dying are rooted in one simple thing: economic development. Our current dilemmas about the end of life are those of economically developed societies. Developing societies have slightly different issues. Rapidly ageing, as Figure 1.1 shows, they too are beginning to experience the modern world's dying trajectories, but without the pharmaceutical and palliative care enjoyed by the West (Seale, 2000; Berterame et al., 2016).

GRIEVING

Premature death

By the mid-nineteenth century my locality of Widcombe had become somewhat urbanized. It comprised a small but significant upper and upper-middle class, a fair number of tradespeople, and a large labouring class – many of whom lived cheek by jowl in insanitary housing, typical of the time as Britain rapidly industrialized and urbanized. With more people living close together and before public health measures began to benefit the poor, the death rate – especially of children – increased. This is revealed in many of the stones in the new Widcombe churchyard, built for this new working class (Figure 1.4).

What was it like for Jane Bourn to lose five children over 13 years? What were her thoughts as she herself fell ill and died a year later? Was she concerned about her religious salvation? Or about who would look after any surviving children? Who survived her? Other children, her husband? How did they manage? Did their grief cripple them or, did they simply struggle on as best they could – with one or more children going out to work, or older children looking after any remaining younger children, or the husband re-marrying?

FREDERICK BOURN
died 21 January 1838 aged 15 months

EDWIN BOURN
died 6 January 1842 aged 1 year 9 months

ALBERT BOURN
died 2 February 1842 aged 6 months

MATILDA BOURN
died 21 July 1850 aged 4 months

LOUISE BOURN
died 16 September 1851 aged 6 weeks

JANE BOURN mother to above children
died 22 December 1852 aged 43 years

Figure 1.4   Bourn gravestone, Widcombe, Bath

Safely Gathered Home

FRANK PARSONS
Died Oct 24th 1870 Aged 3 years

EMMA PARSONS
Died Jan 31st 1881 Aged 15 years

SARAH PARSONS
Died May 12th 1882 Aged 19 years

JOHN PARSONS
Father of the above
Died June 26th 1896 Aged 55 years

LOUISE wife of the above
Died March 13th 1902
Aged 63 years

"Rise, He calleth thee"

Figure 1.5   Parsons gravestone, Widcombe, Bath

The Parsons family (Figure 1.5) were doubtless thankful that their children survived infancy, but then experienced the sadness of first a 3-year-old, and then a 15- and then a 19-year-old dying. And what about the religious inscriptions 'Safely gathered home' and 'Rise, he calleth thee'? Do they indicate a faith that provided comfort in the face of such loss, as some historical studies suggest (Rosenblatt, 1983)? Or was this simply a conventional form of words expected in a more religious era than Britain today?

What we do know is that multiple infant and child deaths within a family characterized not only rapidly urbanizing nineteenth-century Britain but also the slums, favelas and shantytowns of the global South as urban populations exploded in the later twentieth century. Historians (Dye and Smith, 1986) and anthropologists (Scheper-Hughes, 1990) have enquired into how parents, especially mothers, dealt with multiple child deaths. They certainly knew that young deaths were natural, part of the order of things. But did that reduce their sense of loss? Did they limit their attachment until the child had got through the dangerous early years, as Philippe Ariès (1962), who wrote influential books on the history of both childhood and death, argued? Even a deeply attached mourner, with practical matters of survival dominating and so many other mouths to feed, may have had to put grief on hold, perhaps indefinitely (Stroebe and Schut, 2008).

What about infant and child death in advanced industrial societies today? When I show the Bourn and the Parsons gravestones to my first year sociology class, there is shocked silence. Young people today do not expect their siblings, their peers or – when they become parents – their children to die. Today's 'natural' (but in truth, historically recent) order is that parents should raise to maturity not only enough children to reproduce their genes but *all* their children. Child death, once all too common, is now deemed unnatural. Modern parents who lose a child may also lose their faith in a god who should not let such a thing happen. Few if any would echo Montaigne, the sixteenth-century French philosopher who wrote 'I have lost two or three children in infancy, not without regret, but without great sorrow.' Expecting some of his children to die perhaps gave Montaigne resilience.

The underbelly of general longevity today, by contrast, is that premature death has become an obscenity; it challenges what Parkes (1988) terms the mourner's 'assumptive world', in this case the assumption that people ought to live to old age. Some bereaved parents report that other parents who had been their friends now avoid them, for they have become reminders of the unmentionable. This is not, as is often supposed, an example of 'disenfranchised grief' (Doka, 2002), a loss that is not recognized; rather it is what I would call 'hyper-enfranchised grief' – a grief so terrible that others fear to come close to those enduring it. Consequently, support groups for bereaved parents, and research into how modern parents cope after the death of a child, are major growth areas. If others do not know how to support the grieving family, then those with special knowledge – other grieving parents and experts – may be able to (Riches and Dawson, 2000). What was once all too normal has become a specialist field, whether the specialists be professionals or other grieving parents.

The rise of intimate grief

As societies modernize and death rates in infancy and childhood decline dramatically, so do birth rates and family size. Instead of five, six, or seven births, only around two births per family are needed in order for family and society to reproduce themselves. The consequence is that close personal attachments (parent–child, sibling–sibling, grandparent–grandchild) are made with fewer people, and are likely to last many decades. Offspring may be in their sixties when the parents eventually die; a sibling relationship may last 80 or 90 years before eventually being sundered by death (or by dementia). Even a grandchild–grandparent relationship may last several decades. So when a close family member dies, grief may be felt by relatively few people, but very intensely. This is especially likely in societies where nuclear rather than extended families are the norm (Lofland, 1985).

But there is a contradiction. Though the death of an old person may be intensely mourned by a few intimates, the social, economic, and political gap they leave is often minimal, both within the wider family and within the workplace (Blauner, 1966). Children have long since left home, grown up, and become economically self-sufficient. The old person's death does not impact the workplace, because he or she had retired – and the bureaucratic organization of work means that, should a worker die, they may be replaced. Though social activities may increase on retirement, in later old age social connectedness may decrease as the person becomes frail and housebound and as peers die. In their final years, the old person is unlikely to wield much power within society or family: no longer head of a household responsible for young children, they may also have stood down from any leadership roles within the community. Pensions, life insurance and welfare benefits mean their survivors are not left destitute in the way survivors were in times past when a breadwinner died. So the world goes on much as it did before, yet a bereaved spouse and maybe one or two other family members are devastated. When in times past people died 'in harness' as workers and as raisers of children, many social and economic adjustments had to be made and, as in urban Senegal today (Ribbens McCarthy et al., 2018), loss was talked about largely in terms of these adjustments – children having to go out to work, other family members stepping in to help raise children, and so on (Marris, 1958). Now loss is talked about less as a social and economic matter, and more as an inner psychological process – loss has been internalized, individualized, psychologized.

This shift is illustrated by Cruse Bereavement Care, the UK's internationally respected leading bereavement charity. When founded in 1959 it focused on the social and economic concerns of widows whose working-age husband had died (Torrie, 1987). Its first Fact Sheets dealt with income tax, housing, health and diet, pensions, insurance, children's education and training for work. Only later, as more and more people died in old age, as welfare benefits expanded and as more women entered employment, did Cruse's focus shift from economic welfare to psychological counselling. Cruse also began to work with anyone who has been bereaved, including a significant number of adult daughters whose elderly parent had died; inheritance meant they were more likely to gain than suffer economically from the person's death, yet the personal pain of losing a parent to whom they had been close for many decades could prove hard.

Because of the high cost of raising a child in contemporary society, another group of bereaved people who stand to gain financially by the death yet who find themselves devastated and whose loss is indeed often seen today as the cruellest of all, are parents who have lost an infant or young child. In agricultural societies and in the early decades of industrialization, children are economic assets to the family who put them to work; in advanced industrial societies, they comprise the family's biggest expenditure (after perhaps the mortgage) yet are prized in themselves beyond value (Ariès, 1962), so a child's death leads to perhaps the most intense pain known to post-industrial men and women.

This lack of fit between personal loss and socio-economic-political readjustment finds expression in the funeral. Whereas the depth of grief depends on personal attachment, the scale of a funeral depends on something else: social recognition. Throughout human history, the scale of a funeral within any one society – measured by its cost and the numbers of mourners attending – depends on how involved the person was in social, economic, and political life, on their social status and on how many people depended on them. So I can guarantee that the funeral of a monarch or a serving political leader will be a far grander affair than my own! Their deaths will create far more organizational disruption and require more organizational readjustment, not to mention possible jockeying between contenders for the position of power that the death has made vacant. Pop stars and celebrities with major followings also leave a big gap in their many fans' lives, reflected in their funeral or in social media mourning.

At the other end of the spectrum, the funeral of a 95-year-old who is deeply mourned by her children and perhaps a surviving sibling may attract only a handful of mourners; many of the deceased's peers have themselves died, while connections with friends, neighbours and others may have withered as infirmity kept her housebound or in a care home. A sad little gathering of perhaps only a dozen people gather in the crematorium to say their farewell. This picture characterizes societies such as Britain where people attend the funerals of those they know. However, in some modern countries – for example Ireland and Japan, and to an extent the USA – you go to a funeral if you know the deceased *or* one of the chief mourners, which means that several hundred may attend the funeral of an elderly person. (When I ask my students if they have attended the funeral of someone they didn't know, or whether they would attend the funeral of their boss's mother, the British majority look perplexed or even aghast; the few who raise their hands and say 'Of course!' are usually Irish or Japanese.) This illustrates this book's main argument: that what modernity produces – in this case a gap between intimate grief and organizational adjustment when an old person dies – may be responded to differently according to culture, national history, and other factors. Modernity structures death and loss, but it never determines people's responses.

MIGRATION, HOME AND WORK

There is another structural reason for the contemporary construction of bereavement as a psychological rather than socio-economic process, and it has to do with the interaction of longevity with two other phenomena that are common in the modern world: migration, and the separation of home and work. Let me illustrate.

Although ancient Rome at its height had a population of one million, most people in pre-industrial societies lived in small, stable rural communities of often no more than one or two hundred people. With high child and infant mortality, families needed to be large in order to reproduce the population. Death, usually of a child or a parent with dependent children, left behind a household in mourning, comprising one or both parents and a number of children, typically living in poverty within a one-room dwelling. Grief was therefore inevitably a shared experience, with mourners crammed together in the same small space. 'Shared' did not necessarily mean good or comfortable, for individuals grieve in different and sometimes mutually incomprehensible ways (Doka and Martin, 2010); so the potential in the cramped pre-industrial cottage for mourners' behaviours, feelings and reactions to disturb one another would have been considerable. Beyond the household in mourning was the village, whose inhabitants, though not all related to the deceased, at least had known the deceased so were all co-mourners, even if lesser mourners. In rural Europe, the tolling church bell announced that the village as well as the family had lost a member.

The longevity, geographical mobility, and separation of home and work that typically accompany urbanization and industrialization have created a radically new social context for mourning. Today's typical death of an old person leaves behind, if they are the first to go, an elderly spouse and also adult children, each of whom may live in a different town or even continent and who go out to work with colleagues who never knew the deceased. Thus the main mourners are no longer co-resident, and may spend much of each day in the company of people who never knew the deceased. This means that grief becomes a more private experience. Some of those encountered in a typical day may 'support' the mourner, but they do not share his or her grief because they did not know the deceased. They are positioned not as co-mourners but as potential supporters; it is in this context that we hear talk of 'supporting the bereaved'. With the decline of mourning dress in many post-industrial societies (Taylor, 1983), others may not even know that the person is grieving. Grief becomes hidden (Gorer, 1965).

In the pre-industrial village, for better or for worse everyone knew each other. By contrast today, many people have disparate social networks – not only their family and their work colleagues, but also perhaps fellow members of a sports club, a veterans club, a faith community, individuals they met on holiday decades ago and have kept in touch with, and so on. When a member of one of my social networks dies, other members of that network become my co-mourners, but not those in my other networks as they did not know the deceased. So I may mourn the death of a fellow sports player and share my feelings and my memories with other players, but my family, my colleagues at work and the couple I've kept in touch with since that great holiday 24 years ago, did not know the deceased. This is illustrated when a young person goes away to university. If a student's university friend dies, her grief is not shared by family or friends back home; or if her beloved grandmother dies, her grief is not shared by friends at uni – however supportive they may be.

This historical emergence of grief as a private, lonely, inner experience which others met in the course of a typical day can 'support' but cannot share does not need to be explained in terms of some uniquely modern 'denial' of death. It can be explained more simply, and more demonstrably, as I have done above, in terms of the social and geographical consequences of economic forces.

Social media

This 'privatizing' of grief is, in part, being reversed by a recent technological development: social media. All communication media since the invention of writing have enabled humans to communicate at a distance, and twenty-first century social media comprise the most recent major development in communication (to be explored more in Chapter 4). In life, general social media such as Facebook enable members of my various social networks to know about, and even communicate with, each other. When I die, these people will be my mourners and – like mourners in a pre-industrial village, but unlike mourners in pre-social-media modernity – they will post messages of grief and condolence which will be read and possibly responded to by others. And just like in a pre-industrial village, differences in grieving styles may become an issue. New issues may arise, such as the intimate grief of close family getting taken over by the volume of upbeat social media posts by those who are far less deeply affected by the death, raising the question who will manage the deceased's social media page and how (Walter, 2015a). Social media afford possibilities to transcend the fragmentation caused by geographical mobility, separation of home and work, and disparate social networks that characterizes the lives and deaths of so many people in the modern world. In raising the profile of a wider range of lesser mourners, social media unravel grief's typically modern intimacy.

SOCIAL CONSEQUENCES OF LONG LIVES

The radical drop in infant and child mortality, and the likelihood that most people will now die in old age after a long life, have marked consequences not only for dying and grieving, but also in many other areas of life not necessarily associated with mortality, such as education, family life and feminism (Goldscheider, 1971).

The old

First, the elderly no longer have rarity value. This can reduce or enhance their status and power in society. On the one hand, their increased numbers may come to be perceived as a 'burden' by the working population, especially in those countries which experienced a post-1945 baby boom which in coming decades will become an ageing and dying boom, supported by the comparatively smaller numbers born since the 1960s. The Japanese population is experiencing unprecedented ageing, while China's 1979-2015 one-child policy will in due course make it a hyper-ageing society dependent on relatively few of working age. On the other hand, the sheer numbers of the elderly contain the potential to become a major economic and political force. For example, with more older than younger Britons voting in the 2016 referendum to leave the European Union, 'Brexit' was in part a result of the grey vote. As was noted after the referendum, the 'democratic' one-person-one-vote system gives old people with only a few years left to live as much influence over a country's long-term future as young people with 60 years still to live. Whether viewed positively or negatively, today's elderly really matter economically and politically.

The young

Second, as already noted, because parents no longer need produce many children to reproduce the population, birth rates have dropped dramatically; children are no longer valued workers but emotional treasures and a major cause of consumption. Socially expected mourning for a deceased child now greatly exceeds that for an elderly person, whereas traditionally the death of a child required little formal marking. Historically, the drop in infant mortality and the greater

solicitude given them have probably been both cause and effect of each other –
assuming your children will live enables parents to take greater delight in them,
and looking after them with more care helps them live longer.

Education, career, divorce

Third, the reduction in family size together with an expectation of 65 or more
years between puberty and death make all kinds of new social formations possible. Educating people until their mid-twenties becomes a rational investment.
And with pre-school children occupying only a few of her 65 or more years
post-puberty, a woman can now plan what to do with her life as well as, or
indeed instead of, bear and rear children. It is only in low-mortality societies that
higher education, feminism, and women's careers become mass possibilities.
Meanwhile many marriages end not in death but in divorce, as couples face
strains of longevity unknown to most couples in pre-modern societies.

Social arrangement	1813	2013
Childbirth	Dangerous	Safe
No. of children	6–10	2
Infancy	Several die	Very few die
Marriage	Divorce unavailable	Half end in divorce
	Usually ends in death	Half end in death
Spouse dies	After 5–20 years of marriage	After 40–60 years
Average marriage	10–20 years	10–20 years
Children	Lose parent through death	Lose parent through divorce
	May not outlive parents	Expect to outlive parents
Parent dies	When child is young	When child is middle aged
Babies occupy	All of woman's adult life	<5 out of 65 yrs post-puberty
Work	From age 7 till death	From 16/22 till 60/65
		(half total lifespan)

Figure 1.6   Social consequences of the mortality revolution

It is not that longevity causes these new social arrangements; rather, longevity
makes them possible. Like social media, it affords possibilities. Religious, cultural
and other factors shape people's attitudes and hence which of these possibilities –
such as liberal divorce and abortion laws, higher education, and equality for
women in the workplace – individuals or entire societies decide to opt for.

The mortality revolution that makes these new social arrangements possible
may be summarized in Figure 1.6. This compares 1813 – the year from which I
extracted typical years of death from my local church records – with 200 years

later. The numbers given in each column are not exact, but indicate what was common and therefore to be expected then and now – not only in my own locality but in most countries that urbanized and industrialized in the nineteenth and twentieth centuries.

CONCLUSION

This chapter briefly outlined how modernization causes a demographic transition in which high death rates and high birth rates are replaced by low death and birth rates. Dying in old age after a long life has moved from ideal to reality for most of the developed world's population and for many in the developing world too. Dying today of degenerative disease typically takes months or years, rather than the mere week or two that infectious disease often needed to kill. This necessitates a whole new 'craft of dying' (Lofland, 1978).

The demographic transition profoundly shapes grief. In small families there can be more intense attachments between parents and children, and between siblings. The death of an old person who is no longer economically active or raising children can leave a big emotional and relational hole for family survivors, but does not cause the economic loss that the death of a working-age parent caused pre-modern mourners. And in small, mobile families whose members go out to work, mourners are separated from each other, making grief a more private, inner experience. The proliferation of long lives also affords new possibilities in many other areas of life, such as the political power of the elderly, the solicitude now given to children, mass higher education, and careers for women as well as for men. The changing profile of death has widespread consequences for life.

FURTHER READING

- Blauner, R. (1966) 'Death and social structure', *Psychiatry*, 29: 378-94.
- Goldscheider, C. (1971) 'The mortality revolution', in C. Goldscheider (ed.), *Population, Modernization and Social Structure*. Boston, MA: Little Brown.
- Kellehear, A. (2007) *A Social History of Dying*. Cambridge: Cambridge University Press.
- Lofland, L. (1985) 'The social shaping of emotion: the case of grief', *Symbolic Interaction*, 8 (2): 171-90.
- Riley, J. (2001) *Rising Life Expectancy: a global history*. Cambridge: Cambridge University Press.
- United Nations (2017) *World Mortality 2017*. New York: United Nations Population Division.

Questions to discuss

- Imagine you live in a society in which few live to old age. How would this affect living, dying and grieving?

- Considering societies in which infant mortality is common, do you think it possible for a baby to die and its mother not to be grief stricken?

Note

1. This picture is simplified. On some Pacific islands and on the Pacific coast of Canada, hunters whose main prey is an ample supply of fish have lived in settled communities for millennia.

MEDICINE

This chapter discusses not specific medical and health technologies, such as drugs, MRI scanners, or sewage systems, but health techniques: practices, policies, modes of organization, and power that place dying, death, and bereavement firmly, though not totally, within the orbit of medicine and health. These practices and modes of organization can shape how lay people as well as professionals think about dying and loss. When the family of a gravely ill person are asked how she or he is, the answer may well comprise, or at least include, a report on their physical condition couched in medical terms: 'The nurses are giving him morphine and that has helped' or 'The operation failed, and she's declining fast'. Non-medical answers such as 'He was pleased the priest came to give him the last rites' or 'She accepts that it won't be long now' may or may not supplement an otherwise medical answer.

This chapter first sketches how dying, death, management of the physical remains, and even grief are all placed under regimes of medicine and health – what has been termed the 'medicalization of death' – before digging a bit deeper to unearth related processes – rationalization, professionalization, institutionalization. Then I look at how this adds up to a 'death system', before exploring recent attempts to re-centre dying and grieving within family and community, with medicine as servant rather than master.

MEDICALIZATION

Dying

Until the nineteenth century, the priest had more power to help the dying soul to heaven than the doctor had to ameliorate bodily pain and symptoms, so families were more likely to call the priest than the doctor to attend the dying person. Today by contrast, the doctor is widely thought to be of more use than the priest. Even in hospices committed to holistic care of mind and spirit as well as body, new patients expect to be assessed by a doctor as a matter of course;

seeing a religious professional or 'spiritual care provider' comes later and is optional. The dominant discourse is secular and medical; religion is an optional extra, even in hospices with a religious foundation.

In pre-modern times when death usually occurred at home and followed the swift and linear-decline trajectory of infectious disease, most adults and even children had witnessed enough deaths to tell whether a sick family member was dying. That this intimate knowledge of dying is rare today is cause for thanksgiving, but it does mean that lay people now usually need doctors and other health professionals to tell them that someone they love is dying. Whether they are told, and how they are told, is another matter. In English speaking countries, both the individual person and their family are usually now told in good time if a person's cancer is terminal, but this is much less likely with multiple organ failure or the prolonged dwindling of late old age (Figure 1.3). In these scenarios, predicting how long the person will live is an inexact art (Christakis, 1999), and health professionals may focus on trying to treat or at least manage each new symptom as it develops – often at the request of patient or family. Without any conversation about impending death, the actual death may come as a surprise to the family – at best they may receive just a few days' or hours' notice. At this late stage, if a hospitalized patient is not in a good enough condition to participate in decision making, it can be stressful for health professionals to meet a shocked family and work with them to make joint decisions in the patient's best interest (Wilson, 2017).

Whether dying is recognized sooner or later, it continues within the medical frame of illness. A key question for dying people and their families is what type of medical assistance they wish or can afford. Kellehear (2016) identifies four kinds of such assistance, or what he calls 'medical rescue'. One is palliative care, which aims to rescue the person from pain and symptoms so she or he can put affairs in order and death can take its natural course. A second, in those jurisdictions in which it is legal, is 'euthanizing medicine' – medically assisted dying, which rescues the person from a lingering death. Third, are repeated stays in hospital until attempts to patch up one organ after another fail. Fourth, the frail aged may experience dying in care homes, in the hope they will be rescued from the abandonment and isolation that might otherwise accompany the erosion of their physical and cognitive capabilities. In each case – apart from the 10 per cent who die suddenly and unexpectedly – dying is managed by health care professionals.

Critics of the modern way of dying, from Illich (1976) onwards, have often been disturbed by its medicalization. Two points need to be made here. One is that few of the critics would wish to return to a pre-modern world when modern painkillers and other kinds of medical assistance were not available. The other is that though people may say in good health that they would like a natural death at home among their family, when it comes to actual dying they may prefer skilled professional care in hospital. This was a common response in a recent ethnographic study with people dying in Germany. As one woman being cared for at home said:

Being in love with me doesn't teach my husband how to change a catheter, right? And then there's this stuff that's always existed between us. I tell him how to do things right, and he can't, and I get a little angry, and he feels criticized ... when I am lying in bed and he has to do everything, then I don't dare say anything. He feels that he does nothing right, and once I say one little thing about how he should turn me in bed, for example, he explodes and thinks that he does everything for me but that I always criticize him ... Then I feel guilty ... what's the good in that? (Menzfeld, 2017: 317)

Dependency, one of the greatest fears of individualistic westerners, can be easier to handle if one depends on paid professionals rather than on family members. Some do not want a son or daughter to see them naked, and to wash them. Others are all too aware that the family member who cares for them also has a job, children to look after, and a household to run, and do not want to over-burden them.

Death

Medicalization continues at the moment of death and in its immediate after-math. As the UK's National Health Service website puts it:

Confirming death used to be straightforward. Death was said to occur when the heart stopped beating and a person was unresponsive and no longer breathing. The lack of oxygen, which occurred as a result of no blood flow, quickly led to the permanent loss of brain stem function.

Confirming death is now more complex, because it's possible to keep the heart beating after the brain stem has permanently stopped functioning. This can be done by keeping a person on a ventilator, which allows the body and heart to be artificially oxygenated ...

To save a person's family and friends from unnecessary suffering, once there's clear evidence that brain death has occurred, the person will be disconnected from the ventilator.[1]

This new definition of death as cessation of brain stem rather than of heart/lung activity results from two medical technologies. One, as the quote suggests, is the ventilator which may be routinely used in certain conditions or during and after some surgical operations; this creates ethical problems and difficulties for staff and families because putting a patient on a ventilator is an easier decision emotionally and ethically than is removing it in the knowledge that the person will die. The other medical innovation is transplant surgery, which in the case of major organs requires the dying/dead person to be kept artificially ventilated – and hence their organs oxygenated – until the relevant organs can be 'harvested'.

After every death, a certificate must be signed by one or more doctors confirming its cause; before this can be done, post-mortem examination of the body or, in certain legally prescribed circumstances, referral to a coroner may also be necessary. Death certification has two purposes, one medico-legal, the other curative-medical, and both concern the modern state's regulation of its population (Foucault, 1973). The first purpose is to assure the state that the person did not die by illegal means, either directly (say, through murder or arson) or indirectly (perhaps through medical negligence or sub-standard workplace safety measures). The second purpose is to enable the subsequent collation of annual statistics of the causes of death among the population as a whole; only thus can health services within a jurisdiction know whether or not progress is being made in reducing each cause of death, both among the total population and among various sub-groups (age, gender, social class, etc.). Death certificates and the ensuing statistics are a key health technique. Whether through transplant surgery or death certification, the personally known and loved dead are used to enhance the health of society's living members.

How does the family experience the death certificate's continuation of medicalization even after death? It can be both painful and positive. On the one hand, a known and loved individual with all her quirks and oddities is reduced to data for collation with other data into statistics. There is a profound mismatch between the personal grief of family and friends, and the impersonal needs of state and society. Family members may find it painful to learn the exact cause of death, or to see listed on the certificate contributory factors such as alcoholism that they feel stigmatize the deceased's lifestyle and amount to an officially negative final judgement on the life. On the other hand and more positively, many families want to know what the person died of. The idea that a person can die of nothing identifiable is unacceptable to most modern people, for reasons I explore below in the section on 'rationalization'. To know that the state will not allow a body to be buried or cremated until all measures to establish the cause of death have been exhausted, to some families, speaks of an official concern and care for each individual, however lowly their social status. Either way, whether experienced positively or negatively, state-sponsored medicalization cannot be avoided after death in any modern country.

The body

In addition to the certification required after all deaths, some bodies may continue as medically useful objects for some time after their demise. The person before death, and/or their family after death, may agree for organs to be donated for transplant surgery, or for the whole body to be donated for dissection in the cause of medical research or teaching.

Dead bodies can harm as well as benefit the health of the living. Almost all bodies – or what is left of them after dissection or organ removal – are either buried or cremated, processes which national laws ensure do not endanger the living. Though legalities and practicalities differ between countries, this almost always means disposal in a legally designated burial ground or in an officially approved crematorium or (in the USA) crematory. A crematorium or burial ground may or may not be designed with religious needs in mind, but in the modern world it will certainly be designed according to public health and environmental regulations. For example, graves are not to pollute water courses, and cremation exhausts should be scrubbed clean of airborne mercury from tooth fillings. In other words, the disposal of the dead is not to endanger the health of the living.

Mourning

Even after the body has been safely buried or burned, medicalization continues. Mourners who are not coping well are more likely to see a doctor than any other kind of professional (such as a therapist or priest). Irrespective of whether or not the mourner seeks medical relief from their suffering, bereavement is increasingly seen as a psychiatric condition – and psychiatry is a specialty within medicine. If pre-modern mourning was governed by religious and community norms, modern mourning is instead, or also, seen as an inner psychological process whose workings have been revealed by the researches of medically qualified psychiatrists such as Sigmund Freud (1984), John Bowlby (1980) and Colin Parkes (2008) as well as by non-medically qualified psychologists such as William Worden (2003) and Margaret Stroebe and Henk Schut (1999).[2] Whether or not mourning is timetabled according to religious rites at set times after the death – as in Judaism, Hinduism, Roman Catholicism and Eastern Orthodox Christianity – it is increasingly understood in terms of the temporal dynamics of 'the grief process' (Wambach, 1985). As well as, or instead of, religion and community, it is psychology that provides guidance and a timeframe. Formally classifying grief, or certain forms of grief (e.g. complicated, or prolonged) as a psychiatric condition, however, is contentious, for it opens the door to treatment by psychiatrists – who might welcome this as it enhances their client base and enables them to assist in the relief of suffering, but health care organizations and insurance companies might not welcome the cost implications. Chapter 13 looks at this in a bit more detail.

We now look at some processes linked to medicalization, namely rationalization, professionalization, and institutionalization.

RATIONALIZATION

Statistical death

Before the scientific revolution started in seventeenth-century Europe, across the world a person's death was generally seen throughout the world as an act of God, the result of supernatural forces, of someone's misdemeanour, or of witchcraft. At the start of the Jewish/Christian scriptures, for example, the book of Genesis depicts death not as natural but as the result of human sin. There was no telling when death would come. In the late European Middle Ages, death came to be pictured as a skeleton – the Grim Reaper – with his own power; a common image in European art became the man or woman going about their daily business but with a skeleton, personifying death, tugging at their coat tail or tapping them on the shoulder. In 'death and the maiden' pictures, the skeleton was portrayed embracing, violating, a young woman. Mortal illness could strike anyone, not just in times of plague, with little warning and with death following in a matter of days; death was capricious, its timing known only by God.

This changed in the 1680s with the mathematical notion of probability (Hacking, 1975; Prior and Bloor, 1992). Applied not long after in France to church records of deaths, it became apparent that mortality was patterned, your chances of dying early being higher, for example, in town than in the countryside. In the gaze of the statistician, death afflicts not individuals but populations and sub-populations, and its modus operandi is not capricious but predictable. Once this became apparent, the state took an interest in collecting mortality data; it became possible to start what we now call the 'life insurance industry'; and ordinary individuals came to realize that death is no longer the Grim Reaper, an act of God, but the result of identifiable medical causes. It is in this context that the possibility of a person dying of no known cause became unacceptable, abhorrent even. So today, citizens give their personal mortality data to the state, and in return the state provides the family with a rational, verified cause of death.

In the eyes of the late twentieth-century social philosopher Michel Foucault, this was a political as well as a mathematical achievement. In his eleventh lecture at the College de France in 1976, Foucault described how late eighteenth-century France supplemented the state's longstanding sovereign power over individual life and death with regulatory technologies of life, controlling not individual bodies but whole populations, intervening in the birth and death rates, controlling biological disabilities, and manipulating the environment. All this became necessary 'to govern the economic and political body of a society that was undergoing both a demographic explosion and industrialization' (Foucault, 2003: 249). Public health measures and population control, in other words death and life, become central to how modern states regulate and manage their populations. Birth and death certification are foundation stones of this regulatory technology.

Science – sponsored by state and by business – continues to make death known rather than capricious. Only since the early 1960s when the theory of plate tectonics was confirmed has there been a unified schema in which 'volcanoes, earthquakes and other geologic upheavals are viewed as ordinary and ongoing manifestations of the planet's crustal dynamics' (Clark, N., 2014:23). Environmental science tells us that floods may be caused by human action, such as deforestation hundreds of miles upstream. Hitherto, such natural disasters had been categorized by insurers as 'acts of God' and were uninsurable. They may still be uninsurable; or with improved local geological or environmental knowledge, insurance premiums may rise in risk areas.

Science is likewise promising to revolutionize medicine. Because not every breast cancer is the same, and because individuals differ genetically, twenty-first century research into individualized medicine goes a step further, using micro-biology and genetics to tailor drugs to the individual, not to a disease category. The hope is that treatment will succeed with every individual, not just with a statistical proportion of those given a diagnosis. Over time, predicting the vulnerability of particular communities to earthquake or volcano, and the responsiveness of individuals to specific medical treatments, promises to become ever more accurate. However religious individuals or communities may be, death is now understood and controlled through the application of human reason, empirical evidence, and scientific and statistical analysis.

Bureaucracy

Death's rationalization occurs not only because of scientific advance, but also because of the bureaucratic organization of health care. Modern hospitals, general practice, and social care provided to frail people living at home operate on bureaucratic lines, and could hardly operate at scale any other way. Anthropologist Sharon Kaufman (2005) shows how American hospitals shape the end of life has changed since the 1960s when Glaser and Strauss (1965) and Sudnow (1967) conducted their classic sociological studies of hospital dying. The drivers of change are technology and funding systems which replace a passive waiting for death with active choices between ethically tricky and financially consequential options.

Kaufman (2005: 17) observed that hospital and medical language 'emphasizes problem-solving and decision-making ... Such language ignores or redirects incoherence, anxiety, breakdown, diffuse suffering, and any other expression of affect that lacks rationality.' Favoured terms such as 'control' and 'choice' are neat, abstract concepts assuming individual autonomy, but Kaufman shows these to be illusions. Improved sharing of information between doctors, nurses, patients, and families has not reduced inappropriate aggressive treatment or resuscitation. 'First ... patients and families ... do not know what to want, other than recovery or an end to suffering in a general sense. Second, [in hospital] ... health professionals' ability to act with conviction is constrained' (pp. 34–5). The choices available to patients and families are 'guided and limited by the options physicians and others present. Those, in turn, exist within a system of institutional directives' (pp. 47–8). Patients and families are required to choose, but only at certain times, and only certain choices are available. Patients, families and often staff themselves understand neither the system that drives all this, nor the organizational and financial constraints on choice.

Such processes may also be observed in hospice care in the USA. Hospice care is reimbursable by Medicare, but only for those with a diagnosis of less than six months. This means that people with considerable pain or symptoms but an uncertain or lengthy prognosis (as is often the case with conditions other than cancer) may be ineligible for care, while those suffering much less but with a clear diagnosis within the approved timeframe receive hospice care. Since resources are not infinite, any health care system has to devise rational and equitable ways to allocate care; inevitably, the consequences for some individuals are perverse and inequitable.

McDonaldization?

If Max Weber saw rational organization as key to western modernity, George Ritzer sees McDonald's fast-food restaurant as the epitome of contemporary rational organization (Ritzer, 2018). Around the world, organization after organization, like McDonald's, is characterized by efficiency, calculability, predictability, control, and an irrational rationality. So is health care, and in particular care of the dying and dead, McDonaldized? The medical management of the dead body and of body parts certainly seems to be organized this way. Care of the dying is more debateable. On the one hand, there are clear systems to ensure efficiency, calculability, predictability, and control. Bed occupancy and use of operating theatres in hospitals are kept as near 100 per cent as possible. Dying patients for whom active treatment is no longer warranted may be sent home or to a care home in order to release the hospital bed for more treatable patients. Should a patient die in hospital, as many do, there is no time for the dead body to rest there in peace, for the bed is needed by the next patient; the body has to be moved promptly to the morgue. Personal care for those dying at home is costed as 'care packages', and care plans are drawn up to maximize use of the carer's limited time; staying competitive in the care market entails cutting costs.

On the other hand, though McDonaldized care systems are devised by managers, accountants and – in socialized medicine, politicians – who are remote from actual face-to-face, hand-to-buttock care, those who do the actual care have to relate to real suffering human individuals and to struggling households. It is not surprising if such workers attempt and may often succeed in injecting a humanity that is not costed in the 'care package'. This has been observed in studies of care work; aides find satisfaction in exercising autonomy on behalf of their clients, so they can care *about* as well as *for* them. In other words, they may go the extra – uncontracted – mile (Brown and Korczynski, 2017). Likewise, a study of low-paid front-of-house funeral home employees who meet with the family to arrange the funeral often allow their humanity to over-ride company targets for selling unnecessarily expensive coffins (Bailey, 2010).

As Zygmunt Bauman (1989) argued in his book *Modernity and the Holocaust*, impersonal – and often inhumane – bureaucracy thrives in large organizations with a long chain of command between executives and those who actually work with customers, clients or patients. Therefore those making organizational deci-sions never meet those affected by the decisions. The degree of freedom of the 'foot soldiers' to subvert inhumane bureaucracy is certainly greater in twenty-first century health care than in the Nazi death camps to which Bauman compares modern mega-organizations. A senior nurse was recently asked on British televi-sion what advice she would give to her daughter currently training to be a nurse; she replied, 'Never stop caring'. She knew both the organizational pressures to stop caring, and the possibility of resisting those pressures.

PROFESSIONALIZATION

Critics of death's medicalization have often supposed that doctors were the first professionals to claim authority at the deathbed, expropriating and undermining lay knowledge and expertise. But as I noted in Chapter 1, Kellehear's (2007) historical survey questions this; doctors are simply now the most significant of a range of professionals who claim knowledge of dying. The problem with modern death is therefore not so much that it has become medicalized, but that it has long been professionalized.

In modern societies today, death has come to be managed not only by doctors but also by an increasing range of health and related professionals. This includes nurses with fancy titles such as 'clinical nurse specialist in palliative care' which clearly proclaim that dying requires considerable expertise (however down-to-earth the nurse herself may be). Also helping to care for those near the end of life are occupational therapists who support patients whose health prevents them from doing the activities that matter to them; art and music therapists who help patients express and communicate their feelings about dying; social workers who advise with financial or family problems; care workers who operate within care homes or in the person's own home; not to mention highly trained ambulance crew who transport dying people to hospital after a life-threatening event or care crisis. After death, in many countries a funeral director removes the body as soon as practicable from the place of death to the funeral parlour where care of the body is performed by the parlour's staff rather than the family, though some religions insist on lay members caring for the body. Families increasingly defer to professionals, especially to those who care directly for the dying or dead body; such care therefore becomes removed from families, who may then come to fear the dying, and especially the dead body.

This process of differentiation – in which more and more functions (in death as in life) are split off from the family into separate institutions which become more specialized and focused on their core functions – is one of modernity's core processes (Parsons, 1966). To explain the proliferation of death-related professional expertise we do not need to make recourse to death-related explanations (such as a supposed 'death-denying' society); it's just that the increasing division of labour and the increasing specialization of expertise are what happens as societies modernize.

Dying's professionalization does not mean that the dying person is cared for most of the time by professionals. On the contrary, most care is given by family members. And there are significant inequalities, especially between those dying with cancer who are most likely to qualify for hospice and palliative care, and the frail elderly who are least likely to qualify. Thus in Denmark,

> while nursing staff in the hospices are highly trained, this is not always the case elsewhere, particularly in nursing homes and home care. Likewise, while the staffing in a Danish hospice is one nurse to a handful of patients, the night staffing in a Danish nursing home involves one nurse assistant being responsible for (and alone with) between 24 – 48 residents of whom around 80% may suffer from dementia. (Timm, 2018)

Denmark is far from alone in this disparity. Across the modern world, medical and professional expertise in care of the dying can go hand in hand with poorly trained, low paid or unpaid daily care. And in most modern countries, most families have totally delegated caring for the *dead* body to paid functionaries (i.e., to funeral directors and their staff).

INSTITUTIONALIZATION

The location of the dying, and especially of the dead, body is crucial, for possession of the body grants a kind of ownership (Sudnow, 1967; Howarth, 1996). Paid staff who care for a dying or dead body in hospital, nursing home or funeral parlour have considerably more control over the body and hence over decision making than do those working in the patient's own home. However 'open' a hospital, care home or funeral parlour announces itself to be, it still controls who may visit and when; even it does not restrict who may enter, staff retain the right to request visitors to leave because, for example, institutional schedules require the body (living or dead) to be prepared for the night or to be prepared for medical or post-mortem procedures.

The institutionalization of the dying has been increasing throughout the modern era, first in sanatoria, then in hospitals and nursing homes and now in hospices (Elias, 1985) so that in many advanced industrial countries today around three-quarters of the population draw their last breath in an institution (Gawande, 2014). Despite their name, care homes are where people die as well as are cared for; nursing homes are where people die as well as are nursed; and hospitals designed to cure their patients are where many, sooner or later, die. Countries vary as to which kind of institution is the most likely place of death – in Norway, for example, it is the nursing home; in the UK, it is the hospital. But whatever the kind of institution, the management of dying by specialist professionals and the institutionalization of dying are parallel consequences of modernity.

One consequence is that dying is somewhat hidden. Many people in the modern world arrive at adulthood, even middle age, without ever having been present when someone draws their last breath – the deathbed's location within an institution conspires with longevity, small families and geographical mobility to remove the deathbed from life's everyday arenas. Again, one does not need to invoke notions such as death 'denial' to explain this removal of the deathbed, this 'sequestration' (Mellor and Shilling, 1993) of the dying from the living. It is a simple matter of modernity's differentiation of social institutions. The family's functions are split off and extended; we place children in school, and the dying in hospital.

Limits to institutionalization

That said, though the last breath is more often than not taken in an institution, much of the time spent dying may have been spent either at home or in a de facto home such as a residential facility for the elderly (Kellehear, 1990, 2016). In the modern world, the living therefore have witnessed dying even if they have not witnessed the last breath or the hours immediately preceding it. Here we may note Kellehear's (2014: 9) non-medical definition of dying as 'the personal expectation and acceptance of death as an imminent event' where 'imminent' may mean seconds (e.g. in the case of being shot), minutes, hours, months or (e.g. in Alzheimer's) years; dying means being aware that something is killing me, whether that be violence, accident or illness. As Chapter 1 showed, most of us nowadays spend a long time dying, in and out of institutions.

Nor should we assume that all institutions are, in sociologist Erving Goffman's (1961) term, 'total' – excluding outsiders and degrading their inmates. Though old-style hospitals and institutions where once many were born and where many died were difficult for outsiders, even family members, to access (Townsend, 1964), we have come to understand the dehumanizing effect of such institutions. This is an example of science (in this case, social science) revealing some of the risks (in this case, dehumanization) caused by early modernity's management of life and death, to be explored further in Chapter 6. Consequently, institutional boundaries in late modernity have become much more porous (Walter, 2017b); visiting hours, for example, are much more relaxed. At the same time, in some countries such as India where hospitals do not always provide hotel as well as medical services, other family members may be a regular fixture at the hospital bedside, feeding and toileting the sick family member.

In addition, the smart phone, a technology to be considered further in Chapter 4, is beginning to break down the clinic's walls. A study of Swedish women with terminal cancer found that when a woman visits the hospital clinic for chemotherapy or for tests it is not unusual for her to take a selfie and then immediately post it, generating short empathic responses in the form of hugs, hearts and smileys (Lagerkvist and Andersson, 2017). Even when physically alone with machines and with health professionals, she is surrounded by as much love from family and friends as is the Indian hospital patient. Hospital inpatients may use social media and other communication technologies to link with the outside world, even in the long hours of the night. The main limit to such activity is age; almost everyone is now online apart from some of the very old, who – comprising many of the dying – remain particularly vulnerable to the isolation from the outside world that institutionalization can bring.

THE DEATH SYSTEM

Medicalization, rationalization, professionalization and institutionalization add up to what Kastenbaum (2007) terms a country's 'death system' – an integrated set of practices for managing the dying and then the dead body and the grieving family. Most modern countries' death systems display fundamental similarities, including much of what this chapter has described, similarities caused by each country having to manage the same demographic facts or by copying other countries' responses (Beckfield et al., 2013). But each country's death system also has its peculiarities, often rooted in national institutional histories (see Chapter 13). To give just one example, the coroner system in all English-speaking countries can be traced back to the medieval English coroner, but the modern coroner's duties have evolved somewhat differently in each country.

Kastenbaum writes as though the death system in any one country is functional for managing death and the dead, and for minimizing the disruption of death for society. However, most modern legal-medical systems and their associated death system struggle with some all-too-common features of many contemporary deaths.

First, modern medicine is good at preventing, curing or managing single diseases and conditions: inoculation against particular diseases, setting a broken leg, treating an infection with antibiotics, or managing diabetes. But as we saw in Chapter 1 modern dying is usually more complicated, entailing an older person suffering multiple morbidities, many of which cannot be cured or managed without affecting other organs (Kellehear, 2016). Elderly people in this position often find themselves in and out of hospital, enmeshed in a system geared to treating single conditions. Geriatrics, the medical specialism that looks at the old person holistically, is in many countries of low status compared to more high-tech curative specialisms and so skilled geriatricians can be in short supply.

Second, in many countries most complaints about hospital care follow a death. Even taking into account that natural shock and anger at any death can be irrationally projected onto those in whose care the person died, this still leaves many deaths caused in part or whole by iatrogenic (medically caused) conditions (Illich, 1976), medical error (Makary and Daniel, 2016) or organizational dysfunction. Medicine remains an inexact science and doctors acting in good faith and without any negligence on their part can act in ways that, with hindsight, contributed to a patient's death. This kind of medical error is an inevitable if regrettable part of the practice of medicine; medical negligence, by contrast, is avoidable and much rarer. There is also the possibility of organizational routines and managerial priorities that contribute to a patient's death.

Countries vary in how they respond to hospital death complaints, whether through suing, leading to defensive medicine and high insurance premiums for practising doctors; or through more open communication between hospital staff and family both before and after death. But whereas an airline will conduct a thorough investigation after a fatal crash, often revealing human and organizational rather than technical failings, fatalities in hospital are too frequent for intensive investigations to become routine. So poor management of death can become endemic within the organization. Even more troubling, death certification in 117 countries relies on the World Health Organization's (2019) *International Classification of Diseases*, which does not capture human and system factors, including medical error. So medical error is not publicized as a cause of death. Independent research, however, has concluded that in the USA medical error is in fact the third leading cause of death, after cancer and heart disease (Makary and Daniel, 2016). It is not surprising if official failure to acknowledge its role in a death angers the surviving family.

Third, the individual is peripheral to the post-death system in most modern countries, however humane the professionals operating the system. As explained in the section above on 'rationalization', these systems are geared to protecting the health of living society as a whole, not soothing the battered and bruised emotions of the bereaved. Determining the cause of death has to be accomplished, however distressing to survivors, as does informing the family if the death has not occurred at home. Where the death is stigmatized, as for example where drugs are implicated, even a process such as face-to-face informing the family may be performed as little more than a cursory duty. One British study found that people bereaved by a drug or alchohol-related death struggled to navigate a death system comprising potentially over 30 different kinds of agencies (police, coroner, funeral directors, clergy, counsellors, GP, hospital, etc.) whose focus was either the dead or the bereaved; and that was not including solicitors, banks, utilities, the local press, or people who were not 'officials' such as family, friends or those who had been dealing drugs to the deceased (Valentine, 2018: Fig. 6.1).

Modern death systems therefore contain tensions, not least − in the case of medical error and organizational malfunction − the failure to perform the essential function of determining the cause of death. Compared to the larger legal-medical system of which the death system is a part, the death system commands little public or political interest − except when a particular death or series of deaths becomes a national scandal. A British example is GP Dr Harold Shipman who was able to murder several hundred patients because the death certification process assumed GPs to be honest. Another is the *Daily Mail* newspaper campaign that highlighted failings in the Liverpool Care Pathway. Intended to provide high-quality care for dying patients in their last hours and days, this pathway was successfully developed in well-resourced palliative care settings but failed to work reliably in more pressurized health care settings where quality control could degenerate into a superficial 'tick-box' exercise. Reform by scandal, however, produces new systems that lock the proverbial stable door out of which several horses have already bolted; systems produced this way are rarely efficient or humane.

BEYOND MEDICALIZATION

As death becomes more and more medicalized, movements have arisen attempting to 'de-medicalize' it, to make death once again 'natural'. Examples include resisting high-tech but futile medical interventions, hospice programmes to enable people to die at home rather than in hospital, the compassionate community approach, and the home funeral and natural burial movements. Here I wish to make just a few observations about such movements: (1) Many are initiated by doctors themselves, and arguably extend medicalization even in the name of de-medicalization. (2) Others are initiated by allied health professionals who may succeed in a degree of de-medicalization, but in the process further death's professionalization. (3) Most of the time, families just have to get on with caring for a dying member or coping with grief.

Hospice and total care

One major initiative to make death more natural is the hospice and palliative care movement. This rejects heroic but ultimately futile medicine that keeps the terminally ill person alive for as long as possible, whatever the quality of life. Hospice and palliative care aim to manage physical and even existential pain so the person can maintain a quality of life until death comes naturally. The hospice movement was started, and in many countries is still largely led, by doctors. Indeed, Cicely Saunders, widely credited for founding the first modern hospice, St Christopher's in London in the 1960s, had retrained from social worker to doctor in order to be taken seriously; medical authority was needed to challenge medical authority (du Boulay, 1984).

Over thirty years ago, American sociologists Arney and Bergen (1984) observed that the movement to humanize death and dying came not from outside medicine but from within it. American psychiatrist Elizabeth Kübler-Ross's best seller *On Death and Dying* (1969) taught millions about psychological and emotional aspects of dying of cancer. British paediatrician Dr Hugh Jolly was probably more influential than bereaved parents themselves in getting health care professionals to become more sympathetic to parents of stillborns and miscarriages (1976). Arney and Bergen ask whether the attempts of such medical entrepreneurs to make medicine more humane have at the same time inadvertently enabled medicine to colonize more and more areas of life. The holistic hospice doctor or paediatrician now enquires not only into the patient's physical symptoms but also into their inner emotional and spiritual life. The doctor who asks me 'How are you, in yourself?' is seeking to gaze into my soul as well as into my body (Clark, 1999). The stethoscope, X-ray and CT scanner are complemented by techniques of holistic care. Information leaflets for cancer patients in the UK now describe in some detail possible emotional responses to cancer, alongside factual information about diagnostic and treatment procedures. Many patients and families may well welcome this more holistic practice of medicine, but it nevertheless medicalizes more and more areas of life.

Some innovations are introduced by health professionals who are not doctors. Though I know of no research documenting this, my impression is that many of those promoting the radical home death movement are experienced nurses and social workers who have seen the failings of hospital dying and have moved outside 'the system' to help families enable a member to die, and be cared for after death, at home. Within the system, some hospice services are nurse-led and pride themselves that, though they recognize the doctor's art, medicine is not dominant. Art and music therapists promote their expertise in enabling patients to express their feelings as they face the end of life as a way of making end-of-life care more holistic. Indeed, the hospice philosophy presumes that what Saunders called 'total pain' – the pain of soul and mind as well as body – requires a holistic, multi-disciplinary team approach to end-of-life care in which doctors play a role but do not dominate. In relocating medicine as servant rather than master, a more human approach to dying values the expertise of a wide range of professionals and semi-professional volunteers as people near the end of life. In other words, end-of-life care, when resources allow, requires ever wider professional expertise. Medicalization is replaced by professionalization. What may appear a more natural death seems to require considerable multi-professional expertise.

Compassionate community

Is there no escape from the gilded cage of medical colonization of life and professional colonization of death? Is escape desirable anyway? Many people are grateful to experts who manage dying and dead bodies on the family's behalf, or who provide advice and support.

The 'compassionate community', 'health promoting', or 'community development' approach offers a means of escape in which communities themselves take (more) responsibility for end-of-life and bereavement care (Karapliagou and Kellehear, n.d.). The aim is not to build yet more professional capacity but to build community capacity. A 'compassionate community' is one where all organizations and informal networks behave and organize as though their members are mortal rather than immortal. Examples include humane HR policies for employees who need to take time off to care for a dying family member or in the aftermath of a death; including end-of-life issues in school curricula; enabling existing social networks of friends and neighbours to help families care for a dying member. This approach has been pioneered in Australia, and most notably in the (relatively prosperous and left-wing) Indian state of Kerala where large numbers of non-medical volunteers from all strata of society provide hands-on care. Volunteers there soon learned that patients' concerns were more often social than medical – 'children dropping-out of school, families falling into poverty because of out-of-pocket health expenses, starvation, social isolation, and stigma' (Vijay, 2018). The volunteers provide regular support to patients and families, bringing in medical professionals as and when needed.

At the beginning of life, birth is a family and social event in which medical expertise plays a valued role, but is not routinely dominant; so, it is argued, the end of life needs to be firmly re-located within the social, in any society at any level of economic development.

What then are the chances of this approach succeeding in de-medicalizing death, not by proposing some illusory notion of 'natural' death but by firmly re-inserting death, like birth, into the social? The Kerala volunteer movement was founded in 1993 by two medical doctors, though the main global publicist for the compassionate community approach, Allan Kellehear (2005), is a sociologist.

In the second decade of the twenty-first century the concept is being embraced in several highly industrialized countries not so much by community organizations but by palliative medicine and the hospice movement. Only time will tell whether it will migrate from being a fashion within palliative care to a movement in which 'communities themselves independently create the policies and practices for their own end-of-life needs' (Karapliagou and Kellehear, n.d.: 13). Clark (2018) has raised doubts about the potential of compassionate communities significantly to reduce the need for professional services, while Chapter 14 exposes several barriers that limit easy transposition of the Kerala model to post-industrial societies like the UK.

To my knowledge, the compassionate community movement has given little or no consideration to the vexed question of euthanasia/assisted dying. Policies in countries that have legalized such practices, and debates in those which have not, usually remain within a medical framework, and ethical dimensions are generally considered part of medical ethics. A doctor has to certify that euthanasia in any particular case is allowable in law, and a doctor has to provide or enact the necessary practical means. The question might be asked why this should be the responsibility of a doctor? If society deems that terminally ill people with untreatable pain or symptoms should, if they so wish, be helped to die, then why should responsibility for enabling this essentially non-medical act be passed on to doctors? Is it not a community responsibility? If end-of-life care in general is to be seen as a community responsibility, should this not also include euthanasia/assisted dying? What this might look like has yet to be explored.

CONCLUSION

This chapter has shown how death, dying and bereavement are seen in modernity primarily as health issues in which medical expertise is needed, supplemented by an increasing number of other professionals. All this adds up to a complicated 'death system' for managing care of the dying, determining the cause of death, taking care of the dead body, and supporting the bereaved – a complex bureaucracy for rationally and predictably managing the irrational and the emotional. Also significant is institutionalization in which the body, whether dying or dead, is located in hospital, care home or funeral home, locations which maximize control by professionals.

Critics of this modern way of death have moved the dying/dead body out of institutions, developed a more holistic and multi-professional approach to care, promoted dying at home, and returned responsibility for end-of-life care to the community; however, most of these innovations have been initiated by doctors, and arguably represent more a humanistic extension of medical and professional work than de-medicalization.

Modernizing society entails *rationalization* in which rational action supersedes traditional reasons for doing things, *differentiation* in which social institutions are split off from one another, and *domestication* or the instrumental control of nature. All these are expressed in the management of modern death through medical and health techniques. Finally, late modern attempts to humanize death and dying reflect a fourth feature of modernity, namely *individualization* with respect to each individual's personality (van der Loo and Willem, 1997).

FURTHER READING

- Arney, W.R. and Bergen, B.J. (1984) *Medicine and the Management of Living*. Chicago, IL: University of Chicago Press.

- Clark, D. (1999) '"Total pain", disciplinary power and the body in the work of Cicely Saunders, 1958-1967', *Social Science and Medicine*, 49: 727-36.

- Illich, I. (1976) *Limits to Medicine*. London: Marion Boyars.

- Kaufman, S. (2005) *... and a Time to Die: How American hospitals shape the end of life*. Chicago, IL: University of Chicago University Press.

- Makary, M. and Daniel, M. (2016) 'Medical error - the third leading cause of death in the US', *BMJ*, 353 (3 May).

- Prior, L. and Bloor, M. (1992) 'Why people die: social representations of death and its causes', *Science as Culture*, 3 (3): 346-74.

Questions to discuss

- What tensions can you identify in your own country's medicalization of death, dying and loss?

- Should the health of the living determine how society deals with its dead?

- Can you imagine a developed modern society in which professional expertise is not the main authority for managing dying and grief? What would it look like? Would it be desirable?

Notes

1. www.nhs.uk/conditions/Brain-death/ (accessed 3/6/19).

2. Curiously, these researcher-practitioners' major contributions to psychiatry and psychology have received little recognition within these disciplines.

3

COMMODIFICATION

LIFE: COSTED OR SACRED?

Modernity has created two kinds of human life. On the one hand, capitalism has fostered an economic calculus in which lives can be used by business and/or the state, a calculus in which life itself is costed. Some early nineteenth-century plantation owners calculated that it was cheaper to work a slave to an early death and then buy a new one than to treat each slave well – slaves were literally commodities. After the 2008 financial crash, neo-liberal governments cut health care spending – knowing that it would lead to extra deaths. Yesterdays' slave owners and today's policy-makers may or may not wrestle with the ethics of this costing of human life.

At a more everyday level, capitalism accelerated the move from craft and subsistence production to wage labour, separating workers from what they produce, which may be bought and sold impersonally. More and more things are bought and sold – commodified – forcing us to become waged workers and consumers who depend on what we can buy. By contrast, 'in the Middle Ages it was not the labor contract, but the family, the church, or the lord that decided a person's capacity for survival' (Esping-Andersen, 1990: 35). These earlier forms of social protection were first undermined by capitalism and then replaced by the welfare state, insurance and new forms of charity (the mix varying from country to country) which provide health care, education, and so on free at the point of access. Esping-Andersen refers to welfare and charity as 'de-commodification'. But everything has a cost. In ill health and at the end of life, we may be more or less aware of cost, required to pay more or less, depending on the welfare/charity/insurance/market mix.

On the other hand, modernity also fostered the revolutionary idea that every human life is sacred. Since the sixteenth-century Protestant Reformation and then the eighteenth-century Enlightenment, concepts such as individual liberty, human dignity, and civil rights have steadily gathered force; at first applicable only to upper-class white men, these concepts have been extended to one group after another until in the twentieth century human rights came to be enshrined in international law. In this perspective, the living body is sacred, inviolable; the anti-slavery movement held (and still holds) that humans should not be bought and sold; the body belongs to the person inhabiting it and to no-one else.

Examples

This extends to body parts, before and after death. In several advanced industrial countries, blood and organs (such as kidneys) may be donated but cannot be bought and sold, and there is public horror at revelations of an international trade in these. After death likewise, whole bodies may be donated but not sold, and public dismay follows the occasional media revelation of a commercial trade in bodies and body parts for surgery, dissection or display.

When waging war, the armies of advanced industrial economies now attempt to limit loss of life on their own side and even on the enemy side – very different from the slaughter of the First World War and from the slaughters still enacted by undemocratic countries today. Late modernity's sanctity of life seems progressively to have undermined the earlier ideal of sacrifice for country. And yet advanced industrial countries still go to war for economic reasons, not least the protection of oil supplies.

So human life in modern times has become both sacred and more and more commodified. The two may not be utterly opposed. Pinker (2012) has argued that the market requires buyers to trust sellers whom they do not know personally; historically, this fostered the idea that traders outside my own little tribe may also be human, like me. He argues this is one reason (among many) both for the reduction in violence over many millennia and for the reduced tolerance for violence over recent decades.

Whatever the merits of Pinker's argument, it is clear that death in modernity lies within a contradiction between the economic calculus and the sacredness of each life; between costing each item of care and the state's commitment to care for the vulnerable; between commodification and de-commodification. This is reflected in health care, which on the one hand strives to save life, since life is sacred; on the other hand, every medical procedure and treatment plan is costed and, the more limited the resources, each life/death has to be valued against another.

Patients and their families are often all too aware of this contradiction. They may be amazed at heroic life-saving efforts, free at the point of access, made available through their health care plan or through socialized health care; or immensely grateful for hospice care for which no payment is asked. Yet just a few weeks earlier or later, they may be dismayed at how their insurance plan excludes certain medical conditions, or how help at home to wash and toilet a dying family member is rationed to just two 15-minute slots each day.

An old story

Commodification of the dead is not, however, new (Jupp and Gittings, 1999). Theologically, the Protestant Reformation in sixteenth-century Europe hinged on the question of whether the soul got to heaven simply through God's free grace, or whether the surviving family needed to pay priests to pray for the deceased's soul. The time a Catholic soul spent being purified in purgatory while on its way to heaven could be reduced by the pre-deceased buying 'indulgences' from the church – Pope Leo X, for example, offered indulgences to those giving alms for the rebuilding of St Peter's Basilica in Rome. Even after it had left earth therefore, the medieval soul's progress was caught within an economic nexus – an abuse which plenty had criticized before but which drove the reforming monk Martin Luther to challenge the church itself.

What though about the corpse? The dead body and its constituent parts have long been both sacred, and traded. In the European Middle Ages, relics – small bones purportedly from a saint's body – were venerated, yet were also stolen and traded in order to maximize a church or monastery's income from pilgrims (Bynum, 1991). After the Battle of Waterloo in 1815, local people and camp followers scavenged among the dead, extracting teeth which could be sold to dental surgeons. Eighteenth- and nineteenth-century museums were keen to display anatomical specimens from aboriginal people who were not considered fully human and therefore were more easily objectified and their remains turned into commodities (Fforde, 2004); there is a long history of entrepreneurship in the commodification of corpses for anatomical display (Knoeff and Zwijnenberg, 2015). Today, though organs from the dead are more likely to be donated, after donation they are treated as commodities; behind the scenes, they may or may not be traded for money.

Is the body/life/death/care/salvation sacred, not to be bought or sold? This question has vexed many, both before and during modern times. But the ever increasing extension of the market into every aspect of life, along with the ever-deepening notion of life as sacred, make the question ever more salient to the modern management of death, dying and loss.

VARIETIES OF DE-COMMODIFICATION

Esping-Andersen (1990) identified different kinds of welfare regime in the West, based on three kinds of de-commodification. The *conservative* approach considers social stability to be based on church and family, so they should continue substantially to provide for the population's welfare. The *liberal* approach – the most commodified – relies on the market, but recognizes that the market will always leave gaps, which have to be filled by charity and the family. Finally there is the *socialist* approach, reflected for example in state funded universal health care such as the UK's National Health Service (NHS), at least in its first decades.

Esping-Andersen did not consider the death system, but his approach raises the possibility that countries with different welfare regimes may differ as to which aspects of death care are commodified and which are de-commodified. For example, the Anglo-American liberal/market approach to welfare retains a significant place for charity, not least in end-of-life care, while the social democratic Swedes prefer to use services paid for by taxation. Or, as President Calvin Coolidge famously observed in 1925, 'the chief business of the American people is business',[1] so it is not surprising if Americans tend to be more comfortable than Europeans with a funeral industry that makes profits out of dead bodies and out of grief.

Within any one country, some parts of the death system are more commodified than others. In the UK for example, end-of-life care provided by the NHS or by hospices is de-commodified, that is, not paid for at the point of access and therefore experienced as free; bereavement care is mainly provided for free by voluntary organizations. Sandwiched in between, however, is the funeral, for which the surviving family pays funeral directors, cemeteries and crematoria, florists, clergy and celebrants. In other words, the British funeral is very heavily commodified – except perhaps for the post-funeral tea (on which more later in this chapter).

Care for the dying person, however, is uneven: NHS health care is de-commodified, but the NHS does not provide social care to assist with washing and feeding at home, nor does it provide residential care for the frail elderly; both social care and residential care, provided by profit-making companies, have to be paid for by the family, though the local municipality may assist those on low incomes. This oscillation between being looked after for free, and having (and often struggling) to pay for care, is something that dying people and their families can be acutely aware of. After free NHS care in a high-tech hospital, the cost of home care, residential care or the funeral can come as something of a shock. (By contrast, in some developing countries the cost of drugs for those nearing the end of life may exceed the cost of the funeral.)

Despite this variety between and within countries today, and despite the medieval commodification of saints' relics and prayers for the dead, it is clear that in pre-modern times much less was commodified than now. In medieval and early modern Europe, if you were looked after on your deathbed, it was by members of your household or possibly by a charitable or religious foundation; you were unlikely to have to pay specially for care, even if you could afford it – not least because you were likely to be ill for only a few days before death released you. For the funeral, the family might pay the village carpenter to make the coffin and the sexton to dig the grave, but much else was provided by church, family and community; a local woman might lay out the deceased, a communal hand-bier used to wheel the coffin to the church, family members carried the coffin into the church and lowered it into the grave. It was the rise of the undertaker in the nineteenth century that dramatically commodified funerals – a process being replicated today in many developing countries.

I will now look at how modern institutions and their publics oscillate, or perhaps more accurately lurch, between commodification and de-commodification in the management of dying, funerals, and grief.

DYING

Health care

As Chapter 2 showed, modern western publics look to health care systems to manage dying, so the degree of commodification in the health care system profoundly affects people's experiences of, and access, to care at the end of life. In a system that is totally socialized, taxation or compulsory insurance covers the health care of everyone living in the country. In other words, the experience of giving and receiving medical and nursing care is de-commodified. In the UK which has socialized medicine, families rarely mention the cost of healthcare (dementia excepted), unlike in the USA where it is one of the most frequent topics of conversation (Miller, 2017: 33–4).

However, it is not that simple. Even when provided free at the point of access, care can be commodified, and under the influence of neo-liberal ideology increasingly so. This occurs both backstage and frontstage. Backstage, 'care' is transformed from a verb – the activity and attitude of caring – to a noun, a thing to be delivered, a service to be traded. In contemporary English usage, whereas families care for their members (care as verb), health care is 'delivered' (care as noun) as though it were a package. Referring to a health service as 'delivering care' or even 'providing care' rather than 'caring' neatly avoids any promise that the service, and those who work for it, actually care. Language is used to turn care from an activity into a thing. In the UK, social care at home is actually described to the family as a 'care package'. Whether or not the person delivering the package actually cares about the sick person depends on their personal attitude; it is not contracted as part of the package (Bolton and Wibberley, 2014). If this commodification is produced by language, it is *a fortiori* produced by neo-liberal economics. When, as is increasingly the case, there is an internal market in which various private agencies bid for contracts to provide care on behalf of the state or a health care organization, it becomes clear that care has indeed become a commodity to be traded.

Frontstage, the commodification of care goes hand in hand with the rise of the consumer. 'Patients' who patiently accepted what care the doctor, nurse or care aide gave are now replaced by 'consumers' with the right to make informed choices as to what care they wish to receive, irrespective of whether or not they have to pay. 'Doctor's orders' are replaced by 'informed consent'. Care and treatment are divided up into a menu from which the consumer may choose – either at point of need, or beforehand via advance directives. Some items, notably euthanasia but also drugs and treatments the state or the insurance plan will not cover, and in much of the world morphine, may be off the menu.

Both health care professionals and patients/consumers vary as to whether, or how far, they welcome health care's consumerization. My discussion of advance directives in the previous chapter noted that Europeans are less likely than North Americans to see themselves as health care consumers, as are those nearing the end of life. For old people experiencing frailty and multiple health issues, hours each day are spent on the tedious routines of bodily survival: getting up, getting washed, getting dressed, eating, resting, getting to the toilet. Time is structured by these imperatives; life has to be lived day by day, rather than making plans for the future, including end-of-life care (Bramley, Seymour and Cox, 2015).

Media coverage and the experiences of family and friends may more or less accurately inform healthy people about the variability, availability and quality of end-of-life care, for example between one care home and another, between hospital and hospice, between cancer and dementia, between one post code and another, or in the USA between those with a prognosis of less than six months and those with a longer prognosis. In this scenario of inequality, as one long-time observer of Danish palliative care observes, the best way to help people feel more comfortable about death may not be to engage them in discussions about their mortality or encourage them to make advance choices which perhaps cannot be honoured, but 'to assure them, that they will be properly cared for when the time comes' (Timm, 2018). In other words, what many people may want at the end of life is not choice, but to know they will be looked after (Walter, 2017b). In the UK context, citizens want the NHS to uphold this guarantee of patient care (D. Davies, 2015), and many are sceptical about its transformation into a guarantee of consumer choice.

Hospice economics

How hospice services are funded varies from country to country, and can change over time. British hospices, for example, are charities. On average, one-third of their funding comes from government while the rest comes from donations, lotteries and investments. The high proportion of funds coming from donations, either by living members of the local community or in post-death bequests, reveals a particular form of economy which Titmuss (1970) in his classic study of blood donation called the 'gift relationship'. Titmuss argued that British blood donors, who, unlike American donors, were never paid, chose to donate blood as a thank-you to the NHS for its free care: one gift led to another. It seems that British hospices rely on a similar, and very impressive, model of reciprocal gift giving. The hospice provides really good care to local people as they are dying. In response, many change their wills to allocate some of their estate to the hospice; donations at the funeral may be directed to the hospice. Many who have friends or family who benefitted from hospice care, or are simply aware of the good reputation of a hospice, volunteer for their local hospice, for example by tending the hospice garden, driving patients to day care, or helping to run one of the many local hospice charity shops. It is not unusual for a British hospice to have 400 or 500 local volunteers. A significant proportion of hospice volunteers are themselves retired, receiving a guaranteed income through their pension and therefore comprising the biggest group of adults who do not need to sell their labour in order to live; in other words, their lives are relatively de-commodified, enabling them to give their labour for free to the hospice. With this abundance of voluntary resources far exceeding that available to local state-funded NHS services or for-profit residential elder care, the quality of hospice care continues to excel and the virtuous circle continues.

Of course, this generates inequality in end-of-life care; those eligible for hospice care, primarily those with cancer, benefit and those with other conditions risk missing out. But the economics of reciprocal gift giving provides an alternative to both a health care market and to socialized medicine. Or a supplement to them. My local NHS hospital has over 400 volunteers and a significant income from donations, many of them from grateful patients and their families. By contrast, few for-profit care homes for the elderly have extensive volunteer programmes in the UK, and many have none. I would predict, though this needs testing, that in any country, donations and volunteering will be much higher in not-for-profit than in for-profit institutions. Reciprocal gifting combines high levels of paid professional expertise with a large volunteer army in what, from the perspective of family and community, adds up to de-commodified care. If family and community give back to the hospice (or hospital), it is not because the hospice 'delivers good end-of-life care' but because it cares, skilfully. The hospice cares for its local community, the community cares for its hospice, and so on in a virtuous de-commodified circle.

American hospices began with similar economics. Since the 1980s, however, Medicare has reimbursed American hospice care for patients with a prognosis of less than six months. This financial windfall has proved a mixed blessing for it has enticed for-profit companies to enter hospice care; caring for the dying has become big business in which there is an economic logic to maximizing patient admissions and minimizing levels of care (Whoriskey and Keating, 2014).

Compassionate communities

Chapter 2 introduced the compassionate community movement as a reaction against hyper-professionalization; here we consider its potential to de-commodify dying.

While British hospices combine de-commodification with highly professional expertise, other initiatives – such as the home death movement and the compassionate community movement – combine de-commodification with de-professionalization. One critique of the hospice model is that its promise of total care for total pain has led to the expansion of professional capacity, that is, more paid professionals of ever expanding speciality and expertise, whereas what is needed is an expansion of community capacity to support those in the community who are dying. This would entail some de-commodification, with unpaid labour replacing some paid labour.

What de-commodification in a compassionate community would look like is open to question. With the last year of life currently taking a significant share of health care expenditure in all advanced industrial countries, the compassionate community ideal could be co-opted by governments wishing to cut health care expenditure. And there is the question whether it romanticizes community. Daniel Miller's (2017) ethnography of how dying people in rural England maintain or lose social connectivity reveals an unhelpful and inaccurate romanticizing of a mythical past 'community', at least in the villages he observed. He was disturbed by a significant minority of those he talked to, especially older men, who had lived in the village all or most of their life, yet were isolated and lonely. They do not fit the stereotype of cosy, friendly village life.

English villagers whose pride and sense of privacy did not allow neighbours to enter their house were grateful to professionals who visited, as they were to the paid gardener or cleaner who took time to befriend as well as to garden or clean. On getting older, some English people cultivate their garden more than relationships, which in any case are withering as peers die. And then they can no longer garden. So middle-class people pay a local person to do the garden; gardeners often understand their role as friend, and may spend half their employed time chatting over coffee or getting their spouse to come and fix a few things in the house. Thus 'commercial contacts remain when other social contacts have fallen away' (Miller, 2017: 175). Professionalism and commodification can be accompanied by real care by one human for another.

By contrast to Miller's English village, Horsfall et al. (2011) have documented how in the suburbs of western Sydney, Australia, dying people and/or their family carers mobilize their wider social networks in order to gain support. I myself have observed something similar in my own middle-class urban street in southern England (Walter, 1999a). At present, why and to what extent neighbourhoods do or do not enable mutual care and thus partly de-commodify the end of life, is not well understood. While the commodification/de-commodification tension is endemic as late modern individuals near the end of life, the actual geography of de-commodified care is complex and variable.

FUNERALS

In pre-industrial societies, funerals can be elaborate affairs. For at least three centuries, funerals in southern Ghana (West Africa) have displayed social and economic status, 'family exercises in self-congratulation' in a 'game of honor and shame' (van der Geest, 2000: 124). Once this game of conspicuous consumption has become socially normative, it is very hard for a family to try to break it. So is anything different about funeral expenditure as societies modernize? Van der Geest shows how from the 1960s to the 1990s, Ghanaian funerals became commercialized and professionalized, with families delegating hired outsiders to perform activities the family once did, and the very ability to hire an outsider in itself became a matter of prestige. Similar patterns have been found in many societies around the world, in both the global North and the global South; in death as in life, modernization entails structural differentiation in which new institutions arise and are paid to do what families once used to do for themselves or to do what before was never done (Parsons, 1966).

Status insecurity

Anthropologist Gordon Childe (1945) reviewed evidence over many millennia and concluded that the scale of funeral expenditure may not reflect a family's social and economic status so much as its level of status insecurity. When status is vulnerable, and made more vulnerable by the death, then funeral rites are used to display the family's resources, even if the family goes into debt in order to perform the expected display. Status insecurity is typically rife in the early decades of industrialization as thousands leave a settled life in the countryside to make their way as industrial labourers, moving from a feudal or peasant economy into a brave but uncertain new capitalist economy, whether in their own country or abroad. Maintaining security of income and knowing where one fits in this new unfamiliar order can generate an obsession with 'keeping up appearances' or 'respectability' – whether through keeping the front of the house clean, or wearing smart clothes to church on Sunday, or 'putting on a good show' when organizing a wedding or funeral.

Funeral expenditure can be particularly high during this transition to industrialism. In Victorian Britain when millions moved from country to city, high funeral expenditure was lampooned by novelist Charles Dickens. In mid twentieth-century USA millions of poor migrants from around the world managed to make some kind of a living in the American land of opportunity; on their or their children's death, the family would hire a fancy hearse and solid mahogany casket to display that they had 'made it'. This 'American way of death' was mercilessly critiqued by British writer Jessica Mitford (1963) who, whether because of her aristocratic pedigree or her communist ideals, seemed blind to the reasons why people would want such an extravagant funeral; instead she – like Dickens – blamed the high expenditure entirely on the funeral industry's greed and sharp sales strategies. The cost of an average funeral in post-war Japan, currently around US$25,000, is three times higher than in the USA and can likewise be seen as resulting from very rapid modernization and upward social mobility. Japan's funeral industry also has its critics, such as the Buddhist Soka Gakkai sect which provides not only much simpler funerals but also a belief system that justifies simple rites and empowers families to leave behind the expected 'game of honor and shame' (van der Geest, 2001: 124).

Once the transition to urban industrialism is largely complete and people know better where they fit in society, funeral expenditure often declines. In the USA since the 1970s it has usually been lawyers and doctors rather than factory workers, those who have been Americans for several generations rather than recent immigrants, who have approved of Mitford's views and opted for cut-price cremation without any ceremony. Their social status, well established in life, did not need to be paraded in death. Both Mitford herself, in 1996, and pop singer David Bowie in 2016, neither of whose reputations needed any further enhancing, opted for a non-ceremonial cremation costing just a few hundred dollars.

Personalized funerals

Increasingly in several advanced industrial countries, rather than display the family's status, funerals celebrate the deceased's unique personality and life (Garces-Foley and Holcomb, 2005). Personalization may partly de-commodify the funeral, but not necessarily. In the UK and the USA I have observed what I call 'mass-produced individualization'. Here, the family have a sense of co-constructing with the funeral professionals a personal and unique ceremony (Holloway et al., 2013); but many funeral professionals, however much they might deny it, have a template into which they slot poems, songs, readings that reflect the particular individual (Cook and Walter, 2005). Clergy and funeral celebrants often operate this way, as do funeral directors. In one American funeral parlour I visited in the early 1990s when personalization really began to get under way, the funeral director proudly showed me his latest range of caskets; in each casket's top corner a different figurine could be screwed: a golfer, a baseball player, a bird, a dog, and so on, depending on who had died – sportsman, nature lover, devoted dog owner. The economic model is the same as contemporary automobile production. Henry Ford's mass-production motto 'Any colour so long as it's black' is long gone; today's customers can choose not only the colour but any number of variations (leather seats, wire wheels, a particular music system, sat nav, etc.). The result is a vehicle that is personal, not quite the same as anyone else's; yet the manufacturer still benefits from mass production. Personal rarely means de-commodified.

That said, in the UK personalized funerals can be arranged and performed partly, or more rarely fully, by the family themselves. Though systematic research has yet to establish this, it seems to be people well established within the upper or middle classes who are most likely completely to de-commodify the funeral by opting for a DIY funeral which they arrange without a funeral director, cemetery, priest or celebrant, digging the grave themselves and burying the body on private land (Gittings and Walter, 2010). They could easily afford a normal funeral, but they find a de-commodified one more meaningful. Doing it yourself is not legal in all countries.

Culture and institutions

The theory that status insecurity may be managed through costly funerals does not explain all variance in funeral commodification and expense. Later parts of this book emphasize the importance of culture and how institutions and practices evolve in any one country, and these factors certainly influence funeral commodification.

Funeral food

A case in point is funeral food. In many regions of the USA, a country where everything is supposedly commercialized, funeral food is homemade by friends and neighbours and may be consumed after the funeral in non-commercial premises such as the family home or a church hall (Graham, 2018). In the supposedly less commercialized UK, though the family rather than the funeral director arrange the post-funeral tea, the food itself is often purchased from a commercial caterer and the tea held in commercial premises such as a hotel or pub. What in the USA is the community's gift to the family, in the UK is often a commodity purchased by the family.

Within the USA there are variations. Thus while Anglo-American funeral food is often home-made, Mexican American funeral food is more likely to be bought in order to sustain mourners as they sit with the dead in the funeral parlour. And before the funeral in the UK, neighbours may bring homemade food to the house – but this is not *expected* as it is, for example, in the Jewish community or the American South.

Funeral directing in America

In mid twentieth-century America, white funeral directors often chose to present themselves as stalwarts of the local community, involving themselves in the local Lions Club and raising money for charity (Pine, 1975). This helped create an image of themselves as caring and trustworthy, so was good for business – most of all, grieving families want to feel cared for and that the funeral was being looked after by someone they could trust. This economic model may be represented thus: care/exploitation → profit → charitable giving → caring image → more business → profit → and so on.

The history of black funeral homes reveals more complex ambiguities. Cann[2] documents how, because white funeral directors did not want to touch bodies of colour, black funeral homes became the cornerstone of many African-American neighbourhoods, and funeral directing became one of the few routes to upward mobility for African Americans. Handling the funeral following a racist killing put the black funeral director at the heart of a highly emotional and political rite, and several became civil rights activists. To this day, black funeral homes continue to provide a focus for African-American identity. So, the very people who turned the mutual aid African-American funeral[3] into a capitalist product to be bought and sold are the very people who courageously proclaimed that all life is sacred, or in today's phrase, that black lives matter. Yes, black funeral directors made money out of the dead, but they also lifted their community and advocated civil rights. And yet they have not always been willing to help the destitute who could not afford a funeral. The relation between commodification and de-commodification is never simple.

Paying for the funeral

Given their often considerable cost, how do low-income families pay for the funeral? Various ways are culturally approved, or even expected, depending on the society concerned. Each involves more or less de-commodification.

At need

In the early decades of modernization when millions are impoverished and struggle to afford a funeral, sharing the cost with other poor families is one solution. This may be done at the time of the funeral, as in contemporary Kenya's *harambee* (Swahili for 'all pull together') – a tradition of community self-help that co-funds funerals along with many other events and community projects. Other African countries have similar systems (Bonsu and Belk, 2003; Jindra and Noret, 2011). Even affluent Japan, where funerals are among the most expensive in the world, funds funerals this way. Everyone attending a Japanese funeral brings a financial gift for the family; after a few months, the family return a somewhat lesser value gift.

This process affirms social bonds through a typically Japanese rite of reciprocal gift giving; donors know they in turn will be receiving either in a few months' time or the next time they have to arrange a funeral. This places commodification within a gift economy.

Pre-need

Another collective system, more formal and often less personal, pools resources pre-need. In the early days of the labour movement, in both the USA (Dowd, 1921) and the UK (Richardson, 1989), local burial clubs and co-operatives enabled working people to pool resources for burial. Mexican Americans have voluntary self-help associations (Moore, 1980), while in South Africa burial *stokvel* members regularly contribute a fixed amount of money to a common pool (Lukhele, 2013) from which they can draw when a funeral has to be paid for.

In Victorian Britain, burial clubs – where a penny a week contribution guaranteed a payout to cover funeral expenses when the time came – were the first successful example of social insurance in which regular contributions insure against future financial hardship (Richardson, 1989). The principle was then taken up in the twentieth century by the British state which came to provide social insurance, first against old age (1906) and then against unemployment, sickness, disability and other risks, including in the late 1940s a universal Death Grant, payable to anyone on death. The grant's original value was sufficient to pay for a simple funeral, but in time failed to keep up with increases in funeral costs, and was abolished in 1987 (Foster and Woodthorpe, 2013). Recent years in Britain have witnessed examples of funerals for widely-loved but destitute local individuals being crowd-funded through social media, a twenty-first century digital *harambee*.

In advanced industrial societies like the USA and the UK, pooling resources through a pre-need funeral plan is now big business for insurance companies and trust funds. Either a lump sum or regular instalments are invested by the provider to cover most or all of the cost of the funeral, whenever that may be. This system in no way challenges the funeral's commodification; to the contrary, it offers a way for a funeral company to increase its market share by signing up customers years or even decades pre-need.

As funerals become more and more commodified, such schemes continue to find customers among those entering the modern urban world. Though in East and West Africa people are used to everyone contributing, on moving to England their African networks in the UK may not be extensive enough to pay for anything like a lavish funeral. English friends are not used to helping to pay for another family's funeral; and mourners living back in Africa may be unwilling to help pay for a funeral they cannot attend. This leaves a serious shortfall between cultural expectation and financial reality. At least one British insurance company is therefore promoting itself to this group in the hope that £30 per month to guarantee a £10,000 funeral will be perceived as good value.[4]

Alternatives

An entirely different approach is the American memorial society, as championed by Mitford. This is an association of hundreds or thousands of consumers who join together to negotiate better terms with funeral providers: its collective buying power makes the memorial society a match for funeral corporations in bargaining for a fair price.

The only way to take the funeral entirely out of commerce and back into family or community is for mourners to do the funeral themselves. The most common example is in some religious groups where it is a religious duty to care for the congregation's dead. Thus many Jewish congregations have a burial society comprising volunteers who perform many of the functions that would otherwise be done by a commercial funeral director. Islamic mosques may have facilities for washing the dead. Caring for the dead in such communities is not a commercial operation, but a sacred duty.

In sum, though funeral costs vary considerably between economically developed societies, the funeral typically involves a high degree of commodification. The funeral industry, though generally quite conservative (death is not when most people want to become cultural revolutionaries), is experienced in taking new ideas and putting a price tag on them. Natural burial, for example, where the body (or in some countries, the cremated remains) is buried in a wood or field in a simple biodegradable container, is very rarely do-it-yourself. The UK has over 250 natural burial grounds which sell plots to consumers, the vast majority of whom also employ a funeral director. The American cemetery industry has proved adept at monetizing and commodifying green burial as a new option for families to purchase, almost always at a higher price than conventional burial, thus subverting the movement's desire for family-organized de-commodified funerals (Sloane, 2018). Families wishing to avoid their corpse's commodification may need considerable determination and resourcefulness, not to mention resources (such as their own land or station wagon).

GRIEF

Sociologists have argued that capitalism requires both a producer ethic that values hard work and motivates the worker, and a consumer ethic that attaches values such as family, love, status, happiness and personal fulfilment to consumption so that people will want to go out and consume ever more and more, far beyond what they need for material subsistence. Both were and are essential for capitalism's twin engines, production and consumption; the consumer ethic helped create a demand for ever more goods, the producer ethic helped produce the goods. In early industrial Britain and North America, according to Max Weber's much discussed Protestant Ethic thesis (1930), the producer ethic of hard work was an offshoot of Calvinist religion; a parallel 'romantic' consumer ethic, rooted according to Colin Campbell (1987) in Protestant pietism, valued personal experience and family love, still very much in evidence today. Each ethic has endured well beyond its religious origins.

The two ethics link to two different normative worlds at home and at work. At home people are expected to be expressive, loving and committed for life; at work they are expected to be instrumental, to seek advancement up the career ladder and/or be flexible to seek employment elsewhere if need be. This creates two very different contexts for the performance of grief.

In the private sphere of home and family, love – between spouses, and between parents and children – is supposed to be eternal. In grief this is both a comfort and a sign that grief will never end, not a pathology to be 'got over' but a new way of being with the beloved. As a beautifully carved headstone for an 11-year-old boy in an English country churchyard near my home puts it: 'Brief is life but love is long.' This idea is found in romanticism, from the grand opera of Wagner's *Tristan and Isolde* and Puccini's *La Bohème* to contemporary pop songs. Then, boy lost girl to consumption; now girl loses boy to car crash or drugs; but the message is the same: there will never be another. The same idea is found on many gravestones and in newspaper death anniversary messages, as on this 1998 gravestone in a London cemetery: 'Those you love don't go away/ They walk beside you every day.'

Everlasting grief is good business for publishers of books on grief; certainly in English speaking countries, such books are flourishing, including grief auto-biographies, collections of poetry about loss, and self-help grief therapy books. But it is hard to see how it is good for business if workers are incapacitated by grief indefinitely, looking to a lost past rather than the future orientation on which capitalism depends. So there is another view of grief, first articulated in 1917 by Sigmund Freud (1984), which Stroebe et al. (1992) have dubbed 'modernist'. In this view, grief is something which can be got over. It is understood as the pain that accompanies the sundering of the bond linking two people; in time, though, the mourner will 'let go' of the deceased and be restored as an autonomous individual, able to make new relationships. It is consistent with a cultural norm that anthropologist Geoffrey Gorer (1965) identified in early 1960s England, namely that grief is time-limited. This is a much more hopeful, future-oriented view of grief, more compatible with a work ethic. With support, care and perhaps therapy, the mourner can be restored to full functioning, both at home and in the workplace.

The consumer ethic of loving, consuming families underlies the romantic understanding of bereavement, while the producer ethic underlies the modernist imperative to let grief go and move on. It is not surprising that a capitalist economy that requires both a producer and a consumer ethic should generate two bereavement ethics; but whereas the two capitalist ethics complement each other and enable capitalism to function, the two bereavement ethics contradict each other and complicate grief. Mourners get conflicting messages about the nature of grief. And workplace bereavement policies, typically offering only a few days off – and that only for a close family bereavement – rarely offer the time that even modernist psychologists would consider necessary. But conceptually, if not in terms of timescale, bereavement leave policies are modernist in that their time-limited concept of grief expects the worker to return to normal functioning as soon as possible. Bereavement is seen as a glitch, not a way of being. Capitalism struggles to value grief, whether conceived in romantic terms (continue the bond) or modernist terms (let go).

Commodified grief care

However grief and its remedies are conceptualized, capitalism can make money out of grief. That, at any rate, is Nancy Berns' thesis (2011) about how the word 'closure' has been used since the early 1990s in the American economy and in American culture. She documents varied, even opposing, meanings of 'closure' – closing a chapter, remembering, forgetting, getting even, knowing, confessing or forgiving – all are promoted as ways of ending the pain of loss. This means that virtually any policy, practice, commodity or service – from techniques for letting go, to memorials for remembering, from taking revenge through witnessing capital punishment, to forgiving via restorative justice – can be sold by business or claimed by politicians as providing closure. 'Closure' is the promise that sells caskets, funeral services, political programmes, public memorials, and much more. Grief itself is perhaps not commodified, but – at least in American capitalism – the remedy is. 'Buy this, and your pain will end' is closure's promise.

Cemeteries in rapidly growing East Asian cities, both capitalist and communist, are often seen by business and government as locking up valuable land that would otherwise be used for development; some families, however, believe that urban development driving super-highways through old cemeteries undermines traditional relationships between the living and the dead (Aveline-Dubach, 2012). But are economic development and the needs of mourners necessarily opposed? Lim's (2018) study of the modernization of cemeteries in Kuala Lumpur, Malaysia, suggests not. In the 1990s, vast new commercially operated 'memorial parks' began to change 'official representations of cemetery space from dangerous, wasteful and a hindrance to modern development to valuable (in the sense of being monetised) modern public spaces … in which meaningful intimacy between the living and the dead is emphasised and fear suppressed' (2018: Abstract). Lim argues that these modern cemeteries dispel traditional taboos and fears, modernize practices of filial respect, and evoke personally more meaningful ways to relate to the dead.

Historian David Sloane's book (2018) on the past, present and possible futures of the American cemetery offers a more critical account of commodification and of the myriad ways the American cemetery industry sells its wares as remedies for grief. The challenge of green burial has been rather easily co-opted by the industry and sold back to consumers at inflated prices. More significant challenges to grief's commodification since the 1990s have come from the proliferation of everyday, participatory memorials which mourners themselves create at little or no monetary cost. The two most vibrant locations for such memorialization are currently the street and the Internet. Probably more mourners post memorial messages, photographs and songs on social media at zero cost than purchase space in any commercially provided 'internet cemetery'.

In line with folklorist Jack Santino's (2006) earlier research into spontaneous shrines, Sloane sees street memorials and social media memorials as personal and yet communal 'expressions of Americans' struggle with state and private institutions for control of memory' (p. 232). He gives an example of an African-American woman: 'Why would she come to the cemetery and look down at a plaque with her son's name when she could sit by an RIP mural near her home, and have her neighbours stop by and talk with her about her loss?' (p. 188). Unlike the home death and natural burial movements, the exponential growth of everyday memorials in the street and on social media are not the result of any organized movement. Rather, they are grass-roots de-commodified memorialization.

Exploitative or meaningful?

The previous section poses a key question about grief's commodification. When grieving people pay the death care industry for their services, are they being helped or exploited, or both? Radical critics such as Jessica Mitford are clear that the name of the game is exploitation of people when they are at their most vulnerable. But the death care industry is equally clear that its services help people through a difficult time in their life. This divergence of opinion is not new. As mentioned above, sixteenth-century Protestant reformers saw medieval Catholic selling of prayers and 'indulgences' for the dead, who could thereby proceed more swiftly to heaven, as a cynical ploy to make money for the church. In another view, however, Catholic rites provided families a way to care for their dead and to articulate grief, whereas the paucity of Protestant rites left mourners emotionally empty. And I have noted that elderly middle-class widows in England who maintain rather distant relationships with their neighbours may receive the most meaningful encounter of the week from their paid gardener or cleaner. For as long as there has been money, its relation with grief has been ambiguous; modernity's increasing commodification of life and death simply extends the ambiguity so none can now escape it.

CONCLUSION

This chapter has argued that modernity is characterized by a heightened tension between an economic calculus that puts a price on life and death, care and grief, living and dead bodies; and the view that humans — their life, soul, and bodies, alive or dead — are sacred, priceless. I have given examples of how health care systems, the funeral industry, churches, governments and business, along with individuals, families, communities and social movements dance, sometimes elegantly, sometimes flat-footedly, between economic calculation and the sacredness of life, between the commodification of life/death and its de-commodification. The dance differs between countries, and between sectors (e.g. health care, the cemetery industry, the Internet), but dancing between these two poles is something that modern people cannot avoid as they approach the end of life, as they try to cope with the death of one they love, or as they work for an organization that sells care — for the dying, the dead or the grieving.

FURTHER READING

- Berns, N. (2011) *Closure: The rush to end grief and what it costs us*. Philadelphia, PA: Temple University Press.

- Childe, V.G. (1945) 'Directional changes in funerary practice during 50,000 years', *Man*, 45: 13–19.

- Jindra, M. and Noret, J. (eds) (2011) *Funerals in Africa*. Oxford: Berghahn.

- Kellehear, A. (2005) *Compassionate Cities*. London: Routledge.

- Mitford, J. (1963) *The American Way of Death*. London: Hutchinson.

- Sloane, D.C. (2018) *Is the Cemetery Dead?* Chicago, IL: University of Chicago Press.

Questions to discuss

- In your country, what aspects of dying, funerals, memorialization and bereavement are most fully commodified?

- What aspects have never been commodified, or not fully?

- What examples of de-commodification can you identify in your country? Why and how has this occurred?

- In your country, what happens when a family cannot afford to pay for health care or for a funeral?

Notes

1. www.thisdayinquotes.com/2010/01business-of-america-is-business.html (accessed 3/6/19).

2. www.candikcann.com/saving-and-selling-black-bodies and www.candikcann.com/whiteout-death-in-the-21st-century (accessed 3/6/19).

3. https://socialwelfare.library.vcu.edu/eras/colonial-postrev/free-african-society/ (accessed 3/6/19).

4. Information from John Harris, February 2019.

4

COMMUNICATION

Death is irreducibly physical, but it is also social. Getting frail or terminally ill and then dying disrupts family and other social networks; bereavement restructures social engagement with both the living and the dead. The Internet is also, and increasingly, social, so much so that nowadays the term 'social network' is as likely to mean online as offline networks. So this chapter seeks to show how communication technologies – a key part of modernity – affect experiences of dying, and of grieving (Walter et al., 2011–12).

'ICT' refers to information and communication technology. As well as communication, people may need information at the end of life. We die only once, so dying presents an entirely new situation for each individual who faces it, and possibly also for close kin. There is a lot to learn, and fast. Most knowledge about dying, however, is tied up in the heads, textbooks, and procedures of health professionals (Chapter 2), so the modern family faces, at the very least, urgent information needs. The Internet is fast replacing books (which in turn replaced orally transmitted knowledge) as the go-to medium through which modern people search – and are expected to search – for information, and indeed the Internet and social media have become increasingly important sources of information for sick, elderly and dying people and their carers. This may be positive, but can also be negative. Some elderly people whose lack of IT skills prevent them from accessing services, even services specifically for old people, are unable to access application forms and helplines that are entirely online. And as well as reliable information, it is not hard to find persuasive but unreliable claims online for alternative treatments that can offer seriously ill people false hope.

Those thinking about their own death, or who are grieving the death of someone close, may have another need for information – about life after death. Who is disseminating ideas and beliefs about the afterlife, and how, is also part of end-of-life communication.

So this chapter is about information and communication technologies and media. We will see how over the past two centuries modernity has witnessed the arrival of one new communication technology after another, each with the potential to undermine processes described in the preceding three chapters:

- Whereas Chapter 1 argued that increasing longevity renders death less visible, modern media often make death and the dead more visible.

- Whereas Chapter 2 highlighted the professionalization of death and dying, contemporary social media can engage a wide range of friends and wider family as a person is dying, and expands people's access to alternative as well as to conventional medical knowledge.

- Whereas Chapter 3 analysed death's commodification, contemporary social media enable people to share experiences of terminal illness or memories of the deceased, for free.

- And, though modernity has fostered secularization in some, though not all, parts of the world (Chapter 10), each new communication technology offers new ways for the dead to be present among the living, making new forms of spirituality plausible.

The rapid evolution of new communication media, a key aspect of modernity, therefore complicates how other modern technological and economic factors shape death and dying.

I hope that by the end of the chapter it will be clear that communication media, like the factors described in Chapters 1–3, do not *determine* anything. Rather, they open up possibilities, and make some things more plausible. How this works out in any one country, and whether and if so how possibilities are taken up, varies for reasons discussed later in the book. Quite a bit of this chapter's history of communication media draws on examples from Europe and North America, the part of the globe with which I am most familiar. I am not suggesting that what the West does today, the rest of the world may do tomorrow, far from it. My aim is simply to give examples of how each new technology has afforded mortal humans new possibilities; it is up to you to explore how, if at all, such possibilities have been shaped and developed in your own part of the world.

Much of the chapter will be about how communication media have offered new ways for the dead to be present in the lives of both individuals and society. It is no coincidence that 'media' is the plural of 'medium' – a word referring to people who claim to put the dead in touch with the living. Both spiritualist mediums and communication media enable an absent person, another reality, another place, another time to be present here and now. Starting with the first – and pre-modern – communication technology to enable people to communicate with others who are physically absent, namely writing, I move swiftly on to inventions produced by modern science: electricity, the telegraph, photography, recorded sound, mass media (radio, television, cinema), digital war, and finally the Internet and social media which build on these earlier technologies.[1]

WRITING

Before the invention of writing, and more particularly before the beginning of mass literacy, communication with the living meant talking face to face with those physically co-present (Ong, 2012). Stories about both the living and the dead were shared orally within a community of known individuals, and therefore reflected the world of family and community. It was in this context that shamans performed rites to help the dead to wherever they were destined, that those of some status within family and community were transformed post-mortem into ancestors, and that rites were performed to keep these ancestors happy and/or to persuade them not to cause trouble.

Modern understandings of the afterlife, however, have been profoundly shaped by the teachings and practices over three millennia of what are now, perhaps misleadingly, called 'world religions'. In the main, these are religions of the book: teachings originally delivered orally were written down into what eventually become sacred scriptures (Horsfield, 2015), enabling people's horizons and their identity to expand way beyond family and local community. Millions across the world identify as children of Abraham, worship Jesus, claim Mohammed as the prophet, or respect the teachings of the Buddha. In each instance, writing, printing and literacy enable a dead person – Jesus, Abraham, Mohammed, the Buddha – to continue as a presence in the lives of millions (Goss and Klass, 2005). And as we shall see in later chapters, monotheistic Judaism, Christianity, and Islam have had an uneasy relationship with family ancestor worship.

But let's move on to specifically modern communication media.

ELECTRICITY AND THE TELEGRAPH

The young Mary Shelley published her novel *Frankenstein* in 1818. She had recently attended scientific lectures on electricity by a Dr Wilkinson who had suggested that electricity, though at the time still in its infancy, might be used to bring inanimate matter to life. Mary, who had experienced nightmares in thunderstorms, was intrigued by this idea. That electricity could bring dead matter to life resonated not only with her imagination, but also with that of millions who have subsequently read her book and seen movies based on it (Frayling, 2017).

This vignette introduces one of this chapter's recurrent messages: everyday technologies can make plausible the possibility of bringing the dead, if not to life, then at least nearer. The next stage in the story comes 30 years later in 1844, when Samuel Morse electrically transmitted a message from Washington to Baltimore. Before his invention of the telegraph, the only way that physically distant people could communicate in real time, avoiding the delay inherent in sending and receiving letters, was by visual semaphore systems that used flags to communicate from ship to ship or beacons to communicate from hill to hill – laborious, limited in the distance they could be seen, and prone to being misread. The telegraph, however, enabled what media studies calls co-presence; the telegraph wire almost instantly channelled the physically absent minds of others.

The telegraph helped make spiritualism, where mediums channel the dead to the living, plausible (Nelson, 1969). And indeed western spiritualism is commonly dated to originate from just four years after Morse's demonstration, when in 1848 the young Fox sisters in Hydesville, New York, claimed that the spirit of a murdered pedlar communicated to them through rapping noises, leading to intense public interest in the possibility of mediumship between the living and the dead. It may seem fanciful to twenty-first century rationalists that a technological invention could have fostered widespread interest in what some might consider hocus-pocus, but everyone at the time was aware of the connection. Talk about mediumship frequently invoked electricity, the telegraph, and another recent invention – photography (of which more anon).

By collapsing time and distance, the telegraph also enabled news of a death to be transmitted almost instantly across vast distances. Before the telegraph, news of family members living, sailing, fighting and dying on the other side of the world could take months to reach home, as Fitzpatrick (1994) movingly shows in his study of letters sent and received by Irish immigrants to Australia. That the telegraph could inform the family back home the same day was revolutionary.

In the American Civil War (1860–1865) the telegraph raised a further possibility. Fallen soldiers had hitherto been buried on or near the battlefield, but near instantaneous transmission of the news immediately involved the family. Embalming techniques, used in the 1850s to preserve bodies for anatomical instruction, were quickly developed by quick-off-the-mark entrepreneurs to preserve the bodies of fallen soldiers which, carried on the new network of railroads, could be brought home for burial. Or at least the bodies of officers whose families had the resources to pay (Farrell, 1980; Faust, 2008). So began the American burial custom of 'bringing our boys back home' rather than burying soldiers where they fell. This in turn led to further developments in embalming so that viewing the body in its casket (originally, an ornamental box for jewels) became the central rite in the American funeral, civilian as well as military – certainly not something Morse had envisaged his invention would lead to! How technological innovation affects the dying, the dead and the bereaved is rarely as originally envisaged. This is also true of the next pair of communication inventions in the modern era, namely photography and recorded sound, as it is also of twenty-first century social media.

PHOTOGRAPHY AND PHONOGRAPHY

A nineteenth-century romantic death culture that celebrated grief for the beloved (Ariès, 1981) stimulated interest in the new inventions of photography and phonography. (By phonography, I mean machines for recording and playing back sound.) Many Victorians wanted their beloved dead to live on, and these new technologies promised to make this possible. Hitherto, only the rich could afford an ongoing visual representation of the deceased in a painting of the person made while alive, or a sculpture made from a death mask. Photography was much more democratic, and by the end of the nineteenth century, middle-class and even some working-class people could afford at least one commercial photographic portrait of each family member, including dead children for whom a post-mortem photograph might provide the only visual record (Burns, 1990). Edison's invention in 1877 of a phonograph to record sound aroused interest for much the same reason, as it enabled family members' recorded voices to be preserved beyond the grave. Nipper, the dog on the famous His Master's Voice (HMV) label, was originally (1899) portrayed sitting on a coffin listening to a phonograph recording of his dead master's voice – hence the record company's name. New technologies give the deceased's face or voice an enduring presence; at the same time, a desire for this presence stimulated interest in these technologies (Peters, 1999; Sterne, 2003).

In the twentieth century, both photography and phonography developed in new ways. The spread of cheap and easily portable cameras in the first half of the twentieth century meant there are now few families in modern societies whose memory of their forebears is not shaped by the family photograph album (Riches and Dawson, 1998) or more recently by digital photos. Unlike staged studio portraits, these candid photographs – and even more so home movies, videos and a short sequence captured on a smart phone camera – have a remarkable capacity to capture a moment in time that, uncannily, enables subsequent generations to witness the dead as though alive (Barthes, 1993). Taking and displaying photos helps us imagine kinship.

However, until the widespread use of smart phones to obtain multiple sound-plus-motion recordings of friends and family, the main use of sound recording in the twentieth century was not, as originally envisaged, to provide a record of the voices of family and friends. Instead, its commercial success in the twentieth century was to record music played by professional musicians. So while the modern twentieth-century family lived with pictures of both living and dead family members – on the mantelpiece, in photo albums, and in their wallets – the recorded sounds they lived with were those of professional musicians and composers, living and dead (McCormick, 2015). When grandad died, they might struggle to recall the sound of his voice; but they instantly recognized Frank Sinatra's.

HMV made a fortune selling recordings of professional musicians, not selling devices to enable us to record our family members' voices.

The result is that much of our lives is spent in the visual and aural presence of the famous dead, and we think nothing of it. An example: eating in a restaurant whose walls are adorned by posters of Che Guevara, Marilyn Monroe and Elvis Presley, and whose piped music includes John Lennon singing *Imagine* or Yehudi Menuhin playing Mozart. Before the invention of the modern technologies of photography and phonography, this kind of 'living with the dead' was impossible – though other kinds, now less plausible, were possible (Baudrillard, 1993). Technology offers new possibilities for *how* to relate to the dead.

Photography and phonography come together in cinema, television and video, but it is the smart phone that brings them together for everyday recording of family and friends. Social media enable sound-accompanied pictures of everyday life to be forwarded and re-forwarded to any number of friends and acquaintants, in life and after death – contrasting with the much more private family photo album. Mobile social media at long last fulfil Victorian hopes that those we know and love will live on after death in sound as well as sight, for friends as well as family, with ease and at zero cost.

MASS MEDIA

Much research has been conducted on death in the mass media (Hanusch, 2010), so there is space here for only a few examples of how movies, soap operas, news media, and so on, offer possibilities to re-locate death and dying in modern society. Death abounds in mass media – news media disproportionately cover death, whether the natural death of a famous person or the violent deaths of ordinary citizens; death and loss are often key to a movie's plot; they spice up the everyday life of soap operas, and provide a means of escape for the character when an actor leaves the show. Mass media brought the deaths of strangers, of famous and fictional characters into the twentieth-century living room and now, with twenty-first century mobile devices, anywhere the viewer cares to watch his or her screen, which means everywhere.

At the same time, the actual deaths of intimates are hidden from sight in hospitals and care homes. For Jacobsen (2016), the media's 'spectacular death' which we witness 'at a safe distance but hardly ever experience upfront' partially reverses death's invisibility (Chapter 1). The media consist of representations, of appearances, and viewers and audiences know this, though some are genuinely distressed at the death of a celebrity or iconic figure who represents their hopes and dreams or is in some other way part of their identity. Real-time exposure to the events of 9/11 was certainly spectacular, but – despite its cinematic quality – surely shocked and traumatized many Americans living hundreds or thousands of miles from the Twin Towers, even more so those living in New York. Pictures of the 2017 Grenfell Tower fire, in which a block of flats in London went up in flames, disturbed many across the UK.

The mass media have transformed the visibility of violence, war and disaster in the eyes of western publics, though what kinds of violent death may be shown in which media varies over time and from country to country. The more authoritarian the government, the more direct control it has over media coverage, not least of bad news. But even in democracies, there is censorship and self-censorship. I recall some decades back attending an Andy Warhol exhibition of a sample of the over 90 per cent of press photographs of car crashes that do not pass the censor. It was a sobering experience not only to witness these terrible pictures, but also to realize how audiences are protected from them. Since the 1950s, the effect on viewers, especially young viewers, of witnessing both factual and fictional violence on television has been a topic of both research and public contention.

Highly-censored newspaper and newsreel coverage of the Second World War acted as effective propaganda in many combatant countries, including the UK (Jalland, 2010). Two decades later, however, television news and other media coverage of the Vietnam War, even though censored, helped turn large sections of the American public against the war. Exposure by *Newsweek, Time* and *Life* magazines of the 1968 Mỹ Lai massacre by American troops was particular powerful. Likewise in October 1984, Michael Buerk's BBC news images of millions of starving people in Ethiopia led to Bob Geldof and Midge Ure's charity single *Do They Know It's Christmas*, which became the UK's fastest selling single ever, raising £8 million, followed the next year by the Live Aid concert. The combination of television news and the pop music industry, catalysed by individuals such as Buerk and Geldof, turned media images of starving children into mass compassion, continuing to this day in highly organized media compassion-fests.

DIGITAL WAR

War today is itself fought with digital media which may transform the experience of killing. Consider military drone operators living and working in the American Mid-West (Pinchevski, 2016). Every day for eight hours a day they monitor a target in the Middle East, getting to know the target's mundane daily routines and his or her family, perhaps even beginning to identify with them as fellow human beings. Then as the drone strikes, the operator watches these people blown apart – in close-up detail rarely witnessed by traditional troops on the ground and never by aircrew bombing from thousands of metres up. After eight hours watching people's mundane lives and then watching them being killed, the operator then drives home and in 20 minutes is asking the kids about their day. How such operators deal – or fail to deal – with this psychologically is very likely different from the traditional coping mechanisms of soldiers on active service who are separated from their families for months on end and rely on group solidarity with comrades on whom their lives depend. Replacing hand-to-hand combat with killing at a distance – a trend in warfare since the invention of gunpowder and increasingly so since the invention of the airplane and the rocket – may now no longer protect the killer from visceral knowledge of the consequences of his violent actions. New media create new possibilities not only for distancing humans from violent death, but also for digitally-induced trauma. Digital media can cause us to be haunted by the dead.

THE INTERNET

Is the Internet a free space in which all manner of grass-roots, youthful, and idealistic views may be expressed and undermine hegemonic (official, dominant) views of reality, including medicalized dying? Or is it a multi-billion dollar industry which functions to reproduce hegemonic views while giving the impression of being a free space?

The answer is that it is both (Miah and Rich, 2008; Curran et al., 2012), in death as in life. The Internet enables dying people and their carers to access and to purchase, sometimes at considerable cost, alternative/holistic treatments that may fruitfully complement conventional medicine or may be pseudo-cures that exploit desperate people. Also on the Internet may be found personal blogs and tweets by dying people, including dying medical personnel, which balance the medical with the experiential. At the same time, the Internet implicitly promotes death's medicalization by providing far more up-to-date information about medical procedures than were ever readily available to patients in print.

Online suicide pacts and pro-anorexia sites may feature writing about death that is markedly counter-hegemonic:

> The self-inflicted deaths of a man and a woman who met online on a forum for people contemplating suicide has raised concerns over the role the internet has in helping or harming those thinking about taking their own life. Suicide pacts are rare events – even more so when they are made over the internet … Japan and South Korea have seen a sharp rise over the last few years. (Barford, 2010)

Anorexia is a life-threatening condition. Dias (2003) argues that pro-ana sites offer anorexic women a sanctuary, a safe place, where there is no judgement, no pathologizing and no well-intended but useless advice from outsiders, a sanctuary where non-recovery narratives are accepted, a space where women 'can support each other and break the isolation they feel' (p. 40). But such counter-hegemonic narratives can deeply worry parents and other family members who press the authorities to close such sites down.

In sum, the Internet, like the printing press before it, purveys both hegemonic and counter-hegemonic versions of reality; and like the printing press, it is feared as well as used by the establishment, not least the medical establishment.

SOCIAL MEDIA

Mortality becomes visible again

One of modernity's major achievements has been to move death from the province of infancy and childhood to the province of deep old age, with the happy consequence that many people now get through childhood without personal experience of bereavement (Chapter 1). This can mean, however, that they enter adulthood ignorant about death and loss, or even unconsciously assuming they are immortal. Social media, however, make ignorance largely a thing of the past. More common now is the experience of one of my sociology students:

> Although I have not lost a friend, in the past three years I have noticed four deaths of 'friends of friends' on Facebook. I became aware of these deaths through status updates and pictures posted by those left behind. Being one contact away from these people meant that I was allowed access to some of their personal pages, though we had never met before. All four were in their early twenties; two had died in accidents, one committed suicide and one had a recessive genetic disorder.

In the sociology of death undergraduate module that I taught until 2014, I began by asking the class (comprising mainly white, middle-class students in their early twenties) how many knew someone who had died. When I first started teaching this in 1994, about a quarter of the students put their hands up, but 20 years later it had risen to around three-quarters. The most plausible explanation is not a massive increase in the death rate of juveniles or grandparents, but the effect of social media. While traditional mass media often profile the death, loss and destruction of those not personally known to readers and audiences, new social media publicize the deaths of friends of friends, bringing mortality just that bit closer to home. Unlike 1990s Web cemeteries which (rather like physical cemeteries) visitors had to choose to enter, death announcements, status updates and commemorations now pop up on people's phones in the midst of everyday life. Death is no longer separated from everyday life (Walter et al., 2011–12; Brubaker, Hayes, and Dourish, 2013).

Social media can also, of course, publicize the dying and death of those not personally known. In 2010, murdered American teenager Chelsea King attracted huge social media attention (Phillips, 2011). In 2013, terminally-ill British teenager Stephen Sutton used social media to raise £4 million for his teenage cancer charity. His death the following year prompted both heavy online traffic and considerable physical foot traffic to pay respects to his body lying in state in Lichfield Cathedral, not to mention headline coverage in traditional news media.

Chapter 2 mentioned a hospital oncology clinic in which women post selfies and receive hugs, hearts and smileys back from family and friends. I described this as breaking down the clinic's walls. This works both ways: the technology enables not only the woman to feel supported, but also her friends and family to accompany her, at least in spirit, each step of the way. Her encounter with a life-threatening illness and its treatment becomes part of their hour-by-hour lives as well as of hers (Lagerkvist and Andersson, 2017). Other studies have reported how bereaved people who may not find face-to-face encounters supportive can access social media at any time and in any place and find someone who is supportive. Social media make it harder to forget the dying, the dead, and the bereaved. And though social media are largely designed by men, it seems to be women who are making the most of their communicative capabilities around the end of life.

Presenting the self online

It is not, however, that simple. Humans have always taken care how they present their self in face-to-face situations (Goffman, 1959), and social media present particular challenges. A Danish researcher quotes a bereaved father:

> I do perhaps have the need to write something several times during a month, or even a couple of times during a week. But then I think to myself, oh no, I have to be careful not to let it get out of hand, I mean to avoid the 'now he writes something about that dead child, again!' (Raun, 2017)

Raun goes on to discuss 'the special kind of vulnerability that is attached to mourning in the semi-public space of Facebook ... where one is expected to enact a private public self, not a too official public self and not a too transgressive intimate self.' Online, mourners want to share, but are anxious not to overshare. This is why some mourners join a dedicated online group for their particular life-threatening illness or their kind of loss, though – as with face-to-face mutual help groups (Wambach, 1985) – online groups also impose their own implicit norms as to what can and cannot be said, and how.

One of my sociology students describes the complexities of navigating mourning 'netiquette':

I have viewed and 'liked' RIP Facebook pages even though I have no personal connection to the deceased. This was firstly because the death was particularly tragic and covered in the news therefore the lady and her family deserved to be honoured and respected and second, because I felt I had to. I have 'liked' memorial pages because I have seen that 20–30 of my Facebook friends have. Therefore I 'liked' the page because I did not want to be seen as disrespectful of the dead.

However when my Grandad died my sister wrote as her Facebook status 'RIP Grandad' and this really annoyed me because I felt that no one on Facebook knew my Grandad so why was this any of their business to share or know about our family's grief.

Once a person has 'liked' a memorial page on Facebook, after what period of time is it ok to 'unlike' the page? Is it ever acceptable? I personally have never 'unliked' a memorial page and this is possibly due to peer pressure and the worry does this make me a disrespectful, inconsiderate and heartless person?

This student clearly shows how Facebook norms look very different depending on whether she was 'liking' a memorial page for someone she did not know personally, or whether she was grieving her own grandfather. Along with the Danish father, this British student shows not only that users of social media are together co-creating new norms for mourning and memorializing, but also that individual users can struggle with these norms and/or find them inappropriate. Each online platform has its own evolving norms with which users may be more or less familiar, leaving them more or less open to censure by others.

A free space?

This suggests caution about the sociological hypothesis that the Internet provides a free space where griefs that are otherwise disenfranchised may be expressed. 'Disenfranchised grief' refers to grief that is not socially acknowledged, such as grief for a friend, for a suicide or for a miscarriage, for a pet, or grief experienced by children or by people with cognitive impairments (Doka, 2002). Researchers have for some time argued that, even if such grief is not acknowledged in everyday settings or in specific settings such as the funeral or when requesting bereavement leave, online it can be both expressed and acknowledged, especially in sites that allow anonymous posts (de Vries and Rutherford, 2004). And indeed several specialist online memorial sites are specifically for griefs that are disenfranchised in face-to-face interaction, such as pet grief, grief following AIDS, and grief for a celebrity. There may be more freedom, within limits, in these specialist sites.

As well as acquaintances of the deceased posting messages with the potential to disturb other mourners, the very openness of some sites opens them up to complete strangers and therefore to trolls, especially if the site allows anonymous posts. Trolls may lash out at Facebook 'friends' or those who never knew the deceased who post condolences and commemorations. Trolls articulate, in deliberately provocative ways, the reservations about 'look at me' mourning, the social pressure to mourn online, that others – like the student quoted above – privately wrestle with. Arguably, many trolls are attacking not individual mourners but online mourning norms (Phillips, 2011) yet, when read by bereaved family members, can cause offence.

Traditionally, there is an assumption that – with a few exceptions such as the deaths of heads of state, political leaders, and the military – chief mourners (usually close kin) have the right to control the funeral and to choose the form of memorialization. When a young person dies today, however, this right can easily be undermined (Hutchings, 2012). As a British funeral celebrant told me in 2013:

> The funeral I did yesterday was fraught due to the family's requests for no memorial Facebook page, being ignored. The distraught Mother shouted to me, 'When will they realize he was sick, then he was dying and that now he is dead!'

Though some family members may feel strengthened by the extent of online condolence and commemoration for a young person, others can feel disturbed by superficial and relentlessly upbeat posts from young peers who hardly knew the deceased, posts which make a mockery of the intense grief the family themselves are feeling. Attempts, successful or not, by parents to close such pages are not unknown. At the same time, some parents may not appreciate how important it is for their deceased child's peers to have a place where they can share their memories (Pennington, 2013). In the mid-2010s, Facebook responded to such conflicts by introducing a new feature in which account holders can nominate a 'legacy contact' to manage their account post-mortem (Brubaker and Callison-Burch, 2016).

Talking to the dead

Recall how in the mid-nineteenth century the telegraph and photography fostered interest in communicating with the dead through a medium. Contemporary social media also afford the possibility of new or revived spiritual practices concerning the dead.

Mourners have probably spoken to the dead since time immemorial, but in a twentieth century that framed mourning in secular and psychological terms, mourners in some countries came to fear that talking to the dead might be seen as evidence of insanity. So they talked to the dead in private, often at home or at the graveside, when no-one else was around, or silently. Social media posts, however, often address the deceased (Brubaker and Hayes, 2011; Kasket, 2012) in the knowledge that others are reading and watching; thus the previously private practice of addressing the dead has become socially acceptable. Kasket found on Facebook considerably more direct addressing of the dead (as 'you' rather than 'she or he') than Roberts (2004) had found on an earlier generation of virtual memorials. The more formal the site and/or the relationship, however, the more likely she or he is to be used. Thus, on UK Ministry of Defence online memorials to soldiers killed in Afghanistan, whereas the deceased's mates and subordinates sometimes address the deceased directly ('I still can't believe you're gone'), his superiors always address the living ('He always led from the front').

Online, the dead also address the living (Kasket, 2019). Apps enable the dead to send timed greetings (e.g. on birthdays) to those they love; messages from cyberspace are literally messages from the grave. More startlingly, some entrepreneurs are developing artificial intelligence software to analyse a person's unique communication style so that, after death, messages can be autonomously generated that appear to come from the deceased. This technology is, at the time of writing, far from perfected, and may remain in the realm of science fiction for some while. And, given that customers are likely to be young adults who may live for many decades until they die and can start posting autonomous messages, by then the software is likely to be outdated and the company gone out of business. In the meantime, however, digital technology can preserve text messages and emails, outgoing as well as incoming, after the co-respondent has died; in so far as these replace telephone calls rather than paper letters, they constitute a new way that conversations can live on after death. Whether all this positively keeps memories alive, enhancing the bond with the dead, or prevents mourners from letting go, is a matter of some debate in the West. In East Asia, where ancestor veneration continues as part of urban modernity, apps enable ritual interaction with the dead without the need to visit the physical shrine at which such rites are traditionally conducted (Gould, Kohn and Gibbs, 2019).

Afterlife

It is remarkable, even in secular countries such as England, Germany or Sweden where personal religious belief is expected to be kept private, that a significant minority of online memorial posts presume the dead to be residing in heaven, as in 'See you in heaven' (Jakoby and Reiser, 2013). Why is this? First, if I am directly addressing somebody, they have to be somewhere, and the most readily available location for a deceased addressee in a Christian or post-Christian society is heaven. Second, the upbeat positivity of sites such as Facebook means that wherever this perfect person is must be a perfect place, which can only be heaven.

'Angels' are another spiritual term commonly used in social media memorialization, not only in religious USA but also in secular Scandinavia. Posts increasingly refer to the deceased not as a soul (a passive being in a heaven cut off from Earth) but as an angel – a being with agency, specifically the ability to fly from heaven to Earth, to look after and to guide the living (Walter, 2016). Two aspects of the online environment may encourage this. First, angels – like cyberspace – connect the living and the dead, carrying messages back and forth. Second, the physical activity of writing and posting an online message to the dead is the same as sending an online message to the living – unlike a paper letter to the dead whose envelope cannot be addressed and posted. Writing offline to the dead may be experienced as private therapy; writing online to the dead is a normal social activity. It is perhaps not surprising that the very normality of online writing to the dead causes some writers to feel that the dead are receiving and reading the message, commented on by a number of Facebook writers: 'Even though it seems silly to talk through facebook, I know u can see and understand every word I type' (Kasket, 2012: 65). This 'assumes an active listener who keeps up with the day-to-day comings and goings of the living' (de Vries and Rutherford, 2004: 21); that is to say, it assumes the dead have agency. Angels have agency, souls do not, so angelhood is the logical post-mortem state for the online dead.

Online memorialization therefore often includes a spiritual language for talking about death, the dead and mourning. In so far as it naturalizes such a language, which is the implication of the preceding two paragraphs, this super-high-tech yet everyday environment may foster a partial reversal of secularization, at least within online memorialization.

Digital legacy

Digital property can be inherited not only by individuals but also by communities. By contrast, an item of physical property, including (if the negative is lost) a traditional photo, can be bequeathed to just one individual; hence I can remember the deceased by using her furniture or placing her picture on the mantelpiece – a rather personal memory. But digital content can be copied to any number of recipients, or put on the Web for anyone and everyone to see. So, distributed digital content can enhance the deceased's communal or public presence, as well as their private presence. If writing and printing allow words to go beyond the confines of face-to-face conversation, digital dissemination of artefacts such as photos or music allows inheritance beyond one-to-one inheritance. I have on my laptop, for example, a photo of a member of a hiking club to which I belong, taken on his last climb before his death by another club member and circulated to the club by a simple click. This locates him more securely as a club 'ancestor'. Digital technology thus enhances the potential for ordinary ancestors to move beyond the family to all kinds of formal and informal groups and organizations.

Digital immortality, however, is not assured. While digital materials such as the photograph of my hiking pal, once forwarded, may spin around cyberspace indefinitely, other digital assets may disappear just as soon as the Internet host is informed of the death, though few users read the fine print and know which digital assets will suffer this fate. Just as it is unpredictable which bits of paper or other material possessions will outlive you or for how long, so there is considerable uncertainty about the post-mortem longevity of your digital bits.

Back to orality?

Yet with all the digital chatter about mortality, people in many countries across the world are being urged to communicate about death in old-fashioned face-to-face talk. Since the first *café mortel* held in Switzerland in 2004, the death café movement has spread to many countries and at the time of writing (early 2019) over 7,000 cafés have been held worldwide. At these cafés, 'people drink tea, eat cake and discuss death. Our aim is to increase awareness of death to help people make the most of their (finite) lives'(https://deathcafe.com/).

In his sociological study of death cafés in Los Angeles, Fong (2017) employs Habermas' theory of communicative action. Fong sees death in America as a colonization of the life world in which a trinity of social institutions – medicine, the market, and the media (corresponding to Chapters 2, 3 and 4 of this book) – 'monopolise the framing of what death and dying should be'; these three macro institutions infiltrate grass-roots communication about death and dying. Death cafés, Fong claims, provide a free communicative space where participants can explore what reclaiming death from this unholy trinity might mean for themselves, so they can author not only their deaths but also the rest of their lives in the light of their mortality.

But medicine itself is inciting people to talk about dying (Arney and Bergen, 1984). Several countries are witnessing doctor-led campaigns to increase patient choice and control over what kind of care they receive as they are dying (Chapter 2); campaigners are concerned that many doctors, patients, and families may be reluctant to address this issue. For this to change, doctors need to initiate conversations with patients, and dying people need to talk to their families. Campaigns encourage people to talk about death and dying, both when they are dying and in advance, and provide the tools to start such conversations (Royal College of Physicians, 2018).[2]

After two centuries of innovative communication technologies that (often unintentionally) provide modern humans with more and more ways to be aware of death, dying, and the dead, why are modern people being urged to put down their cameras and televisions and tablets and smart phones and just talk about death, face to face with others? After all, blogs and social media as well as face-to-face talk provide a 'free communicative space'. The seventeenth-century French producer of memorable maxims, François de La Rochefoucauld, pronounced that 'Death is like the sun. It cannot be looked at directly.'[3] Is it that mediated death is easier than face-to-face talk – an indirect way of addressing death? Is it that I find it easier to post a condolence on social media than to ask the mourner round for a coffee? Easier to look at a photo of my grandmother than speak about how her death affected me? Easier to watch media reports of the latest terrorism attack than to talk to others directly about my own fears? Easier for a doctor to talk to a patient about how to treat the latest flare-up or how to manage symptoms than to ask her what she thinks her prognosis is? I don't know. But something odd is going on, for in an era when the world has never before been pervaded by so many technologically mediated representations of mortality, one campaign group after another is urging us simply to stop and talk.

It is possible the Dutch find it easier to talk about death. In their country, where doctor-supervised voluntary euthanasia has been practised since 2002, American anthropologist Frances Norwood (2007) describes this less as an act than as a series of face-to-face conversations between general practitioner and patient, in nine cases out of ten ending not in euthanasia but in a natural death. I am told by a Dutch anthropologist working in the UK that this also means that talking personally about death – at any time in the lifespan – is relatively easy in the Netherlands, because talking about when I want to die (which could include requesting or at least considering euthanasia) is unproblematic.

CONCLUSION

The past two centuries have seen an unprecedented explosion of new information and communication technologies, each of which has afforded new possibilities in the period before and after death. This chapter has demonstrated several aspects of these possibilities. First, technology determines very little, but offers many possibilities. Second, these possibilities may come into being through users' evolving everyday practices, as with social media; or through commercial interests, as with phonography's shift from recording the voices of the family dead to those of professional musicians. Third, these possibilities are rarely anticipated by the inventors of the technology, as with Facebook which has had to play catch-up with post-mortem practices. When, as with photography and phonography, the invention from its inception *was* intended to expand relationships between the living and the dead, subsequent practice has rarely turned out quite as expected. Fourth, new communication technologies, far from accelerating secularization, can have the opposite effect when it comes to the dead, offering new ways for the living to remember and even communicate with them, whether within a framework of Christian/post-Christian angels or Asian ancestral rites. Fifth, these new ways may strengthen existing community practices, as in Asian rites, or run counter to existing trends, as with secular Swedes who start tweeting about heaven.

How people use technology depends on culture and on institutions. This is clearly shown in Cann's (2013) study of QR codes engraved on tombstones that enable smart phones to show text, pictures and sound related to the deceased. She compares their use in Japan, South Korea, China, the USA and the UK. In parts of Asia, tombstone QR codes enable ancestral rites and are popular, but in the USA and UK they are optional sales items which are not so popular or play an educational heritage function. QR codes were developed in 1994 by the Japanese automotive industry, and literacy about them is high across East Asia; they appeared on tombstones from 2008 and quickly generated a large consumer market. In Japan, they allow 'family and friends to tap into a virtual treasure trove of memories, photos, videos and info about the dead .... They often allow users to make offerings, giving such virtual gifts to the deceased as food, incense, or even clicking a virtual button and having a Buddhist funeral chant or prayer said for the dead' (2013: 103). In South Korea, by contrast, tombstone codes never really took off, despite high familiarity with the technology. In China, the government promoted a modified QR system in order to reduce foot traffic to cemeteries at the grave cleaning holiday; that is, to counter the negative effects of religiosity rather than (as in Japan) to enhance religiosity. In the UK and the USA, there is much less general awareness of QR, reducing interest in their use in the cemetery. The tombstone QR story doubtless will have a limited lifespan, as QR becomes rendered obsolete by image recognition software.

Why have tombstone QR codes been more successful in Asia? Cann (2013: 110) argues that because Shinto Japan tends 'to see the world as a network of animated spirits' and Daoist China also recognizes the spiritual in nature, 'embedding the extra-ordinary, or virtual realm, into the physical, concrete world is not such a stretch.' In historically Protestant Christian countries, by contrast, 'the sacred realm is firmly located outside the physical one.' To test this explanation, we might enquire how QR technology is used in Catholic Latin America where matter and spirit are deeply interconnected after death.

FURTHER READING

- Barthes, R. (1993) *Camera Lucida*. London: Vintage.

- Brubaker, J.R., Hayes, G.R. and Dourish, P. (2013) 'Beyond the grave: Facebook as a site for the expansion of death and mourning', *The Information Society*, 29: 152–63.

- Cann, C.K. (2013) 'Tombstone technology: deathscapes in Asia, the UK and the US', in C. Maciel and V.C. Pereira (eds), *Digital Legacy and Interaction*. Santa Barbara, CA: Praeger, pp. 101–13.

- Kasket, E. (2019) *All the Ghosts in the Machine: Illusions of immortality in the digial age.* London: Little, Brown.

- McIlwain, C.D. (2005) *When Death Goes Pop: Death, media and the remaking of community.* New York: Peter Lang.

- Walter, T., Hourizi, R., Moncur, W. and Pitsillides, S. (2011-12) 'Does the internet change how we die and mourn?', *Omega, 64* (4): 275-302.

Questions to discuss

- How, in your experience and observation, do people use ICT in death, dying and bereavement?

- How does this vary by the user's age, nationality, or other factors?

- Why do you think people in some countries are being urged to *talk* about death rather than communicate about it through other media?

Notes

1. For more detailed treatments, see Walter (2015b) and Walter et al. (2011–12).

2. www.dyingmatters.org (accessed 3/6/19).

3. Maxim26: https://wikiquote.org/wiki/Fran%C3%A7ois_de_La_RacheFoucauld (accessed 3/6/19).

DEATH DENIAL?

Part I has pointed to several technological and economic aspects of modernity that shape death, dying and bereavement:

- Advances in food production and distribution, sanitation, and medicine have produced unprecedented longevity in which death now normally comes in old age, allowing all kinds of new possibilities in life as well as transforming expectations about death and loss (Chapter 1).

- Death now primarily falls within the arena of health and bureaucratically organized health institutions; doctors and other health professionals are looked to for knowledge not only about dying, but also management of the dead body and mourning. Over half of modern populations in advanced industrial societies die in hospitals and other health-oriented institutions. And it is doctors who oversee assisted dying / voluntary euthanasia in those jurisdictions where this is legal (Chapter 2).

- While doctors, nurses and emergency personnel strive to save life, health care systems put a price on life; modernity is caught between a typically modern view that all human life is sacred and an economic calculus that prices everything. Modern death practices are caught between sanctifying and commodifying human life (Chapter 3).

- The unprecedented invention in the modern era of one new communication technology after another has opened up new ways for the living to relate to the dying and to the dead, and for mourners to relate to each other (Chapter 4).

Throughout, I have argued that how all this works out in practice varies widely, depending on culture, institutions, national histories and other factors covered in the rest of this book.

Before leaving Part I, though, I want briefly to explore one particular question that has exercised both death reformers and scholars of death and modernity. Is there something inherent in modernity that causes death to become invisible, unfamiliar, sequestered, or denied? Let's briefly look at each of these possibilities.

The chapter title has a question mark, as its content is a lot more contentious than that of the previous four chapters.

INVISIBLE/UNFAMILIAR

Part I has shown how modern dying typically occurs in old age and in institutions; this separates it from everyday life and reduces its visibility. If witnessing the death of close family members was the all-too-common lot of children growing up in a one-room hut or cottage in pre-industrial times, now it is possible to get to old age without ever having witnessed someone draw their last breath (Chapter 1). This means that death becomes, to use Ariès' (1981) term, unfamiliar; we therefore rely on experts and professionals to manage it for us, which in turn renders it even less familiar (Chapter 2). As with many things that pre-industrial people did for themselves, so also with care of the dying and the dead; we now pay others to do this for us, whether that payment be directly through a market transaction, or indirectly through insurance, socialized health care, or even charitable organizations (Chapter 3). This is part of what sociologists term 'structural differentiation', in which different areas of modern life – health, education, religion, politics, and so on – get split off from each other into separate institutions and even separate ways of thinking. These institutions (school or hospital for example) then develop their field (education or health care) far beyond what the pre-industrial family did for itself. Chapter 4, however, showed that advances in communication technology from the nineteenth right through to the twenty-first century render mortality, death and loss *more* visible to modern humans who thus become more familiar with it, at least in a mediated way. So modernity makes death both less and more visible, less and more familiar.

But is something more subtle going on than simple visibility or familiarity? The sociological theory of sequestration and the psycho-cultural theory of terror management suggest so, but – as I argue in this chapter – should be used with considerable caution.

SEQUESTRATION

Sociologists Antony Giddens and Ulrich Beck have written much about how economic and technological change prompt modern people to think about themselves and their lives in new ways. Key concepts here are detraditionalization, individualization, reflexivity, and sequestration (Beck and Beck-Gernsheim, 2002). As modernity proceeds, as the market comes to commodify more and more of life (and death), and as globalization and instant electronic communication disembed people from place, they become more free-floating, looking for guidance in everyday action to neither traditional routines nor collective ideology. Such detraditonalized individuals become highly reflexive, determining their own life in their own way, carving out a life of their own.

For some, this could mean liberation from the expectations of religion, family and community; for others, being required to make too many choices when body and mind are failing can be a burden – they may just want to be looked after (Walter, 2017b). Giddens (1991) focuses on the existential aspects of this freedom. For him, reflexivity – constantly having to work out what furthers my own life project – induces in late-modern people an 'ontological insecurity'. Death, revealing the ultimate frailty of each individual's life project and of the body on which it depends, therefore becomes existentially threatening. If everyday life is to continue unruffled, death must be sequestrated, sidelined from the mainstream of social life.

Peter Berger (1969: 52) wrote that 'Every human society is, in the last resort, men [sic] banded together in the face of death'; in other words, communal efforts – especially religious rites – to manage death have throughout history been the glue of society. Inspired by Giddens, however, Mellor and Shilling (1993: 427) point to the decline of religion and ritual, which creates in the face of death what Durkheim termed 'anomie' – normlessness. They therefore modify Berger's statement thus: 'Modern society is, in the last resort, people standing *alone* in the face of death (emphasis in original).' Like Giddens, they argue that this is so terrifying that death is sidelined, sequestrated by modern society, rendering those personally facing death or bereavement even more alone.

Critique of sequestration

How credible is this sequestration thesis? First, though reflexivity may in part result from individualization and detraditionalization, it is also something *required* of citizens and patients living in neo-liberal regimes, including neo-liberal health and welfare regimes – not least twenty-first century palliative care and funeral celebrancy (Arney and Bergen, 1984; Árnason and Hafsteinsson, 2018).

Second, if we want to identify people who stand unsupported in the face of death, we should look not at affluent members of peaceful democracies, but at those who lack not just religious ritual, but also the protection of the state and of medicine – concentration camp inmates, genocide victims, sub-Saharan Africans with HIV/AIDS, and frail elderly people in poorly-run institutions (Agamben, 1998; Noys, 2005). If anyone has a motive to sideline death, it may be such people; yet they cannot, for it stares at them every day.

Third, there *is* good empirical evidence that many people in many modern societies, at least before the advent of social media, have been relatively unfamiliar with death – other than in its spectacular mass-media representations

(Jacobsen, 2016) – which can make it difficult to talk about (Chapter 4). But the evidence that death has been sidelined from society because of a specifically modern existential fear is questionable. Consider for example the claim that 'The more people prioritize issues relating to self-identity and the body, the more difficult it will be for them to cope with the idea of the self ceasing to exist' (Mellor and Shilling, 1993: 414). But Scandinavian countries prioritize issues of self-identity and the body, yet – despite the famous image of Nordic existential angst – surveys rate these countries rather low on fear of death (Zuckerman, 2008).

True, many studies have revealed high levels of death anxiety in the USA – but this finding is not replicated in all age groups or in all modern societies. In affluent countries that, unlike the USA, have well-developed welfare states and/or low levels of economic inequality, many citizens' lives become not only long, but also healthy, materially secure and suffused with general wellbeing (Wilkinson and Pickett, 2009). In such conditions, this life may prove sufficient for personal contentment (Inglehart et al., 2008). Thus Danes and Swedes display rather little fear of death and are content to find meaning in more proximate things: family, a bike ride through the forest, the company of friends (Zuckerman, 2008). Japan, 'with its lack of monotheism and comparatively widespread acceptance of death with nothing beyond, except for the groups one has been committed to that live on beyond oneself', likewise suggests widespread death anxiety to be not universal across all modern societies (Mathews, 2013: 46). Even many Americans, but noticeably more in affluent California than economically insecure Detroit, have embraced Abraham Maslow's ideal of self-actualization – in this life.

So if anxiety about death is not inherent in modernity, how do modern societies manage mortality? Sociologist Talcott Parsons argued that post-war Americans deal with death as they do with any problem – through what he termed 'practical activism': life insurance, medical check-ups, going to the gym, and so on. Far from being excluded from society, death management is part of the warp-and-woof of society and of the economy (Parsons and Lidz, 1963). Further, the process of certifying the cause of each death is central to the operation of health care, industrial safety, and criminal justice. Death statistics reveal unsafe practices in workplaces and medicine's success or failure against life-threatening diseases, and information on any one death can indicate whether or not a crime has been committed (Prior, 1997). One Australian study of the role of the dead in modern systems of governance shows how

> [t]echniques of filing … transform the speech acts of civil servants, registrars, coroners and pathologists into institutional narratives, formal records, and technocratic reports. They position the dead as neither things nor persons, but cases, records and names in an expanding bureaucratic archive. Narrating biographies of the dead, recording their lives and honouring their memories through the technology of the file has come to signify today one of the most important functions of the modern state. (Trabsky, 2017)

Whereas sequestration theorists such as Mellor and Shilling see modern death as present in private but absent in public, those who research the role of death in state bureaucracies conclude the opposite: with death typically postponed till old age, it is not so often encountered in private life, but is routinely present in bureaucratic practices. That said, even with today's culture of transparency, state files are not exactly in the public eye.

Finally, even if modernity did sequestrate death, it is highly questionable that it still does – for reasons outlined in Chapter 4. Some aspects of death may be characterized more as pervasive in society than sequestrated (Walter, 2018).

My conclusion is that death in the modern world is profoundly subject to medicalization, professionalization, rationality, and bureaucracy, and is often located in hospitals and other institutions – separated from mainstream social life. This all occurs for reasons outlined in Chapters 1 and 2; we need not look to existential anxiety to explain these processes.

TERROR MANAGEMENT

Nevertheless, theories rooted in existential anxiety continue to pop up in death studies. Inspired by Ernest Becker's (1973) book *The Denial of Death*, proponents of terror management theory (hereafter TMT) (Cave, 2012; Solomon, Greenberg and Pyszczynski, 2015) argue that a universal but largely repressed fear of personal extinction motivates humans to construct symbolic immortalities, which in turn drive not only religion, but also culture and civilization. Culture protects humans from the terror of their mortality, and thus enables them to deny it. If Freud saw civilization as built on the repression of sexuality, Becker and TMT see it as built on the repression of mortality. Sociologists Peter Berger (1969) and Zygmunt Bauman (1992) have argued on similar lines, and TMT has some similarities to sequestration theory. However, TMT publications and sociological publications on sequestration rarely cite each other and seem to have separate audiences, perhaps reflecting low levels of sociologists and psychologists citing each other in any field.

TMT has now been tested in over five hundred social psychology experiments in several countries. For TMT to say anything specifically about death in modernity, however, there must be something about modernity that destabilizes the age-old process TMT posits of culture protecting individuals from anxiety about their own extinction. As in sequestration theory, the decline of religion and of community are the most likely candidates. Elsewhere (Walter, 2017a) I have argued that fear of death is not universal but is likely a side-effect of the afterlife offered by world religions over the past three millennia, an afterlife conditional on faith, or right living, or predestination – none of which are certain. Where these religions are in decline (mainly Europe), anxiety about post-mortem destiny may linger or even grow for a while, but after a generation or two of secularization, especially in societies – such as the Nordic countries – which combine affluence with economic equality and a welfare state, death anxiety largely dissipates. Death anxiety may therefore fester during the process (but not the end stage) of secularization, and the process of industrialization so long as this is marked by economic inequality and insecurity. Stable, secular, egalitarian, advanced industrial societies do not seem to be marked, let alone driven, by death anxiety. This question of material security and insecurity, and how this complicates a simple story of 'modern death', is the theme of Part II.

My death and thy death

Brinkmann (2019) has rightly critiqued Becker for assuming that our fundamental anxiety is our own death rather than the death of those we love. He points out that as children and young adults we learn about death from others dying, long before we ourselves die. And Toynbee (1968) pointed to the other end of life where old people may fear being left alone if their lifelong partner dies first; it is the other's, not their own, death that they fear most. At both beginning and end of the lifespan, death of the other has more prominence than death of self. Brinkmann and Toynbee write as though this is universally true; they replace one universal (Becker and TMT's fear of my death) with another (fear of your death).

Historian Ariès (1981), however, provides ample evidence that each kind of fear develops in particular kinds of society. Thus church teaching in the European Middle Ages fostered anxiety about the individual's own post-mortem destination, followed in the Italian Renaissance by a celebration of individuality which was particularly vulnerable to personal extinction. Nineteenth-century Europe, by contrast, idealized romantic love and family relationships, leaving Victorians vulnerable to death of the beloved, whether spouse, lover, or child. Their anxiety about bereavement shattering an intimate relationship continues into the present century. Poll almost any group of westerners today what they most fear about death, and losing an intimate will trump fear of one's own death.

TMT experiments typically divide their subjects into two groups, one of which is subliminally exposed for a micro-second to an image of mortality such as a cemetery, and the other a control group. The two groups are then compared for some socio-political attitude, such as racism against other groups, and typically the subliminally death-aware group is the more hostile. TMT researchers interpret this as meaning that when made aware of your own mortality, you cling to your own culture, for culture is what defends humans against the terror of extinction. But from Brinkmann, Toynbee and Ariès, it seems more likely that a picture of a cemetery will conjure up in modern people a fear of bereavement rather than of their own extinction. This is no minor matter, since TMT is rooted in Becker's interpretation of existentialism and an existential fear of extinction; without that particular fear, the theory collapses.

No-one is immortal, so it can certainly be argued that all cultures are systems for enabling society to survive the deaths of the members of society. This entails sub-systems for managing 'hatching' and 'matching' as well as 'dispatching'. Rules are put in place for who may marry whom and how families and kinship systems are to be organized; socialization enables each new generation to learn society's rules; and death rites limit the damage done to groups by the death of members. (The particular challenges death poses can vary, as Ariès showed, and so the cultural solutions will vary.) To see culture as primarily a system for assuaging the individual's fear of his or her own extinction seems to owe more to existential philosophy than to empirical evidence.

In this section, I have not critiqued the idea of death denial in detail as this has been done elsewhere (Dumont and Foss, 1972; Kellehear, 1984; Walter, 2017b: Ch. 1). What I have explored, however, is whether there is anything specifically about modern societies that causes their members and their social institutions to deny death. Though there are plenty of theories suggesting this, the empirical evidence is far from conclusive. What is clear is that death reformers frequently invoke the mantra that ours is a 'death-denying society' and have done so since at least the 1960s. Sociologist Lynn Lofland (1978) brilliantly shows how this claim, despite its lack of empirical evidence, functions not as social science but as rhetoric, justifying the programme to talk more about death and bring it out into the open. The claim therefore does not need evidence to be self-perpetuating.

CONCLUSION

There are clearly many ways in which death and dying are split off from everyday life in modern societies, but I have argued that this is most convincingly explained in terms of the structural differentiation of social institutions that characterizes all areas of modern life. We do not need sociological theories of sequestration caused by existential crisis or psychological theories of denial, repression, and terror management. Though I admire these theories' ambition to relate individual psychology, even the unconscious, to society, culture and politics, they are too broad brush to pay much attention to inter-group differences. So I do not find them particularly helpful for this book's agenda – to tease out what in modern deathways results from a shared modernity, and what results from much more specific aspects of different cultures and different national histories and institutions.

FURTHER READING

- Bauman, Z. (1992) *Mortality, Immortality and Other Life Strategies*. Cambridge: Polity.

- Bayatrizi, Z. and Tehrani, R.T. (2017) 'The objective life of death in Tehran: a vanishing presence', *Mortality*, 22 (1): 15–32.

- Becker, E. (1973) *The Denial of Death*. New York: Free Press.

- Kellehear, A. (1984) 'Are we a death-denying society? A sociological review', *Social Science and Medicine*, 18 (9): 713–23.

- Lofland, L. (1978) *The Craft of Dying: The modern face of death*. Beverly Hills, CA: Sage.

- Mellor, P. and Shilling, C. (1993) 'Modernity, self-identity and the sequestration of death', *Sociology*, 27 (3): 411–31.

- Solomon, S., Greenberg, J. and Pyszczynski, T. (2015) *The Worm at the Core*. London: Penguin.

- Walter, T. (2017) *What Death Means Now*. Bristol: Policy Press, Ch. 1.

Questions to discuss

- Is there anything about modernity that causes humans to be particularly concerned about their finitude?

- Do modern societies address human finitude in a characteristically modern way?

- In answering, assess evidence not only from your own experience but also from different age groups, social classes, ethnic or national groupings within the modern world.

PART II

RISK

Part I outlined common factors that impinge on all modern societies and influence how they manage death, dying, and grief. But there are also significant differences, both within and between societies at the same level of economic development, and these interact with the common factors in complex ways. In other words, modernity – in death as in life – is multiple (Eisenstadt, 2000). Part II looks at some variations in modernity in terms of the 'landscape' of risk and inequality; it also considers variations in the physical environment itself.

Modernity is often believed to have greatly enhanced human control over nature. Certainly modernity's control of nature has drastically reduced some of the risks to life that have afflicted humankind for millennia, including many infectious diseases, certain kinds of famine, and precarious access to clean water. As Chapter 1 showed, this is why the average lifespan in a country typically doubles over the course of modernization. At the same time, modernity has increased other risks, not least the rapidity of infection from germs carried around the globe by contemporary transport systems, diseases of affluence, famine and war caused by human-induced environmental change, and the risk of ultimate extinction of the human species caused by a mix of global warming, pollution of the oceans, soil degradation and loss of biodiversity. The early years of modernity typically prove especially risky.

An example is shipwrecks, forever a hazard in sea travel. Nineteenth-century capitalism and colonialism greatly expanded global trade; this meant much more shipping, and a colossal number of wrecks – an average of several each day and loss of life equivalent to 50 jumbo jets or more a year. Ship-owners resisted change as they benefitted from insurance claims, so it was left to various Victorian moral entrepreneurs like Samuel Plimsoll who battled to introduce shore-to-ship cannon-fired lifelines, lifeboats, lifejackets, and the Plimsoll line to prevent overloading – all highly effective measures. It was not a matter of a modern economy controlling nature, but of an expanding economy expanding risk – as indeed was also the case with mine and factory accidents. So the industrialism that improved life for consumers, made it more dangerous for workers (and with steamships, both crew and passengers); and as is often the case, it was not high-tech that eventually reduced the carnage, but simple innovation and mandatory regulation.

Sometimes consumers are at risk; tobacco smokers, for example, risk getting cancer and other diseases. Their risk, as with all human-induced environmental or medical risks, was established by scientific research; and as with shipwrecks, mandatory regulation has been the most important measure in reducing risks from smoking – along with health education.

The Iranian capital Tehran today illustrates this mix of lives both saved and lost in the process of modernization. From 1960–2016, life expectancy in Iran rose dramatically from 45 to 76 (Figure 1.1), yet 'death is literally written all over Tehran' (Bayatrizi and Tehrani, 2017: 20–1). Even the city's more westernized and modern suburbs visibly display death and risk, some of it caused by modernity: murals to the martyrs of the war with Iraq, unpreparedness for likely earthquake, fatal traffic accidents, and killer smog caused in part by ageing cars that do not meet today's emissions standards.

What about those of us now living in cleaner, safer late-modern, post-industrial societies where everyday convenience depends on massive exploitation of the planet, its resources and many of its poorer inhabitants? Do you appreciate living in an unprecedentedly safe, secure and convenient world, in which light comes at the flick of a switch, clean water at the turn of a tap, and food in abundance at the supermarket? Or do you take this all for granted? Or are you anxious that living on an increasingly precarious planet will sooner or later revive violence, disaster, pandemic disease, familiarity with death, and even extinction of our species? Or are such anxieties, stemming from the mediated ideas of others, eclipsed by everyday personal experience of convenience and safety? If not, are your perceptions of danger and estimates of risk based on good evidence (Furedi, 2002)? How then does perception of risk impinge on everyday life and death?

Other risks of modernity are not directly environmental. The displacement of populations from their home may be related to resource scarcity, but not always. Many Jews in 1930s Warsaw, or middle-class Syrians in early 2000s Damascus, had little idea of the death, destruction and loss to come just a few years later.

Moving from physical to psychological or even existential risk, Chapter 4 demonstrated not only the benefits of social media, but also some of the risks; performing the bereaved self may, for some, be trickier online than face-to-face. As we shall see in Chapter 6, modern death's medicalization, rationalization, and commodification risks de-humanizing people – giving rise in some countries to a reaction in the form of innovative and more personal end-of-life, funeral, and mourning practices. And all the while, the protection from death, disease, and violence that modernity promises is unequally distributed, between and within societies, with poorer people getting sick more often, more often at the receiving end of violence, and dying earlier than richer people. And as we saw in Chapter 1 (Figure 1.2), economic inequality within a nation increases not only poorer people's risk of death from almost all causes, increasing the health divide; it also increases everyone's risk of poor health outcomes. Looking at risk opens our eyes to inequality, in death as in life.

Psychological and emotional insecurity has been central to attachment theories of grief (Parkes, 2008), but economic and material insecurity – though central to epidemiological (population level) research into the socio-economic correlations of ill health and mortality – has barely featured in studies of how societies respond to death, dying, and bereavement. Part II attempts to remedy this.

6

SECURITY AND INSECURITY

This chapter introduces two socio-political theories about how, as societies modernize, objective levels and subjective perceptions of risk change. The theories are Ronald Inglehart's theory of post-materialism (which might be better termed 'post-scarcity'), and Ulrich Beck's theory of risk society. I then do something which has not been done before, namely apply these theories to death, dying, and bereavement. The chapter concludes by combining the two in an attempt to explain the rise of the death awareness movement that has for some decades been challenging modernity's medicalization, commodification and supposed denial of death and dying.

POST-SCARCITY

Karl Marx argued that our values and beliefs derive in large measure from our economic position. This seminal idea then informed American political scientist Ronald Inglehart as he analysed data from successive waves of the World Values Survey from the 1970s to the 2000s (Inglehart, Basanez and Moreno, 1998; Inglehart and Welzel, 2005). Inglehart and his colleagues found that people whose daily lives are preoccupied with physical survival or who risk falling into poverty have different value systems from those he terms 'post-materialists' who can take economic security for granted – as do, for example, many post-war baby boomers. People value what is in short supply, so if the material goods necessary for survival are scarce, then they are what people on the breadline will value (Inglehart, 1981). As people become economically secure and move to the suburbs, other things may become relatively more scarce, such as a sense of belonging or a sense of purpose.

To feel economically secure, you are likely to have had economically stable parents so you grow up taking economic security for granted. Post-materialists are typically not the first generation enjoying an affluent society, but second and subsequent generations (Inglehart, 1981). And the more unequal a society, however affluent overall, the greater the unease that economic security cannot be taken for granted; the absence of a comprehensive welfare net further undermines the sense of security. The USA is therefore a less consistently post-material nation than Sweden. Even millionaires in a country such as the USA may have a 'fear of falling', an insecurity that without earnings or capital they will lose everything and become destitute.

Values

So how do values change as people come to feel economically secure? Those preoccupied with survival, Inglehart argues, often embrace traditional values; scarcity means that if you do not do things right, as defined by your society, then you or your family might die. You feel threatened by other cultures that do things differently, and are likely to distrust foreigners. Entertaining other worldviews is too risky; you know what works in your own society and will keep you alive, and you stick with that. But as economic security comes to be taken for granted, priorities evolve from striving for economic and physical security to quality of life, wellbeing, individual freedom and self-expression. Along with these come a concern with environmental issues, appreciation of cultural diversity and a more participatory democracy, linked to tolerance, trust and political moderation. Economic security frees people to widen their horizons and choose their own values, in death as much as in life. For example, the religion handed down by parents is replaced by personally chosen spirituality – which has implications for end-of-life care.[1]

The result is a clear divide between materialists and post-materialists not only on religion but also on tolerance of outgroups such as foreigners, refugees, gays and lesbians. In 2016 this kind of divide was clearly seen in the UK's referendum decision to leave the European Union and in Donald Trump's election as President of the USA; in both countries, those whose economic prospects had been damaged by globalization voted very differently from those who were benefitting from globalization. Another example is the global fracturing of the Anglican Church in which economically secure western churches broadly accept homosexuality while many African churches do not. Materialists and post-materialists tend to vote differently, to feel differently about the world, and to have different value systems. Post-materialists who consciously value self-expression, individual freedom and personal wellbeing are more likely to choose employment in what Bernice Martin (1981) calls the 'expressive professions' such as teaching, health care, social work, journalism and the arts rather than commerce. Those who work in palliative care and bereavement care (though not perhaps funeral directors) are therefore often more post-material than their patients and clients, rather less often the other way around.

Inglehart himself clearly values post-materialism. He sees its emphasis on trust, political participation and individual freedom as precisely the values needed by democracy. He offers a socio-economic-political version of Maslow's (1954) 'hierarchy of needs' in which, once a person's basic needs for safety, belonging and esteem are met, she or he can attend to the higher need of self-actualization. In this chapter, I am not so concerned to promote post-material values or self-actualization, nor indeed with criticisms of Inglehart's work. Rather, I intend to use his theory as a tool to understand developments and differences in how people in modern societies think about and manage the ultimate insecurity of death and dying – just as they help us understand the election of Trump or splits in the Anglican Church.

In this chapter, I adapt Inglehart's terminology. 'Materialism' has a negative connotation, and 'post-material' could be taken to imply that people, however non-material their values, turn their back on material goods, which is clearly not the case. Affluent 'post-materialists' in California consume far more of the world's resources than do 'materialists' in the global South. While continuing to use the term 'post-materialism', I more often use the terms 'scarcity' and 'post-scarcity' that point more directly to the economic base of people's values and also which do not risk implying any disrespect for much of the world's population.

Scarcity's origins

We need to note one caveat about the term 'scarcity'. In his much cited article 'The original affluent society' (1974), anthropologist Marshall Sahlins argued that hunter-gather societies were the original affluent society:

> Hunter-gatherers consume less energy per capita per year than any other group of human beings. Yet ... all [their] material wants were easily satisfied. To accept that hunters are affluent is therefore to recognize that the present human condition of man [sic] slaving to bridge the gap between his unlimited wants and his insufficient means is a tragedy of modern times. There are two possible courses to affluence. Wants may be easily satisfied either by producing much or desiring little. (p. 181)

Hunter-gatherers desire little, and so feel they have all they need. There is considerable evidence that scarcity arose when people settled down and became farmers. Though this increased the amount of food available per acre, it also increased the hours spent producing food, along with rendering populations vulnerable to poor harvests and economic inequality (Boserup, 1965). Such precariousness continues for many subsistence farmers today, just as it does for waged labour in the early years of industrialization. Meanwhile, today's few remaining hunter-gatherers find their traditional hunting lands encroached on by local farmers and/or agri-business, so they are neither as cut off from modernity nor as affluent as they once were. Scarcity therefore increasingly has become the common lot of humankind since Neolithic times when hunters first turned to farming, and then again in recent times when settled farmers lose their land and become landless workers in an industrializing society. Only since the mid-twentieth century, and only in the First World, has a significant minority of humans enjoyed an economically secure, post-scarcity era. That said, since the early 1990s collapse of Japan's post-war boom (Allison, 2013) and throughout much of the West since the 2008 financial crash, economic security is now proving elusive for many of the grandchildren of Inglehart's baby-boomer post-materialists (Standing, 2011).

Even within mature industrial societies, and even before these financial crises, not everyone felt economically secure. The expansion of white-collar jobs through much of the twentieth century along with post-war prosperity were followed in the late twentieth century by the collapse of secure factory jobs, leaving a much expanded middle class, along with an increasing 'precariat' of workers (both white collar and manual) depending on casual jobs and short-term contracts, and an underclass unable to sustain itself through paid employment (Standing, 2011). The more unequal the society, and the less comprehensive its welfare services, the more vulnerable is a sizeable portion of its population to economic insecurity. The consequence of such inequality is higher death rates, along with higher rates of other manifestations of societal dysfunction, including homelessness, mental illness, suicide, and violence (Wilkinson and Pickett, 2009). Another consequence, I will argue, are perspectives on end-of-life care, euthanasia, funerals, grief, abortion, and capital punishment that can be markedly different from those held by the more secure who live in a post-scarcity bubble.

Managing the end of life

Living with insecurity, never knowing whether one will be out of a job tomorrow or whether this year's harvest will fail and the family starve, does not foster a sense of control over one's life. On the contrary, it can lead to fatalism (Hoggart, 1957), or to seeking protection by trusting God, placating the ancestors or performing magical rites. If I am powerless, believing in an all-powerful God may be immensely reassuring – at least someone is in control of things. The power of ritual to influence events can also reassure. By contrast, families who have experienced economic security for more than a generation more readily have a sense of personal control over their life; the ability to predict circumstances tomorrow, next year or even ten years ahead enables choices and decisions that feel well founded.

Of course, not everyone fits this pattern. Some who have experienced catastrophic economic or political circumstances but who have managed to migrate to another country do so with great determination to take control of their life, against the odds. If the country to which they migrate is the USA, this personal determination is supported by a national culture that affirms that anyone can succeed. And there are plenty of modern societies, Japan and India for example, where religious ritual as well as scientific/medical technique are regularly employed to help individuals and communities stay safe.

There is evidence that these two orientations – a sense of personal control, and handing control over to God or fate – greatly affect the experience of dying. A study of preferences about control at the end of life among 65–85-year-old Canadians distinguished 'activists' from 'delegators' (Kelner, 1995). Delegators – found equally in middle and working class – left decisions about end-of-life care to the doctor, to God, or to fate. Activists – much more likely to be middle class and well educated – had more confidence in their ability to control their own destiny, and therefore were more likely to make their own decisions and not uncritically accept the doctor's authority. The difference is expressed in these two women: 'I would leave it to the doctors; it's a sin to try to control your dying. We must just accept our fate and wait until we die' and 'I want the control myself; it's my life and I should be the one to make the choices'. Kelner (1995: 542) comments that '[t]he current ideology of greater consumer participation in medical decision-making has clearly had little impact on … delegators.' This fits widespread evidence that in North America the more religiously devout are more likely to trust modern medicine.

A more recent study of non-institutionalized San Franciscans aged 67–98 with a life expectancy of less than a year (Romo et al., 2017) found they 'generally delegated decisions to others'. This enabled them to 'achieve a sense of control without being in control of decisions.' Like Kelner, the authors conclude that their findings 'challenge the prevailing view of personal autonomy.' If one would expect a strong sense of personal autonomy, surely it would be in San Francisco? Why then is it not expressed as these residents face the end of their long lives?

One possibility is that this particular sample does not represent the generation most likely to value personal autonomy, namely the post-war baby boomers who are only now beginning to enter old age. Another possibility, which to my knowledge has yet to be researched, is that elderly frailty can reduce even lifelong post-materialists to a preoccupation with basic survival. They may spend hours each day getting dressed, struggling to the bathroom, washing, preparing a simple meal, often having to rest after each of these operations. Any movement risks a fall, so care has to be taken at all times. As an elderly friend with Parkinson's told me, 'It's like all your life you'd been flying your plane on auto-pilot, but now every single movement has to be done consciously, manually. It's very, very tiring.' Every minute, every move, risks catastrophe. The physical security that underlay the youthful and middle-aged experience of personal control is eroded. It may be rational at this point to hand control over to others.

Abortion and Euthanasia

Abortion and euthanasia are very specific forms of death that each society must decide whether, and if so how, to allow. During periods when there is pressure to decriminalize or legalize them, there can be considerable parliamentary, public and media debate that reflects and/or shapes public opinion and personal attitudes. Abortion and voluntary euthanasia/assisted dying are likely to be chosen by individuals who want control and mastery over their life, and unlikely to be chosen by those who accept fate or God's will; so we might expect attitudes to these two issues to be related to economic security or insecurity. And indeed it seems clear that liberal views on each of these issues are more likely to be held by post-materialists. Those whose lives are preoccupied with survival are more likely to be fatalistic – in turn associated with conservative or fundamentalist religion which sees life and death as ultimately in divine, not human, hands (Cohen et al., 2006).

The more economically unequal a society, the more torn it is likely to be between scarcity and post-scarcity values, and hence between support for and opposition to abortion and euthanasia (not to mention other life-and-death issues such as capital punishment, gun control, suicide, and AIDS). The USA, one of the most unequal of advanced industrial societies, is sharply divided between the economically secure and the insecure; and it is host to some of the bitterest conflicts on life-and-death issues. Each side not only disagrees with its opponents but often cannot even comprehend the other's sincerely held views. They inhabit very different worlds.

This polarization has become even more marked with the arrival of social media. Search engines suggest to each user sites consistent with his or her browsing history. Thus a conservative Catholic with a history of viewing pro-life anti-abortion sites, and a liberal Episcopalian with a history of viewing of feminist pro-abortion sites, on entering the same search term will find their computer, tablet or phone listing very different sites, these sites supporting the user's pre-existing views. And worse, unlike the days of old media when readers of right-wing tabloid newspapers knew they were reading content different from that in liberal broadsheets, online the Catholic and the liberal may not realize they are being fed different information. The mutual incomprehension of, and disdain for, each other therefore grows: 'Given what I know and surely they must also know, how can they believe *that*!' But online, what they read and what I read are not the same, so what they know and what I know are not the same.

Searching for meaning

Palliative care aims to be holistic, encompassing spiritual, psychological and emotional as well as physical needs. At least in English speaking countries, palliative care defines spirituality as an individual search for meaning; this search is considered primordial, universal – unlike religion, which only some people embrace (Bramadat, Coward and Stajduhar, 2013). Seen from the perspective of this chapter, however, individual spirituality appears as post-material. Over recent millennia most humans, struggling to survive, have accepted the beliefs and rites of their society that provide a secure framework for living in a materially insecure world. It is only when material security is guaranteed that people can afford to break free and explore the meaning of life for themselves, wherever it might take them. Of course, throughout history there have been exceptional individuals who have done that. But here I am talking about most people, and what is culturally expected of them. The expectation that each individual should work out the meaning of life for themselves is very recent, and – I suggest – located within the post-material condition.

Put this way, the individual's search for meaning could mean positive liberation from externally imposed meaning. It could also be more negative, or more challenging. It could be that existential security – trust that 'people, things, places, and our sense of self are more or less consistent' (Lagerkvist, 2017: 102) – is undermined by modernity's erosion of tradition (Chapter 5) and specifically by consumer society, social and geographical mobility, and the precarity of post-2008 austerity. For existentialist media studies scholar Amanda Lagerkvist (2017: 107), the human being is no autonomous sovereign but one 'who sometimes stumbles, falls, misunderstands, struggles, is vulnerable, hurting, speechless, and finds no solution; but who may also experience moments of ultimate meaning, community, support, and fullness.' The question is whether this is *the* human condition, as Lagerkvist suggests, or more the post-material condition as I am suggesting here. She comes from Sweden, perhaps the ultimate post-scarcity society.

Whatever the answer, it is clear that palliative care workers whose background and/or training fosters post-material values can have very different understandings of spiritual care from many of their patients (Garces-Foley, 2006b). Some palliative care staff consider spiritual care – understood as helping patients find their own meaning in life and death – to be integral to their work, yet are illiterate about religion (Pentaris, 2018). How these differences are then negotiated in clinical encounters needs researching.

Outside of Western Europe, things are often different (Coleman, 2016). In post-communist Serbia where everyday survival continues to preoccupy much of the population, traditional religion has revived, not only to sustain a revived national identity but also in the personal encounter with death (Pavicevic, 2015: 119). Across East Asia, ancestral rites evolve as societies de-colonize and urbanize (Endres and Lauser, 2011); or may be replaced by a secular acceptance that the visible, material world is all there is (Reader, 2012). In many parts of the world, the idea that each individual be required to make their own sense of life and death is incomprehensible.

Funerals

In Chapter 3, I argued that families whose social standing is not entirely secure may – as far as they are able – spend rather lavishly on funerals (and weddings) as a show of economic respectability. As families become more settled and economically secure, the funeral may no longer be needed to display economic or ethnic status; instead, it is used to celebrate the deceased's individuality. But post-material funerals can display other things as well as the deceased's uniqueness. I give two examples here: cremation in the USA, and green burial.

Stephen Prothero's (2000) history of cremation in the USA asks why that country's mid twentieth-century cremation rate, so much lower than in most other developed countries, only began to rise, slowly, from the 1970s. Prothero argues that cremation fitted many baby boomers' anti-materialist, environmental style. (Late twentieth-century boomers were beginning to organize their parents' funerals; they were not themselves yet dying in significant numbers.) Some had read Jessica Mitford's (1963) searing critique of the mid-century American way of death; what resonated was not so much her exposé of the industry's pricing tactics but of the products being crass, over the top, baroque. Fine for manual workers or for first/second generation migrants to ride (when dead!) in a Cadillac, but for financially secure and longer-established Americans 'the secret of end-of-century cremation's success was not that it was cheap but that it was not tawdry' (Prothero, 2000: 210).

Another kind of post-material ending is green or natural burial, where the body is buried in a wood or meadow without embalming and in an easily bio-degradable coffin, with minimal or no marker. Several countries offer variations on this theme. In some European countries and in Japan (Boret, 2014), natural burial may refer to the unmarked burial of ashes in a natural environment. Natural burial may be no cheaper than a conventional burial (Sloane, 2018), and if it entails mourners driving a long way to a favoured site may even have a higher carbon footprint than conventional burial or cremation. The only fully natural way for a large mammal such as a human to be disposed of is for it to lie on the ground and there be eaten by predators, bugs and worms. No natural burial fans are advocating that! Natural burial is therefore as cultural as any other kind of burial, even if it consumes somewhat fewer resources. What matters is its symbolism, representing post-material ecological values.

Bereavement

In unpublished teaching material, Susan LePoidevin identified several dimensions of loss: identity (the person's self-concept, values, self-esteem), emotional (their emotional equilibrium, how they express emotions), spiritual (the meaning given to the loss, religious comfort or distress), practical (learning new tasks), physical (effects on health), lifestyle (need to move house, take a job), family/community (change in family/community roles). She does not specifically list a material dimension, but this is implied in the practical and lifestyle dimensions. Which dimensions of loss are culturally acknowledged depends, I have argued elsewhere (Walter, 2017b), on economics.

For many on the edge of survival, bereavement's primary challenge may be material. This is clearly shown in a recent study of bereavement in urban Senegal; the loss of a breadwinner may mean that some children can no longer go to school – school uniforms may now be unaffordable or children may now have to go out to work. Unlike well-to-do mourners in the West, bereaved family members had few words with which to tell the researchers about their emotions, and often could say little more than 'It was hard' (Ribbens McCarthy et al., 2018).

To take another example of dire loss, refugees have myriad practical concerns that take priority if they are to survive, however bereft they feel after the loss of spouse, parent, child, or homeland. At the time of writing, many thousands of migrants attempt to cross the Sahara and then the Mediterranean to get to Europe; their families may have borrowed heavily in order to fund the passage, in anticipation of future remittances when the migrant gets to Europe and finds work there. If the migrant dies en route, as many do, the family is left penniless and without hope, as well as bereft.

Economic security enables the emotional dimension to be prioritized as what grief is 'really' about, as in much of twentieth-century grief psychology and counselling. Exploring grief's emotions through individual talk and therapy (rather than prescribed ritual) becomes culturally possible, and even normative (Wortman and Silver, 1989). By contrast when survival dominates, so too do practical concerns, along – often – with a culturally expected stoicism that consciously puts emotions on hold (Stroebe and Schut, 1999; Merridale, 2000; Jalland, 2010).

A heroic story

Inglehart sees the move toward post-material values as progress, furthering democracy. The preceding paragraphs have outlined various ways that the shift from preoccupation with survival to a sense of economic security also radically affects how people manage death, dying, and loss. Significantly, this 'post-scarcity' death and dying is also seen as progress by many in the 'death awareness movement'. Patient autonomy instead of passive acceptance of doctor's orders, palliative care's focus on the whole person (including spirituality), personalized funerals, expressing grief's emotions – these are all components of a 'good death' as seen by those who work in palliative and bereavement care, whether or not their patients, clients and customers want this. The death awareness movement is a post-material movement – to be explored toward the end of this chapter.

RISK SOCIETY

There is, however, a less heroic view of security, insecurity and risk in late modernity. Marxism points to inequality and insecurity as inherent in modernity, while ecological thinking highlights all manner of new risks created even as some older risks are eradicated. Though there is considerable evidence that violence tends to decrease over the very long term (Pinker, 2012), it is also true that modernity was born in violence. This includes the violence of civil wars of liberation - from the English Civil War, the French Revolution, and the American Civil War, right through to the twenty-first century. It also includes the violence of global trade – whether directly through the slave trade or indirectly through colonial and neo-colonial domination. At the time of writing (2019), war and civil war, not least in the Middle East, have created more refugees in Europe than at any time since the Second World War. If the superpowers once managed to outsource violence by waging proxy wars in the global South, now the survivors of violence are arriving in their millions at the borders of affluent countries.

At the same time, modernity's environmental consequences create new risks by the minute. Paradoxically, these risks can often only be identified through modern science – examples being the discovery of the hole in the ozone layer and the documentation of global warming. Then there are the political risks of globalization, as manufacturing moves from Europe and North America to parts of the world where labour is cheaper. Many of those left behind in the First World's de-industrialized 'rust belt' feel that political elites no longer represent them, leading in 2016 to the dramatic election of Donald Trump in the USA and the UK referendum vote to leave the European Union.

Whereas the International Labour Organization talks of rights, and the United Nations of human needs, the World Bank (2013: xii) – arguably more powerful than either – focuses on risk, both managing risk and taking entrepreneurial risks: 'Building resilience to risk is essential to achieving prosperity … whether one is grappling with natural disasters, pandemics, financial crises, a wave of crime at the community level, or the severe illness of a household's chief provider.' The seminal sociology text on risk is Ulrich Beck's *Risk Society* (1992), which analyses both the risks modernity creates and its need to manage risk.

A key question is whether a late-modern world is preoccupied with managing risk because the world has become potentially more dangerous, or because we are now more aware of risk. Bruno Latour (2003: 36–8) argues the latter:

> 'Risk' does not mean that people are nowadays leading a more dangerous life than before – this would fly in the face of all the life expectancy tables and would be an insult to the masses still dying in the throes of typically modern engineered famines. … 'Reflexive' does not signal an increase in mastery and consciousness, but only a heightened awareness that mastery is impossible and that control over actions is now seen as a complete modernist fiction.

As to 'risk', it does not mean that we run more dangers than before, but that we are now entangled, whereas the modernist dream was to disentangle us from the morass of the past.

We never have been modern, in that modernity never described its deeds accurately: it only believed it controlled nature.

By choosing not to look at side effects and externalities, for example that the industrial revolution depended on colonial exploitation or that economic growth is wrecking the planet, modernity gave the impression of heroic mastery of nature. As Latour (2003: 40) puts it, 'The incredible freedom and creativity of the moderns was due to nothing but the ability for their right hand to ignore what their left hand was doing.' Ecological thinking that shows how everything is connected is now making such ignorance less and less possible.

Risk aversion

As physical and social environments become safer, awareness of – and aversion to – risk increases (Furedi, 2002). Health and safety legislation has made workplaces measurably safer, yet at the same time can limit individual initiative. The requirement to check on the police record of anyone working with children or vulnerable adults reflects increased awareness of potential abuse, yet can discourage volunteering, neighbourliness or spontaneous help to a stranger.

According to some recent British studies, this can impact end-of-life care, for example in the requirement that anyone, other than a family member, coming into contact with a dying person has to be trained, not to mention police checked. What does this do to neighbourliness and friendship? It seems to define care as the domain either of professionals (who have relatively little time) or of families (who may be exhausted). Risk-averse health care professionals can be protective about 'their' patients being helped by non-family non-professionals. As a frustrated volunteer said:

We've got health care so wrapped up in risk aversion and … bureaucracy that nurses were saying 'I'm not sure about this and that', but for goodness sake, people have gone to have a cup of tea in people's houses for centuries. (Zaman et al., 2018: 142)

Suresh Kumar, a leading Indian advocate of community action in palliative care, notes:

A system that does not have the room to use the various capabilities of lay people is an 'underdeveloped' system. This is why I would call the health systems in many European countries 'undeveloped'. (Unpublished, quoted in Zaman et al., 2018: 142)

Risk-averse systems foster a risk-averse mentality, which in turn, Zaman et al. fear, limit free-flowing compassion at the end of life as in the rest of life.

In his ethnography of how rural English people use communication media toward the end of life, Miller (2017) became concerned about another manifestation of risk aversion – health care organizations' obsession with patient confidentiality. He concluded this was 'the single major cause of harm to patients other than disease itself' (p. 214). He found palliative care staff frustrated by confidentiality regulations that prevented the easy sharing of information about patients between professionals; staff from different agencies, night staff, hospice workers who were not part of the NHS, any of these might not have access to a patient's record when they needed it. Designed to protect patients, 'confidentiality' did the opposite. Professionals could give many examples of this, but none could recall a single instance of a patient who had been protected by such regulations. In the 1950s, Cicely Saunders, the founder of the hospice movement, challenged doctors' reluctance to give morphine to dying patients because the drug is addictive; Saunders pointed out that risk of addiction is not an issue for someone who is dying. Sixty years later, those who work in palliative care – not to mention their patients – are still struggling with practices designed to reduce patient risk that actually increase it.

THE DEATH AWARENESS MOVEMENT

Inglehart welcomes the shift from scarcity to post-scarcity; for him, it represents modernity's greatest triumph. Beck, Latour, Furedi and other theorists of risk are much more ambivalent about the shift from triumphant modernism to risk society. Yet these very different theories can each contribute to an understanding of a death awareness movement that seeks to challenge death's denial, commodification, and medicalization.

First risk. As we saw in Chapter 1, modernity has succeeded in controlling the life-threatening infections that throughout history led to premature death for at least half the population. Some progress is now being made in reducing death from non-infectious diseases such as cancer and especially heart disease, even though modern living makes these diseases more prevalent. And the risks created by death's medicalization include the inhumanity of hospital dying, loss of agency in many people's dying, being kept alive as a vegetable, and life extension into an unwanted frail and demented deep old age. Physical successes in the battle against the Grim Reaper have been won at social, psychological, spiritual, and economic cost. A significant proportion of modern health care systems is spent in the last months of life, yet people end up dying wired to life-support systems that isolate them from family and friends, or dying in institutional warehouses for the demented elderly. Family, friends, and health care workers struggle with health care bureaucracies whose rules and practices may limit patient wellbeing and undermine expressed wishes. 'Choices' offered by neo-liberal health systems can reflect legal and financial constraints more than what patients and families might want. People who have exercised agency throughout life are denied agency in their dying. The result is that post-materialists have to trust medical and care systems they may not actually trust. The problem of modern dying is a classic problem of risk society in which modernity has created new risks whose management has become an obsession.

The death awareness movement as a whole is a response to the physical, psychological, social and spiritual risks caused by modern medicalized, bureaucratic dying. Movement members try to create a more humane way of dying. This is clearly what the hospice and palliative care movement intends. It is also what the right to die movement intends, along with those promoting advance directives. And death cafés aim to provide a free space where people can reclaim grass-roots communication about death and dying from framing by medicine, the market and the media (Fong, 2017).

At this point, Beck and Inglehart's theories offer illumination, for the death awareness movement is, it seems to me, a post-material response to risk society. Focusing on talk, on spirituality, on psychological wellbeing, on achieving a good death, it is a post-scarcity – and largely female – response to the risks engendered by modernity's (mainly male) marginalization of death and loss. A Serbian ethnologist, all too familiar with death, displacement, and civil war, told me she considers the American and British death awareness movements to be a response by a rather safe and secure society that has become unfamiliar (Ariès, 1981) with death, a society that can afford the luxury of end-of-life care plans, advance directives, and self-actualization in dying. She doubted that the movement's values and policies easily translate to those parts of the world, or even those parts of otherwise affluent societies, preoccupied with survival.

As Francis (2019: 97) observes of the American death awareness movement, its leaders 'are middle-class, college-educated white women. Eager to bring conversations about dying to marginalized communities, [they] sometimes fail to recognize conversations already taking place. How might the movement engage with the death activism of *Black Lives Matter*?' Many African Americans are concerned about the risk that their teenage sons may be shot by the police, not that an elderly death may be over-medicalized. Many mothers in Mexico are terrified their children will get caught up in drug violence. Britons living in inner cities may be anxious that their son will be stabbed by another teenager, and of their powerlessness in reducing such stabbings. For many such communities, getting to old age and dying in hospital of cancer is no risk but something to be thankful for, and cause for far less comment than violent teenage death. The contrast with the death concerns of the post-materialists who populate death cafés can hardly be more striking. Death by violence, overdose or starvation does not fit the death awareness movement's agenda to turn existential anxiety about mortality into anticipation of customizing one's own natural, self-expressive death (Lofland, 1978). Meanwhile, some hospice workers valiantly serve those dying homeless under damp, cold bridges in Britain, or dying of AIDS in sub-Saharan Africa, of fading away with dementia in care homes.

CONCLUSION

This chapter has considered 'high modernity', in particular how people's values change as they come to feel economically secure and how this contrasts with those who continue to live a life of insecurity. Two theories have been used. One, post-materialism, suggests that economic security frees people to be more self-expressive, concerned with personal self-fulfilment, and wanting to exert personal control over their lives. This agenda clearly resonates with that of palliative and bereavement care, and with liberal views on euthanasia and abortion. The more economically unequal a society, however, the more likely it is to be split on such issues.

The other theory, 'risk society', more pessimistically perceives a high modern obsession with managing the risks that result from modernity – risks to the environment, to health, and to the human soul. The death awareness movement identifies risks to the quality of dying induced by modern bureaucratic health care and seeks to manage them through humanizing end-of-life care, and injecting post-material values of personal expression, personal autonomy and personal spirituality. This may be welcomed by well-off baby boomers in the West, but misses the mark entirely for those preoccupied with their own and their children's survival in rust-belt America, in drug-ridden Mexico City, or in unseaworthy boats bearing refugees across the Mediterranean to Europe. These too are part of modernity, part of the modern way of dying.

FURTHER READING

- Beck, U. (1992) *Risk Society: Towards a new modernity*. London: Sage.

- Cohen, J., Marcoux, I., Bilsen, J., Deboosere, P., van der Wal, G. and Deliens, L. (2006) 'European public acceptance of euthanasia: socio-demographic and cultural factors associated with the acceptance of euthanasia in 33 European countries', *Social Science and Medicine*, 63 (3): 743–56.

- Garces-Foley, K. and Holcomb, J.S. (2005) 'Contemporary American funerals: personalizing tradition', in K. Garces-Foley (ed.), *Death and Religion in a Changing World*. Armonk, NY: M.E. Sharpe, pp. 207–27.

- Inglehart, R. (1981) 'Post-materialism in an environment of insecurity', *American Political Science Review*, 75: 880–900.

- Inglehart, R. and Welzel, C. (2005) *Modernization, Cultural Change and Democracy*. New York: Cambridge University Press.

- Kelner, M. (1995) 'Activists and delegators: elderly patients' preferences about control at the end of life', *Social Science and Medicine*, 41 (4): 537–45.

- Ribbens McCarthy, J., Evans, R., Bowlby, S. and Wouango, J. (2018) 'Making sense of family deaths in urban Senegal', *OMEGA – Journal of Death and Dying*, 25 October.

- Wilkinson, R. and Pickett, K. (2009) *The Spirit Level: Why equality is better for everyone*. London: Allen Lane.

Questions to discuss

- Choice in dying, voluntary euthanasia, personalized funerals, and addressing the emotional needs of bereaved people are rarely valued in economically insecure families or societies. Other priorities dominate – what are they?

- How does economic inequality in your own country affect attitudes or practices concerning death, dying and loss?

Note

1. There are some similarities with terror management theory (see Chapter 5), in that each theory argues that a sense of vulnerability causes individuals to cling more tenaciously to their culture. Inglehart posits economic insecurity as the chief cause of vulnerability, TMT posits mortality awareness. Since economic insecurity increases risks to life and often increases awareness of life's fragility, there is potential for integrating the theories. The introduction to Part III hints at some implications of this.

7

THE PHYSICAL WORLD

Though modernity has to some considerable extent domesticated nature, the physical world remains both a very real constraint on and enabler of human behaviour. Humans act in a physical and social environment; they have a body. This is true of the end as well as of the rest of life: death may be social, spiritual, existential but it is also irreducibly physical. Social, economic, and political factors greatly influence the risk of dying, but death always has immediate physical causes and dying is experienced in a body which occupies a space, whether that be a small apartment, a hospital bed, or a killing field. Dead bodies have to be disposed of. Even our afterlife imaginations are geographical, physical: death is imagined as a journey from here to there, heaven is imagined as a place, reincarnation is into another body.

DISPOSING OF THE DEAD

The physical environment has clearly shaped traditional ways to dispose of the dead. The very dry air of Egypt and of the Andes made it possible naturally to dry and mummify the corpse. Religions originating in hot climates, such as Judaism and Islam, typically bury the body within 24 hours, while humans living in the Arctic may keep the bodies of those dying in winter until the spring for burial. Those who die at sea – until very recently – have had to be buried at sea. Disposing of bodies is a physical affair, so it is not surprising that the physical environment limits what forms of disposal are possible.

The physical environment has also helped shape concepts of the afterlife. The idea of death as a journey across a river emerged in Mesopotamia and Egypt, civilizations founded on rivers.[1] Islam – a religion whose origins lie in the desert – came to see paradise as a garden, an oasis in an otherwise dry land. The Bible depicts heaven both as a garden (referring back to the original Garden of Eden) and as a city (perhaps inspired by Jerusalem, the holy city). It is not surprising if the landscape of heaven is pictured in relation to the landscapes that the living both endure and enjoy (Tuan, 1974).

To an extent, modern technology can sidestep some environmental constraints. Mechanical diggers make lighter, though never light, work of rocky and frozen ground. Refrigeration enables corpses in hot climates to be kept for longer. Fast marine engines, helicopters and airplanes enable some of those who die at sea to be transported home. That said, notions of what comprises culturally proper disposal of the dead, especially if enshrined in religion, can continue for many generations if not indefinitely after modern technology has rendered redundant the original environmental reason for the practice. When modern technology is embraced, as with refrigeration facilities for the dead in some parts of West Africa, this may be esteemed as a mark of modernity; or it may be seen pragmatically – with extended family spread across the globe, it can enable the funeral to be delayed until everyone can attend.

CONSTRAINING NOT DETERMINING

The environment rarely determines human behaviour. More often it constrains, creates limits, makes certain courses of action relatively easy, others more difficult. Or it may suggest possibilities – doubtless mummification originated in 'natural' mummies where the climate dessicated the body. But though this option was taken up in the high Andes, in Tibet's similarly frozen, rocky, tree-less high plateau where both burial and cremation are difficult, the preferred option came instead to be sky burial, that is, leaving the body out in the open for vultures and other creatures to consume. And sometimes a society engages in practices that, on purely environmental grounds, seem unnecessarily difficult. Thus the Toraja of Sulawesi, Indonesia, despite their damp tropical climate which might suggest speedy burial or cremation, instead allow the corpse to dry and mummify over a period of months or even years until they can afford to give it a proper funeral. In the meantime, the body remains part of the household. Torajan mortuary customs have been the subject of anthropological studies (Tsintjilonis, 2007), and now attract tourists as well.

Western burial practices

In countries that traditionally bury, shortage of land influences but does not determine practices. Rapid urbanization in nineteenth-century Europe and North America led to a population explosion and a drastic reduction in readily available land for burial, but this was responded to in three very different ways.

Continental European countries responded by systematizing the old ad hoc medieval practice of re-using graves; instead of gravediggers simply relocating any bones they unearthed as they had done for centuries, the new rational practice provided grave leases for a set number of years after which the body would be decomposed and the grave could be re-used. On expiry of the lease, families could choose to extend it if they so desired, a sustainable system which remains to this day.

Victorian Britain, however, chose to develop new and large out-of-town cemeteries in which bodies could rest in perpetuity; as each cemetery filled up and the city encroached around it, the cemetery was intended to evolve into a nature- and monument-filled haven of recreation and moral uplift; and a new out-of-town cemetery would be started on the city's new periphery (Loudon, 1981). Unfortunately, the public's will to visit declined, both because memories faded and because the urban park movement provided competition for Sunday strolling; maintenance of graves declined as families lost interest and the number of grave lots sold declined. Some cemeteries went bust; municipalities took over, and promoted cremation as a pragmatic solution to financially unsound burial (Jupp, 2006).

The USA was different again; it too opted for large out-of-town cemeteries, but cemetery owners and managers knew that American families were mobile and might not be able to look after graves themselves; so plot prices included a sum to fund maintenance by the cemetery company; the lawn cemetery was then developed with absent families in mind – with no headstones, maintenance by the cemetery company was cheap and easy (Sloane, 2018).

An Icelandic volcano

The environment can shape not only burial but also other life-and-death-related practices. A few years ago while on holiday in Iceland, we intended to climb one of its many volcanoes. The hotel we stayed at prior to the climb provided tourists with very clear instructions what to do should signs of volcanic activity become manifest while on the mountain. The recommended 14-point escape plan could be reduced to one: Get off the mountain pronto! That evening I asked the young waitress at the hotel what she did when the volcano showed signs of erupting, which it does every decade or so. It turned out she lived on the farm next door, and she answered: 'We put on our motorcycle helmets, get on our quad bikes and head toward the mountain to get our horses and sheep off the mountain.' There is clearly logic in this: why save your life if your means of livelihood – your precious livestock – have all perished? And there is also logic in the advice to tourists: the last thing the area needs is tourist fatalities. So, how humans respond to this regularly erupting volcano depends on whether they are farmers or tourists.

The home

Environments are social as well as physical, none more so than the home. The meaning of home varies and can change over time, not least at the end of life.

Surveys in several western countries show that people – at least when surveyed in good health – would like, if possible, to die at home, surrounded by family. This is also what many non-westerners see as a good death (van der Pijl, 2016). Not so in Singapore. In this crowded little island city state, most purchase a small apartment in a high-rise Housing Development Board block; adults do not qualify for a HDB apartment until they marry, so it is common for single adults in their twenties or thirties still to be living in the parental apartment. With home being rather crowded, most Singaporeans go out to eat, drink, and socialize. For the same reason, they also prefer to go out to die, that is, to hospital.

PRESENT HAZARDS

Technology and technique may reduce traditional environmental risks and eliminate some environmental constraints (such as day and night, or having to walk to fetch water), but even in modernity the physical environment continues to present traditional risks to life, which this section explores. A later section discusses future and potential environmental risks to life that modernity itself creates.

I am British, and it is easy for Britons to imagine that modernity has controlled nature. But Britain is one of the most geologically, climatically, and biologically benign parts of the globe. We are not threatened by volcanoes, earthquakes, tsunamis, hurricanes, tornados, drought, or extremes of temperature or rainfall; we have no significantly poisonous or dangerous animals or insects; and harvests are more or less guaranteed. Perhaps the main exception is the sea, which for many millennia has provided Britons with a convenient yet dangerous means of transport.

Most modern societies, however, inhabit less amenable territory. In south eastern Australia, where most Australians live, suburban houses and gardens are designed to resist bushfires; and their inhabitants are cautious lest their little children encounter a potentially lethal redback spider in the garden. The country is one of the most urbanized in the world, in part because so much of the terrain is inhospitable to anything other than very low-intensity ranching or hunter-gathering. Driving across the outback requires preparation for how to survive in the event of a breakdown. So urban Australians are less prone than Britons to romanticize nature; they know only too well it can kill.

It is no coincidence that Australia was one of the first places to pioneer the compassionate community approach to end-of-life care in the 1990s. In remote outback communities where travel to access specialist health care can take hours or days, people have got used to caring for one another; survival, let alone health and wellbeing, depend on, to use the sociological jargon, mobilizing your social capital and your local social networks. Sociologist Allan Kellehear, working at La Trobe University in Melbourne, had the insight that what works in the outback could also benefit urban communities. However well-resourced health services might be, most of a sick or dying person's time is not spent in the company of health professionals; mobilizing the supportive capacity of friends, neighbours, families, employers, colleagues, and so on is therefore central to wellbeing as life comes towards its end.

The sea

A significant amount of the Netherlands is polder – land reclaimed from the sea. For centuries, windmills have been pumping water out of the polder, and dykes have been built and maintained to keep the water away from farmland and settlements. Without constant vigilance, much of this country – one of the first to modernize – would be inundated.

From accompanying Dutch general practitioners in their home visits to dying patients, American anthropologist Frances Norwood (2009) concluded that Dutch euthanasia – physician-assisted dying – can be understood in terms of Dutch history, culture, and institutions. Her conclusion that 'policy is not transferable to other countries without consideration of both structural and cultural contexts' (p. 229) chimes with the approach of this book. Norwood shows how euthanasia in the Netherlands is not just an act, but a series of conversations between patient, family and GP; for every ten dying patients who initiate a conversation about euthanasia, only one is likely actually to be helped to die by their doctor. She roots this process in several aspects of Dutch life such as single-handed GPs who get to know their patients well, and a consensus culture based on a low power differential between workers and bosses, and between lay people and professionals. Such features, absent in many modern societies, foster informed, honest, open, trusting conversations.

Norwood also considers Dutch euthanasia practices to be rooted in a characteristically Dutch emphasis on order and control, based, she argues, on a historical and present relationship to nature: 'It is the process of euthanasia talk, not the final decision made, that creates the order for which Dutch people … strive' (p.112). Controlling nature by maintaining dykes and taking control of the natural process of dying are variations on the same theme. Whereas in Norwood's home country – the USA – euthanasia typically entails a discourse of choice and freedom, in the Netherlands it comprises a discourse of control. Not everyone agrees with Norwood's analysis, but she raises the possibility that – as with Australia's development of compassionate community policies – historical and present experience of the natural environment can open up new ways of imagining and managing the physical process of dying.

From Viking travellers to coastal fishermen to contemporary oil workers, the sea has been central to Norwegian society and economy, a resource for living – and a cause of death. Most communities in northern Norway have memories of local people and their boats lost at sea, and folklore about the *draug* – the ghost of a drowned mariner who may return to haunt the living – is well known. In this culture, the sea – like nature in Australia – is too dangerous to be romanticized. Yet of the small number of Norwegians who apply for permission to scatter ashes, 63 per cent choose to scatter on the sea (Høeg, 2019).

Violent geology

The Pacific 'ring of fire' refers to the lands that bound the Pacific Ocean – clockwise from New Zealand, through Indonesia, Japan, Kamchatka, and down the American west coast through Oregon, California's San Andreas Fault, and along the Andes to Chile. This geologically unstable ring is host to some of the world's most active and dangerous volcanoes, earthquakes, and associated tsunamis. Volcanic ash is very fertile, so volcanoes traditionally attract sizeable farming populations to their slopes: like the sea, they both give life and take it away. Indeed, seismic and climatic forces that threaten human life are intrinsic to a planet that is hospitable to humans. The earth's hospitality and its dangers are inextricably linked.

Some of the better known examples of Pacific ring disasters include the following. The 1883 eruption of Krakatoa in the then Dutch East Indies darkened the sky across the world for several years and reduced summer temperatures in the Northern Hemisphere by up to 1.2 degrees centigrade, temperatures not returning to normal until 1888; the 1906 earthquake and the consequent fire in San Francisco destroyed 80 per cent of that city's buildings, and led to Los Angeles taking over as California's premier city; the 2004 Boxing Day tsunami in the Indian Ocean produced waves up to 100 feet high and killed a quarter of a million people in 14 countries; the 2011 earthquake in Christchurch, New Zealand, killed 185 and destroyed the city's central business district; soon afterwards, the Great East Japan Earthquake killed nearly 16,000 people and damaged a million buildings, while the associated tsunami caused reactor meltdowns at the Fukushima nuclear power plant.

Such events are often reported by western media as unexpected and unprecedented. But local families retain a folk memory of them, along with norms such as how to behave when they occur, reinforced today by government advertisements giving instructions about appropriate life-saving behaviour. *Tendai tendenko* has long been a saying in North East Japan – meaning that when the tsunami approaches, you should run immediately to higher ground without stopping to pick up others. This maximizes the chances of community survival, even though it goes against the norm of looking after those in your care such as children, old people, or patients. In the 2011 tsunami, some people's first instinct was to fetch their patients or their children, and died along with them. This survival norm therefore conflicts with the norm of self-sacrifice for those you love, doubtless leading to guilt, shame, or regret. Westerners concerned with life-and-death ethics may wrestle with issues such as euthanasia or when to turn off life support; they do not have to wrestle with how to behave in a tsunami.

Like suburban Australian properties designed to survive a bushfire, some buildings in the ring of fire are designed to withstand earthquakes. In Japan, both traditional and modern design mitigate the force of earthquakes. But in other countries, traditional building techniques can render homes vulnerable to earthquake. In societies experiencing rapid urbanization, such as China, Iran, or Nepal's Kathmandu valley, speed of construction may trump earthquake awareness. In colonial times, the early years of colonization often ignored indigenous folk memory and imposed inappropriate European building styles that could render inhabitants vulnerable to, for example, bushfire or earthquake. It can take generations after colonization or urbanization for more appropriate designs to become standard. And innovative building techniques and standards can, ultimately, only be tested in a real disaster to demonstrate their resilience or lack of it – as Japan found in the 1995 Kobe earthquake where supposedly earthquake-proof office blocks and flyovers buckled or collapsed.

Vulnerability and resilience

The same natural disaster can affect different communities very differently. Development agencies and research organizations that have traditionally been involved with disaster response are therefore refocusing on disaster resilience. Incorporating resilience into buildings is relatively straightforward in terms of design, but may be complicated politically and economically; incorporating resilience into health care systems so they can function in a major disaster is another challenge; identifying other factors that make a community resilient is a work in progress (Mishra et al., 2017).

The big historical picture seems to look like this. Small-scale hunter-gatherer societies have been relatively resilient to natural disaster; with no permanent houses and few possessions, they can respond to flood or drought simply by moving to a safer area. But when humans settle down in permanent homes and rely on growing crops, they may become vulnerable to drought, flood, earthquake, hurricane, and famine. Living together in cities increases the vulnerability still further, especially when – as in much of the world today – cities are host to millions of poor migrants from the countryside who struggle to survive in substandard accommodation with poor infrastructure. It is the most economically developed and politically stable societies that today have most successfully built disaster resilience into their building codes, health care systems, and communities. Lessons learned from Japan's 1995 Kobe earthquake enabled better preparedness for the 2011 earthquake and tsunami. In general, the death rate from disaster in affluent countries is much lower than in poor countries, and in stable democracies than in corrupt dictatorships (Kellehear, 2016: 21–2). What protects humans in the face of disaster is risk management – a particular form of late modernity.

FUTURE HAZARDS

If the prophets of ecological doom are right, modernity's 'conquest' of nature may prove short-lived. Or, if Latour is right, it was always imaginary. Since the middle of the twentieth century, it has become clear that atmospheric, geologic, hydrologic, biospheric and other earth system processes are all affected by human activities. This heralds, some argue, a new geological time period, the Anthropocene.[2] Its origin can be traced variably to 10,000 years ago when hunter-gatherers in balance with their natural environment began more intensive extraction of food from the land through agriculture; to the start of the industrial revolution in the mid-eighteenth century; or to the mid twentieth-century's rapid acceleration of human impacts on earth systems (Steffen et al., 2015).

If and when these impacts begin to make the planet so much less hospitable for humans that death rates begin to increase, probably first in poorer parts of the world and then extending to the richer parts, is impossible to predict. And precisely what combination of factors might make the planet inhospitable – global warming, climate change, sea level rise, loss of ecological diversity, drug-resistant bacteria, soil degradation, famine, fuel shortage, or resultant population movements, inter-group conflict and wars – is also impossible to predict. In the meantime, for most readers of this book – educated, materially comfortable members of affluent, peaceful societies – human-induced environmental catastrophe is a fable of total destruction that has not yet happened, but which preys, more or less, on the imagination. Real and unreal at the same time. In that sense, though not in others, it is like the prospect of nuclear Armageddon during the mid twentieth-century Cold War.

To see what life in such a global catastrophe might be like for a hitherto relatively advanced urban society, consider the 872-day siege of Leningrad from September 1941 to January 1944 in which death rates peaked at 2,000 per day (Merridale, 2000). The state introduced mass graves in order to combat epidemic disease; gravediggers survived by topping up their formal wage with informal extras for families; families wanted to venerate their dead with a decent burial yet feared using precious resources to bribe a gravedigger which might imperil their own survival. Hass (2015: 56) concludes that how the state and civilians responded to this extraordinarily high death rate was a key facet of the social order of the siege. The human planet has yet to witness environmental catastrophe at this level, but in the meantime non-nuclear wars, civil wars and local disasters occur daily, leading to more deaths – whose management in turn impacts back on society. Less dramatic examples of social and economic collapse leading to increased death rates, such as Russia after 1989, were mentioned in Chapter 1.

So, how might 'post-materialists' in safe societies who have lived all their lives with economic security (Chapter 6) manage the event of major, long-term catastrophe? Not a one-off earthquake, volcanic eruption or terrorist strike, but reversion to an ongoing life of struggling to survive scarcity? This is why I mentioned Leningrad. How would a refamiliarization with death (Ariès, 1981), a reversion to 'bare life' (Agamben, 1998; Noys, 2005) in which the state and medicine lose their power over premature death, affect individuals and society? How would it affect the 'assumptive worlds' that psychological experts argue are so important in enabling bereaved people to make sense of their loss (Parkes, 1988; Neimeyer, Klass and Dennis, 2014)? If local social capital (social networks, trust, solidarity, etc.) is key to resilience after disaster (Aldrich, 2012), how long can such capital be maintained in the face of extended catastrophe?

Might this sort of scenario demand a re-thinking of twentieth-century theories of bereavement that were developed in peaceful western societies? These theories focus on how individuals cope with the loss of another individual, and would have to be modified in at least two ways in extended disaster. First, losses are likely to be of whole families and communities, of jobs and farms and a way of life, as well as of an individual loved one. Second, as has often been the case in poor communities and in wartime (see Chapters 1 and 6), mourners' own survival and their family's survival may take precedence over dealing with their emotional response to loss.

Disaster and social change

Moving from short-medium term coping to long-term consequences, there are many historical instances where it has been argued that a major disaster, war, or mega-death has precipitated long-term social change (e.g. Behringer, 2018). It is not just that society influences how humans manage death, but mega-death can also influence society. Three much discussed examples are the Lisbon tsunami, the Black Death, and Chernobyl.

In 1755, after three centuries of a golden age of discovery and prosperity in which its fleets opened up the oceans as highways for trade, a tsunami destroyed Portugal's capital, Lisbon. This shook its citizens' faith in the order of things, not least their 'philosophy of optimism that held the present world has taken the best possible form due to the grace of God' (Kabayama, 2012: 41). Explanations of the tsunami therefore focused on why or how the residents of Lisbon had incurred God's displeasure. With the population disoriented, Portugal's enterprising prime minister took the opportunity to rebuild Lisbon in the image of fashionable eighteenth-century beauty, turning it into the visually splendid city it remains today (a process that Naomi Klein, who I discuss below, would recognize). One of Europe's greatest natural catastrophes was turned into a triumph.

But if we are to get an idea of what eco-catastrophe might lead to, the Black Death is a better place to look. Possibly caused by bubonic plague, between 1346 and 1353 it killed 30–60 per cent of Europe's population, rampaging through each country in just a year or two. It is by far the biggest single tragedy to have afflicted the continent (Herlihy, 1997). In Western Europe, unused land and shortage of labour weakened both the power of landowners and the obligations of peasants to their overlords; wages rose, peasants could choose where to work and who to work for; serfdom effectively ceased. Attempts by the upper class to peg wages were largely ineffective, and were a cause of England's 1381 Peasants Revolt. In Eastern Europe, by contrast, new stringent laws were more effective, tying people to the land as serfs more tightly than before. In various parts of Europe, Jews had a lower death rate and, in the absence of scientific explanations, were identified as causing the Black Death; several Jewish communities were massacred, while other outsiders such as Romani and lepers were also targeted. More positively, by destroying feudalism's tranquil economic growth, the Black Death may have prepared the ground for the Italian Renaissance (Kabayama, 2012).

If the Black Death catalysed the demise of feudalism in Western Europe, the 1986 Chernobyl nuclear reactor disaster in Ukraine, spreading radiation contamination over a very wide area, catalysed the demise of the Soviet Union and of communist regimes in Eastern Europe (Plokhy, 2018). Though the number of deaths directly attributable to the disaster may not be large, the political consequences were enormous. Moscow's attempts to pin blame on a few managers failed to reassure the public in a new era of openness, undermining faith in the Soviet government. Economically, the cost of the clear-up was the final nail in the coffin of public finances fatally weakened by spending on the arms race. Nuclear power had been seen as a symbol of communist modernity and efficiency, but the disaster revealed both technical incompetence and the nuclear industry as a symptom of Soviet imperialism in non-Russian republics such as Ukraine. This helped power the nationalist revolts that underlay the Soviet Union's collapse in 1991. The Soviet system was already in trouble; Chernobyl pushed it over the edge.

The Black Death and Chernobyl demonstrate that mega-disaster can be a catalyst for the destruction of socio-political systems that have lasted for decades (communism) or centuries (feudalism), especially if the system in question already has structural weaknesses. It is not inconceivable that a mega-disaster, possibly some form of eco-catastrophe, in the present or future centuries could threaten contemporary western capitalism.

Disaster capitalism

Canadian critic of corporate globalization Naomi Klein is not so sure. She cites many examples where disasters have been used by big business to further entrench their domination or by free marketeers to take over governments (Klein, 2008). The Boxing Day 2005 tsunami, for example, destroyed beach-side communities around the Indian Ocean. In Sri Lanka, beach cafés and the boats of poor fisherman were wiped out, but these local businesses were not allowed to re-start. Instead, humanitarian aid was spent on new beachfront hotels, many operated by multinational companies. Though the first few weeks saw grassroots co-operation across the religious and ethnic divides of the country's bitter civil war, this was soon overtaken by the state's plan to use the disaster as an opportunity for multinational investment in the country's tourism industry.

How 'disaster capitalism' works out depends on context. In order to fend off communism, the post-1945 Marshall Plan aimed to woo Europe and Japan back to their own kind of capitalism; so the USA invested in Germany and Japan to help them get their own industries up and running again, rather than plundering them by opening them up to Ford and General Motors. But 60 years later, after the Iraq war, without the threat of communism, the USA implemented an 'anti-Marshall' plan of plunder by American corporations (Klein, 2008: 251–2).

Klein does not see this is as mere opportunism. She defines 'disaster capitalism' as 'orchestrated raids on the public sphere in the wake of catastrophic events, combined with the treatment of disasters as exciting market opportunities' (2008: 6). Klein argues that free-market theorists, starting with Milton Friedman, have for decades seen disaster – which may include political collapse after war or civil war – as an occasion to implement radical new ideas (i.e. a pure free market) that would be seen as unrealistic in more normal times. This is 'the shock doctrine' – people are in such shock that they may welcome someone who promises to fix things with a radical solution. Friedman's view is that 'Only a crisis – actual or perceived – produces real change. When that crisis occurs, the actions that are taken depend on the ideas that are lying around. … [We] develop alternatives to existing policies, keep them alive and available until the politically impossible becomes politically inevitable' (Klein, 2008: 6).

Stephen Holmes (2008) criticizes Klein for conflating the open competition eulogized in free-market ideology with the (often monopolistic) interests of big business, but the wider argument is surely correct that powerful actors can use catastrophe as an opportunity to profit, to get into power, or to bring in policies they could not in normal times. And Friedman is right that the actions taken in crisis depend on the ideas that are lying around. But those ideas are not necessarily free-market ideas (Jones, 2018). In 1945 the British electorate voted out their wartime hero Winston Churchill in favour of post-war reconstruction based on the nationalization of industry and a welfare state along the lines of William Beveridge's 1942 report on social insurance. A welfare state chimed with the wartime experience of people pulling together, with the wartime state's proven ability to organize at scale, and with the hope that the war had to be followed by a better society. Another example from the same period entailed the construction of an entirely new nation state: without Hitler's extermination of six million European Jews, the state of Israel may never have been formed.

The moral of all this? Quite simply, there is no telling what kind of major social or political change will occur in the wake of the disruption and chaos that follow war, civil war, genocide, and natural disaster. Or the old system may be further entrenched. Just as death can transform the individual mourner, so mega-death can transform society – often in ways less predictable than Klein supposes.

That said, Klein's advice for recovery from catastrophe is worth quoting:

> The universal experience of living through a great shock is the feeling of being completely powerless ... The best way to recover from helplessness turns out to be helping – having the right to be part of communal recovery ... Such people's reconstruction efforts represent the antithesis of the disaster capitalism ethos, with its perpetual quest for clean sheets and blank slates on which to build model states ... These are movements that do not seek to start from scratch but rather from scrap, from the rubble that is all around ... They are building in resilience – for when the next shock hits. (2008: 465)

In terms of Stroebe and Schut's (1999) dual process model of bereavement, this means that communities where survivors rebuild immediately – rather than nursing their catastrophic emotions while others rebuild – are more likely to survive and become resilient. Solnit (2009) writes about the extraordinary communities that can arise after disaster, offering a vision of a society that is less authoritarian and fearful, more collaborative and local. Anthropologist Victor Turner (1974), however, warns that the intense sense of togetherness found in extraordinary circumstances rarely continues indefinitely into mundane everyday life. Thus the question for Solnit is how to sustain extraordinary community in the long run – how to keep at bay the predations of big business and of national politicians seeking to gain the glory of rebuilding? How simply to persevere in the face of intransigent, unpredictable insurance companies, government agencies and other bureaucracies which can cause as much mental ill health as the disaster itself?

THE BODY

My own body is the part of the physical world that is closest to me. It is a part of 'nature' that is superficially tameable through healthy body regimes (diet, exercise, lifestyle, a safe environment) but sooner or later, short of suicide or voluntary euthanasia, becomes untameable (Ehrenreich, 2018). We are stuck with the body we are given, and ultimately this shell in which we live will die, along with our very selves. Our minds and our emotions – how we think about death, how we feel about loss – are also rooted in the body. Modernity influences all bodies, not least dying and grieving bodies, in various ways which I will sketch; as always, the influence is modulated by class, income, nationality, age, and gender.

The cultured body

In his massive two-part work *The Civilizing Process*, Norbert Elias (1978) argues that control of bodily functions emerged in eighteenth-century France as a sign of civilization. Urinating and defecating in designated places, blowing your nose, or using a knife and fork rather than just stuffing food into your mouth with your hands, came to be seen by the upper class as a hallmark of good manners. By the late nineteenth century, washing body and clothes became a mark of bourgeois respectability, distinguishing them from the labouring classes. Inculcating such habits into young children tamed and civilized the naturally wild infant. As anthropologist Mary Douglas (1966) shows, such body regimes regulate the symbolically dangerous boundary between the body's inside and the outside: skin, and the various orifices that allow fluids to pass in and out of the body such as nose, mouth, ears, anus, vagina, and penis. Controlling the emotions also became part of the civilizing process, though the extent of emotional control varies across countries. All this turns the physical body into a manifestation of culture.

If infancy is when this transformation starts, frail old age and terminal illness can reverse it to a greater or lesser extent in what Clive Seale (1998: 149) aptly calls 'falling from culture'. One body regime after another collapses as the person returns to a state of nature. Incontinence is for many the most shameful. But eating is also highly significant, for eating together is an important way that humans socialize, both within families and in other settings. The liquid or intravenous diet of some very ill people denies them the human company of the breakfast or dinner table; eating ceases to be at the heart of sociality, and is reduced to a mechanical operation. The frail or dying person becomes less and less a social being, more just a body to be fed, watered, and cathetered.

National differences

This raises the question of national differences. American culture values health, happiness, and the perfect body, all of which imply control over the body. Anyone can do anything, become anything. How does this fare when the body begins to pack up? Some have argued it leads to a denying of ageing and mortality, with both the elderly and the dead cosmeticized to look youthful and healthy – a 'denial of death' that is not generically modern but specifically North American (Samuel, 2013). English culture, by contrast, can be more accepting of social and bodily limitations; traditional working-class culture can indeed be quite fatalistic (Hoggart, 1957). Does this mean that ageing and mortality are less an offence in England than in the USA? Anyone travelling to Britain from the USA notices in the streets both frail old people, and the occasional glass-sided hearse displaying the coffin within. These public manifestations of ageing and dead bodies can shock the visitor from the USA (C. Davies, 1996). Of course, it is not quite this simple. American mourners are much more likely than Brits to view the deceased in the funeral parlour (Harper, 2010), and elderly Americans may well be out in public, but unlike their British counterparts they are not taking the bus or hobbling along to the local shop on their withered limbs but driving to the mall. The question for readers is: in your society, how do cultural attitudes to the body affect the visibility of the ageing, dying, and dead body?

When people tell me why they cremated or buried a close family member, I have been struck by how often they explain their choice in terms of earlier experiences of dying or dead bodies: 'My wife's body was riddled with cancer. I didn't want that preserved, so I chose cremation.' Others relate their choice to previous experiences of death: 'I saw too many rotting bodies during the war. Cremation is cleaner, quick, final.' If Elias (1978) is correct that modern civilization values the clean, controlled body, does this help explain the shift to cremation in most modern societies? And if Miner (1956) is correct that North Americans are particularly obsessed with washing and cleanliness, then does this help explain American disposal practices?

Possibly. The previous chapter described how Americans waited till the turn of the millennium before adopting cremation in any numbers, long after their hygiene obsession had been noted by Miner. Twentieth-century Americans had abandoned the nineteenth-century practice of burial in a softwood coffin in direct contact with the soil in favour not of cremation but of placing the body, embalmed and preserved, in a strong hardwood or metal casket, deposited in a concrete-lined vault beneath the cemetery's manicured lawn. Such American corpses are surely putrefying and decaying like any others, but the *image* is of the body resting within the sacred American soil, yet protected from physical contact with actual messy soil's ability to initiate decomposition. In death as in life, dirt is anathema in America. There are surely other interpretations and explanations of choice of disposal (Walter, 1993a), some of which are raised in Chapter 14's discussion of migration, but it is always worth considering how cultural ideals of the living body affect disposal of the dead body.

CONCLUSION

This chapter has explored how the physical world, from our own body to the planet itself, shapes and is shaped by culture, shapes and is shaped by death. I have discussed how individual death challenges and transforms the civilized individual body; and how mega-death can challenge and transform the social body, society itself. Modernity – whether manifested in the individual body that has the good manners to eat and urinate in culturally approved ways, or in a global economy that purports to have controlled nature – is ultimately vulnerable precisely because this so-called control of nature is always provisional, even (Latour, 2003) imaginary.

FURTHER READING

- Harper, S. (2010) 'Behind closed doors? Corpses and mourners in American and English funeral premises', in J. Hockey, C. Komaromy and K. Woodthorpe (eds), *The Matter of Death: Space, place and materiality*. Basingstoke: Palgrave Macmillan, pp. 100–16.

- Herlihy, D. (1997) *The Black Death and the Transformation of the West*. Cambridge, MA: Harvard University Press.

- Klein, N. (2008) *The Shock Doctrine: The rise of disaster capitalism*. London: Penguin.

- Norwood, F. (2009) *The Maintenance of Life: Preventing social death through euthanasia talk and end-of-life care – lessons from the Netherlands*. Durham, NC: Carolina Academic Press.

- Seale, C. (1998) *Constructing Death*. Cambridge: Cambridge University Press, Ch. 7.

- van der Pijl, Y. (2016) 'Death in the family revisited: ritual expression and controversy in a Creole transnational mortuary sphere', *Ethnography*, 17 (2): 147–67.

- Walter, T. (1993) 'Dust not ashes: the American preference for burial', *Landscape*, 32 (1): 42–8.

Questions to discuss

- Has the physical environment in any way shaped your country's approach to death and dying?

- Investigate the socio-political consequences of a particular war or disaster.

- In your society, how do cultural attitudes to the body affect ageing, dying, and dead bodies?

Notes

1. 'Crossing the river: the journey of death in Ancient Egypt and Mesopotamia', available at http://religionandtechnology.com/2009/08/21/crossing-the-river-the-journey-of-death-in-ancient-egypt-and-mesopotamia/ (accessed 13/6/19).

2. www.anthropocene.info/ (accessed 13/6/19).

PART III

CULTURE

Whereas Parts I and II considered modern societies in general, Parts III and IV examine the factors that cause modern societies to differ from one another in how they manage death and loss. Part III looks at culture, Part IV at the nation.

Though there are national cultures (Herzfeld, 2014), nation and culture are not the same thing. Several nations may broadly share a culture, for example one that is individualistic, or hierarchical, or Confucian, or family-centred. Then there is mono-culturalism and multi-culturalism: a nation's celebration of one culture or of its diversity of cultures. Some nations, such as Japan, are rather mono-cultural; others such as the USA, Australia, or the UK are more multi-cultural. Sweden used to be mono-cultural, but over recent decades has become quite multi-cultural. And within any one culture, there can be subcultures – such as the subculture of a hospital, care home, or prison. A black man dying in an American prison, for example, may find his dying influenced by several cultures and subcultures (American, African-American, prison), in addition to institutional structures and regulations (prison, health care), laws (relating to health, death, and imprisonment), resources (are staff available to provide escort to hospital appointments?), social class, and racism.

CULTURE AND DEATH

Culture comprises the ideas, customs and social behaviour expected of a group of people. Ernest Becker (1973) and his terror management (TMT) disciples (Solomon, Greenberg and Pyszczynski, 2015), along with sociologists such as Zygmunt Bauman (1992), Michael Kearl (2010) and at least in his earlier writings Peter Berger (1969), have all argued that, in one way or another, human cultures are a response to mortality. The individual has to die, but culture continues. Culture offers people projects, immortality strategies – such as family, religious faith, charitable projects, fame, property, Facebook pages – that endure beyond the individual's life and provide that life with meaning. Facing death without these culturally provided immortality strategies would, some argue, be intolerable.

As discussed in Chapter 5, TMT argues that the more people are aware of their mortality, the more they cling rigidly to their culture; they become, for example, less tolerant of outgroups. Inglehart's (1981) cross-national analysis of survey data, discussed in Chapter 6, is potentially consistent with this; he shows that economically insecure populations preoccupied with their own and their family's survival tend to cling to traditional cultural mores and feel threatened by those who are different or who seek cultural change. By contrast, economically secure, long-lived populations – increasingly common in late modernity – are more likely, in Frank Sinatra's words, to do things 'my way' and to have less need to do things the traditional way; they feel much less threatened by outsiders, by change and by other cultures. For them, survival and death are not everyday anxieties, so it could be argued that culture becomes less salient. In other words, the thesis that mortality awareness drives culture which in turn shapes people's values may be becoming less true in late modernity. But whatever drives culture and however individuated some late-modern individuals may be, culture remains important in both life and death.

Some countries have very specific death cultures. Most famous perhaps is the Mexican Day of the Dead, but there are also the Caribbean Nine Nights (a wake rooted in African religion that lasts several days), the annual Japanese Bon festival (when the ancestors are welcomed back for a day), the Christian All Souls' Day practised in many Catholic countries but now also a major festival in historically Protestant Sweden, and so on. Part III, however, does not focus on specific customs, exotic and interesting though they can often be to outsiders; information on them is widely available in other books and on the Internet. Rather, my intention is to identify some key cultural orientations and ask how they shape death and dying. Unlike exotic festivals, these orientations can be so taken for granted that people are largely or totally unaware of their influence.

CULTURAL VARIATION

How then do cultural orientations vary within modernity? Cross-cultural analysts – notably Inglehart (1981), Huntington (1993) and Hofstede (2001) – have cut the modern cultural cake in various ways. Schwartz (2006) synthesizes these into seven transnational cultural groupings: West European, English-speaking, Latin American, East European, South Asian, Confucian-influenced, and African and Middle Eastern. He identifies three dimensions: mastery versus harmony, hierarchy versus egalitarianism, and embeddedness (group conformity) versus autonomy. Autonomy and egalitarianism tend to increase with modernization, while mastery/harmony seem to be independent of modernization.

Part III does not take as systematic an approach as Schwartz. Instead I examine three aspects of culture that influence how any one modern society deals with death and loss. These are: group embeddedness versus individual autonomy (Chapter 8), family (Chapter 9), and religion (Chapter 10). Individual autonomy tends to undermine the traditional hold of religion and family over the individual, but this need not mean that religion and family cease to be important. Rather they become more fluid, with individuals choosing their own spirituality (Heelas, 2002) and negotiating what kind of family they wish to form (Smart, 2007).

CULTURAL COMPLEXITY

Cultures are complex, and often contradictory (or at least seem so to outsiders). To give just two examples. The USA appears in all cross-cultural surveys as commercial and highly individualistic. Yet in small town America, especially in the South, neighbours bring home-cooked food to the house of mourning, sometimes for weeks or months after the death (Graham, 2018). This local solidarity and partial de-commodification is not found in some European welfare societies which pride themselves on being more solidaristic. Another example is the Swiss city of Zurich, a major hub of international capitalism; yet the city pays for most of the cost of each resident's funeral.

So we have to distinguish between ideology and practice. Both Denmark and the USA have a highly individualistic ideology, but in practice can be quite collectivist, even conformist. De Tocqueville, in his classic 1835 study *Democracy in America* (1988), noticed this. If I am expected to 'be myself', then I may look anxiously around at others to see what kind of selves they are being, and imitate them. To know how to behave, I therefore end up looking not to tradition but to my peer group (Riesman, 1950). This phenomenon clearly characterizes many teenagers, and may characterize a whole nation. It can also characterize those facing the, for them, new experience of terminal illness. Honeybun, Johnston and Tookman (1992) noted how in multi-bedded hospital rooms, dying patients learned much from observing room-mates who were a bit further on in the dying process. And the proliferation in individualist societies such as the USA and the UK of books and blogs offering first-person accounts of dying or grieving (Hawkins, 1990) presumably finds an audience among those anxious to know how others have dealt with such matters. Conversely, anthropologists have shown how in supposedly conformist or collectivist societies in which certain deathbed, funeral, or mourning rites are prescribed, some individuals may exert considerable creativity in how they perform them.

Consequently, culture can provide more than one script for how to behave and feel; people and groups may pick and choose between scripts. Terminally ill people may follow different scripts depending on whether they are talking to their doctor, to a community nurse, to a family member, or to a researcher (Seale, 1998; Long, 2004). There is also the possibility raised in the previous chapter of 'falling from culture' as a person nears their end, with the availability of scripts reducing by the day (Seale, 1998).

FURTHER READING

Schwartz, S.H. (2006) 'A theory of cultural value orientations', *Comparative Sociology*, 5 (2-3): 137-82.

INDIVIDUAL AND GROUP

MODERNITY AND THE INDIVIDUAL

Both Hofstede (2001) and Schwartz (2006) see cultures as spread along a continuum between social embeddedness in family, community and society, and personal autonomy. Hofstede defines the difference as follows:[1]

> Individualism can be defined as a preference for a loosely-knit social framework in which individuals are expected to take care of only themselves and their immediate families.

> Its opposite, Collectivism, represents a preference for a tightly-knit framework in society in which individuals can expect their relatives or members of a particular ingroup to look after them in exchange for unquestioning loyalty.

> A society's position on this dimension is reflected in whether people's self-image is in terms of 'I' or 'we'.

Many scholars argue that modernity fosters individualism. Following Giddens (1994) and Beck and Beck-Gernsheim (2002), Mouzelis (2012: 209) argues that in the early stages of modernization 'traditional certainties are replaced by collectivist ones (e.g. ideologies on class, nation, party) which provide … a meaning in life and clear guidelines.' In late modernity, 'both traditional and collectivist certainties decline or disappear … From whether or not to marry and have children, to what life-style to adopt … the individual has to be highly reflexive, and must construct his or her own biography.' Some elites in some pre-modern societies may also have done this, but it is 'only in late modernity that ... subjects on the non-elite level are called ... to create "a life of their own".' And, I would add, a death of their own. There is evidence, for example, that middle-class Chinese are beginning to articulate preferences for their end-of-life care or what kind of funeral to purchase.

Arguably, this requirement to be an individual is driven by capitalism's requirement that late-modern individuals and families be avid consumers. If early capitalism had to kick-start a revolution in productivity, late capitalism has to ensure that populations continue to want to consume more and more once all their basic needs are fulfilled. More and more of life – including personal fulfilment – is marketized, requiring people to become economic actors making endless consumption decisions rather than acting according to traditional mores. In this argument, affluence makes everyone more individualistic.

Another factor could be family size. Chapter 1 outlined how modernization causes a drastic reduction in this. It is hard in a large family for parents to give each child as much attention as in a small family; each child just has to 'fit in' to the busy social group that is the large family. Small families, by contrast, offer greater possibilities of bringing up each child as a distinctly unique individual and nurturing each child's unique hopes and talents. For this reason alone we might expect some correlation between modernity and the reflexive individual, though this possibility is not taken up in every modern society. Two modern societies with exceptionally small families are contemporary Japan (which fosters group loyalty) and China (which fosters loyalty to the state).

Family, community, state

Indeed we find that equally advanced industrial societies can score very differently on Hofstede's individualism score, for example: USA 91, Sweden and France 71, Japan 46.[2] Rapidly industrializing and urbanizing China scores 20. Different scores may partly be explicable in terms of *which* in-group – family, community or state – is given loyalty and looked to for support. Swedish historians Berggren and Trägårdh (2010) argue that Swedes, and to an extent other Nordic peoples, fear the loss of individual autonomy entailed in personal dependency on family and neighbours; in social democratic Sweden, therefore, the state protects individual freedom against family and local community. Swedes embrace public collectivism in defence of private individualism, though this is being undermined by increasing marketization of welfare services. This means that, in old age, Swedes who in theory believe in state welfare provision may with some justification fear moving into a care home (Socialstyrelsen, 2017); many are in fact cared for in their own home by (usually female) family members (Ulmanen, 2015), which does not fit the Swedish model in which full employment for both sexes funds welfare provision through taxation of income. In conservative Germany, by contrast, the state supports more the family than the individual – at least according to Berggren and Trägårdh.

In the USA, it is the state not the family that is widely believed to pose a risk to personal freedom; individual, family, and community therefore co-operate to keep the state out of their lives. Many Americans, though distrusting the state, volunteer and socialize with their neighbours. 'American individualism is something of a doubled-edged sword: it fosters a high sense of personal responsibility, independent initiative and voluntarism, even as it encourages self-serving behaviour, atomism, and a disregard for communal goods' (Hayes and Lipset, 1993–94: 69).

To summarize Berggren and Trägårdh's thesis. In the USA, epitomizing Esping-Andersen's (1990) liberal regime, individual and family co-operate to keep the state out. In Germany (Esping-Andersen's conservative regime), state and family trump the individual. In Sweden (Esping-Andersen's social democracy), state and individual ally themselves against the family. So Swedish individualism is not like the USA's, nor is its statism like Germany's. A single individualism/collectivism scale, or a one-directional modernization theory, may miss such nuances.

It is therefore possible that individuals who are reflexive in their own personal life – including wanting control over their dying – might nevertheless embrace collectivist policies such as nationalized health care, or they might be very active volunteering for their local charitable hospice. Even if late modernity tends to turn people into reflexive individuals, modern societies vary in the extent that members feel responsible for one another – and *how* they exercise that responsibility, whether through paying taxes or through looking out for their elderly next door neighbour. Bearing these nuances in mind, I will now consider how collectivism versus individualism – responsibility for others versus responsibility only for self and family, deference to the group versus personal autonomy – affect death, dying, and grief. I look first at death rates in individualistic and collectivist societies, before looking at differences in how they manage dying and grief.

CAUSING DEATH

Can individualism or collectivism actually contribute to causing death? There is considerable evidence suggesting the answer is 'yes'.

In his classic 1897 study of suicide, Emile Durkheim sought to understand why in Western Europe the suicide rate was higher in countries where Protestants predominate than in countries with a majority of Catholics (Durkheim, 2002). His conclusion was that Protestantism leaves the believer alone before God, while Catholics are integrated into a universal church; the Protestant is expected to meet God through his or her own reading of the Bible rather than through accepting church dogma. This leaves the Protestant in a state of moral individualism, reliant on self and God rather than a social group – the church. Durkheim further argued that social integration helps immunize people from taking their own life; hence Protestants are more prone than Catholics to suicide.

However, Durkheim also identified another form of suicide – altruistic suicide – where the person is so integrated into the group that he may kill himself out of duty. Examples include followers and servants upon the deaths of their chiefs. Some decades after Durkheim wrote, the Japanese kamikaze pilots of the Second World War became classic examples.

Durkheim's argument has been subjected to considerable criticism over many decades; my reason for presenting it here is simply to raise the possibility that both individualism and collectivism might help explain why particular death rates may differ between social groups and over time. Let us explore further examples.

Inequality

Wilkinson and Pickett (2009) have collated a wide range of evidence showing that the more economically unequal a society, the higher the incidence of social and physical malaises – including many that impact on life expectancy, such as obesity, mental illness, infant mortality, and murder (Figure 1.2). Their recently updated review of the evidence confirms this (Pickett and Wilkinson, 2015). Though people in affluent countries on average live longer than those in poorer countries, it is very clear that the more economically unequal countries such as the USA and the UK have lower life expectancy than would be expected from these countries' overall wealth (Day, Pearce and Dorling, 2008). Those European social democratic societies that have well-developed welfare states that redistribute income and provide high-quality health care to all, along with Japan where wages are not so unequal to start with, are at the top of the longevity league. The economically unequal USA and UK also score very highly on measures of individualism. There is further evidence that (1) the early years of industrialization increase economic inequality, (2) the establishment of effective trade unions and welfare provision then reduce inequality, but (3) since the 1980s inequality has begun to rise again significantly; many health indicators, including overall life expectancy, have declined in this last period in many countries (Therborn, 2013).

Establishing causation in social science is never easy. Does individualism *cause* economic inequality? And does economic inequality *cause* ill health? Or is the relationship more complex? There is strong evidence that neo-liberal policies which began in the USA and the UK in the 1980s and then spread to many other countries – including to some extent the social democratic Nordic countries – have undermined both income equality and many health outcomes (Schrecker and Bambra, 2015). Neo-liberalism as a philosophy is clearly linked to individualism. In neo-liberalism, individuals are responsible for their own welfare, and social problems are expected to be solved not through collective action but through the individual actions of millions of individuals operating within markets. The neo-liberal 'austerity' response to the 2008 global financial crisis cut health care and other services, causing deaths that otherwise would not have occurred (Stuckler and Basu, 2013). Has neo-liberalism peaked? Possibly. Both President Donald Trump's policies and the UK's dramatic vote to exit the European Union 'suggests that economic nationalism has now replaced neoliberalism as the central organizing idea of the political right' (Morris, 2017: 125).

Collectivism

In sum, it does seem that, at least within mature industrial societies over the past century, there has been a relationship between a country's level of individualism and a range of poor health outcomes. In other parts of the world, however, collectivist societies such as China and Zimbabwe display great inequality of income. And historically, feudal and imperial societies were often both collectivist in orientation and very unequal. Collectivism entails loyalty to one's own group, often positioning outside groups as 'other'. Within any one country or empire, this may simply mean fewer resources going to outgroups. Or it may mean ruthless suppression, as with Mao's persecution of intellectuals during the Cultural Revolution, or the Zimbabwean army's slaughter in the 1980s of Ndebele civilians in Matabeleland who supported opposition politician Joshua Nkomo; the operation was termed *Guykurahundi*, a Shona term meaning 'the early rain which washes away the chaff before the spring rains'. Another example, from 2017, is the burning of hundreds of Rohingya Muslim villages in Rakhine State, Myanmar, the Rohingya comprising an ethnic and religious minority within Myanmar. Or it may mean full-blown genocide, as with the Holocaust's ambition to exterminate Jews and certain other groups perceived to be non-Aryan, such as Roma and ethnic Poles.

In such societies, the underlying inequality is not economic but ethnic; of the two, ethnic inequality can prompt more vicious and intentional deaths. More individualistic societies, believing every individual to be of equal worth regardless of group membership, have made great strides, unimaginable only a century ago, towards equality of race, gender and sexuality (Therborn, 2013: 79f). I say 'unimaginable' because racism – a pernicious form of collectivism – was part and parcel of eighteenth-, nineteenth- and even twentieth-century expansionist capitalism, whether expressed through slavery in the American South, imperialism by the European powers, or appropriation of Aboriginal land in several countries. The formula was: individual rights for my race, discrimination against or even extermination of your race (Chakrabarty, 2007). All this was clearly reflected in different death rates for rulers and ruled, whites and blacks, free man and slave, and (still today) white settlers and indigenous peoples.

Paradoxically, the individualism that drives modern western inter-group equality also tends to exacerbate within-group economic inequality; racism's explicit danger to life and limb is traded for egalitarian individualism's hidden dangers to life. This is not to say that any society yet treats all groups equally. Even countries that pride themselves on inter-group equality may not extend full rights to all citizens, such as those with learning difficulties, dementia, and prisoners, often resulting in excess deaths among such groups. In my own country, the UK, excess deaths among elderly hospital patients in North Staffordshire and among adults with learning difficulties at Winterbourne View care home led to public scandals in the early twenty-first century.

So in certain circumstances, individualism causes excess deaths; in other circumstances, collectivism does. The safest societies today include those modern social democracies whose reflexively modern citizens retain a sense of collective responsibility for all those living within their national borders, a sensibility enacted in public policy. Whether this collective responsibility can readily extend beyond national boundaries is a crucial question at the time of writing, with millions of refugees being turned back at European and American borders.

MANAGING DYING

Contemporary cultures that prioritize the individual produce medical ethics and policies that embrace informed decision making by the individual patient. This is not to say that the views of doctor, nurse, or family are irrelevant, but that the individual patient's choice is, subject to available resources, paramount. American textbooks on medical ethics emphasize patient autonomy, contrasting with French texts which emphasize beneficence (the doctor's responsibility to do good and not harm) and the doctor's professional judgement.[3] Then there are cultures (e.g. in the Mediterranean and East Asia) which prioritize the patient's family; here the individual patient may or may not be an informed participant in discussions between doctor and family. Gordon and Paci (1997: 1446, 1449) contrast American oncology's autonomy-control narrative ('In the beginning there was the individual') with Italy's social-embeddedness narrative ('In the beginning there was God and the family who created the child and who protects the weak in times of trouble'). Family members may be more scared of the person dying than is the person him/herself, which can influence treatment decisions. In Singapore, for example, over-treatment is more likely if caregivers rather than patients are making the decisions.[4] The historical shift to informing terminal cancer patients of their diagnosis started in the USA in the late 1960s and took only a decade or so. The equivalent transition in Mediterranean Europe started much later and continues to conflict with a family-centred culture (Marzano, 2009).

An unusual case is provided by Aotearoa/New Zealand, one of the world's few officially bi-cultural nations. Health care workers must pay attention to the needs of indigenous Māori – which would not be the case if the official policy were multi-culturalism. Whether they like it or not, Pākehā (New Zealanders of European origin) have to respect the rights and needs of indigenous Māori (though not of other minority groups, such as Pacific Islanders or Chinese). Palliative care nurses understand that to engage with a Māori patient they must engage with the *whānau* or extended family. In Māori culture, personal identity is rooted in family and place, so any conversation between strangers has to begin with each introducing themselves, identifying their *whānau* (family), *iwi* (land, community) and *whakapapa* (genealogy). So, for a nurse–patient relationship to develop, nurse as well as patient has to identify her/himself in these terms; this goes against western nursing ethics in which the professional nurse is expected to keep her non-professional life private, not to mention western health care economics which do not allow time for such rituals. That is only just the beginning; the clinical encounter is likely to include several family members, whose voices may be as important as the patient's.

Dependency and relatedness

Face-to-face dependency (in adults) has negative connotations in many western countries where the mantra for elderly and for disabled people is to maintain their independence for as long and as much as possible. But in many parts of the world dependency does not have such a bad press. In China, filial piety requires the young to look after the old in their family, though this poses problems if the young live in the city and the old in the countryside. In Bangladesh, people feel it right that the old come to depend on younger family members; even if the old person has reservations, she will still do this.[5] It some poorer countries, including western countries in the earlier stages of industrialization, dependency on family and neighbours has been an economic necessity, but with affluence and welfare states households can be more self-sufficient when afflicted by hard times, including mortal illness. Indeed, in the UK one reason many working-class households fiercely resist asking neighbours for help is that it would imply that the family has slid back into poverty and is no longer 'respectable'.

Amae

But valuing dependency cannot always be explained as a product of hard times. In one of the world's most affluent societies, Japan, adults value dependency, the word *amae* referring to the pleasurable state of depending on the benevolence or goodwill of others – a pleasure which Doi (1981) notes we first experience as a baby. This means that Japanese people are expected to look out for others in any setting, not just within the family; they become skilled in reading non-verbal cues and anticipating what others need without having to ask. I experienced this in a traditional Japanese tea room in Tokyo; from where I was sitting the view into the garden was nice, but not quite perfect. After a few minutes, without my trying to attract her attention and without either myself or her saying a word, the waitress quietly moved a screen to give me the perfect view. What I experienced was *amae*, the pleasure of being looked after without having to make my needs known. The implications for end-of-life

care are obvious: good nursing care around the world entails the nurse anticipating the person's needs, but in Japan this is not only a professional practice
but also a widespread cultural practice. Crucially (Yamazaki, 2008) it means
that a comatose patient should receive as good care as a conscious patient. By
contrast, westerners fear that, unable to articulate needs, the comatose or cogni-
tively impaired patient is vulnerable to care not of their choosing – hence the
need for advance statements and the like.

This is not to say that end-of-life care in Japan is better than elsewhere – there
is no evidence for this. Nor is it to say that *amae* is the only script for dying in
Japan, which like any modern other country holds in tension multiple scripts for
dying (Long, 2004, 2005). It is to say that how people think about end-of-life
care, and what they fear as they near the end of life, are profoundly shaped by
how their culture values dependency or autonomy.

A concept without a word

Britons value both individual autonomy *and* the unconditional care provided
by the National Health Service. While British health care ethics and neo-liberal
health policies increasingly promote personal choice, popular opinion identifies
being looked after by the NHS, in other words *amae*, as a central if not *the* central British value, amounting almost to a national religion that no politician
dare explicitly challenge (D. Davies, 2015). But since the English language has
no word for *amae* and no way of talking positively about dependency, health care
ethics – including palliative care – continues to promote autonomy and choice.
There is literally no language to articulate what people value. In the
Netherlands, a new term – *professional loving care* – has been coined to give
words to this concept, which is now formally at the heart of nursing practice
(van Heijst, 2011).

This raises the possibility that some practices may exist and be valued in a
society that cannot easily be 'read' from that society's culture. Bellah et al.'s (1985)
study of values in America found precisely this, namely that citizens whose main
language was of personal autonomy and individual achievement struggled to find
the words, let alone an underlying philosophy, to name the profound bonds they
experienced within communities and between generations. They also struggle to
name the bonds they feel with the dead. The concept of 'continuing bonds' in
bereavement (Klass, Silverman and Nickman, 1996), now widely accepted in
Anglophone bereavement care, did not come into focus until American psychologist
Dennis Klass encountered Japanese ancestor rituals which enabled him to name
what Americans routinely do but have no words for (Steffen and Klass, 2018).
Terms such as 'continuing bonds' and 'professional loving care' have to be consciously invented; they do not arise naturally from the culture. And it can work
the other way around too. There is some evidence that ageing Japanese baby

boomers no longer value *amae* as they do not want to burden their children. So the Japanese have a concept, *amae*, that some Japanese no longer value or desire.

Stating wishes in advance

The theory of possessive individualism (Macpherson, 1962) teaches that my life and my body are my own, and I have the right to control them. This is one basis for arguing for abortion and for voluntary euthanasia. It is clear from debates about each of these in the USA, however, that the liberal belief in individual rights can conflict with, and for believers be trumped by, the religious idea that our lives and our bodies are God's. The conflict between these two views is more pronounced in the USA than in most other countries because the USA both embraces a profoundly individualistic culture in which each individual is responsible to make something of his or her life, *and* has a very significant proportion of the population who embrace conservative religion – mainly fundamentalist versions of Protestantism and conservative understandings of Catholicism.

A considerable challenge for the 'my life and body are my own' philosophy is to what extent my body can or will continue to be my own should I suffer severe cognitive and/or communicative incapacity, as in major stroke, coma, or advanced dementia. With increasing longevity and medical advances, such conditions are on the increase. In other kinds of dying, such as cancer and heart disease, cognitive and communicative capacity is typically maintained for months, years, or decades, only to be surrendered in the last few hours or days – which may well coincide with emergency hospitalization and being cared for by people with whom one has no previous relationship. How might carers – whether professional or family – know my wishes in such circumstances? This is an issue not only for patients, but perhaps even more so for doctors. With medical paternalism being reconfigured, at least in Anglophone countries, into a regime of patient choice where the patient's 'informed choice' replaces 'doctor's orders', then how is today's non-paternalistic doctor to act when the patient is incapacitated from making or communicating a choice?

This is the cultural and political context in which advance decisions (ADs) – otherwise known as 'advance statements' or 'living wills' – are being promoted in more individualistic counties. An advance decision is a written statement of the specific circumstances in which I would wish to refuse treatment, should I lose the capacity to make or communicate decisions about my treatment and care. Rather more general are advance care plans (ACPs), co-produced by patient, family, and health care practitioners at the start of treatment or care, outlining the kind of care the patient desires as their condition deteriorates and in particular as they near the end of life. Both ADs and ACPs have been heavily promoted in North America, and more recently in the UK. Terminology varies somewhat between countries.

Challenges

ADs and ACPs are more likely to be embraced by those who have been used to exercising control throughout life. Even in countries whose culture promotes personal autonomy, those with less control in their life, most likely those from lower social classes or migrants, are unlikely to consider that they can predict the future and may therefore not see the point in ADs and ACPs. They would rather trust their family and the doctor (Zivkovic, 2018). And studies in Norway and England suggest that the idea of controlling the future does not sit well with the lived experience of frailty in old age (Pollock and Seymour, 2018). A recent British doctoral study found that frail old people typically take one day at a time:

> Frail older people experience profound uncertainty, associated with rapid changes to their physical and/or mental state and complex challenges in everyday life. Consequently, their attention is focused on day-to-day maintenance of quality of life, rather than on future care or advance decision making. Many had difficulty imagining a future ... The end-of-life orientation of current ACP policy and practice is at odds with the dynamic nature of frailty ... The liberal idea of auton-omy as self-determination and self-interest presented by the legalistic and ideo-logically driven policy of ACP is out of step with the lived worlds of frail older people. (Bramley, Seymour and Cox, 2015)

What I value may change as I get sicker. How can I know in good health what I would or would not want were I to develop advanced lung disease or demen-tia? I simply do not know what it would be like to struggle for breath, hour after hour; to be conscious but unable to communicate; or to be so forgetful and confused that others have to look after me. I may anticipate that without inde-pendence or privacy, life would not be worth living, but there are enough reports of sick people finding new meaning in dependence to cause me to doubt my ability to state in advance what I would want. One response to this is for ACPs and ADs to be continually revised, but we have just seen that the older and frailer I become, the more likely I am to live from day to day and resist, or at least be ambivalent about, future planning. If *amae* risks others misjudging what I need, ACPs and ADs risk my falsely predicting what I would want. Anthropologists see magic as the belief that you can predict and influence the future through ritual action; with magic defined thus, ACPs and ADs function as a magical rite (Zivkovic, 2017).

In practice, a country's law does not *require* citizens to believe in such magical thinking. England's 2005 Mental Capacity Act, for example, offers three possible paths for those contemplating what they would want should they lose mental capacity. The first is an AD for those who want to state certain things in advance. Second, a Lasting Power of Attorney (LPA) is appropriate for those who wish to delegate care decisions to a friend or family member, should they lose mental capacity. And the third option, which comes into force when there is no AD or LPA, is to leave things to a best-interest decision at the time, made by doctors in consultation with family. Some people may chose more than one option, for example an AD concerning resuscitation in order to relieve the family from making this life-and-death decision, together with an LPA for general decision making about care.

ADs and ACPs are by no means always acted upon, for a whole range of reasons – not least lack of awareness of their existence. Thus an ambulance may be called to the house where someone has collapsed, but the ambulance crew may not know that the patient does not wish to be resuscitated – even if this has already been communicated to the general practitioner or family. Modern health care systems are highly complex and, even with the latest communication technologies, advance directives and plans may not come to light in time. Some argue that the best technology is old fashioned – tattoo 'DO NOT RESUSCITATE' on my chest!

In conclusion, faith in the individual requires me to trust my judgement to predict what I would want, should the dying process entail my, sooner or later, losing mental capacity. Faith in the group requires me to trust professional or family carers to do what is best for me. Many western societies allow for both possibilities, though the more religious and the more group-oriented, the more faith is put in family and doctors.

Independence and privacy

Two key values that are associated with individualism are independence and privacy. Atul Gawande writes perceptively about the desire for personal independence, which he sees as a hallmark of modernization. Thus in China, Japan, and Korea, the proportion of elderly people living on their own is rapidly rising, linked to an erosion of the shame at leaving elderly parents on their own. What's venerated now is not youth, but 'the independent self' – at all ages. There is one problem with this, namely that it takes no account of what will very likely happen sooner or later, and may last quite some time. 'Serious illness or infirmity will strike. It is as inevitable as sunset. And then a new question arises: If independence is what we live for, what do we do when it can no longer be sustained?' (Gawande, 2014: 23). The question is put off by many entering old age and those who care for and advise them. Newly retired people often want to fulfil all kinds of projects and ambitions, and may not care to think of eventual decline. Geriatrics is all about enabling older people to maintain independence, not preparing them for dependence.

Privacy is the handmaid of independence. By contrast, surveillance by family, neighbours, or the police may undermine my freedom to act as I wish. That said, privacy norms vary considerably from one culture to another. Some Swedes may cherish privacy from the prying eyes of neighbours, but accept state regulation. Some Americans, especially in the South and Mid-West, may be in and out of their neighbours' houses but profoundly distrust state interference in their lives.

As part of a major global study of how people use social media, Daniel Miller (2017) conducted an illuminating anthropological study of the social connectedness of rural English people living at home with terminal or long-term illness (I mentioned his study in Chapter 3). Miller found that connections were maintained, distanced, or lost in a very English way. The traditional telephone, for example, was 'extremely un-English because it was exceptionally intrusive' (p. 12). But 'now people can text if this is a convenient time to phone, and then phone to find if this is a convenient time to call around' (p. 109). The non-intrusive text allows people to say I'm fine when I'm not or vice-versa; or to say I'm okay, but not up to a chat.

Engagement in the public domain goes along with respect for privacy. The English villagers were sociable enough in public (over the garden wall, in the pub, golf club, or charity shop) but do not invite each other into the house; the chief exception is young families as children gaily invade the private spaces of neigh-bouring families, and also some middle-class adults who may invite neighbours to coffee or dinner. Working-class people in particular do not like to depend on neighbours – a reminder of the poverty that forced their forebears to rely on neighbours, like borrowing a cup of sugar to keep them going till Friday pay day. The result is that two neighbours may each need or want to give help, but neither wants to be proactive in asking/giving. But, Miller observes (pp. 204–5), 'these same neighbours feel free to engage in public support through volunteering. Indeed, they may end up giving support, through the hospice, to people they might have cared for, but cannot otherwise support, as members of the same community or neighbourhood.' If Swedes rely on the state, and Americans on the individual and on voluntary local action, English people rely on institutions, a highly relevant institution today being the local hospice.

I have discussed Miller's study in some detail not because the English are in any way significant, but because his is a rare example of the kind of fine-grained ethnography that can reveal how, at the end of life, self and others interact within one community in one society and culture. He notes how different his mainly white villagers are from the multi-cultural streets in London observed in some of his previous ethnographies. The point here is not to say 'this is how the English do privacy, pride and dependence at the end of life', but to invite you the reader to ponder how such values work out in your own family, street, and community.

GRIEF

Chapter 1 identified some demographic reasons why modern societies tend to define grief as a private experience. This can be modified by culture, and there are certainly modern societies, such as Ireland and Japan, where funerals are typically attended by large numbers of people. I want to sketch here a few ways that notions of group and individual can influence how modern cultures, to use Jakoby's (2012) term, 'frame' grief.

Cultural historians have argued that western individualism has over at least the past three centuries focused on feelings and the inner life. Fostered at first in novels, plays, and poetry, by the early twentieth century it led to psychoanalysis and eventually to 'therapy culture'. It also provided fertile soil for the idea of grief as an inner journey – rather than a spiritual trial, a social requirement, a practical crisis, or simply a difficult time made bearable by connection to others. This culture's emotional literacy has produced a rich vocabulary to describe 'the grief process'. Four hundred years ago Shakespeare urged us to 'Give sorrow words; the grief that does not speak knits up the o-er wrought heart and bids it break' (*Macbeth*). But it was not until the second half of the twentieth century that an entire new psychological vocabulary of grief gained currency.

Individualism is also associated with the idea that each individual should determine their own life and be able to vote for who is to run their country and local community. This nexus of political ideas has profoundly shaped how grief is framed. Feminist historian Lou Taylor (1983) shows how British Victorian mourning customs – imposed largely on upper-class ladies – mirrored not the depth of grief but power relations in a patriarchal society. Thus a woman had to be in full mourning for longer on the death of her husband's father than on the death of her own baby. The women who in the 1890s challenged this also supported votes for women; they wanted freedom to decide who their leaders were, and for whom they should mourn.

Disenfranchised grief

Over the coming decades, this idea that mourning should reflect personal feeling not social expectation filtered down the social classes. In the USA it found formal articulation in the 1980s in American gerontologist Ken Doka's (2002) concept of 'disenfranchised grief'. It is no coincidence that Doka chose a political concept – disenfranchisement – to describe how some kinds of grief are not socially acknowledged or legitimated. He could have termed this 'socially unacknowledged grief', but instead he used a political word, 'disenfranchised', with the clear implication that all griefs *should* be enfranchised. It is as much a right to have one's grief – whether for a gay partner, a friend, a pet – acknowledged as it is a right to have the vote.

Cann (2014) discusses the proliferation of grass-roots memorials in public places in the USA – on car decals, T-shirts, tattoos, and social media. She sees this as driven by those whose grief is disenfranchised. This may be because the mourners, such as Hispanic Americans, are marginal, or because the deceased is a child, or because the group's traditionally more public style of mourning is banished by twentieth-century America's requirement that grief be private. These new memorials, equivalent to the Victorian black armband, express the person's desire to be identified as a griever. And these memorials are quintessentially American. Memorial car decals are not seen much in other countries, but in the USA cars are an extension of the self, not just a means of transport. And cars and T-shirts are 'everyday artefacts of contemporary American life – instantly recognizable and ubiquitous. Turning these quintessential items of consumer culture into instruments of bereavement forces others to acknowledge death and participate in a dialogue of grief and bereavement' (2014: 103). Sloane (2018) has a similar analysis of vernacular street memorials.

Yet societies that formally espouse individual rights will continue to take some griefs more seriously than others and see little or no problem in this. Robson and Walter (2012–13) show how English people acknowledge a hierarchy in which grief for a friend or schoolteacher is recognized but not considered as serious as grief for a child, spouse, or parent. Social institutions also have to prioritize. Thus most workplaces specify how much leave is allowable for specific kinds of bereavement – an employee who claims a week's compassionate leave for the death of his pet goldfish is unlikely to receive sympathetic treatment, not only from his employer but also from colleagues who will have to cover for his time off. Funeral directors also have to know who can claim authority to organize the funeral, and they reflect a widespread cultural understanding that this is the right of close family – even if it gives the family power to disenfranchise the grief of mourners outside the family (Walter and Bailey, in press).

CONCLUSION

This chapter has argued that the extent to which a culture privileges group over individual, or individual over group, along with *which* groups are privileged, can influence death rates, how dying is managed, and how grief is framed. In individual-focused cultures, the concept of individual rights and personal autonomy over group conformity and medical paternalism are particularly important in shaping dying and grieving.

But societies are always complex. In theory, the upside of individualism is freedom and choice, the downside is anxiety and loneliness. In practice, individuals still live in groups and, required to exercise choice, observe their peers to gain guidance; and individualistic cultures still find ways to look after each other, whether that be through the Scandinavian state, American face-to-face sociability, or English hospice volunteers. In theory, the upside of collectivism is guaranteed support, the downside is a lack of freedom. In practice, the lack of reciprocity entailed in receiving care can cause shame for some dying Māori (Gott et al., 2017: 272–3), while many Japanese find ways to do their own thing. In any one culture, people often choose creatively from a range of scripts – for dying as for living (Long, 2004).

FURTHER READING

- Berggren, H. and Trägårdh, L. (2010) 'Pippi Longstocking: The autonomous child and the moral logic of the Swedish welfare state', in H. Mattsson and S-O. Wallenstein (eds), *Swedish Modernism*. London: Black Dog, pp. 11–22.

- Doka, K.J. (ed.) (2002) *Disenfranchised Grief*. Champaign, IL: Research Press.

- Durkheim, E. (2002 [1897]) *Suicide*. London: Routledge.

- Gawande, A. (2014) *Being Mortal: Illness, medicine, and what matters in the end*. London: Profile.

- Gordon, D.R. and Paci, E. (1997) 'Disclosure practices and cultural narratives: understanding concealment and silence around cancer in Tuscany, Italy', *Social Science and Medicine*, 44 (10): 1433–52.

- Hayes, J.W. and Lipset, S.M. (1993–94). 'Individualism: a double-edged sword', *The Responsive Community*, 4: 69–80.

- Hofstede, G. (2001) *Culture's Consequences: Comparing values, behaviours, institutions and organizations across nations*. Thousand Oaks, CA: Sage.

- Jakoby, N.R. (2012) 'Grief as a social emotion', *Death Studies*, 36: 679–711.

- Long, S.O. (2004) 'Cultural scripts for the good death in Japan and the United States: similarities and differences', *Social Science and Medicine*, 58 (5): 913–28.

- Miller, D. (2017) *The Comfort of People*. Cambridge: Polity.

- Wilkinson, R. and Pickett, K. (2009) *The Spirit Level: Why equality is better for everyone*. London: Allen Lane.

Questions to discuss

- In your society, what is the relative power of group and individual? Which groups are privileged – state, local institutions, family, the medical profession, or …?

- How does this affect: a) death rates, b) fear of death, c) how dying is managed, d) funerals, e) grieving?

- How do notions of privacy operate in your society, and with what consequences for people who are dying or bereaved?

Notes

1.　www.hofstede-insights.com/models/national-culture/ (accessed 13/6/19).

2.　www.hofstede-insights.com/country-comparison/ (accessed 13/6/19).

3.　Personal communication from Ros Taylor, 26 October 2018.

4.　Erik Finkelstein, 'The cost of a medicalized death', Lancet Commission conference The Value of Death, Bristol, UK, 26 October 2018.

5.　Cross-national panel discussion on dependency, Lancet Commission conference The Value of Death, Bristol, UK, 26 October 2018.

9

FAMILY

Westerners are increasingly claiming the right to die and grieve as they see fit, and this idea is promoted by the death awareness movement, palliative care, advance directives and the euthanasia and abortion movements. But death affects not only individuals; it also threatens to tear apart the *social* fabric, and death rituals often function to help repair the torn fabric. A major part of the social fabric typically torn by death is the family. So the family shapes both death's threat, and how the threat is dealt with. This is true in any society – but families are not the same in all societies (Todd, 2019).

Each family is an arena of norms and everyday practices – it is part of culture. At the macro level, each society has expectations as to what counts as a family, what practices families should engage in, and how family members are to 'do family'. At the micro level, each family has its own unique practices, its own ways of doing family which have to be worked out as husband and wife, or partners, bring their own practices and expectations from their family of origin (Morgan, 2011). Some practices concern family time: when does the family eat together, when do couples, and parents and children, find time to talk? Others concern the division of labour within the household: who cares for the children, who cares for ageing relatives, who is responsible for managing emotions within the household, who completes the annual tax return and other official forms?

Such practices shape a family's answer to questions such as how to care for dying members, what counts as a respectful funeral, how and for how long to mourn, how – if at all – to engage with the dead. Gender differences, for example in how to grieve, complicate things; after a child's death, the mother may want to talk and talk, the father goes off fishing by himself, each failing to understand the other, each person's way of grieving either validated or invalidated by societal norms about men, women, and grief (Riches and Dawson, 2000; Doka and Martin, 2010). When society itself is changing, as for example in the UK where stoicism is being challenged by the idea that it's good to express feelings, expectations within a family may need considerable negotiation and re-negotiation. And that is just between partners. Children may develop their own expectations about appropriate death-related behaviour and feelings, with migration from one country to another particularly likely to cause differences between the generations; children growing up in, say, the USA may see things rather differently from their parents who grew up in, say, Mexico or Iraq.

As well as being part of culture, the family is also a social and economic institution, governed by laws (e.g. on inheritance, euthanasia, abortion, children's rights), by tax and welfare regimes, by entitlements to services, and so on (Edwards, Ribbens McCarthy and Gillies, 2012) – all of which can affect death and dying. What families can legally do and what public resources they are entitled to varies between countries. 'The family' is also a political ideology, co-opted by or undermining government; and a religious ideology, co-opted by or undermining religion (Mount, 1982). This raises questions of power. Who has most power and influence at the deathbed, when organizing the funeral, and disposing of the deceased's possessions – the individual? the family (in which case, *who* in the family?) religion? the state? lawyers? health care professionals? In any one country, the answer may depend on the type of death: expected death, coma, dementia, suicide, assisted suicide, abortion. And the answer may differ as between deciding terminal care, organizing the funeral, inheritance, or how mourners should act and feel.

This chapter looks first at some consequences of filial respect in East Asia for how people die and grieve, before going on to look at the increasingly fluid and negotiable ideas of what counts as family in some western countries. The chapter then goes on to consider whether and how religion, the state, and the medical and nursing professions promote or undermine family death practices – and how the answers can vary between societies.

FILIAL RESPECT

In Confucian philosophy, 'filial piety' means respect for parents, elders, and ancestors. It also entails the duty to procreate and continue the family line. For over 2,000 years filial piety has deeply influenced Chinese culture, along with several other East Asian societies such as Korea and Japan. It has profound implications for care of the dying, for suicide, for relationships with the dead, and for who should mourn whom.

Making ancestors

Filial piety does not end when the elder dies. It extends into ancestor veneration, found across East Asia (Endres and Lauser, 2011), not least in economically developed countries. Traditional Chinese funeral rites transform the polluted corpse into a revered ancestor, legitimating the patrilineal line and assisting descendants' prosperity; otherwise, the deceased may become a wandering soul causing trouble to the living (Watson, 1982; Tong, 2004). Subsequent ancestor rituals maintain a two-way reciprocal relationship between the living and the dead (Baudrillard, 1993), typically between the eldest son and male ancestors. The relationship is essentially one of mutual care, in which each side looks after the other; more negatively, it can sometimes entail rites to placate the dead so they do not cause trouble for the living.

Filial piety shapes who is required to mourn whom. Thus family members are expected to mourn their elders, especially male elders; they are not expected to mourn those younger than themselves. This is reminiscent of upper-class society in Victorian Britain where ladies were expected to mourn their husband's father for a longer period than their own baby (Taylor, 1983), as mentioned in Chapter 8. This illustrates how, in a patrilineal family and a patriarchal society, cultural norms about mourning may function not to assuage grief but to maintain patriarchy and the patrilineal line. In late Victorian Britain, this was challenged by women fighting for personal liberty. In China, it was challenged by Mao's Cultural Revolution which replaced traditional funerals with socialist memorial meetings; by displaying the deceased as a model socialist citizen, these legitimated not filial piety but socialism (Goss and Klass, 2005). In Vietnam, the state converted traditional family and community shrines to commemorating the revolutionary dead (Kwon, 2008).

At the same time, ancestral veneration survives, adapting to new political or economic circumstances. Many Vietnamese are worried about the war dead; dying violently, and without proper burial, what has become of their soul? They become hungry ghosts, and require rituals to transform them into ancestors or deities. Mediums make a living identifying the location of remains and conducting the appropriate rites (Kwon, 2008; Endres and Lauser, 2011). In one Chinese village, when Mao's Great Leap Forward banned traditional ancestral practices, villagers feared that the improperly buried dead – 'famine-corpse ghosts' – were bringing misfortune to surviving family (Thaxton, 2008). In the present century, a Chinese colleague described to me a medium-size company headquarters which housed on the top floor a shrine where executives would consult with the ancestors before making business decisions: capitalist businessmen in a communist society consulting the company ancestors in order to make profit! Despite the formal ideology, whether Confucian or socialist, people often find ways to bend customs to their own needs. Everyday practices may match neither formal statements of ancestor veneration nor political ideology.

Abandoned elders

In Chinese culture, to die before your parents, especially if you have not produced any offspring to continue the line, is one of the most unfilial things you can do. China's one-child policy (1979–2015) produced two generations of

Chinese parents with only one child to look after them as they age and die – though there are exceptions, for example rural parents could have a second child if the first was a daughter. Some of these one-child parents have suffered or will suffer the misfortune of their one child dying before them. They will experience not only economic hardship in old age but also the shame of having no children to continue the family line, no children to care for them as they age and to look after their post-mortem wellbeing as ancestors. Confucian filial piety together with the one-child policy places these grieving parents in a uniquely difficult and stigmatized position.

The population stabilization produced by the one-child policy certainly helped China's spectacular economic growth, but it was a high-risk strategy in terms of care for elders, for the dying and for the ancestors – all of whom depend on the one child surviving its parents. This is now causing particular hardship and anxiety for two generations of bereaved parents in a particular culture at a particular time – illustrating how the challenges posed by death and bereavement depend on social and political context.

In Fang's (2018) interviews with Chinese parents whose only child had died, many spoke of financial loss caused by the costs of looking after their sick child. In 2009, nationwide health care insurance was introduced, covering most health care costs, but many parents lost their child to illness before 2009 so even some middle-class parents had used up all their savings and even borrowed money for medical treatments. Other parents were worried about who will look after them in old age. More fathers than mothers spoke of there being no-one to continue the family line.

There was also shame at no longer being part of the community of parents. As they age, they are both too poor and feel too stigmatized to move to a private old person's home. To counter this, some parents have advocated that the government fund old people's homes for childless old people where they can recover a sense of family and interdependency by exchanging care and support with other bereaved parents. Yet the parents Fang spoke to also expressed hope that, after decades of consistently high economic growth and improved living conditions, state provision will in due course improve. Moreover, having sacrificed themselves for the nation's one-child policy, they feel the government is responsible for their care in old age

If dying before your parents is unfilial, then choosing to die is very much so. Suicide among young Chinese is deemed terrible, not so much as in the West because of the perceived waste of a life with so much promise, but because it is shameful to abandon your parents. Suicide among the old, while not welcomed, does not offend against filial piety and is not uncommon; China has the world's second highest elder suicide rate. The one-child policy means that many millions of Chinese couples have four parents to look after, with no help from non-existent siblings, so it is not surprising if some older Chinese feel abandoned by their children – though they may use kinder terms such as 'they are too busy' or 'they are under too much pressure' (Leong, 2018).

CHOICE IN FAMILY RELATIONSHIPS

In stark contrast to Confucianism, the sociology of personal life in western societies nowadays emphasizes the variety of family forms, the fluidity of relationships, and the many and varied attachments that contemporary westerners can develop (Smart, 2007). Far from all Britons, Finns, or Americans live in a nuclear family with mum, dad, and two kids. Following separation or divorce, many live in reconstituted families. After a spouse is divorced or dies, many women live alone while retaining significant friendships. Some choose to remain childless. Others live with gay or lesbian partners. And binary categories such as male/female and straight/gay are dissolving as a younger generation comes to see gender identity as fluid. The question this section asks is: If fluidity increasingly characterizes how people choose to live their lives, does it also characterize their dying and subsequent funeral and mourning? Or do conventional, 'old-fashioned' assumptions about family creep back in?

It is a bit soon to say for certain. To my knowledge, no research has been conducted specifically into this question. And, apart from divorce and remarriage which in some countries grew rapidly from the 1960s to the 1980s, it is only in very recent decades that openly gay, bisexual, or transgender identities have been widely acknowledged; many of those whose relationships are based on such identities are yet to die.

Bereavement theories have long reflected this fluidity. Thus attachment theory has since the mid-twentieth century seen the depth of grief as connected to the mourner's particular attachment to the deceased, which in turn goes back to how securely the mourner was attached to his or her mother in infancy (Parkes, 2008). And the concept of disenfranchised grief (Doka, 2002) aims to validate grief for whomever it is felt, regardless of formal relationship.

So much for theories, but what about culture? In practice, do twenty-first century people expect caring, grief, and funerals to reflect attachment rather than formal and even traditional family structures? It seems not, or not yet. Let's look at some evidence.

Funerals

One early twenty-first century study in which several hundred Britons wrote about the last funeral they had attended (Walter and Bailey, in press) found that these funerals had little to do with individuals or even grief and everything to do with family – defined very conventionally. Drawing on Finch's (2007) concept of 'displaying family', Walter and Bailey argued that the funeral is a rite in which family is displayed, indeed accomplished. Where there was conflict between acknowledging grief and displaying family, then family almost always trumped grief – thus relatives who were not close to the deceased were often criticized for not attending the funeral: whatever they felt, they were 'family' and should attend. Or a close friend deeply distraught at the death might sit at the back since the front seats were reserved for 'family'; no respondent challenged this 'disenfranchising' of a non-family member's grief. And however warmly invited, friends and neighbours did not always attend the post-funeral tea, saying 'We're not family.'

Though more and more British funerals are 'personalized' in that they reflect and even celebrate the deceased's individuality, the funeral ceremony is devised by the priest or celebrant in conjunction with 'the family' (who are typically paying the bill). Eulogies therefore typically highlight family relationships. So, though the twenty-first century 'life-centred' funeral in theory reflects the uniqueness of each life and the diversity of contemporary living arrangements, in practice these funerals continue to display family in quite conventional ways. Most of the funerals in Walter and Bailey's study were of older, middle-class Britons, and in time more funerals may reflect the diversity of living arrangements; and doubtless even now, many celebrants and priests could describe exceptional funerals they have conducted which broke the mould. Structurally and culturally, however, the British funeral lies securely in the hands of 'the family', and this is expected both by the general public and by the funeral industry.

Grief

This confirms an earlier study by Robson and Walter (2012–13), mentioned in Chapter 8, that showed how British people have remarkably consistent expectations that the depth of grief is likely to flow from relational closeness defined in conventional family terms. A clear hierarchy emerged:

- Blood relatives and spouse experience more intense grief than in-laws.

- Primary kin (parent, child, sibling, spouse) grieve more than secondary kin (such as grandparent, niece, cousin, in-laws).

- Fictive kin (e.g. a friend who becomes godmother) may grieve as much as in-laws but not as much as blood kin or spouse.

- Neighbours, work colleagues, and so on grieve less than kin.

- Those with a professional or contractual relationship to the deceased suffer significantly less grief than any kin.

This hierarchy emerged from the responses of free individuals. It is formally embedded in policies such as company bereavement leave, which typically prioritizes the death of a close family member, conventionally defined.[1]

As Edwards, Ribbens McCarthy and Gillies (2012) comment, the family does not just consist of its members' practices; it is also an institution, with traditional family structures powerfully embedded in policy, law, and politics, irrespective of how people actually live.

Care

As well as hierarchies of grief, there are also hierarchies of care. Quereshi and Walker (1989) found that Britons expect hands-on care for sick or dying people at home to be given by resident kin; if none exist, then by non-resident kin; and only if these are not available, will friends and neighbours step in. Neighbours play an important role in generally 'looking out for' a frail or sick neighbour, and may be first on the scene if, for example, the person falls and presses their personal alarm button. But hands-on care is then immediately handed over to professionals and/or kin. Neighbours can be great at calling an ambulance; they are not expected to wipe bottoms – not least as this could undermine norms of neighbourliness that hinge on reciprocity and privacy. Britons value their neighbours but do not want to depend on them if they cannot reciprocate (Walter, 1999a; Miller, 2017).

In twentieth-century Japan, care of the elderly was the responsibility of the eldest son whose family was expected to live with his ageing parents – in practice his wife often did much of the hands-on care. By the end of the century, many grown-up sons did not live near, let alone with, their elderly parents. So it has become increasingly common for care to be negotiated: if another son or a daughter, or their spouse, lives nearby and likes the elderly parent or parents, they may agree to do the caring. But it remains understood that care is the next generation's responsibility. Thus, filial piety is maintained via more flexible arrangements than had hitherto operated.

Of course, in economically less-favoured circumstances, non-standard living arrangements are widespread, deriving less from choice than from necessity. In nineteenth-century Europe, orphans were often cared for by aunts and grandparents. In sub-Saharan Africa where AIDS has decimated the middle generation, it is not unusual for children to be raised by grandparents. Many African fathers work away from home, returning maybe just once or twice a year – as also do Indian construction workers in Singapore or the Middle East. And in fatherless families, common in sub-Saharan Africa, the mother may work away from home, often on another continent. Many live-in carers in the UK come from Zimbabwe; their earnings from looking after an old person whose children are not prepared to care for them full time are remitted back home to Africa in order to support others to look after the carer's own children. Children can become deeply attached to the substitute parent-figure, such as grandmother or aunt, and deeply mourn them on their death – not to mention finding themselves, once again, having to devise other living arrangements.

In sum, it seems that rapidly modernizing societies disrupt traditional relation-ships, leading to varied and fluid family arrangements; some post-industrial societies also have varied and fluid living arrangements, enabled by highly developed concepts of equality, diversity, tolerance, individual rights, and choice. In between, mature industrial societies – such as post-war North America, Western Europe and Japan – seem to have more structured family arrangements. Deep-seated assumptions and feelings about death, funerals, and grief may, however, lag behind – hence the shame of the childless Chinese old person, or the family-focus of the twenty-first century British funeral.

RELIGION

This section introduces religion's role in promoting or undermining family death practices.

As we have seen above, Confucianism fully supports ancestral veneration as it is consistent with Confucius' notion of filial piety. But the priests and prophets of monotheistic religions – notably Judaism, Christianity, and Islam – have often feared the passionate loyalty and love that humans show for family, fearing it undermines worship of the one true God. In other words, love for family is a form of idolatry. Buddhism, though non-theistic, expected many men to leave their family responsibilities to become monks; family was just another attachment, another encumbrance of mortal life, to be left behind on the spiritual path. Polytheistic Hinduism, by contrast, seems able to accommodate the family dead among myriad gods and goddesses, major and minor; loyalties can be multiple.

The result is that, whereas ancestor veneration and its reciprocal relationships between the living and the dead have continued to thrive under Confucianism, the opposite has been the case with monotheistic religions and with Buddhism, which have had an altogether more complex relation with the family in life, and with family ancestors in death. The more hardline versions of these religions have suppressed ancestor veneration, sometimes ruthlessly and murderously (Douglas, 2004; Park, 2010). Only God was to be worshipped. But, given people's desire to care for their family dead, there has also been syncretism (amalgamation) as with Roman Catholic saints through whom prayers may be made for the family dead; and as in Buddhism which selectively modified its teachings in China and Japan to incorporate family ancestors. And all the while, whatever the theologians and priests may have been teaching, ordinary folk were doing their own thing – as in popular Irish Catholicism where prayers are made not only to the Virgin Mary but also to grandmother Mary, as much a saint in her family as the Virgin herself.

In his book *The Subversive Family*, Ferdinand Mount (1982) argues that natural loyalty to the family undermines any ideology demanding total loyalty to God or to the state. If some religions, and some totalitarian states (such as Mao's China), have responded by downgrading the family in favour of God or the state, others have co-opted the family, as did Nazi Germany and as does contemporary Christian fundamentalism. But though fundamentalism validates the family in life, in death the fundamentalist belongs not to his or her family, but to God.

THE STATE

If religion can promote or oppose particular family death practices, so too can the state.

Promote

Japan provides an exceptionally clear example of the state promoting a particular kind of family and controlling the family through care of the family grave. From 1868, the Meiji reforms signalled the country's retreat from isolationism and its intention to join the modern world. One reform promoted the *ie* or three generational patrilineal household, comprising grandparents, eldest son, his wife and their children; *ie* also refers to their house, garden and rice paddies, and the *ie*'s section in the cemetery. All households are registered, with one person – almost always male – as head of the household. This system echoes the rest of society. The household head is responsible for looking after the ancestral grave, just as the emperor looks after the nation, and – later in the twentieth century – the company looks after its employees. Tsuji (2002: 192) observes that 'Many Japanese companies build collective graves for their deceased employees and worship the spirits of corporate "ancestors". This role of the company parallels the *ie*'s role in ancestor worship and the state's role in worshipping "glorious" military dead.' The family grave became the focus of ancestor worship, complemented by the *butsudan* or household shrine (Tsuji, 2002; Rowe, 2007).

Nowadays, however, many Japanese families are not three-generation stem families, but nuclear, comprising only a couple or a single person; hence 'the growing number of people without "proper" descendants to take care of their graves' (Tsuji, 2002: 184) This has led not only to new challenges in elder care but also since the 1990s to considerable innovation in where and how human remains are deposited (Boret, 2014).

Inheritance

Inheritance laws may both reflect and support cultural assumptions about family and individual. English kinship, and by extension, kinship in the USA, Canada, Australia, and some other ex-British colonies, is peculiarly individualistic, so that kin relationships operate between persons rather than positions (Strathern, 1992).

'Knowing someone to be my brother or my aunt reveals little about the type of relationship I have with that person; it depends *which* brother or aunt' (Finch and Mason, 2000: 18, emphasis in original). Each individual therefore constructs their own kinship system. According to Alan Macfarlane (1978), this goes back a long way; as far back as the thirteenth century, English wills revealed the possibility of people choosing whom in the family to leave stuff to. Wills and inheritance thus became a way in which English individuals create their family.

This English system differs from the law of patrimony found in some European countries and in Japan where the eldest son holds property in trust for the transgenerational family (Déchaux, 2002) – as also do English aristocrats and royals. Distribution of the remaining parent's assets among all the children is required by law in some other European countries, but Britons and Americans are free to will their property to whomsoever they wish – even if most English parents choose to distribute their property equally among their children (Finch and Mason, 2000). Inheritance laws therefore have considerable power to support particular family structures (Gilding, 2010).

Assume

The state may well assume that certain family members will care for a dying person, according to some variant of Quereshi and Walker's (1989) hierarchy of care. Likewise, welfare benefits may be available to carers who fit the state's assumptions about families and care. This may also pertain after death. The British government's funeral payment scheme reimburses poorer families for part of the cost of a funeral; a spouse, parent, or close family member is eligible to claim. Woodthorpe and Rumble (2016), however, found that who in a family takes responsibility for paying the funeral director depends – as we would expect from the previous section on the fluidity of English concepts of kinship – on the quality of the relationships particular family members have with each other. Consequently, who the government assumes should take responsibility for the funeral and who in the family has actually paid the funeral director may not be the same, in which case the person who has paid may be unable to claim reimbursement. This shows how family relationships are both internally negotiated *and* subject to external constraints.

Using Esping-Andersen's (1990) typology of European welfare regimes, Britain is a liberal regime that tends to restrict benefits to those most in need, yet it seems that – in the case of the funeral payment scheme – eligibility requires a particular kin connection to the deceased as well as low income. Corporatist welfare regimes – Belgium, France, Germany, Spain – are 'typically shaped by the Church, and hence strongly committed to the preservation of traditional family-hood' (1990: 27), so it would be interesting to see how this operates in death as well as in life. Valentine and Woodthorpe (2014) sketch funeral welfare payments in these countries; we await more fine-grained research to determine how assumptions about kinship shape the operation of these different national (and in the case of Germany, local) schemes.

Oppose

The power of love for family can challenge not only monotheistic religion and Buddhist detachment but also the state. In Sophocles' play, Antigone insists on proper burial for her brother who died on the losing side in a civil war. This incurs the wrath of Creon, the king and her uncle, who is determined that the political order be upheld by leaving traitors to rot without dignity where they fell. Sophocles' depiction of this conflict between the law of kinship and the law of the state has exercised subsequent political philosophers from G.W.F. Hegel (Avineri, 1972) to Judith Butler (2000).

This theme has been taken up by Gail Holst-Warhaft (2000) in her book *The Cue for Passion: Grief and its political uses.* Following Durkheim (1915), both sociology and anthropology have taught that through funeral and other rites, mourners gather together to affirm the solidarity of the group over against death. Holst-Warhaft, however, shows how the passion of grief can be the cue not for stabilizing society, but for transforming it. Grief is probably the most powerful emotion that humans feel, carrying us to the edge of madness; in many societies, it was indulged, performed, shaped into song and lament. But authority figures in church and state have feared it, banning songs, laments, and wakes, and making mourning a dull business. They turned the energy of grief into depression.

But Holst-Warhaft gives examples over 2,000 years of how grief has powered mourners (acting together, rather in the isolation into which modernity usually thrusts them) to challenge authority. The most dramatic example is The Mothers of the Plaza de Mayo, the mothers of Argentina's disappeared, who refused to be bought off with (probably fake) bones being returned to them and with talk of the need for 'closure'. As their newspaper put it: 'Let there be no healing of wounds. Let them remain open. Because if the wounds still bleed, there will be no forgetting and our strength will continue to grow.' The Mothers' collective mobilization of their grief played a key role in political change in Argentina.

Funerals

The preceding paragraphs gave dramatic examples of conflict between the political order and family grief. Chapter 12 will consider the treatment of the war dead by democratic states which somehow have to both honour family grief and display the dead as national heroes. There are also examples of the state imposing a new kind of funeral that does not, as in Japan, support the family but downgrades it and displays instead the political order. In most cases, Durkheimian sociology is correct: in funeral rites, mourners gather together to affirm the solidarity of the group over death. The question is: which group? In the American or European war cemetery, the group is manifestly not family but nation. But family is not undermined. In some communist countries, by contrast, funerals that display the deceased as a model citizen affirm socialism in an effort to undermine the family.[2]

I have mentioned already China and Vietnam. China's Cultural Revolution stopped the veneration of family ancestors; funerals were simple, with family no more important than workmates; only the funerals of important local or national party members (ultimately Mao himself) were on any scale (Whyte, 1988). But in a more capitalist twenty-first century economy, some rural Chinese are reverting to family ancestors; for others there is anomie, uncertainty. According to one informant, 'No one knows the old ritual, and no one believes in the old religions anymore, but the practices put in place by the CCP [Communist Party of China] are discredited' (Goss and Klass, 2005: 202).

A more recent study, 'Dying socialist in capitalist Shanghai' (Liu, 2015), tells a somewhat different story. Secular civil funerals were invented by the Republican government in the early twentieth century before the 1949 Communist Revolution. They were then promoted by the CCP from the late 1960s, with the following format (p. 253):

- The Master/Mistress of Ceremonies announces the beginning of the memorial meeting.

- All commemorate the deceased in silence while the funeral dirge is played.

- The work unit representative gives a memorial speech.

- The representative of the bereaved gives a thank you speech.

- All collectively bow to the deceased three times.

- Farewell Ceremony.

At the ceremony's heart is the memorial speech. Here is a recent example (Liu, 2015: 260):

> Comrade Wang Dashan was diligent and hard working. No matter what posts he worked, he was always concentrating on working. He loved his job and was good at it. He was dedicated to his job with his full heart. Comrade Wang Dashan was an honest and frank man. He was humble and cautious as well as friendly and kindly. He was frugal and simple and had endured hardships and bitterness. He was very strict in educating his children so all his children are law abiding and studious people.

The death of Comrade Wang Dashan made us lose a good comrade. Although he has passed away, his spirit of selfless dedication to work, his bitter, hard, and diligent, as well as frugal life style, his decent, honest, and frank morality are examples for us all. Although human beings cannot return to life once they have died, we can transform our grief into a powerful force. Having this model, we can commemorate Comrade Wang Dashan by having even more passion to devote ourselves to the work of socialism.

Comrade Wang Dashan, please rest in peace!

The memorial speech always identifies person with citizen. In this example, the only mention of family is to show how Comrade Wang ensured his children grew up to be good citizens. The subsequent 'thank you speech', given by a family member, memorializes the deceased from a family perspective but may also echo much of the language of the memorial speech.

Having liberalized the economy, the CCP now discourages socialist funerals, and Shanghai funeral parlours actively promote personalized funerals. However, socialist funerals remain popular in Shanghai, usually with religious additions (either Confucian ancestor veneration or Buddhist reincarnation). Throughout the world, mourners are generally unwilling to be cultural revolutionaries, especially in the emotionally challenging early days of bereavement (Marris, 1974). Unless they are forced to adopt a new form or have witnessed it at other funerals, mourners tend to adapt existing funeral forms rather than adopt entirely new ones, temporarily returning to tradition. (We find this, for example, in Europe where many mourners who have not attended church for decades return to a religious format for the funeral.) Maybe something like this is happening in Shanghai? The secular memorial meeting has become traditional, or at least familiar. Whatever the explanation, socialist citizens continue their evolving dance between communism and family ancestors, with those attached to Buddhism, Christianity, or other religions adding their own variations.

I would not want to overplay the state's power over death. Tsuji (2002: 193) concludes his article 'Death policies in Japan: the state, the family, and the individual' as follows:

> The Meiji regime used death policies to exercise tight control over the family and the individual ... [Yet] mortuary practice is not a product of government policies alone, but of a complex interplay among policies, people, traditions, and other situational factors.

No state manages to control all family death practices, and some states make no attempt to control them. In Serbia, a colleague informed me that 'excepting some general features of modern dying, the death of common Serbs is more shaped by family, religion and regional traditions than by state politics.'

HEALTH CARE PRACTITIONERS

This chapter has looked at how religion, the state and the individual interact with family in the governance of dying, funerals, mourning, and inheritance. A further question to be asked in any country is how medical, nursing, and other health professionals interact with families in shaping end-of-life care and how the power to make decisions is distributed between families and professionals?

Chapter 8 identified that in most western European countries, North America, Australia, and among New Zealanders of European descent (*Pākehā*), the individual patient is positioned as the prime decision maker. This means the patient should be the first to hear their diagnosis and prognosis, however bad the news. Health care professionals (HCPs) contract to care for the individual patient, though in disability and palliative care they may also work with family carers – but these are somewhat peripheral to the core work with the patient.

Several studies have shown, by contrast, that in Mediterranean countries such as Italy, along with many Asian countries such as Japan, the doctor tells the family that the patient has cancer, or that the disease is incurable. It is then up to the family to decide whether or not to tell the patient; often, they choose not to (Gordon and Paci, 1997).

But there is a third approach. With Māori, all parties – patient, family, and HCP – discuss the diagnosis, prognosis, and care options together. And in the Netherlands where collaborative decision making is the norm, discussions about euthanasia typically comprise a series of conversations between doctor, patient, and family member (Norwood, 2009). Consultations with Māori and Dutch patients and their families may take far longer than the ten minutes or less allocated in some other countries.

In some cultures, therefore, HCPs talk with the family, which may undermine patient autonomy; in others, they may talk with the patient, which may implicitly or explicitly exclude some or all of the family; in yet other cultures, they may engage in a time-consuming consultation with the entire family including the patient.

In all cases, HCPs have to operate within their country's law. Where euthanasia/ assisted suicide is illegal, however committed HCPs are to the patient making informed decisions – for example about where to die – HCPs cannot countenance a decision about *when* to die. In such countries, it is not unknown for some patients to accumulate a stash of pills, kept secret from both HCPs and family, in case the time should come when they have had enough and wish to end their life.

Last minute negotiations

Wilson's (2017) recent research in an English hospital has shown how the patient-focused Anglo/NW European model can come under severe strain in the patient's final hours. The many patients with complex medical conditions and/or frailty often do not have a predictable 'dying trajectory' (Chapter 1). If they have been hospitalized for a while, doctors and nurses will be interacting mainly with the patient; family members visit to see the patient, and do not always get to see the doctor or the responsible nurse. So, especially in busy general medical wards, there may be little or no relationship between doctor or nurse and the family. Doctors and nurses in such wards regularly identify dying very late, by which time – a day or two or even just hours before death – it is not unusual for the patient to have become confused or comatose, in other words to have lost mental capacity. The family is asked to come to the hospital, but with so little warning, they may find it difficult to accept that their relative is imminently dying. The patient is no longer able to make decisions, and may not have granted formal power of attorney to a family member. At this point, doctor and family – effectively strangers to one another – have to collaborate to make major decisions on behalf of the patient; a tall order in the circumstances. The doctor is legally entitled to make any decision she or he sees as in the patient's best interest, such as ceasing treatment she or he deems futile and likely to cause suffering. Families, or some members of the family, may not agree to this. In other words, though formally the western system privileges the autonomous individual, in practice end-of-life decisions may be made messily between HCPs and family. Both sides find this very stressful, especially when family members refuse to accept HCPs' clinical judgement or HCPs' account of what the patient would want.

In any cultural system therefore, efforts by the patient, family members, and HCPs to control end-of-life decision making may or, especially when death approaches without adequate warning within an institution such as a hospital, may not run smoothly.

CONCLUSION

Because of the attachments humans make with one another, death and dying profoundly affect families. This is the case not only in family-centred societies, but also in post-industrial societies that privilege diversity of lifestyle choice over any one family form, and in communist societies that privilege the collective over the family. In some societies, funeral and mourning rites function to support patriarchy rather than individual mourners.

This chapter has therefore developed the previous chapter's exploration of the relative power over death of individual and group, to focus on one key group: the family. I have asked who controls dying, funerals, memorialization, grief and inheritance. What power does the family have in relation to the individual, to religion, to the state, or to medical and nursing professionals? How is control over end-of-life information and decision making negotiated *within* families?

The chapter has also mentioned some historical instances where overt conflict over family death practices has reconfigured the power of individual, religion, state, or family.

FURTHER READING

- Déchaux, J-H. (2002) 'Paradoxes of affiliation in the contemporary family', *Current Sociology*, 50 (2): 229-42.

- Finch, J. and Mason, J. (2000) *Passing On: Kinship and inheritance in England*. London: Routledge.

- Kwon, H. (2008) 'The ghosts of war and the spirit of cosmopolitanism', *History of Religions*, 48 (1): 22-42.

- Park, C-W. (2010) 'Between God and ancestors: ancestral practice in Korean Protestantism', *International Journal for the Study of the Christian Church*, 10 (4): 257-73.

- Robson, P. and Walter, T. (2012-13) 'Hierarchies of loss: a critique of disenfranchised grief', *Omega*, 66 (2): 97-119.

- Tsuji, Y. (2002) 'Death policies in Japan: the state, the family, and the individual', in R. Goodman (ed.), *Family and Social Policy in Japan: Anthropological perspectives*. Cambridge: Cambridge University Press, pp. 177-99.

- Walter, T. and Bailey, T. (in press) 'How funerals accomplish family: findings from a Mass-Observation study', *Omega*.

- Woodthorpe, K. and Rumble, H. (2016) 'Funerals and families: locating death as a relational issue', *British Journal of Sociology*, 67 (2): 242-59.

Questions to discuss

- In your society, what kind(s) of family are officially or legally promoted?

- How, if at all, is this reflected in end-of-life care, at the funeral, in mourning, and in inheritance? Is this accepted? If resisted, how? By whom?

- In your society, can you identify any conflicts over death practices between family and individual, religion, state, or health care practitioners? How, if at all, are they resolved?

Notes

1. Cann (2014: 4–10) compares bereavement leave policies in different countries.

2. The Soviet state was more concerned to promote funerals that were atheist rather than anti-family, rather unsuccessfully according to Lane (1981: 82–6).

10

RELIGION

This chapter considers how religion can affect death, dying, and bereavement.

Across the world and throughout history, religion has been concerned with death. Indeed anthropologist Bronislaw Malinowski (1925) thought that religion is driven by the anxiety that death provokes in humans. From his study of the Trobriand Islanders, he concluded that religion and magic enable tribal peoples to manage the risks and dangers posed by the natural world, for example when fishing out in the ocean. Others, however, note that religion may cultivate anxiety as well as reassurance in the face of death, for example when religions threaten post-mortem punishment for unrighteousness in this life.

NOT ALL RELIGIONS ARE THE SAME

The most obvious way that religion deals with mortality, at least in the eyes of westerners, is its offer of some kind of life after death. Four very different offers may be sketched, along with their implications for relationships between the living and the dead (Walter, 2017b).

Ancestors

At least since humans began to settle down and become agriculturalists ten or more millennia ago, ancestor veneration has been widespread (Steadman, Palmer and Tilley, 1996; Parker Pearson, 1999: Ch.7; Whitley, 2002). Religious rites, possibly assisted by a shaman, enable the family to transform the dead into ancestors and then to care for them and ensure they cause no trouble. Identifiable ancestors often last only 50 years or so – as long as there are survivors to remember them – after which time individual identity dissolves into general ancestorhood. As Chapter 9 noted, not everyone could become an ancestor, this status often being reserved for males and/or elders.

Immortality

The idea of immortality – not for a couple of generations but for ever – was found in ancient Egypt where this highly desirable status was reserved for royalty and favoured courtiers, later extended to any with the means to pay for the relevant rites. The genius of salvation religions such as Christianity and Islam is that they took the hope of everlasting life and offered it to everyone, whatever their gender, age, wealth, or social status. This appealed to ordinary folk and to the socially outcast; all that was necessary for immortality was faith and/or having lived a good life. As in ancestor veneration, several – but not all – religions provide rites and prayers by which the living can ensure the wellbeing of their family dead.

Reincarnation

The religions of the Indian subcontinent offer a different prospect. In Hindu traditions, accumulating good karma by performing the duties of your caste enables re-birth in the next life into a higher caste, until eventually moksha or union with Brahman, the universal God or soul, is attained. In Buddhism, the end point is nirvana, the realization of non-self or emptiness – very different from Christian or Islamic heaven.

Memory

A few religions, notably Protestant Christianity that emerged in the wake of the sixteenth-century Reformation in northern Europe, taught that the prayers of the living do nothing for the dead. The mourner might gain comfort from knowing the deceased is in heaven, but the only way the living can relate to the dead is by remembering them (Koslofsky, 2002). This is also how atheists and secularists relate to their dead.

Memory and care, body and soul

Some religions and practices enable care for the dead, others enable only memory. Rites that care for the deceased soul often focus on the physical remains or on the grave, as was clearly demonstrated in Robert Hertz's (1960 [1907]) classic essay on the anthropology of mortuary rites in which the transitions of body, soul, and mourners each echo one other. Examples are found throughout the world, from Torajaland in Indonesia where the dead body is kept in the house for months or years (Tsintjilonis, 2007), to Latin American and Mediterranean cults of both the family dead and of saints and martyrs (Chesnut, 2017).

Protestant bodies, Catholic bodies

When, however, the belief system denies that anything can be done for the deceased's soul, then memory practices tend to ignore the body. Cann (2014: 31) writes about cultural variations in death practices across the USA; she observes that 'the empty cross of Protestantism, which focuses on a theology of salvation rather than the Passion, contrasts with Catholicism's stress on the body.' Think of all those tortured Christs hanging on Catholic crucifixes, whether in sculpture or painting, contrasting with the emptiness not only of the Protestant cross, but also of many Protestant church interiors designed simply to enable the congregation to gather to hear the Word of God. In culturally Protestant Britain, there is rarely a public viewing of the body in the funeral parlour, while in the USA criticisms of this practice have often come from Protestant clergy. In the historically Calvinist Swiss city of Zurich, most inhabitants are now cremated; commonly, there is no ceremony at the crematorium; a few close relatives witness the burial of the urn containing the ashes; and then the main ceremony is a memorial service, entirely detached from the body.

Protestant and Catholic corpses are treated differently. In Catholic churches, the body may be received into the church the evening before the funeral for the family and other mourners to pray around it; and the next day, during the funeral service, the priest sprinkles holy water and incense on the coffin as he walks around it praying for the deceased's soul. Prayers for the soul and respect for the body are intertwined. In Protestant funerals, by contrast, clergy rarely give the body any ritual attention or pray for the deceased's soul, though they may commend it to God. At the same time, of course, individuals have their own feelings and preferences – not all Catholics visit family graves, and some Protestants pray for the dead. Lived religion and church teaching are not always the same.

Europe historically is Christian, but within Europe a major influence on the cremation rate is whether a country has a majority of Protestant, Catholic, or Orthodox Christians. When I ask Catholics why they prefer to be buried, they often answer 'Because of the resurrection'. I have asked them a question about the fate of the earthly body, and their answer concerns the soul's eventual destiny as a heavenly body – for them, body and soul, earthly body and heavenly body, are intimately connected. Protestant theologies, by contrast, typically see the specifics of burial as neutral. When in 1944 the (Protestant) Church of England's Archbishop of Canterbury died, he was cremated; he had made clear that how the body is disposed of has no significance for the soul's post-mortem destiny. Thenceforth, theological objections to cremation evaporated in the Church of England (Jupp, 2006). Church members became free to choose cremation or burial on the basis of personal preference, convenience, cost, and so on.

Some twentieth-century Protestant theologians such as Karl Barth rejected the Greek idea of soul; a soul without a body is not a person. They therefore rejected the idea of a soul awaiting resurrection in a body. Instead, when we die the whole person (body and soul) dies, later to be resurrected in its entirety; in this view, cremation's destruction of the body mirrors death's destruction of the person. That said, few Protestants in the global North still believe in physical resurrection; their most popular afterlife belief is that the body dies and what remains is the eternal soul (Walter, 1996) – arguably symbolized in cremation's destruction of the body (D. Davies, 1990).

Table 10.1 overleaf shows the cremation statistics in several European countries for 1986 and 2016. In 1986, the cremation rate was very much higher in Protestant than in Catholic countries. By 2016, the difference is less marked but still discernible. The Catholic church had long prohibited cremation for its members; in 1965 following the Second Vatican Council reforms, the Pope reluctantly accepted cremation without in any way encouraging it. So 20 years later in countries such as Italy or Ireland it was still only exceptional Catholic families who were bold enough to cremate; in any case, some Catholic countries such as Ireland had few facilities for cremation. By 2016, more crematoria had been built in Catholic countries; over time the practice had become more acceptable, child abuse scandals had eroded church authority, and more people had no religious affiliation at all. All these factors pushed up the cremation rate, blurring the difference between historically Catholic and historically Protestant countries.

Comfort?

As well as having very different attitudes to physical remains, religions vary in what they offer the dying and the grieving. Clearly, many gain comfort from knowing that their loved one is now a revered ancestor, or has gone to heaven. Those religions that provide rites and prayers that mourners can perform to help the dead on their way provide not only a task that brings mourners together, but also for some a sense of control – if at the appointed times I perform the correct rites or pray the right prayers, then my mum's soul can rest in peace. Such rites are essentially magical: perform the rite correctly, and things will be okay.

But not all religious teachings about death are comforting. Having introduced the hope of immortality for all, salvation religions make it far from certain that everyone will attain it. How can I know whether or not I am saved and bound for heaven? Fear of hell can provoke anxiety in religions that teach such possibilities. And in Hinduism, there is the possibility of going backwards in the chain of reincarnation. Max Weber (1930) famously argued that anxiety about post-mortem destiny was particularly acute among some seventeenth-century Calvinists who then dealt with their anxiety by living morally impeccable lives – which turned out to include a uniquely Protestant economic ethic which, Weber argued, contributed to the early rise

Table 10.1   Cremation rates in Europe

1986

Protestant	Catholic	Mixed	Orthodox	% Cremated
England & Wales				71
Sweden				59
		Netherlands		42
	Belgium			14
	Spain			11
	France			3.7
	Ireland			1.5
	Italy			0.6

2016

Protestant	Catholic	Mixed	Orthodox	% Cremated
		Switzerland		85
Denmark				83
Sweden				81
UK				77
		Netherlands		63
	Belgium			59
		Germany		57
	Portugal			54
	Spain			50
	Austria			47
Norway				41
	France			39
	Poland			24
	Italy			23
			Serbia	19
	Ireland			18
			Romania	0.4

Source: Cremation Society of Great Britain

www.cremation.org.uk/statistics

of capitalism. Weber's thesis has been criticized; I cite it simply to illustrate the possibility that religious teachings about death can influence not only how humans die and grieve, but also how they live.

Unlike Buddhism which teaches that suffering is at the core of the human condition, Christianity is challenged by suffering. Christianity affirms there is only one God, and he is love. So how can this loving God allow suffering (Berger, 1969)? A tragically young death, or a death that entails much suffering, may challenge a Christian's faith – even to the point of creating a second loss. Not only has the mourner lost her loved one, she has also lost her faith.

So, dealing with death is central to most if not all religions. But how they deal with it varies.

SECULARIZATION

You may say 'I'm not religious' or 'religion is a thing of the past'. Indeed. Secularization as well as religion shapes contemporary death, dying, and grieving (Walter, 2015b).

A religious world

The global pattern of religion and secularity may be summarized quite simply (Berger, 2012). Though it was once thought that modernity, especially education and urbanization, inevitably erodes religion, the world as a whole remains surprisingly religious. Atheism as national policy has proved less than effective; religion is reviving in China; and there are now few if any communist countries that successfully ban all religious practice. Whether or not Japan is secular is a matter of some debate (Reader, 2012), which leaves the world with just two increasingly secular arenas, one or both of which readers of this book are quite likely to inhabit: Western and Central Europe, and an international secular intelligentsia. Since these two secular bubbles have a lower birth rate than the world's religious majority, this creates the paradox of a world that western Europeans and the highly educated experience as increasingly secular, while statistically the world's religious population is growing.

This religious majority is increasingly urban and modern, or modernizing – so modernity does not necessarily mean secularization. In modernizing while retaining and developing high levels of religiosity, much of the world follows the USA rather than Western Europe. Indeed, certain forms of religion in some parts of the world can be a modernizing force, often challenging traditional ancestral death practices – examples being Pentecostalism in South America (Martin, 1990) and Zimbabwe (Maxwell, 1998), Presbyterianism in South Korea (Park, 2010), and the Baptist church in parts of India (Vitebsky, 2008).

Medicine

That said, there are many ways that secularization has affected death and dying across the globe as well as in secular Europe. Institutions, such as health care, may operate on secular lines even in a highly religious society. Chapter 2 examined how, starting in early eighteenth-century France, death came to be seen through rational eyes – no longer capricious, to be managed through prayer, it became statistically predictable and hence manageable through public health measures. And every individual death was seen to have a medically certifiable cause. In other words, modern medicine does not see death as an act of God.

Of course, pre-industrial populations, living in the countryside close to animals, knew the physical realities of animal death, but this was allied to a religious understanding of human death. Priests were more available than doctors, and medicine in any case had little power to prevent or ease death. By contrast, modern urban populations, divorced from animal death, gain their understanding of death in large part from the extensive medical procedures that take over the deathbed which is more often than not located in a hospital, a setting defined by medical and nursing procedures. Calling a priest and/or performing religious rites is an optional extra. Of course, this optional extra may be taken up far more often in religious Manilla than in secular Stockholm, but medicine's secular, scientific practices are global. Exceptions, such as the Mukti Bhavan guesthouse in Varanasi, India, where dying people go to gain moksha, or salvation, are notable for being exceptions to the modern urban norm (Basu, 2014).

In many but not all modern societies, the weeks and months after death may or may not involve religious rites assisting the soul on its post-mortem journey, but this period is also increasingly seen in terms of the mourner's psychological wellbeing. Whether or not there is belief in life after death for the deceased, the focus is increasingly on how mourners are to live after the death. As Philippe Ariès (1981) argued in his overview of the history of death in Western Europe, a 'romantic' concern with 'thy death' (how am I to live after you die?) has since the nineteenth century overlain the older religious concern with 'my death' (what will happen to me when I die?). By the late twentieth century, Christian evangelist Billy Graham's book *Facing Death and the Life After* (1987) said almost as much about the psychology of grief as about eternal life – this by a conservative religious teacher in the world's most religious advanced technological society.

Varieties of secularization

The preceding paragraphs largely concern the post-Christian West. To what extent they apply to parts of the world historically dominated by other religions, readers may better judge than myself. In Japan, there are many shrines both in the home and in public places where people can care for their family ancestors, though the percentage of homes with a household shrine has declined, as has the percentage of household shrines being regularly used for worship (Reader, 2012). Meanwhile, Japan's collective concept of personhood militates against the individualistic Anglo-American notion of the individual mourner's 'grief journey'.

Even within Christendom, there are variations, for example between neighbouring countries. Sweden is more secular and Norway more traditionally religious; but online Swedes are more creative in depicting new visions of an afterlife and, unlike Norwegians, envisage afterlives for their pets (Gustavsson, 2015). Many English hospices have religious origins but now only offer patients religious support as an optional extra. But in much more religious Ireland, Roman Catholicism remains threaded into the warp and woof of many hospices – though this may change as Irish society undergoes very rapid secularization, or at least loss of power by the institutional church (Inglis, 1998, 2014).

Inglehart, Basanez and Moreno (1998: 20–21) found that religion's influence is long-term – how modernization or even secularization proceeds depends on a country's specific religious history. So, for example, historically Protestant Germany and the Netherlands now have roughly equal numbers of Protestants and Catholics (because twentieth-century Catholics had a higher birth rate), but in terms of values even the Catholics in these two countries are more German, or more Dutch, than Catholic; their values differ from those of co-religionists in historically Catholic countries like Italy or Spain. Indeed, the cultural map of the world[1] that Inglehart and colleagues produced from analysing successive waves of the World Values Survey is in large measure a religious map, as is seen from the various clusters they identify: African Islamic, South Asia, Confucian, Latin America, English speaking, Protestant Europe, Catholic Europe, Orthodox, Baltic. So not only is modernity multiple (Eisenstadt, 2000), so too is secularization (Berger, 2014).

Arguably, outside of the very few communist countries which still persecute religion, secularization has proceeded most readily in those countries which have historically been shaped by Lutheran versions of Christianity (which fall within Inglehart's 'Protestant Europe'). The sixteenth-century reformer Martin Luther espoused a 'two kingdoms' theology which distinguished a religious realm characterized by the worship of God from a secular realm in which things such as family, work, or nature are of great value but not to be worshipped (which would be idolatry) (Witte, 2013). This keeping God out of secular matters has enabled Scandinavian countries to develop secular institutions with greater ease than Calvinist, Catholic, and Orthodox regions of Europe. In Lutheran countries there is little or no tension between a doctor's Christian faith and his or her practice of secular medicine, or between a therapist's personal belief in an afterlife and psychological care for grieving clients. A Lutheran can be both religious and secular, without any contradiction.

HOW TO THINK ABOUT RELIGION

This section looks at various aspects of religion and secularization that need to be considered if we are to get to grips with how religion and non-religion shape death, dying, and bereavement.

Three levels

Religion (and secularization) exist at one or more of three levels: society as a whole, specific social institutions, and the individual. Examples at the *societal*, that is national, level include those communist countries that are officially atheist, or Islamic theocracies such as Iran, or even England with its established Church of England whose head is the monarch (originating half a millennium ago in King Henry VIII's determination to divorce his first wife, Catherine of Aragon). Indeed, the birth of many European nations in the sixteenth to nineteenth centuries entailed a religious deal privileging a national church over other Christian denominations, sometimes reflected in the overseas colonies many of these countries founded (Beyer, 2013; Gauthier, 2019). Increasingly, members of persecuted or disadvantaged religious minorities chose to leave Europe and head for America; in due course, the First Amendment of the American constitution rejected the establishment of any one religion. Paradoxically, the USA has very high levels of religious attendance and practice. Rational choice theory (Young, 1997) provides the explanation that, without state sponsorship, religious organizations have to compete with one another, which strengthens them. In such countries, how religion is structured derives as much from national history as from culture.

At the level of *institutions*, we saw in Chapter 5 that modernization has usually entailed a process of differentiation in which social activities such as education, health care, family, law, the state, religion, split into separate institutions, thus separating religious from other institutions. Secularity of social institutions other than religious organizations is therefore widespread, even to some extent in theocracies – an Iranian hospital or university, for example, is not so different from hospitals and universities in other countries. As we have already seen, Lutheran theology actively encourages social institutions such as the law, schooling, or health care to be secular, which is entirely compatible with Lutheranism being the official religion of countries such as Sweden or Denmark. In religiously mixed Germany, however, Protestants and Catholics alike run schools, kindergartens, hospitals, and so on, and the churches have a place in national life, for example on the advisory boards of national broadcasters. The religiously mixed Netherlands has long encouraged different faiths and worldviews to create their own social structures (such as schools and radio stations) which are then funded by the state.

At the *individual* level, religious belief and practice need not correlate with whether or not social institutions or society as a whole are religious. Many Danes (Zuckerman, 2008) and English (Woodhead and Brown, 2016) live secular lives, despite their country having an established church. There are reports of shamanism and fortune-telling thriving in North Korea, the most hostile country to religion in the world (Kang, 2014). And everywhere folk religion can thrive alongside official religion (Bowman and Valk, 2012).

Different mixes

How these three levels relate to each other is specific to each country or cluster of countries. As noted, the American constitution upholds freedom of religion and does not privilege any one religion over another in state-funded institutions such as schools; yet Presidential inaugural speeches traditionally refer to God, and the number of individual Americans who go to church regularly and who believe in God, heaven, and hell is very high compared to other advanced industrial societies; and religion dominates American politics of abortion and euthanasia. England is different again. Church of England senior bishops sit by right in the House of Lords and a daily act of collective worship is required in schools; yet the numbers who regularly go to church are very low and dropping fast (Day, 2017).

In a country such as the USA where social institutions are secular but personal religious faith and practice are buoyant, many people are both religious and secular at the same time. A person may accept without a thought that their work life, or the schools their children attend, or the hospital their mother died in, are organized along entirely secular lines, while they themselves have a deep religious faith or personal spirituality. Conversely, a Dane who does not personally believe in God may not question that his funeral will be conducted by the parish priest prior to burial in the local churchyard.

Because the societal, institutional, and personal mix of religion and non-religion is so specific to each country, it is very easy for readers to misunderstand both religion and non-religion in other countries. For example, the American sociologist Phil Zuckerman has written an intriguing book *Society Without God* (2008) about Denmark and Sweden which he considers the world's most secular countries – more so than atheist Albania in its communist era because Danes and Swedes have chosen, rather than were forced, to live secular lives. He uses social statistics and interviews to show that Danes and Swedes live lives and die deaths as good as any, indeed better than most, contradicting the claims of some conservative American Christians that societies without God will fall apart, become immoral, and be plagued by a fear of dying.

Danish scholar of religion, Anne Kjaersgaard (2017) is concerned that Zuckerman – hailing from the American Mid-West – has defined religion in terms of personal faith and regular churchgoing, which of course would depict

Danes and Swedes as very secular. But societally and politically, Scandinavian countries give religion an official status absent in the USA, while a high proportion of Danes and Swedes who rarely go to church nevertheless identify as members of the Lutheran Church, especially when it comes to funerals and to a slightly lesser extent baptisms (Woodhead and Brown, 2016). In sociologist of religion Grace Davie's terms 'believing' and 'belonging' (2001), Scandinavians belong to the church and at the beginning and end of life this means something to them, even if they don't believe much in God. By contrast, around 50 per cent of the English continue to believe in God, but rapidly decreasing numbers claim membership of any church or – from the 2010's – hire clergy to officiate at funerals.

Pluralism

In the 1960s, American sociologist Peter Berger (1969) argued that literacy, television, travel, migration, and so on had opened up the world so that it becomes easier to know (or know of) people with a worldview different from your own. These plural worldviews relativized the absolutist claims of religion and thus became a secularizing force. But by the late 1980s – with the 1979 Iranian revolution, the rise of fundamentalisms across the globe, and the explosion of talk about personal spirituality – Berger acknowledged that the evidence did not fit his thesis. Rather than producing secularization, modernity produced pluralism, 'a historically unprecedented situation in which more and more people live amid competing beliefs, values and lifestyles' (Berger, 2012: 313). As well as enabling people to be both religious and secular in different areas of their lives, this can revitalize religion – in new forms. Institutionalized religion declines (Bruce, 2002) in the face of 'what works for me consumer religion' (Gauthier and Martikainen, 2016), whether that be the personal spirituality that appeals to many post-materialists in the global North, or the miracle-working new religions thriving in the global South. Just as people negotiate the form of family life that suits them, so they decide on their own mix of religion and spirituality – encouraged by a vibrant and increasingly global marketplace in religious/ spiritual ideas and practices. Old people in Brazil who were born and remained Catholic find their children choosing to become Pentecostals (Martin, 1990); old people in Kansas who were born and remained Methodist find their children describing themselves as 'spiritual but not religious' (Heelas and Woodhead, 2004). Perhaps religion is not in decline so much as, once more, evolving (Gauthier, 2019).

Let me illustrate. In 1982, a friend who was a nominal Anglican (Church of England) and was in the local National Health Service (NHS) hospital with terminal cancer accepted and was comforted by an unsolicited offer from the ward sister, a devout Christian, to pray the Lord's Prayer with her. Today in 2019, such an offer is unlikely to be made, even by a Christian nurse in a Christian hospice; in an NHS hospital, the nurse might risk dismissal for abusing her position of power over patients. She might refer the patient to the hospital's chaplain. Yet at the same time, secular nurses in Britain are now taught that 'spirituality' is part of nursing care, spirituality being defined not as old-time religion but as whatever meaning a person gives to life and death. Contrasting English end-of-life care today with 1982, we see both secularization – the expulsion of traditional religion from nursing practice – and its replacement by individual spirituality.

Official and lived religion

Religion is multi-faceted, comprising ritual, prayer, morality, belief, and/or membership of a congregation. Each religion typically prioritizes some facets over others. Protestant Christianity and Islam prioritize orthodox (that is, correct) belief. Eastern religions are less concerned with orthodoxy than with orthopraxis, right action, especially performing the correct rituals. At the same time, everyday religious practice – sometimes called lived (McGuire, 2008) or vernacular (Bowman and Valk, 2012) religion – may differ from the beliefs or practices taught by religious leaders.

During the era of Europe's colonization of the world from the sixteenth to the mid-twentieth century, Christian Europe's – and especially Protestant Europe's – notion that what defines religion is its belief system as spelt out in sacred texts was imposed on the rest of the world. Thus colonists and missionaries, seeing the very diverse practices and beliefs of indigenous peoples, conceptually re-packaged them as 'world religions' – a concept which now is being deconstructed by post-colonial religious studies (Masuzawa, 2005; Gauthier, 2019).

Arguably, the loss of power by European and North American churches, the emergence of a spiritual marketplace, and the Internet replacing (or augmenting) folk tradition as the disseminator of spiritual ideas, have together enabled a return to the kind of vernacular, bottom-up religious practices that were normal before western colonialism identified so-called 'world religions'. As Linda Woodhead puts it (2012):

> Real religion – which is to say everyday, lived religion – is thriving and evolving, while hierarchical, institutionalised, dogmatic forms of religion are marginalised. Religion has returned to the core business of sustaining everyday life, supporting relations with the living and the dead, and managing misfortune. That's why angels, cathedrals, pilgrimages and retreats are all doing well. And why mind, body, spirit has taken over from theology in the bookshops.

This is what David Nash (2013) terms a 'marketplace of comfort'. If it comforts you to imagine that your deceased grandfather is a guardian angel looking after you, fine (Walter, 2016). If you like the idea of reincarnation, without embracing any other Hindu teachings or practices, fine (Walter and Waterhouse, 1999). If alternative treatments give you hope of beating your cancer, fine. The more people are detached from formal church teaching, the more they 'will hold any number of totally contradictory beliefs and use them in many different circum- stances for many different purposes', especially if it comforts them in the face of death and loss (Stringer, 2008: 32). Linda Woodhead (2012) again: 'In democratic, consumerist societies we believe that we are responsible for own choices … We don't want to be preached at any more, we want to test things out for ourselves.' This underlies western palliative care's practice of spiritual care.

Though palliative care assumes individual spirituality to characterize those living in a post-Christian West, it may treat those with roots in other world religions very differently. Thus health care organizations in increasingly multi-cultural Britain produce 'factsheets' to help health care practitioners understand the religious needs, not least at end of life, of various ethnic groups. These factsheets are usually labelled according to the colonial notion of 'world religions'; thus there are factsheets on end-of-life care for Muslims, bereavement care for Sikhs, and so on, and so forth. Combined with very close listening to patients and their families, such factsheets have their place, but they also pose the danger of lumping together into two pages of 'facts' the very varied practices and beliefs engaged in by quite diverse people. I have argued elsewhere that it can be more helpful to come armed not with a set of so-called 'facts' about a so-called group but with a set of questions that will help the practitioner understand the needs of the particular patient or family they are working with (Walter, 2010).

A related concept to lived religion is *implicit religion* – practices that on the face of it look secular but play a similar function to religion (Bailey, 1997). At the same time, there may be practices that look religious, but are secular in their ultimate commitments – thus a pastoral visit by a priest to a grieving family is on the face of it religious, but if the visit is primarily informed by secular grief psychology aiming to benefit the living rather than the dead, then it may hardly differ from a visit by a secular counsellor; it is implicitly secular.

It can be hard to categorize some practices as religious or secular, explicitly or implicitly (Day, Vincett and Cotter, 2013). Thus in the UK, some time after the funeral a family may create its own little ceremony for disposing of the ashes, a ceremony that is personal, democratic, creative and involves no formal religious institution or its functionaries. Institutionally and formally the cere- mony is secular. But in giving special significance to human remains, in treating them as sacred rather than as just so much rubbish, this could be defined at the individual and family level as a sacred act. How you categorize it probably depends on whether you the reader do or do not consider religion to be of value in human affairs and/or whether you prioritize institutional religion or lived experience.

Superstition

With colonialism identifying 'world religions' as 'proper' religion, non-text based practices got downgraded as 'folk religion', 'superstitious', or 'irrational'. Protestant Christianity, though believing in supernatural events such as Jesus being born of a virgin and resurrected after he had been crucified, is in other ways a rather rational religion. In Protestantism, the world normally operates according to rational principles, interspersed only on occasion – primarily during the life of Jesus – by the miraculous. This worldview readily accepts science and in the seventeenth century may even have laid the foundation for science (Hooykaas, 1972), but struggles with magical practices that suppose the supernatural and non-rational to pervade everyday life, and this still today influences how such practices are perceived in the area of death and dying. Rather than being accepted for what they are, they are judged in one way or another – negatively or positively.

First, such practices may be defined as 'archaic', 'pagan', 'uncivilized', 'non-Christian'. Second, they may be labelled as 'superstitious', a label that is still used by those living in countries once colonized by the West. Thus Singaporean Chinese label a wide range of death practices as 'superstitious', meaning ancestral practices they engage in yet find hard to justify in the terms of the 'rationality' of western science or the teachings of the world religions. Third, and this is very prevalent among advocates of the death awareness movement in the West, is a nostalgia for pre-industrial death practices which supposedly positioned the dying or grieving person within a community and provided meaning that is absent in modernity's mechanistic medicine (Walter, 1995). Fourth, this nostalgia may romanticize ancient practices, especially those that pre-date a Christianity many now consider patriarchal and hierarchical. Thus druidic, shamanistic, and animist death rites are assumed to be altogether healthier than Christian rites and even medical practices.

If dismissing 'superstition' and 'folk religion' stems from Christianity's hegemony as a colonial world religion, romantic enthusiasm for similar ideas and practices stems from the erosion of this hegemony. Neither approach is helpful for the student of society, religion, and death who simply wants to understand such practices.

Religion and culture

Religion always interacts with culture, in death as in life. Wikan's (1988) classic article shows how Muslim death rites differ between Egypt and Bali. Likewise, a Presbyterian funeral in Scotland and in the USA is as much if not more Scottish or American as it is Presbyterian. I have already mentioned how the values of Catholics in the Netherlands and Germany differ from those of Catholics in Italy and Spain. And Buddhism manifests itself very differently in different countries.

Another example concerns hospice. Several British hospices, not least London's iconic St Christopher's, were founded by evangelical Christians, and many British evangelicals today are enthusiastic supporters of hospice and its offer of effective comfort care when aggressive medical treatment is deemed futile. In the USA, by contrast, evangelicals are far more likely to emphasize that God created curative medicine, so giving up curative medicine in favour of palliative care is akin to euthanasia (Long, 2004: 921). This difference could be explained by cultural rather than religious differences. Many Americans believe theirs to be a 'can do' society that can 'fix' any problem, not least illness; by extension, 'can do' Americans readily believe in a 'can do' God. Many Britons, by contrast, are far more fatalistic about life, and hence death. This cultural difference is then expressed in different theologies on each side of the Atlantic. In the USA, there is also a political dimension. Many American evangelicals judge that hospice care, because it gives up any hope of cure, kills patients, and is therefore as sinful as abortion. Thus hospice gets caught up in America's uniquely polarized politics of abortion. On both sides of the Atlantic, most evangelicals oppose euthanasia, but whereas in the USA they may see hospice care as equivalent to euthanasia, in Britain they see it as a positive alternative to euthanasia.

RELIGION AND DEATH PRACTICES

This chapter's final section sketches various ways that religion can interact with a society's death practices. First, I look at examples of religions *promoting*, *opposing*, *accommodating*, *modifying*, and unintentionally *influencing* particular death practices; then I look at how death practices can sometimes *compensate* for what a society's dominant religion fails to offer at or after death.

Promote

Sometimes religions clearly promote or oppose certain death practices, such as burial or cremation. Historically, Judaism buried its dead. Christianity continued this practice; burning came to be associated with Christian martyrdom and in the Middle Ages with the fires of hell; Christians made a point of burning heretics and witches. Burial 'fits' the doctrine of physical resurrection, with medieval Christian art depicting the dead arising out of their graves on the day of resurrection. Islam, also teaching bodily resurrection, likewise promotes burial. By contrast, Hinduism and Sikhism, teaching reincarnation, cremate, while Buddhism, teaching the karmic conservation of moral energy, generally cremates. Burial and cremation have sometimes co-existed, but the overall pattern is that traditionally Christian, Jewish, and Islamic communities buried their dead, while Hindu, Sikh, and Buddhist communities cremated them. Religious minorities within any one community sometimes had to conform to the community norm, often because alternative facilities did not exist; sometimes they created their own facilities. This pattern got complicated in twentieth-century multi-ethnic, multi-cultural, multi-religious societies, many of which offer a choice of burial or cremation. In Denmark, the Lutheran church actually came to promote cremation, especially once it had built some crematoria (Kjaersgaard, 2017). Eastern Orthodox churches, however, still vigorously oppose cremation, so countries such as Greece and Romania have very few crematoria (Davies and Mates, 2005; Rotar, 2015).

Long (2004) interviewed Americans and Japanese about how to die well, and found a number of Japanese 'who linked the idea of a relative's slow, gradual death to the process of becoming an ancestor, and there exists a common notion that demented elderly, in their not fully being in this world, are perhaps already god-like' (p. 923). Linked to the positive idea of *amae*, the pleasure of being looked after like a baby, there is a Japanese acceptance of dementia that many Americans, influenced by the Christian idea of the dying person as an active individual pilgrim (Maruyama, 1997; Baugher, 2008), struggle with.

Oppose

There are many examples of religious opposition to a society's dominant death practices. This book has alluded more than once to monotheism's opposition to ancestor veneration. Today, East Asian converts to Christianity or Islam are under pressure from their new religion to reject ancestor veneration, pressure which their unconverted family experiences as rejection of the family (Park, 2010). This is an everyday conflict, but comes into sharp focus after someone has died. In Madagascar, Pentecostals teach that ancestors have no place in the Bible, so should have no place today in Madagascan families (Phillips, 2006).

Autopsies and using corpses and body parts for medical education or surgery have also generated religious opposition. From the sixteenth to the nineteenth centuries in Europe, many Christians believed that cutting up the dead body destroyed its potential for resurrection, so anatomy schools had to resort to devious means to source bodies for their students (Richardson, 1989). Today, Orthodox Jews and Muslims continue to have reservations about dismembering corpses, not least because their tradition of burying within 24 hours rules out keeping body parts for medical education or research. There are also numerous instances of religion discouraging tears in mourners, perceived as signifying lack of trust in God – though such prohibitions depend on culture as much as on religion (Wikan, 1988).

In many countries, opposition to euthanasia and assisted dying is driven by a religious view that life is given by God so humans have no right to take it away. This can underlie both personal attitudes and organized opposition (Cohen et al., 2006). The more fundamentalist the believer, the more dogmatic the opposition, as Baeke, Wils and Broeckaert (2011) found in a study of Jewish women. In the USA, conservative American Christians' opposition to abortion and euthanasia symbolizes their Christian identity and their opposition to 'secular humanism'.

Another example of religious identity politics concerns Christian converts in Nepal. Nepal is 81 per cent Hindu and 9 per cent Buddhist, so cremation is the norm. Most of the country's 1.5 per cent Christians are Protestant, but though many Protestants cremate in the West, this is not so in Nepal where Christians practise burial as a way to assert their difference (Sharma, 2011).

> Cremation is necessary for Hindus – it's the way the spirit is released to be rein-carnated, and having a son to light the funeral pyre insures conveyance to the next life cycle. In split families, it becomes a sore case of contention: a Christian son may refuse to light his Hindu father's funeral pyre, the Christian son insists on burying his Christian mother while the Hindu son's family really wants to cremate his mother instead, and a community may not want a Christian graveyard near them for fear of lingering ghosts. (Tori, 2014)

If American fundamentalists reject abortion to demonstrate their Christian stand for life over against secular humanism, some Nepali Christians reject cremation to demonstrate that they are Christian, even in a Hindu country. In response, some radical Hindu elements have attempted to deny Christians the right to burial (Sharma, 2011).

As well as conflict between religions, there can also be conflict within a religion – which can express itself within the family if different members of the family adhere to different versions of the faith. Many liberal Christians in the USA do not agree with their fundamentalist co-religionists on abortion and euthanasia. African Pentecostals and Methodists may disagree about traditional ancestral rites.

Accommodate

Sooner or later, religious opposition to a society's death practices may be relaxed or dropped, and accommodations reached (Bowker, 1991; Firth, 1997; Garces-Foley, 2006a). Some Nepali families find compromises to solve the burial/cremation conflict, and some Nepali Christian leaders are developing a theology in which cremation is compatible with Christianity (Sharma, 2011). I have already mentioned how the Church of England accommodated itself to crema-tion in the 1940s, while Catholicism took another two decades and with much greater reluctance. But, unlike Eastern Orthodoxy, the Catholic hierarchy's out-right opposition has gone.

In sub-Saharan Africa, where Pentecostals may vigorously oppose ancestor worship, many other Christians manage to combine respect for family ancestors with being, for example, Methodist or Catholic. In Madagascar, where 41 per cent of the population are Christian and 52 per cent practise indigenous rites in which ancestors' bones are occasionally brought out and turned, one young Catholic priest sees the local ancestors as akin to Catholic saints and their bones akin to the relics kept in many churches (Phillips, 2006). On the American continent, Hispanic death rites – most famously the Mexican Day of the Dead – synthesize indigenous and Catholic practices and beliefs; Catholic prayers for the dead are readily combined with the indigenous belief that deceased members remain part of the living family (Davis, 2006).

Modify

Religion may modulate, or modify, an existing practice. Thus Baugher (2008) argues that the practice of 'presence' or 'being with' that is central to mainstream Christian-influenced secular hospice takes a very different form in San Francisco's Zen Hospice Project. In mainstream American hospices, 'being with' entails the volunteer facilitating the dying person's life review through talk about their feelings; in the Buddhist hospice, 'being with' entails mindfully attending to whatever is going on in the present moment (which may not entail talk or exploring feelings). The mainstream approach can cause volunteers to feel useless if the person has dementia or is at the very end of life and cannot or will not talk; at this point, volunteers may stop visiting. Baugher concludes (p. 279): 'The moral imperative in mainstream hospice organizations of listening deeply to dying persons talk about their experiences may inadvertently lead good-intentioned volunteers to withdrawal from dying persons.' I noted above how the Christian concept of the dying person as an active pilgrim renders the comatose or demented patient deeply problematic, as indeed does the western notion of individual autonomy.

If religion can modify mainstream practice, it can also be the other way around. Legal or funding constraints, for example, may homogenize practice despite different religious perspectives.

Influence

Sometimes, a religion unintentionally influences certain death practices. Chapter 8 discussed Emile Durkheim's famous thesis (2002 [1897]) that European Protestants are more likely to commit suicide than are Catholics – not because Protestantism teaches or promotes suicide, far from it, but because it fails to provide the social integration that Catholicism provides.

Kjaersgaard (2017) provides a more recent example of a statistical correlation, this time of post-mortem organ donation rates which vary between Catholic and Protestant countries in Europe. There are no identifiable differences in formal church teaching that could explain this, so if these two branches of Christianity do indeed influence donation rates then, like suicide, the causation is indirect and unintentional. Like Durkheim's suicide research, Kjaersgaard's is statistical; qualitative research would be needed to unearth how any influence operates; Chapter 13 suggests one among a number of possible influences.

Compensate

Finally, there is the possibility that a society's death practices may compensate for what its dominant religion lacks. After the First World War, the established Church of England's failure to cope with the scale of violent death and bereavement (Wilkinson, 1978) prompted a revival of spiritualism in which bereaved mothers, wives and sisters visited mediums to gain reassurance that their son, husband, or brother, whose body had been blown to bits and had no known grave, was nevertheless spiritually in a good place (Winter, 1995; Hazelgrove, 2000).

Another possible example of compensation concerns mourners gaining comfort through the natural world. For centuries in Europe, burial grounds in which greenery – trees, shrubs, planted flowers, grass – dominate are typically in historically Protestant countries. In the twentieth and twenty-first centuries, woodland and natural burial grounds are far more in evidence in historically Protestant than Catholic countries. By contrast, even rural cemeteries in Catholic countries such as Austria, Italy, and Spain rely on hard surfaces and often have a distinctly urban feel (Goody and Poppi, 1994). In East Asia, nature as consolation has its own, different, religious and cultural associations (Boret, 2014).

How to explain the green Protestant burial grounds, and the hard surface Catholic ones? My explanation, to be the subject of a future article, draws on Draper's (1967) analysis of eighteenth-century English graveyard poetry to argue that, with no rites or prayers through which to help the dead (Gittings, 1984), Protestants have lacked a religious vehicle for expressing grief and turned to nature for solace. Meanwhile, secularists in revolutionary France who had rejected Catholicism turned for comfort and hope to Arcadia, the garden cemetery.

Bereavement memoirs – a genre common today in the USA, Canada, and the UK – are rarely found in Catholic Poland and Orthodox Romania (Małecka, 2012). Might this be because Protestants, lacking religious rites through which to communicate loss, have turned instead to words – whether poetry or other consolation literature? Might bereavement counselling, which typically helps grief not through ritual but through words, also find more resonance in historically Protestant societies? Such hypotheses are yet to be tested.

This section has outlined six ways that religions and societal death practices respond to each other – promotion, opposition, accommodation, modification, influence and compensation. This list is not exhaustive. Another possibility, for example, is *manipulation* where, for example, a dying political leader may be kept on life support for some extra hours or days to allow a large number of mourners to travel and still fulfil Jewish or Islamic expectation to bury within 24 hours of death.

CONCLUSION

Chapter 2 showed how modern secular health care shapes dying is rather predictable, but this chapter has demonstrated wide variation in how religions shape the management of dying, disposal of the body, grief and hope. And long religious histories shape the nuances of secularization in any one country. Reflecting the author's own knowledge and interests, many of this chapter's examples have concerned European Christianity, not least the differences between historically Protestant and historically Catholic countries. But Christianity is also highlighted because it was the religion of those Europeans who colonized the world from the sixteenth to the twentieth centuries, who came to define what is 'modern', 'civilized', and 'rational', and who came to define all religious practices in the image of, or in contrast to, their own version of Christianity. That legacy is now being unpicked across the post-colonial world, in post-colonial religious studies, and in this chapter.

FURTHER READING

- Baeke, G., Wils, J.P. and Broeckaert, B. (2011) 'We are (not) the master of our body: elderly Jewish women's attitudes towards euthanasia and assisted suicide', *Ethnicity and Health*, 16: 259–78.

- Berger, P. (2012) 'Further thoughts on religion and modernity', *Society*, 49: 313–16.

- Garces-Foley, K. (2006) *Death and Religion in a Changing World*. Armonk, NY: M.E. Sharpe.

- Goody, J. and Poppi, C. (1994) 'Flowers and bones: approaches to the dead in Anglo and Italian cemeteries', *Comparative Studies in Society & History*, 36: 146–75.

- Moreman, C. (2018) *Beyond the Threshold: Afterlife beliefs and experiences in world religions* (2nd edn). Lanham, MD: Rowman and Littlefield.

- Parkes, C.M., Laungani, P. and Young, B. (2015) *Death and Bereavement Across Cultures* (2nd edn). London: Routledge.

- Stringer, M.D. (2008) 'Chatting with gran at her grave', in P. Cruchley-Jones (ed.), *God at Ground Level*. Oxford: Peter Lang, pp. 23–39.

- Walter, T. (2017) 'How the dead survive: ancestor, immortality, memory', in M.H. Jacobsen (ed.), *Postmortal Society*. Farnham: Ashgate, pp. 19-39.

- Wikan, U. (1988) 'Bereavement and loss in two Muslim communities: Egypt and Bali compared', *Social Science & Medicine*, 27: 451-60.

Questions to discuss

- How has religion – directly or indirectly – affected how your society deals with death, dying, and bereavement?

- In your culture, are you expected to care for the dead who in turn care for you? Or do the dead exist simply in the memories of the living?

- Can you identify differences between cultural expectations, religious teachings, and/or personal experience?

Note

1.   www.worldvaluessurvey.org (accessed 14/6/19).

PART IV

NATION

Part III looked at cultural differences in how death, dying and bereavement are imagined, organized, and managed; Part IV will now look at national differences. Each nation state has its own very specific history of modernization, which includes the modernization of its death system (Chapter 11). Involvement in war can catalyse new technologies and new policies in managing death and dying, and can influence how people cope with loss and how they remember the past and the dead; each war, and each nation's involvement in the same war, is different; and there may be differences within a nation, as in civil war (Chapter 12). Finally, Chapter 13 looks at laws, social institutions, ideologies and random events which shape death and loss within a nation. Part IV is therefore about national *histories* and how they have shaped death and loss today.

Each chapter uses the concept of *path dependency*: how a group, in this case a nation, starts doing or thinking about something sets up a pattern of enduring behaviour and thought. Even if globalization (Chapter 14) to some extent undermines the nation state, national ways of doing things continue for generations, as do national institutions and national memory. A sense of history is therefore important if we are to understand why a nation does things the way it does.

National differences in death and dying have attracted much less research than cultural differences (e.g. Parkes; Laungani and young, 2015). Why is this? One reason may be that anthropologists have traditionally studied a group sharing a culture, rather than a group sharing a nationality (Rosenblatt, Walsh and Jackson, 1976). Turning to sociological and psychological research, more has been conducted in the USA than elsewhere. Americans tend either to equate the USA with modernity, or to consider the USA to be exceptional and not to be compared with other countries. So what is specifically *American* about the USA is easily left unexplored by American scholars. Cultural differences within the USA, by contrast, attract considerable research. As a land of immigrants, the USA comprises and even celebrates many different hybrid identities: Mexican American, Vietnamese American, African American, Chinese American, Italian American,

Jewish American, and so on. Though all are expected to subscribe to a national mythology of freedom and opportunity, and all find themselves enabled and/or constrained by the same institutional and political structures, Americans are allowed, encouraged even, to retain cultural aspects of their family's country of origin. The USA is therefore tailor-made for research comparing one culture with another. Several studies, while taking the American way of life and American institutions for granted, have compared how different ethnic/cultural groups within the USA value palliative care, practise funeral rites, or perform grief (Kalish and Reynolds, 1981; Cann, 2016). And American thanatology textbooks are often very good on cultural differences, comparing for example Mexican American and Vietnamese American funerals, or Hispanic American and Anglo-American grief. Studies comparing American deathways with those of other countries, however, are rare (Harper, 2010).

Nations

First though, we need to consider the idea of 'nation'. How and when did the nation become a taken-for-granted frame for identity, for assessing who is one of 'us' and who is not, for including and excluding? How and when did the nation state become the taken-for-granted frame for government and for law?

It was not always thus. Many medieval European cities were shaped less by the country in which they were located than by a mix of Islamic, Jewish, and Christian cultures, a mix obscured by nineteenth- and twentieth-century nationalisms (Kwon, 2008). Derrida (2001) argues that the traditional ethic of hospitality to travellers found in many pre-modern cities and in desert oases contrasts with, and was weakened by, the political sovereignty of the modern nation state. People's consciousness and loyalties were once both local and cosmopolitan; national identity was not important (Gillis, 2000). As recently as the nineteenth century, one could travel around Europe without a passport; only in the following century did identification papers, passports, and border controls became the order of the day.

Nationalism

But from the French Revolution until the end of the Second World War, nationalism became increasingly powerful, so that people came to feel as much if not more French rather than Parisian, German rather than Prussian, Spanish rather than Castilian. The modern state typically emerged in the form of the nation state – not as city states (barring a few exceptions such as Singapore) or international states such as the European Union. Though nineteenth- and early twentieth-century colonialism was driven by the profit motive and by capitalist expansion, it was also driven by competition between European nations for political power, exporting European nationalisms across the globe. Moroccans still speak French; Nigerians still belong to the British Commonwealth; Moroccan and Nigerian laws and institutions reflect those of their once colonial masters.

Benedict Anderson sees nationalism as arising out of the religious doubt of the eighteenth-century Enlightenment. If religion once provided meaning in suffering and promised salvation and in the next life heaven, 'nothing makes fatality more arbitrary' than the disintegration of paradise (Anderson, 1991: 11). Into this void stepped the idea of nation, which provided a sense of fraternity and 'a secular transformation of fatality into continuity' – the nation continues when the individual dies. If the individual dies *for* the nation, not only is national continuity assured but also the individual gains a special and enduring place in national memory – individual mortality is subsumed in the nation's collective immortality. Hence my devoting an entire chapter to war.

Nations today

Fascism and two world wars revealed the terrible consequences of the 'collective self-worship' produced by nationalism (Gillis, 2000: 19). A partial correction was found in the internationalism of bodies such as the United Nations and the European Union, and later in people finding identity as members of 'racial and sexual minorities, women, youth, and dozens of new nations and ethnic groups aspiring to sovereign status' (p. 19). But the nation state persists, even as we see the emergence of what Meyer et al. (1997) call a 'world society'. They argue that since 1945, world culture has shaped and sustained nation states (new and old), expecting and even requiring them to have education systems, welfare policies, health systems, universities, citizenship, anti-discrimination laws, reliance on pro-fessional expertise, and so on. I would add that nation states are also expected to have a death system encompassing hospitals, death registration, coroners, post-mortems, funeral directors, cemeteries, crematoria, and so on (Kastenbaum, 2007). For Meyer et al. this means that nation states all look much the same, not least because they copy systems and institutions from each other (see also Robertson, 1995: 34). So even with globalization (Chapter 14), nation states remain the main players, for example as members of international organizations, as signatories to trade deals, as policers of crime, or as wagers of war.

I hope this book demonstrates that the nation state does indeed provide an important frame in which death, dying, and loss are managed, but with more variation between modern nations than Meyer et al. perhaps acknowledge. Of course, variations in geography shape how embedded people are within their own nation. Small states, and people living near borders, are two cases in point. The tiny European country of Luxembourg, for example, had no crematorium until 1995, so Luxembourgers who wished to cremate a family member travelled to Germany. But once a crematorium was built in Luxembourg, Germans – prevented by

German law from scattering ashes – started to travel across the border to Luxembourg to scatter ashes. But even this example of post-mortem internationalism demonstrates the importance of national law and institutions.[1]

To what extent new cosmopolitan identities compete with enduring and newly resurrected national identities is an open question, one in which death is profoundly implicated. Chapter 12 explores how commemorating the heroic deaths of soldiers has played a major role in symbolizing national identity, at least in some countries. From the 1970s, however, a transnational Holocaust memory and from the 1990s a human rights discourse have shifted focus from death of the national hero to death of the universal victim; if heroic deaths were used to promote nationalism, victim deaths are now used to promote cosmopolitanism – at least in the European context.

FURTHER READING

- Anderson, B. (1991) *Imagined Communities: Reflections on the origin and spread of nationalism.* London: Verso.

- Gillis, J.R. (ed.) (2000) *Commemorations: The politics of national identity.* Princeton, NJ: Princeton University Press.

Note

1. I am indebted to Thomas Kolnberger (University of Ghent) for this example.

11

MODERNIZING THE NATION

Nations have modernized in specific ways at specific times. Modernization may entail emancipation from feudalism driven by an emerging middle class (England, France, Sweden); appropriation and development of indigenous land by foreign settlers (Australia, Canada, Israel); colonization (India, Mongolia, Tibet); emancipation from colonization (USA, Finland, India, South Africa); controlling or balancing ethnic, tribal, and clan identities in favour of a national identity (Nigeria, Thailand, Singapore); erasing minor principalities to create a unified nation (Italy, Germany); or revolution (China). In each case, particular interest groups or leaders with the power to drive social and economic change create new institutions or take over old ones, setting up patterns of institutional power for decades to come. This much is clear from classic studies in comparative sociology. For example, Kerr et al.'s (1973) analysis of different patterns of industrialization identified five kinds of elites that, in different countries, got industrialization going: the middle class, dynastic leaders, colonial administrators, revolutionary intellectuals, and nationalist leaders.

So, though all modern nations have a modern system for managing death (Kastenbaum, 2007), their death systems are modernized at different times in different ways by different agents of change. This chapter demonstrates and tries to explain some of the considerable differences in the structure and operation of modern death systems. To hint at just one example: funerals in Serbia and Romania. After the Second World War, Yugoslavia's multi-republic communist regime embraced an atheist ideology that in the Socialist Republic of Serbia was anti-Christian and hostile to the Serbian Orthodox Church that had hitherto exercised considerable power. Rituals of pagan origin, however, were not seen as ideologically dangerous, which enabled Serb folk traditions to survive in funeral rituals (Pavicevic, 2015). In Romania, by contrast, Nicolae Ceaușescu's 1965–89 regime embraced a uniquely nationalist form of communism, in the service of which the Romanian Orthodox Church continued to play a (controlled) role (Coleman, 2016).

In the key period of modernization who takes power? To what end? What is the role of religion at this moment? And what are the consequences for the death system? Such are the questions this chapter invites readers to ask of their own country.

In some countries, just one key time of modernization stands out, such as Britain's industrial revolution, the 1789 French Revolution, or Japan's 1868 Meiji Restoration. (This is, of course, to simplify. England's industrial revolution was driven by demand from a growing middle class that over the previous two centuries had challenged aristocratic and monarchical power, a revolution in itself.) In other countries, especially those experiencing political revolution or colonization, there may be more than one key moment or period. In China, for example, we may identify the 1949 Communist Revolution, the 1958–61 Great Leap Forward, the 1966–76 Cultural Revolution, and socialist China's embracing of capitalism in the twenty-first century; each had consequences for end-of-life care, inheritance, ancestor veneration, and funerals.

The following examples of how elements in various countries' death systems were modernized are not intended to be systematic. Rather, each example is intended to illustrate particular social and historical processes.

MODERNIZATION

Organizing burial: Europe and North America

As we saw in Chapter 1, industrialization and urbanization cause, and are caused by, demographic change. As western societies urbanized and industrialized from the late eighteenth century, populations grew rapidly, but death rates did not begin to decline till the latter half of the nineteenth century. As the number of deaths in expanding European towns escalated, the time-honoured European method of disposal – ad hoc re-use of graves in small churchyards – became ineffective and in dire need of reform. The burial crisis became a major social problem in the cities of all industrializing societies, and each country responded by developing more rational ways of dealing with its dead (Chapter 2). Religious concerns were eroded in the face of public health requirements, though not always without a struggle. Further, mobility from country to town, or from Europe to America, detached mourners from traditional deathbed and funeral customs so they came to rely for guidance on doctors and undertakers. Everywhere, we find two linked innovations. One is increasing use of technical, especially medical, rationality. The other is the rise of new specialists: registrars, pathologists, funeral directors, cemetery entrepreneurs, and managers.

Exactly *who* in the period 1850–1950 succeeded in setting themselves up as specialists, however, varied between countries. In all industrializing western countries the state was concerned that dead bodies were a public health risk, but to whom the state granted control of the dead varied from country to country. Everywhere, for example, new cemeteries were built on new principles of hygiene, rationality, and aesthetics, but *who* built and managed them varied – businessmen (generally, it was men, though that is now changing), municipal officials, or a modernized religious bureaucracy. This resulted in rationalizations of death that differed radically between, for example, the USA, France, and Sweden. Table 11.1 summarizes the three types.

Table 11.1   Control of the funeral industry: three patterns

Institutional control	Example	Key features	Relationship
Commercial	USA	Commercial ownership of both funeral directing and cemeteries	Salesman/customer
Municipal	France	Both funeral directing and cemetery ownership subject to municipal control	Municipal official/citizen
Religious	Sweden	Church responsible for cemeteries, crematoria and (until 1991) death registration	Priest/parishioner

Source: Walter (2005)

Three types

In each pattern, the mourning family is cast in a different role, depending on whether it has to deal with a salesman, official, or priest. The commercial funeral director or cemetery manager casts the family in the role of customer, one offered and able to make choices, though the choices may be manipulated. The municipal official, concerned more with efficient management than with profit, casts the family in the role of citizens entitled to publicly provided (though not necessarily free) funeral and burial services. The priest or religious official relates to the family as parishioners; in the traditionally monopolistic ethnic churches of Scandinavia (Lutheran) and the Mediterranean (Orthodox, Catholic), the family is a parishioner simply through local residence. Thus we have three types of relationship: salesman/customer; municipal official/member of the public; and priest/parishioner (Walter, 2005).

So there are three basic models according to which the modern western dead may be routinely disposed of: the commercial model, the municipal model, and the religious model. Note that these are *institutional* models, whose relation to culture will vary. As she or he talks to a family, the language of a commercial funeral director in Kansas may be more overtly religious than that of a Lutheran minister in Stockholm. Religious symbols typically decorate the American commercial funeral parlour, the British municipal crematorium and municipal cemeteries in Italy. Religious iconography on Swedish or Danish graves may be minimal, despite the cemetery being church owned.

The three institutional types – religious, municipal, commercial – are sociological ideal types which could, in theory, operate in pure form, but rarely if ever do. Their purpose, rather, is to describe and explain the complexity and change that characterize the real world. Some countries show major features of one type, yet never purely – in organizationally religious Sweden, for example, funeral directing is commercial.

Other countries are more thoroughly mixed. In Germany, municipal control of cemeteries co-exists with a powerful state-funded church. England is another mixed example. In the typical late twentieth-century English funeral, a commercial funeral director took the body to a municipal crematorium, at which the funeral service of the non-churchgoing deceased was presided over by a Church of England minister – though the twenty-first century has seen increasing competition from private crematoria and independent celebrants. Meanwhile, in rural areas the Church of England still controls the churchyard where increasing numbers of cremated remains are buried. England is at the same time religious and secular, commercial and municipal.

Explanations

How to account for which organizational type dominates in any one country? I take David Martin's *General Theory of Secularization* (1978), which points to the church's position at the time of each country's key democratic revolution, and extend this to funerals. Where an internal revolution overthrew an absolute monarchy linked to a Catholic monopoly, as in France, the modern state emerged as highly secular; the 1804 Napoleonic decree required municipalities throughout Napoleon's empire to develop cemeteries, and in 1904 munici-palities took control of funeral directing. Strong folk Catholicism (Badone, 1989), however, led to a highly visible Catholic superstructure being built, literally in the case of the cemetery, on this municipal base. In countries like England that tolerated various Protestant denominations, dissent could be carried via churches, so secularism never gained the foothold it did in France. And where (as in Ireland, Finland, and Denmark) the key democratic revolution threw off foreign domination, the 'national' church became identified with liberation, as later happened in Poland. In each case, a more accommodating church–state relationship could evolve, reflected even in some states (notably in Scandinavia) authorizing and funding the church to organize burial on behalf of the state.

Mediterranean Catholic countries and Lutheran Scandinavia are mirror images of one another. In the Mediterranean countries, highly religious people accept that the local state owns and runs the cemetery and, in France and Spain, may have considerable control over funeral directing. In Scandinavia, secular people accept that the church arranges burial and cremation on behalf of all citizens – whether they be Christian, atheist, Sikh, or whatever.

If municipal cemetery provision could be put in place by a secular revolution against absolute monarchy allied to a monopolistic church (France, Russia), municipal provision happened in nineteenth-century England where a strong state (influenced by Methodists and other religious nonconformists) did not see fit to resource a decreasingly monopolistic Church of England to bury the escalating masses of urban dead (Rugg, 1997). Where there is a monopolistic Protestant church, as was the case until 2000 in Sweden, it effectively becomes a state-funded public utility providing a range of welfare services – including funerals, burials, and cremations (Davie, 2001).

In the USA, religious competition, a weak central government, and legal separation of church and state meant that, other than in a few eighteenth-century towns, the churches' historic involvement in burial could never be on a Scandinavian scale. This left a vacuum, easily filled by private entrepreneurs, relatively unconstrained by legislation in a country that distrusts public intervention in routine economic arrangements.

Recent reform

Nineteenth-century funeral reform was substantially driven by concern for public health; reform since the late twentieth century has been driven by affluence and individualism. Chapter 8 explored whether, as societies become more modern and affluent, people and relationships become more individualistic. It certainly seems that around the globe increasing numbers of mourners want more individual control and choice over funeral rites and body disposal (Garces-Foley and Holcomb, 2005). How this individuality is fought for varies, according to whether religious, municipal, or commercial institutions control the funeral industry. Where the *religious* model has dominated, reformers have asked why families with a different religion, or none, must hand their dead and/or funeral rites over to the established or state church (or in Japan, to state-approved funeral Buddhism). Where the *commercial* model reigns, criticism usually comes from those who feel that money, or at least excess profits, should not be made out of the dead. Charles Dickens, Mark Twain, and Jessica Mitford have all criticized the funeral's commercialization. In contemporary Japan, criticism may be heard of the fortune made by some Buddhist monks in the selling of posthumous names.

Where the *municipal* model dominates, reformers have different concerns. In Britain, a widespread feeling grew in the 1990s that a 20-minute service in a municipal crematorium, conducted by a priest who had never met the deceased, was too impersonal for a society that prizes individuality (Walter, 1990). In France, change came in the 1980s from entrepreneurs like Michel Leclerc who introduced funeral supermarkets in an attempt to break the local funeral directing monopolies created by the 1904 state franchise system. Indeed, the municipalization of funeral directing has concerned French critics for over a century (Kselman, 1993: Ch. 6). In Soviet Russia, a non-functioning and un-resourced municipal funeral system was side-stepped by families and neighbourhoods taking responsibility and doing it themselves; since 1990, the local state's formal but hopelessly underfunded control of funerals has continued, so some informal actors have turned themselves into unofficial commercial providers, creating a shadow economy (Mokhov and Sokolova, in press).

Across the developed world, reformers may all want funerals that reflect the individualized relationships and identities of late modernity, yet the systems of sedimented institutional power they challenge and confront are fundamentally different; their campaigns therefore look very different in different countries.

Imitation: cremation in Japan

The preceding section concerned western countries where industrialization was driven by internal demand, not least from a rising middle class. Japan's story of modernization is very different. After 250 years of self-imposed feudal isolation, in 1853 Japan found itself under pressure from a well-armed USA to open itself up to trade. This led to the 1868 Meiji Restoration, which ended the feudal Shoganate and consolidated power in Emperor Meiji. He mandated that Japan should copy modern, especially technological, advances from the West, marrying these to eastern values. During the 1870s, therefore, emissaries were sent to the USA and to Europe to research the most up-to-date technologies and bring them to Japan. It just so happened that during the 1870s a fashionable discussion topic in progressive intellectual circles in countries such as Italy, Germany, and Britain was the possibility of cremation; cremator designs were being published in widely-read magazines. Cremation seemed to the emissaries the perfect example of a modern technology that Japan could adopt. After one or two hiccups (Bernstein, 2000), crematoria were steadily built in Japan and cremation changed from a minority religious practice to a required public health measure, and by the late twentieth century Japan's near 100 per cent cremation rate led the world – by a large margin.

Though this was clearly a process of imitation, Bernstein (2000) reveals the story to have an intriguing twist. The 1870s certainly saw considerable debate about cremation in Europe and North America, but no crematoria had yet been built. The UK's first cremation did not take place until 1885 and the cremation rate did not reach double figures until 1947.[1] The late nineteenth and early

twentieth centuries saw a considerable number of local Italian cremation societies build a local crematorium but, due to Catholicism's influence in family,
social, and political life, it was only in 2007 that the proportion of Italians being
cremated reached 10 per cent.[2] And only since the 1990s have significant numbers
of Americans abandoned burial for cremation. Thinking they were imitating the
West, in the matter of cremation the Japanese have in practice led the West – not
unlike the post-war Japanese auto industry.

I tell this tale simply to illustrate how imitation – of organizational procedure,
of specialization, of technology – is often how a country modernizes (Beckfield,
Olafsdottir and Sosnaud, 2013). What is imitated is always an *imagined* modernity,
what the imitator *thinks* is modern or progressive – something Chapter 14 on
globalization unpacks a bit more. Imitation may not have the intended consequences, and the imitation is always adapted – more or less – to the country's
culture. In Japanese cremation, families witness the body entering the fire and
then, after refreshments, return an hour later with chopsticks to pick the porcelain-
like white bones and place them in a pot for burial in a grave whose upkeep is
determined by a strict protocol of ancestral succession. This is very different from
cremation as practised in the West (which in any case varies from country to
country).

Nation building and burial

New nations typically have to weld together different tribal, clan, regional,
linguistic, religious, class, or ethnic groups into one nation. This requires generating
a national identity that co-exists with, dominates, undermines, or even destroys
these pre-existing identities. In so far as deathbed, funeral, and mourning rites
affirm the deceased's ethnic or tribal group (as classically analysed by Durkheim),
then such rites may function as resistance to the new nation state. The state in
turn may seek to undermine such rites.

Singapore is a case in point. Its British colonial government had left burial of
the Chinese majority to the clan associations that represented different Chinese
immigrant communities as defined by kinship ties. Each clan conducted its own
funeral rites in its own cemetery (Hui and Yeoh, 2002). Singapore became an
independent nation in 1965 and the tiny island's economy and population grew
rapidly. Comprising – as well as the Chinese majority – a significant Malay
minority, temporary construction workers from India, and high-tech and business
expatriates from around the world, the Singapore government has applied
uniquely successful if somewhat authoritarian policies to reduce inter-group
conflict and keep the city-state stable and open for international business. In
1972, the government declared it would close all cemeteries near the city to
conserve land, not least for development. This clearance of ethnic burial grounds
was not just practical, for it transferred power from the clan- and ethnic-based

associations that had run these burial grounds to state organizations (Yeoh and Kong, 2003). The Singaporean state has also promoted cremation and columbaria in which ashes can be stored and ancestors venerated.

The American preference (until very recently) for burial – unusual among highly urbanized western societies – may also be interpreted in terms of integrating the nation (Walter, 1993a), though without Singapore's centralized control. It is understandable that immigrants who have taken the bold step of leaving home and country to cross the seas to the promised land of the USA might prefer burial to going up in smoke. For the family's first and second generation in the States to be buried in the land, the promised land, preferably marked by an expensive stone, symbolizes that the family has arrived, and is here to stay. If sections in the cemetery are organized by ethnicity, that completes the symbolism: our family is Italian American, or Greek American, or Chinese American.

Revolution: forced modernization

In the USSR and China, communist revolutions aimed to transform a largely agricultural economy through directing labour, collectivizing land and factories, and forcing industrialization. In each case, there was massive displacement of population, incarceration of dissidents, and famine. Merridale (2000: 11) estimates that between 1914 and 1953 at least 25 million Soviet deaths – through violence, famine, and epidemic disease – were caused directly or indirectly by state policy, and another 25 million as a result of the Great Patriotic War (the Second World War).

This section sketches how forced modernization caused many deaths and challenged traditional death rites in these two countries. I draw on historian Catherine Merridale's remarkable book on death and memory in Russia (2000), and to a lesser extent on Lane (1981); and on Whyte's (1988) account of changes to Chinese funerals in the four decades following the 1949 Communist Revolution.

Communist revolutions seek a total transformation 'not only of political and economic structures, but of the very way people live – their family lives, rituals and customs, and values' (Whyte, 1988: 289). On coming to power, the Communist Party of China (CCP) found almost every aspect of traditional Chinese death rites objectionable and in need of reform (pp. 292–4). First, the idea of spirits and ghosts to be appeased challenged the CCP's view that there is no supernatural hereafter. Second, death rites reinforced kinship ties over loyalty to party and nation. Specifically, third, the deceased's need to be cared for by male descendants fostered a preference for sons that went against the state's birth control programme – if the first born was a girl, the family would keep trying until a boy was produced. Fourth, the use of feng-shui to locate the placing of graves went against rational land use. Fifth, extravagant funerals impoverished families and tied up resources better used for economic development.

Nevertheless, funeral reform did not come immediately in the People's Republic of China (PRC), and when it did, it was a stop-start process. In the 1950s, collectivization of land indirectly undermined ancestral rites as a person's fate now no longer depended on inheritance of property down the male line. The 1958-61 Great Leap Forward attempted to force industrialization but failed disastrously, the resulting famine causing the deaths of between 16 and 40 million people; it also directly challenged traditional rites by favouring cremation. This lost momentum when the Leap collapsed, to be renewed again in the 1966–76 Cultural Revolution's assault on traditional customs and class-based funeral extravagance in favour of memorial meetings, to be relaxed again on Mao's death in 1976. Apart from appalling suffering, the consequences were an emphasis on the individual, factory, party, and state over kinship and descent groups. 'Individuals and families depend on the favor they win with work-unit authorities, rather than on the favor they may earn with departed ancestral spirits. Descendants depend on jobs, housing, and other resources controlled by the state, rather than on property inherited from the deceased' (Whyte, 1988: 310). This was achieved much more in cities than in the countryside, not least because rural areas lagged behind in access to crematoria; in death as in life, China's urban-rural divide has grown wider under communism.

Disenfranchised grief/memory

Forced modernization by an authoritarian regime typically entails the control of memory, not least who can and cannot be remembered. In the PRC, the erasure of memory was achieved, as noted above, partly through the destruction of private property and inheritance, and partly through funeral reform. Traditionally, the Chinese funeral transforms the polluted dead body into a revered ancestor, thus cementing an eternal patrilineal line and aiding the prosperity of descendants (Watson and Rawski, 1988). Chapter 9 showed how veneration of family ancestors undermined commitment to revolution and to party, so socialist funerals became much simpler, with work colleagues shown as much respect as family; the purpose of the funeral was now to display the deceased as a hard worker and loyal party member. But traditions may die hard, especially in the countryside. During the Cultural Revolution in one village researched by Thaxton (2008), villagers feared that the improperly buried dead became 'famine-corpse ghosts' bringing misfortune to surviving members of the family.

In the Soviet Union, the glorious dead who had died for their country or for the revolution were remembered with honour; victims of the 1932–34 famine, those who died in labour camps or in prison were not to be mentioned. Even heroes had to be commemorated in prescribed ways, memoirs and histories written to prescribed formulae. This systematic manipulation of public memory could undermine private and family memories (Merridale, 2000). It disenfranchised grief

(Doka, 2002), informing families in no uncertain terms that their loved one was not grievable (Butler, 2009).

Survival

Many, many Soviet citizens had no option but to suppress memories not only of the dead but also of atrocity and trauma. They may have participated in atrocities, family members may have disappeared, personal memories might not fit the approved image of the past and expressing them could bring trouble to the family, not least because of the ubiquitous presence of informers. To survive, people forced their memories into the approved mould – as Gulag survivor Varlam Shalamov put it, 'A human being survives by his ability to forget' (Merridale, 2000). If this has been true for some ex-soldiers in democratic societies who participated in two world wars, it was even more true for the ordinary Soviet citizen. In terms of Stroebe and Schut's dual process model of grief (1999), there was little chance of healthy oscillation between feeling the pain of loss and learning how to survive; loss and the memory of trauma had to be suppressed indefinitely, survival was everything. This shaped not just individuals, but an entire culture. Stoicism was and remains the norm; for Russians 'tears are shameful' (Merridale, 2000: 240).

Endurance

Yet before, during, and after the Soviet period, most Russian citizens were and are accepting of authoritarian leadership in defence of their country, a country invaded by both Napoleon and Hitler to devastating effect, invasions whose repulsion came at the cost of immense suffering to millions of Russian citizens. This helped create a culture in which suffering, not least in the Soviet period, could readily be experienced as endurance and heroism. As one of Catherine Merridale's (2000: 417) interviewees told her, 'Dear girl, this isn't your England! ... Of course it was terrible, but we had to rebuild our town. We were carrying everything ourselves, there was no other way. We had defeated the Fascists, and now we were building socialism, right here.' Survival, rebuilding, had a collective purpose and offered hope, even if this meant turning a blind eye to many things. This, Merridale argues, is the frame through which many Russians experienced death and loss.

Similar psycho-political processes of survival, endurance, and collective hope doubtless operated in Mao's China. In addition, the PRC's dramatic economic development – much more successful than the USSR's – depended substantially on controlling population growth, achieved remarkably successfully through the one-child policy. As discussed in Chapter 9, this has subsequently created unique problems for older people whose one child had died.

Migration

Though industrialization entails mechanization that replaces labour, every instance of modernization so far has also required labour moving to where industry is located. As countries modernize, there are three places that labour has come from. First are the country's own rural areas, with agricultural workers moving to the new industrial towns. This is what happened in eighteenth- and nineteenth-century Britain, the first country to industrialize; and is happening now in China, by far the biggest industrializing economy today. Second, workers – most often rural people – may come from other countries to, for example, the USA, Australia, or Singapore. Third, labour may be forced (as in certain parts of the Soviet Union in the 1930s) or enslaved (as in America's antebellum cotton fields).

Migrants face new challenges. In the century and a half following the Great Famine of 1845–62, millions of Irish emigrated and in the process discovered the realities of migrant grief – the loneliness of some emigrant graves, the complexities of sending the body home, or the godsend for mourners today of social media (Ryan, 2016). Wherever they come from, migrants have to modify their death practices. In the days of sailing ships, letters bearing news from home could take several months to get from Ireland to Australia; these letters could be bitter-sweet, helping the isolated migrant retain a sense of family yet also bearing belated news of the deaths of parents or siblings (Fitzpatrick, 1994).

Slaves brutally transported from West Africa to the cotton fields of the American South did not have the comfort of letters; familial connections in Africa were abruptly terminated, a natal alienation that Patterson (1982) describes as 'social death'. Physical death was all too common, yet sometimes slaves were allowed to bury their own dead, unseen and uncontrolled by their masters; these funerals provided a space where the mourning family could be comforted and understood, and even some scope for subversion. The funeral came to be seen, and in the black community is still seen, as a 'homecoming', whether the envisaged home be the Christian heaven or ancestral Africa, or both. From these slave funerals emerged many of the songs and extempore prayers still found in America's black churches.

If migrants typically combine their deathbed, funeral, and mourning traditions with those of the host country, migrants rarely influence the host country's death practices, at least not in 'old' countries. 'New' countries such as the USA may have been more open to immigrant influence. I have just mentioned how slave funerals are the root of contemporary black funerals. And slave cooking habits have shaped white funeral practices in the American South. Well-off antebellum households were cooked for by slave cooks who used the ingredients and techniques they knew – which in time became 'Southern food'. Today in the South, whites cook and bring food to the house where neighbours or co-religionists are grieving, sometimes for months after the death; the dishes they bring are characteristically Southern dishes. So slave food has shaped twenty-first century white funeral food practices (Graham, 2018). It is also possible that the characteristically American public viewing of the body in the days leading up to the funeral was introduced by Irish immigrants.

If migrant practices have sometimes shaped what come to be characteristically national death practices in 'new' countries as they modernize, there are other aspects of migrant death that are generic to many more countries. Chapter 3 discussed how in country after country migration (whether internal or international) has driven both the commercialization and the increasing cost of funerals, while Chapter 14 will discuss some further aspects of migrant death in the globalized twenty-first century.

COLONIALISM

So far, this chapter has looked at how modernization can shape a nation's death system and death culture in ways specific to that nation. The rest of the chapter looks at colonization and de-colonization, processes that have been crucial to both creating nations and modernizing their economies and polities. Colonization and de-colonization have been carried out differently in different countries, in turn affecting each country's death system in identifiable ways. Again, my discussion is not systematic but simply illustrates various ways this has occurred. I look at colonialism's consequences for mortality; attempts to shape a colony's death practices; resistance to colonizing practices; the role of religion in colonization and de-colonization; the unique case of New Zealand's Treaty of Waitanga; and the role of ancestors in post-colonial land redistribution.

Colonizing death

Colonization may dramatically increase mortality among indigenous peoples through explicitly or implicitly genocidal practices; through new infectious diseases against which indigenous people have no immunity; or through relocating people from their traditional lands, thus eroding their culture and bringing despair, unemployment, and alcoholism. A century or more after expropriation of their land, longevity among Native Americans, First Nations peoples in Canada, Australian aboriginals and Māori inhabitants of Aotearoa/New Zealand may have improved since pre-colonial times, but continues much below the national average. Further, infrastructural collapse after de-colonization (e.g. Zimbabwe) or after the fall of communism (e.g. Russia) can reverse what had hitherto been steadily improving longevity (Seale, 2000).

Colonizers often see themselves as more civilized than those under their colonial rule and seek to 'civilize' them. I have already alluded to attempts by Christian missionaries to destroy ancestor veneration in African colonies and elsewhere, though funeral and mourning practices around the world today often synthesize ancestor veneration and Christianity (Park, 2010). In British India, a different practice became identified as unacceptable. The practice of Satī, in which a widow chose immolation rather than suffer the social death that would otherwise be her lot, was initially tolerated by the British East India Company. Campaigning by Christian missionaries and Brahmin Hindu reformers, however, reframed these widows from being victors over a living death to victims (Leslie, 1991) and the practice was progressively banned across India from 1829 to 1861. It was banned in Nepal in 1920.

Whereas some colonial powers simply appropriate land and extract resources, others modernize the economy for the purpose of enriching the colonial power. An example is Japan's colonization of Korea from 1910 to 1945, by which time Korea had become, after Japan, the most industrialized nation in Asia. During the 1920s and 1930s, the Japanese authorities not only identified cremation with modernity (as we saw earlier in this chapter) but also wanted to free up Korean land for farming, mining, and urban expansion rather than have it tied up as burial ground. Consequently, from 1923 to 1935 Seoul's cremation rate rose spectacularly from 5.8 to 76.1 per cent. After independence in 1945, however, the cremation rate declined, dropping to 22 per cent by 1990. Post-independence attempts to promote cremation failed because of cremation's association with the Japanese occupation, and it was not until the 1990s when Koreans came to revalue the environment and fewer Koreans had first-hand memories of the occupation that cremation rose again, rising to 70 per cent by 2010 (Aveline-Dubach, 2012: 207–8).

Resisting colonialism

If cremation is one mode of dealing with the dead body that has been caught up in colonialism and resistance to colonialism, organ donation is another (Hamdy, 2016). Colonial medical schools often used criminal and destitute corpses to educate upper-class medical students. In Egypt, as elsewhere, the 'experience of colonialism … resulted in much less-popular optimism about the potentials of science and technology, as these developments were often deployed to consolidate colonial rule and to mark the cultural inferiority of the Egyptian population' (p. 225). Despite Islamic scholars' approval of post-mortem use of organs, putting the dead to medical use continued to be strongly resisted by many Egyptians who distrusted state-aligned doctors. What changed this was the 2011 Arab Spring when many protesters sustained eye injuries; a campaign for post-mortem cornea donations in that year was unprecedentedly successful. At last, the dead could be used not in the service of oppression but of liberation.

Edo-period Japan (1603–1867) was highly suspicious of outside, especially western, influence, not least in trade and religion. Resolutely opposed to being dominated by any colonial or neo-colonial power, it was particularly concerned about the activities of Catholic missionaries. By the mid-seventeenth century, Christians had been expelled, killed or de-converted, and all Japanese were required to register at a local Buddhist or Shinto temple. Thus began what is known as 'funeral Buddhism', still in operation today, in which the local Buddhist temple and its priests play a key part in most Japanese funerals.

Religion and colonialism

Some of the examples I have given of promoting or resisting colonial death practices indicate the importance of religion. David Martin's (1978) theory of secularization applies not only to democratic revolutions within a country, but also to revolutions against a colonial power. Where a colonized country has a majority religion that differs from that of the colonizers, the home religion can get identified with the nation and with the struggle for national liberation. Though Ireland was not formally an English colony, nor Poland a Russian Soviet colony, the religious dynamics of colonial resistance pertained in each case, with Irish and Poles embracing the Catholic Church as a badge of national identity. After Ireland gained independence in 1922, and Poland regained theirs in 1989, support for the Catholic Church – including Catholic deathbed, funeral, and post-funeral rites – continued to be the norm. Only in recent decades, with Irish identity increasingly linked to the European Union rather than against Britain, and with many Irish rejecting Catholic teaching on abortion and same-sex marriage and scandalized by revelations of priests sexually abusing children, is Ireland now rapidly becoming a more secular society – though this is translating very slowly into funerals.

The Polish and Irish cases could not contrast more dramatically with that of Edo Japan, which perceived Catholicism as an alien religion destabilizing the country.

Bi-culturalism

If most colonial powers have attempted either to eradicate indigenous populations or to 'civilize' them, that is, acculturate them to the colonizer's 'superior' ways, Aotearoa/New Zealand is a rare case of bi-culturalism in which indigenous culture is granted, at least in theory, parity with that of the colonizers. The 1840 Treaty of Waitangi, which recognized Māori ownership of their lands, was in following decades systematically ignored by white settlers, but from the 1950s was increasingly used by Māori to reclaim their rights and is now widely seen as a foundation of New Zealand's bi-cultural society. In few other societies does the indigenous population have a treaty to which it can appeal and on which it can build.

At a palliative care conference I attended in New Zealand in 2014, I was struck by the respect that Pākehā (European descent) participants paid to Māori ways, whether that be the enactment of Māori religious ritual within a secular conference, how Pākehā health care staff interact with Māori *whānau* (extended family) rather than with an individual patient (as described in Chapter 8), or how academics conceive of good research practice. Māori are defined through their *whakapapa* or genealogy, so any meeting (whether clinical or research) between people who have not previously met starts with each describing where they come from, in terms of both geography and kinship. The individual is a person only through membership of a group. In the clinical encounter, in conference papers being presented by a group rather than an individual, in prayers in New Zealand's version of the Anglican funeral rite, or in the pre-match rugby *haka*, Pākehā cannot ignore the strength that Māori find in the group. Indeed, as nurses, researchers, or rugby players, they may be required to participate. Members of the dominant group in a *multi*-cultural society can choose to ignore any or all of that society's minority cultures; in a *bi*-cultural society, they are required to respect and even participate in it. The frequent inclusion of Māori words in Pākehā speech, as in this paragraph, is just one example.

Post-colonial land redistribution

De-colonization may include restoration to the original owners of land taken by colonists. Post-Apartheid claims to land in South Africa were strengthened by the evident presence of ancestral graves on the land, prompting an increase of family groups travelling to white-owned farms to perform rites at their ancestral grave site. In other words, claimants needed to show that this is where their family dead reside, making it not 'my' land but 'our' ancestral land (James, 2009). A Shona friend in post-independence Zimbabwe who is delighted to have 'got back my ancestors' land' enjoys a sense of belonging which I, as an urban westerner, have never experienced, and never can. In Britain, aristocrats whose land has been in the family for generations may have this feeling; but in South Africa and Zimbabwe it is widely felt, and perhaps most intensely felt by those who have reclaimed ancestral land. In these examples, de-colonization increases the importance of ancestral graves and ancestral rites, which in turn influence the operation of de-colonization.

If in these African examples land claims are based on the location of ancestral remains, Verdery's (1999) study of reburial in post-socialist nations has shown how in the Balkans remains have been re-buried in order to mark land ownership. 'To mark new successor nation-states means to mark territories as "ours" by discovering "our sons" in mass graves and giving them proper burial in "our soil", thus consecrating the respective space as "ours"' (p. 98). Using graves to mark territory as 'ours' may go back millennia; some archaeologists argue that round barrows, highly visible in the Bronze Age landscapes of Western Europe, may have communicated precisely this message (Whitley, 2002).

CONCLUSION

This chapter has illustrated path dependency through numerous national examples. Modernization typically entails and often requires changes in the death system, for example when traditional burial becomes impossible in the modern mega-city. How death systems are changed during modernization then sets up patterns – embodied in law, or in the physical landscape (e.g. the building of hospitals or crematoria), or in revised cultural expectations – which shape death practices in that country for generations to come. Though some patterns, such as hospitalized dying, may be similar across modernity, others are unique to particular countries. In some countries, such as Korea, modernization entailed first colonization and then de-colonization, setting up specific colonial and then post-colonial national pathways in how people manage dying, death, and loss.

The next chapter looks at war – another major historical process setting up unique patterns in how each country deals with its dead and with grief.

FURTHER READING

- Bernstein, A. (2000) 'Fire and earth: the forging of modern cremation in Meiji Japan', *Japanese Journal of Religion Studies*, 27: 297-334.

- Hamdy, S. (2016) 'All eyes on Egypt: Islam and the medical use of dead bodies amidst Cairo's political unrest', *Medical Anthropology*, 35: 220-35.

- Martin, D. (1978) *A General Theory of Secularization*. Oxford: Blackwell.

- Merridale, C. (2000) *Night of Stone: Death and memory in Russia*. London: Granta.

- Verdery, K. (1999) *The Political Lives of Dead Bodies: Reburial and postsocialist change*. New York: Columbia University Press.

- Walter, T. (2005) 'Three ways to arrange a funeral: mortuary variation in the modern West', *Mortality*, 10: 173-92.

Questions to discuss

- What revolutionary period(s), political and/or economic, propelled your country into industrialization, urbanization and/or democracy? Who were the key players? How was institutional religion positioned before and after this period? What patterns did this set up that influence how your country manages death, dying, and loss today?

- If your country experienced de/colonization, how did that affect its management of death, dying and loss?

Notes

1. www.srgw.info/CremSoc4/Stats/National/ProgressF.html (accessed 17/6/19).

2. www.srgw.info/CremSoc5/Stats/Interntl/2007/StatsIF.html (accessed 17/6/19).

12

WAR

This chapter considers those who die in war, focusing on (1) how they have been used to shape national identity, (2) how some war deaths are validated while others are unrecognized, and (3) how wartime experience of death and treatment of the war dead can influence peacetime experiences of death and its management. Each country experiences the same war differently, so the path dependencies that follow a war can differ, not least because of whether the country experiences victory or defeat. Within a country, different communities, families, and individuals may also experience the same war differently, with different long-term consequences which can take years or decades to become manifest. Several examples in this chapter come from three particularly bloody past wars – the American Civil War and the two world wars.

Chapter 2 showed how modern death has become medicalized, but war deaths and the collective memory of those who die in war are highly politicized. If in peacetime the state has power to rule over life and death (Agamben, 1998) through laws concerning euthanasia, abortion, and capital punishment and through allocating health care resources, its rule over death is dramatically displayed in war – not only through waging war in the first place, but in decisions to sacrifice, or not sacrifice, this or that military unit, this or that city full of civilians.

This chapter is about war in the modern era. Before the nineteenth century, war was waged between rulers, and the people had no great interest in fighting; mercenaries or press-ganged civilians were often employed to fight. The French Revolution, however, introduced the idea of citizenship, which led to people investing emotionally in their country and in their national identity, which in turn elicited their passions both for glorious imperial expansion and if their country was attacked. So the modern world, at least until very recently, has been characterized by people's wars, or rather state-waged wars embraced by the populace (Pajari, 2015). The new breed of citizen soldier, whether regular or conscripted, enjoyed a moral contract with the state denied the press-ganged or the mercenary. Faust writes (2008: 269) about this new attitude during the American Civil War (1860–65): 'Soldiers were not … simply cogs in a machinery of increasingly industrialized warfare. Citizens were selves – bodies and names that lived beyond their own deaths, individuals who were the literal lifeblood of the nation.' The death of every soldier, not just officers, was now being recorded and in time memorialized.

Since the Vietnam War (1955–73), however, western nations have become increasingly unwilling to sacrifice large numbers of their own citizens in military conflict (Smith, 2005). As we shall see, a new commemorative figure is emerging: war's universal victim. But this does not mean the end of war and violence, for 'the question is never how to get rid of violence, but which set of killing rules we will submit to' (Marvin and Ingle, 1999: 313).

SACRIFICE FOR THE NATION

The logic of sacrifice

From time immemorial, humans have created symbol systems that give meaning to death, more or less successfully (Berger, 1969; Seale, 1998). Examples include religious conceptions of an afterlife, commemorating the dead, propagating off-spring, or personal fulfilment. In war, the state enters the business of meaning making through promoting a new symbol – dying for your country. The symbol most readily applied in wars fought by citizen soldiers is the soldier's sacrifice for nation, a sacrifice which actually constitutes and creates the nation. From the French Revolution until the Second World War, western wars were deeply implicated in nationalism, in building and defending nations, and in affirming a sense of national identity. The symbolic link between war and nation has been what Finnish historian Ilona Pajari (2015) calls the 'logic of sacrifice'. Ernest Becker (1973) considers that culture itself is a system that offers its members meaning through heroic roles which soften the fear of death; in this view, heroic sacrifice in war – far from being exceptional – represents an amplified version of culture in general.

Marvin and Ingle (1999) have argued that, even today and even in peacetime, the key psycho-political dynamic of American nationalism is the myth of violent sacrifice. Exposing this myth, they assert, is taboo, for Americans are reluctant to acknowledge that democracy is rooted in violence. Americans see deliberate sacrifice as a feature of primitive societies, or of religiously motivated terrorist groups today, not of their own society. 'The traditional esteem in which we hold non-violence is misleading … It obscures the violent authority that demands sacrifice … We are meant not to notice. The secret keeps us together' (p. 315).

Russians certainly notice, honouring many of those who died in the Great Patriotic War of 1941–45, but failing to honour those who died fighting the mujahideen in Afghanistan (1979–89) – a war few Russians understood, and having little to do with defending the motherland (Merridale, 2000). Nazi Germany made the connection explicit in the slogan 'blood and soil'. The Nazis saw death as part of a natural cycle in which the buried body fertilizes the German soil; German remains, buried with appropriate rites, make the land German (Black, 2012), a notion found in many communities throughout history and pre-history. If the deceased had died fighting for the fatherland, the symbolism is complete. Burial in German soil of non-Aryans, such as Jews, was problematic, as was the collapse, as the Second World War progressed, of respectful burial of German soldiers and civilians and its all-too-frequent replacement by hurried, coffinless mass burials (Black, 2012).

Writing about Finland's participation in the Second World War, Pajari (2015) argues that the logic of sacrifice applied not just to serving soldiers but also incorporated their womenfolk into this young and vulnerable nation's struggle for survival. By raising and then mourning sons who died in battle, mothers too sacrificed themselves for their country, for the land they loved. And when women took up male occupations, according to the logic of sacrifice 'women are not being unfeminine; they are denying their true selves for the homeland' (p. 183). Yet, first created in the rather peaceful nineteenth century, the logic of sacrifice was difficult to maintain in actual war. For bereaved mothers, either the logic was only skin deep, or if it was deeper, it often did not assuage grief.

Mobilizing passion

For citizen soldiers and their families, death and loss prompt deep emotions that, linked to the meaning given death by the logic of sacrifice, can have powerful consequences, both political and personal. I first realized this in 1982 when the British government sent a task force 8,000 miles south to re-take the Falkland/Malvinas islands from the Argentinian army that had recently occupied them. Like many Brits, I knew little about the islands; a quick look at the *Encyclopaedia Britannica* revealed a convoluted colonial history of the islands' ownership; as the fleet sailed south, questions about the operation's legitimacy arose in my mind and in those of many fellow citizens. All this changed on 4 May when 20 sailors died as *HMS Sheffield*, a British destroyer, was hit by an Exocet missile. Hundreds of Argentine lives had been lost two days earlier when a British submarine torpedoed the *ARA General Belgrano*; justifying this attack has been contentious, but it was the British deaths on *HMS Sheffield* that transformed the psycho-political context in my country. After 4 May, it became much harder to criticize the war. The deaths of British service personnel can be validated if they have died for a noble cause; to suggest the cause is not so noble begins to look at best insensitive to the grieving families, at worst traitorous.

Of course, this is not to say that military deaths cannot turn public opinion against a war, for this happened with western involvement in the wars in Vietnam and

Afghanistan. But such a turn typically occurs later, when it becomes clear that the war cannot be won, or cannot be won without many years of attrition. And the Falklands conflict was European colonialism's last heroic, successful war. Since then, with tolerance of military deaths ebbing, more skilled work is needed for their successful legitimation. Ben-Ari (2005) provides insights in how this is done in twenty-first century Israel, while King (2010) analyses official and media commemoration of British soldiers killed in Helmand province, Afghanistan. These soldiers were identified more as individual personalities than as members of a military unit: 'in grieving for a fallen soldier, the public celebrate the concept of personality as a central collective value' (p. 14). The soldiers' family relationships were detailed – undermining the patriotism that traditionally legitimates military actions, yet making dissent more difficult as media audiences were drawn into mourning an individual and family member more than a soldier. Even objectors to the war, hitherto absent in public mourning for war deaths, found themselves participating in mourning the British dead in Helmand. If King is correct that the British 'no longer live so much in a nation-state but in a community of personalities, united through a shared domestic sphere' (p. 22), then it would seem – as we shall see below – that the image of the hero is being replaced, or at least supplemented, by that of the victim. Nation states may gain through their soldiers dying on the battlefield; families and individuals can only lose (Walklate, Mythen and McGarry, 2011).

Stoicism

As Pajari observes, the logic of sacrifice may never have run very deep. Yes, First World War recruitment campaigns appealed to heroism to get men to enlist, and appealed to sacrifice to prevent mothers, wives, and sweethearts from dissuading their men from enlisting; and padres conducting battlefield burials linked the soldiers' sacrificial death to Christ's (Wilkinson, 1978). But the dominant attitudes among men in the trenches were fatalism and stoicism. Privation, lice, disease, damp, cold, bombardment, disorientation – none of these were heroic, and stoically enduring them with a wry smile or a curse, or both, may have been the main response of soldiers in that war, as throughout history. Notions of sac-rifice and heroism were quickly forgotten once at the front line – even if small acts of sacrifice were indeed a daily occurrence. Endurance, putting up with things, keeping going, looking after your mates, may not be obviously heroic, but it found social legitimation – not least in popular song, such as the British First World War song 'Pack up your troubles in your old kit bag and smile, smile, smile' or the Second World War's 'Keep the home fires burning'. In Russia, narratives of heroism co-exist today with personal stoicism and a refusal to remember, together silencing how war really was (Merridale, 2000).

Not keeping going includes when a soldier psychologically falls apart and is no longer able to function – all too often denigrated by superiors in the First

World War as cowardice, but identified in 1915 by British doctor Charles Myers as 'shell shock', and labelled in the 1980s by American psychiatrists as post-traumatic stress disorder (PTSD), a condition that can torment survivors for years after de-mobilization. Yet many diagnosed with shell shock or PTSD had a few months earlier been exemplary soldiers, heroic even. So we are not here contrasting different people, but different ways of coping, or not coping. Veterans suffering long-term PTSD have truly sacrificed their lives for their country, yet may receive little or no social validation, let alone psychiatric treatment; their attempts to avoid the enduring pain all too often entail alcohol, substance use, and suicide. Victims of war, these living dead do not receive the glory given heroes who die in battle. This is *a fortiori* true in Russia where PTSD is not recognized (Merridale, 2000).

Resistance

Classical Greek scholar and polymath Gail Holst-Warhaft (2000) has identified another response to the pain of loss in war and civil war. She argues that grief, especially for humanly caused deaths, is a 'cue for passion' potentially so powerful that authorities (governments, churches) attempt to regulate it and to dull the passion of grief. But some mourners choose to keep their feelings alive, using them collectively to resist the authorities. Holst-Warhaft gives examples from ancient Greece to the Mothers of the Plaza de Mayo, who gathered daily in front of the presidential palace in Buenos Aires' main square to protest the disappearance of their children between 1976 and 1983 during Argentina's military dictatorship. Doss (2010) shows how various emotional responses to death and loss have motivated women, civilians, ethnic minorities, and other unacknowledged groups to add their own group to the pantheon of those memorialized; at the same time, she shows how any such action risks being co-opted by governments and other interest groups.

REMEMBERING, FORGETTING

In this next section, I look at how the war dead are, or are not, remembered. In particular I consider nationalism's changing fortunes since 1945, not least within the European Union, and how this is linked to changing forms of collective memory. I draw on the interdisciplinary field of collective memory studies which, over the past 30 years, has researched how collective memory shapes group identification – not least through the collective memory of war and the war dead, as articulated in the ever evolving design of war memorials and museums, and in the teaching of history. Drawing on Bull and Hansen (2016), I sketch three kinds of memory – antagonistic, cosmopolitan, and agonistic – along with a fourth, disallowed memory.

Antagonistic memory

If patriotism means love of my country, nationalism includes the additional meaning that my country is better than others. Nationalism implies antagonism – us over against them – and war jacks up this opposition. Most modern nations mythologize themselves as founded on blood shed for freedom and independence, admitting those who die in the struggle to the pantheon of national glory – hence Abraham Lincoln's assassination turned this controversial politician into a sacred symbol of America (Schwartz, 1991). The enemy may be external, as in conventional war, or it may be internal, as in the American Civil War which the Northern states eventually won, after immense bloodshed, over the slave-owning Southern states (Faust, 2008). Or an internal enemy may be eliminated by overt or covert one-sided state action, as in Nazi Germany. 'Within the nation, degenerate elements may be pursued and neutralized or killed in order to homogenise the race. Killing dirt also kills death. Hygienic rationales or metaphors are invoked to justify such action' (Seale, 1998: 55).

Inclusion

Histories of military struggle and victory are the very stuff of traditional school history lessons. Going to school in the 1950s and 1960s, I was taught that England exists because of those who fell at Agincourt (1415), because of Admiral Nelson's death at the Battle of Trafalgar (1805), and because of the brave airmen who defended my country in the Battle of Britain (1940). Thousands of young Israelis, including many born of Russian immigrants whose ancestors were never sent to the death camps, go on pilgrimage to Auschwitz where they learn that their shared national identity as Israelis is built on the Shoah, the mass-murder of European Jews under the Nazi regime 1941–45 (Feldman, 2008). Israel's identity as a national community is based on telling and re-telling the expulsion of the Jews from their homeland in AD 70, and re-remembering the Shoah. Such histories, such pilgrimages, are rites of inclusion in which death functions to include subsequent generations within the nation. The nation exists because of those who died for it.

Exclusion

Rites of inclusion usually also exclude. Who to commemorate and how was a complex and contradictory issue after America's Civil War. Over 600,000 died, as a proportion of the country's population the equivalent of six million today; for those who lived through the war the dominant experience was of death. 'At war's end this shared suffering would override persisting differences about the meanings of race, citizenship and nationhood to establish sacrifice and its memorialization as the ground on which North and South would ultimately re-unite ... Sacrifice and the state became inextricably intertwined' (Faust, 2008: xiii). In 1862, Congress gave the President power to purchase ground for National Cemeteries where every grave was of equal importance – a global innovation in acknowledging the death of every citizen soldier. And yet ... These cemeteries were only for Union dead. After the war, Southerners resented $4m of public funds being spent in five years on dead Northerners. Not until 1898 did the Federal government fund the care of Confederate graves. So in the meantime, in many Southern towns, local ladies started associations to bury their own dead.

Even today, the legacy of the American Civil War is contradictory. While both the Union and Confederate dead are now honoured, the slavery that the war succeeded in abolishing remains barely visible in official commemoration. The often brutal and early deaths of the millions of slaves the Southern states imported from Africa do not receive anything like the same recognition as the soldiers who died in the Civil War (Warner, 1959). Even today, the USA has but a handful of civil rights museums, and almost no slavery museums – nor museums recognizing the near genocide of indigenous Americans. By contrast, the national myth of the USA as a global crusader for freedom, a haven for the world's oppressed and impoverished, is served by Holocaust museums in at least 30 of the country's 50 states. So, some dead are commemorated, some are ignored, all in the name of the same political project. The dead who shame this project's image are ignored, those who enhance it are memorialized. Well, ignored by some. Washington DC's recently opened (2016) National Museum of African American History and Culture, unlike most American museums where black visitors are notable by their absence, is thronged with African American visitors.

Whatever a country's political system, the war dead are subject to symbolic inclusion and exclusion. The Vietnam War was, for the Vietnamese,

> both a revolutionary struggle against foreign aggressors and a vicious civil war ....
> When the war was over and the nation was reunited under the revolutionary state, the memory of the dead from 'that side' (*ben kia*, meaning 'the American side,' as against *bent ta*, 'the revolutionary side') was banned from the new political community of the nation and, by extension, alienated from the moral community of family ancestral worship. (Kwon, 2008: 30)

The Vietnamese revolutionary state converted what it deemed 'feudal' ancestral veneration to commemoration of the heroic revolutionary dead. 'War monuments and war martyr cemeteries were substituted for ancestral temples and graveyards as the village's sacred places' (Kwon, 2008: 30). This resulted in 'ghosts of war', 'a crowd of ancestors uprooted and displaced from their homes' (p. 31). The new revolutionary state was built on excluding the *ben kia* dead as much as on including the *bent ta* dead.

Though Hindus usually get cremated, during Sri Lanka's 1983–2009 civil war the rebel Tamil Tigers chose to bury their military dead. The burial grounds were modelled on western military cemeteries so as to enhance the Tigers' claim to be not terrorists but a regular army, a liberation army. Their founder Velupillai Prabhakaran anticipated that 'The tombs of the fallen Tigers heroes will be the foundation of our new nation' (p. 295). Mourners saw them as places of remembrance (Natali, 2008). After the Tigers' final defeat, however, their cemeteries were destroyed by the government, negating what the Tigers intended them to symbolize and leaving their soldiers un-commemorated.

In all these examples we see that nationhood is built on exclusion as much as on inclusion. Honouring or dishonouring the dead is a powerful symbol of including or excluding the living.

Disallowed memory

Events after civil wars in the USA, Vietnam, and Sri Lanka show how antagonistic memory may disallow collective commemoration of the defeated dead, officially disenfranchising mourning (Doka, 2002) for their families. Chapter 11 described how, from 1917 to 1989, millions of Russians had little choice but to let their dead go and to struggle on, assisted by socialist hope of a better future. Millions who mourned family members killed by Stalin simply had to keep quiet, right through to the Soviet Union's collapse in 1989: 'Some hid their pain from everyone, including their own children, for fear of the damage it might cause. It was dangerous, after all, to mourn the passing of an enemy of the people – and compromising even to be related to one … Silence was their only practical option' (Merridale, 2000: 7, 17). In any case, material hardship, the challenge simply to survive, continued for most of these mourners' entire lives to be more pressing than psychological trauma.

After 1945, all war-torn European countries had to prioritize rebuilding their shattered infrastructure and economy, and in the UK this went alongside a cultural celebration, for example in movies and children's comics, of the country's 'heroic' victory. France found itself in a more ambiguous position, with heroic members of the Resistance movement being outnumbered by ordinary citizens who collaborated with the occupying German forces; remembering the war, whether within families or within local communities, could be fraught (Diamond and Gorrara, 2003).

Defeated Germany and Japan, encouraged and enabled by economic and political aid from the USA, resolutely chose to build a new identity based on modernity and democracy, leaving collective mourning behind. In terms of Stroebe and Schut's dual process model of bereavement (1999), restoration was embraced to the exclusion of mourning. The problem was particularly acute in Germany. How could families, let alone the nation, mourn soldiers who had died for the now discredited Nazi ideology?

There was also the problem of mourning the person who had been, for many, their super-hero: Adolf Hitler. According to Alexander and Margarete Mitscherlich's (1975) influential book *The Inability to Mourn*, first published in 1967, all sections of German society had given Hitler their enthusiastic support, but after Nazism's catastrophic defeat in 1945 regarded themselves as exempt from responsibility. This defence against guilt and shame, the Mitscherlichs argued, rendered them unable to mourn their Führer. Elements of antagonistic nationalism remained visible in that many Germans continued to despise Russians and Poles, and considered that they had a right to a united Germany – eventually achieved after 1989. Nazism itself, of course, born out of Germany's defeat in 1918, could itself be considered a defence against the shame of defeat and the inability to mourn.

Contested commemoration

Post-war Japan was in a slightly different position. Though Nazism in Germany had been totally discredited, Japan retained both its Emperor and a religious vehicle for war remembrance. Shinto – which venerates those who die for the Emperor as *kami* (spirits) – was separated from the state after Japan's defeat, but Shinto shrines still remain. These includes the Yasukuni shrine, founded by Emperor Meiji in 1869 and housing the souls of the war dead as *kami*. This shrine, in the middle of Tokyo, lists the 2,466,532 Japanese who died for the Emperor in war, including 1,068 convicted war criminals, and each day sees many visitors coming to venerate the war dead. Visits by cabinet ministers and from 2001 to 2006 the Japanese prime minister, even if technically personal visits, have been controversial, receiving protests from, for example, China, North Korea, and South Korea. If mourning the war dead was repressed in post-war Germany, in Japan it has been allowed at Yasukuni, inevitably bringing controversy.

Since it did not participate in the Second World War, Spain is a different case again. The Franco era (1939–75) represented a form of fascism that ended not with military defeat but with Franco's death and a peaceful transition to democracy. But like Japan, and unlike Germany, Francoism was and remains informally associated with the country's dominant religion (Roman Catholicism). An hour from Madrid, the Valle de los Caídos (Valley of the Fallen) contains the bones of thousands killed on both sides of the Civil War; at the site's heart is an enormous Catholic basilica containing Franco's tomb. This attracts tourists, along with Maoists who bombed the site in 1999 and Francoists who even today may give a quick Nazi salute after kneeling and kissing Franco's tomb. As in Japan, religion provides a vehicle for memorializing, however contentiously, a defeated ideology and those who died for it.

Cosmopolitan memory

From the 1980s, a new type of memory appeared in Western Europe and North America. Bull and Hansen (2016) argue that this 'cosmopolitan' memory arose first in the late 1970s with the transnational remembering of the Holocaust through, for example, the widely watched 1978 TV series *Holocaust*, then bolstered in the 1990s by the rise of a human rights discourse against fascism, communism, and colonialism – each fatally tied to nationalistic imperialism of one kind or another. The hero disappears, to be replaced by victims and their descendants. I would add that the increasing awareness of PTSD from the 1980s re-cast the soldier from hero to victim. If antagonistic memory arose out of what Ulrich Beck (1992) terms a 'first modernity' characterized by nation states and territorial boundaries, cosmopolitan memory arises from a second, more transnational modernity, epitomized not least by the European Union and more generally by globalization in all its forms (Bull and Hansen, 2016). This second modernity, unlike the first, is more vulnerable than triumphant (Latour, 2003).

Cosmopolitan memory, like antagonistic memory, operates by excluding as well as including. Included is anyone who can be considered a passive, defenceless victim; excluded, or at least minimized, are heroic narratives of soldier sacrifice for the nation, along with commemoration of atrocity's perpetrators. This shift from the nation's hero to war's universal victim then enabled a perpetrator country such as Germany to begin to memorialize the Second World War. Since 9/11, it also enables the memorialization of those who die in terrorism attacks – which both terrorists and nation states see as a global war. Russia, though, has not developed any image of, let alone sympathy for, the universal victim and continues to memorialize the national hero (Merridale, 2000).

Antagonistic memory's return

Bull and Hansen observe that the rise of cosmopolitan memory does not mean the end of antagonistic memory. Beck's globalized second modernity is for Bauman (2000: 13) a liquid modernity which sees 'the settled ruled by a nomadic and extra-territorial elite' comprising Eurocrats, multinational corporations, and transnational pressure groups. This new modernity sees millions seeking community, clear boundaries (whether nationalistic or religious) separating us from them, as an antidote to insecurity. Hence religious fundamentalism and neo-nationalism have increased in many countries in Europe, expressed in the 2016 election of Donald Trump as President of the USA and Britain's referendum vote to leave the European Union. What Goodhart (2017) calls the *somewheres* with roots in a particular place, many of them trapped in poverty in de-industrialized communities, are getting their revenge on the ruling global eliteswho are at home anywhere – the *anywheres*. It seems likely that many of the older *somewheres* who voted to leave the EU recalled the last war antagonistically as Britain standing alone against a Europe dominated by Hitler's Germany; the many *anywheres* who voted to remain in the EU were more likely to see the war as a pan-European tragedy which the EU was founded to prevent ever recurring. Memory of the war dead and contemporary politics are profoundly intertwined.

The four years of television and radio documentaries screened in Britain 2014–18 to commemorate the centenary of the First World War were notable, it seemed to me, for being almost entirely from a British perspective. Yes, the average British soldier was portrayed as a victim of his nationalistic era, but virtually all the footage, all the oral history clips, were of British soldiers and their families. I ached to hear from German or even French soldiers and their families, but waited in vain. Nationalism and antagonistic memory of war is far from dead in second, liquid modernity. The political establishment, meanwhile, became more cosmopolitan than in previous annual First World War remembrances. Thus to mark the centenary of the 1918 Armistice, German president, Frank-Walter Steinmeier, attended London's annual Cenotaph ceremony; and German chancellor, Angela Merkel, joined French President Emmanuel Macron in unveiling a commemorative plaque at the site north of Paris where the Armistice was signed.

Agonistic memory

Post-Marxist political theorist Chantal Mouffe (2005) sees agonism as a democratic respect for conflict; conflict is not to be ultimately transcended as Marx had hoped, but is the eternal stuff of political life. Agonistic memory, therefore, acknowledges all sides to conflict – heroes, victims, and perpetrators – and acknowledges that memories of the same event may differ (Bull and Hansen, 2016). Cosmopolitanism's focus on the victim is as one-dimensional as antagonism's focus on the hero, each erasing any ambiguity between victim, hero, and perpetrator. In the confusion and moral dilemmas of war, however, heroes, victims, perpetrators, bystanders, and spies are not so readily demarcated. We have already seen that PTSD can turn a hero into a victim. Agonistic movies trouble viewers by revealing ambiguities in the divide between good and evil, just and unjust, law-abiding citizen and perpetrator. In certain circumstances, could I too become a perpetrator? Indeed, Britain's heroic wartime prime minister Winston Churchill made difficult decisions that sometimes led to the needless deaths of thousands of soldiers or civilians, on the Allied as well as enemy side; in other circumstances, might this make him a perpetrator of atrocity? Did Hiroshima and Nagasaki save thousands of lives that would otherwise have been lost in a prolonged Pacific War, or were they atrocities? Or both? So much depends on the perspective of the viewer, and from where and when they are viewing such events.

Its ambiguity may explain why the Vietnam Veterans Memorial Wall, completed in 1982 to the design of 21-year-old Chinese American Yale undergraduate Maya Lin, was so controversial, at least in its early years when veterans were expecting an antagonistic, heroic memorial (Wagner-Pacifici and Schwartz, 1991). The Wall's democratic listing of the names of each American soldier who died or remained missing in the Vietnam War and omitting civilian deaths, honours each and every solider in the classic nationalistic war memorial tradition. Yet the Wall's position below ground level rather than triumphantly rising above the ground, its ordering of names by date of death rather than by regiment, was experienced by many as defeatist, unpatriotic and disrespecting military valour. But many veterans and visitors – myself included – have found it profoundly moving. At almost any time, there are visitors tracing or photographing the name of a loved one, or leaving memorabilia at the foot of a name. Quite simply, the Wall does not tell you how to interpret the war and its loss of life: it allows for ambiguity, for conflicting interpretations of history, for diverse interpretations of personal loss, as Maya Lin intended (Lin, 2000).

In turning from heroic statuary and religious symbolism to abstraction, the Wall has influenced almost every subsequent public memorial in the West (Doss, 2010). Publics hesitant about abstraction in art seem to embrace abstraction in post-1982 memorials to war and disaster. The empty chairs comprising the official memorial to those who died in the 1995 Oklahoma City terrorist bombing (Linnenthal, 2001), for example, have been re-invented in the equally profound pop-up memorial to the dead of the 2011 earthquake in Christchurch, New Zealand, and in a square in the former Kraków ghetto in Poland. Is abstraction now popular in memorialization because it allows for the ambiguity denied by both antagonistic and cosmopolitan memory, or because formal representation fails to represent the horror of some catastrophes? Yet at the same time, popular antagonistic war memorials continue to be erected across the world.

A multi-university research programme researching agonism in Europe's remembrance of war considers that agonistic museums and memorials can contribute to peace and reconciliation, yet at the same time the researchers also acknowledge that reconciliation may first be needed in order to build such museums. Thus in Northern Ireland, it has taken two decades of peace for museum curators, aware of the continuing lines of division within the province, to risk an agonist approach to exhibition display. Hitherto, partisan antagonistic displays or cosmopolitan paeans to peace had been the norm.[1]

Francisco Ferrándiz (2013) from the Spanish National Research Council considers that 80 years after the end of its Civil War, Spain is still not ready for agonistic memory.[2] In the post-civil war Franco era (1939–75), church walls listed the local fascist but not the republican dead; in the twenty-first century revising who should and should not be commemorated, and where, still divides communities. With exhumations open to public view, social media are now confusing memory: anyone can photograph remains with their phone and post to social media in real time with whatever caption they choose; pictures from other exhumations around the world are thrown into the mix, and no-one knows which pictures are real and which are fake (Ferrándiz, 2013; Ferrándiz and Robben, 2015). Social media may be more effective in spreading antagonistic ideologies and memories than the fascist and socialist marches of the twentieth century ever were.

How the war dead are included in or excluded from public and private memory is connected to how a country talks about and manages peacetime bereavement. Stoicism and silence learned in war can continue afterwards for a generation or more (Jalland, 2010), while silence learned in a society permeated by informers is not easily unlearned, with good reason (Merridale, 2000). Commemorations that celebrate the heroic war dead or mourn the soldier as victim shape how heroism and vulnerability are valued or devalued in peacetime. At the same time, new conceptions of victimhood shape how the war dead are remembered (Clarke, 2019). Such processes are unique to each nation, since every nation's experience of war is unique.

HOW WAR SHAPES PEACETIME PRACTICES

Innovation

Technological, economic, and social innovations made in war can often influence post-war practices, and this is as true of the management of death and the dead as it is of any other aspect of life. Chapter 4 described how the marketing of embalming for the American Civil War's better-off soldiers and officers was in time used by entrepreneurs to persuade Americans that any decent funeral entailed embalming – not as in war to enable the journey home but to enable a public viewing of the deceased, lying in state within a casket designed for this display. This became the standard twentieth-century American funeral, accepted by millions and functioning not only to sell fancy hardware to the family but also to generate future sales from all the other mourners who file into the funeral parlour and witness its good taste and peaceful ambience (Farrell, 1980). This distinctly American funeral tradition might very well not have come about without the Civil War.

The egalitarian respect shown to the military dead has influenced subsequent civilian burial practice in a number of countries. The already mentioned provision of a grave to each and every soldier, of whatever rank, who died in the American Civil War set a standard for subsequent civilian burial. Something similar happened to the British dead after the First World War. The Imperial (now Commonwealth) War Graves Commission was founded in 1917 to administer the burial and ongoing care of all the Imperial (Commonwealth) war dead in 23,000 sites, including 2,500 war cemeteries in 153 countries around the world. Each grave is marked by a white limestone headstone of standard size irrespective of rank, displaying simple information about the deceased with his regimental insignia at the top and a short personal inscription at the bottom. The stones are cleaned every two years so they look as white and fresh as new, and are arranged in serried ranks rising above a mown lawn like soldiers at attention. This form of kerb-less lawn cemetery – expressing equality in death and ease of lawn maintenance – strongly influenced civilian cemetery design in the UK from the 1920s right up to the present day.

Candles on graves, within Christian Europe a Catholic and Orthodox tradition, are now popular across the (Protestant) Nordic countries. They were first introduced to Denmark on resistance fighter graves in the Second World War and then the custom spread to ordinary civilian graves; the dominant Danish Lutheran Church eventually accepted the practice in the 1990s and now candle lighting is an integral part of the church's All Saints Day commemorative service for the dead (Kjaersgaard, 2017).

State expansion

War, especially total war, requires the state to mobilize and commandeer massive resources and personnel on a scale far more extensive than needed in peacetime. At the same time, fighting a common enemy readily induces in both civilians and fighters a strong sense of solidarity, of working together and making sacrifices to defend the country. This feeling of solidarity and purpose legitimates extensive state activity and state control that otherwise might not be tolerated. As the Second World War drew to its close, this combination is widely thought to have created a unique moment in British history when a good majority of the population looked forward to the creation of a welfare state and the nationalization of major industries such as rail and coal. Over six years of war, the state had proved it could organize at scale and most Britons felt sufficient solidarity one with another to be willing to support one another through state-organized welfare. In the 1945 general election, Labour politician Clement Attlee defeated wartime leader Winston Churchill and the ensuing six years saw the nationalization of key industries, the introduction of the National Health Service (NHS), various welfare benefits, state-funded secondary schooling for all, a strong town and country planning framework, the designation of national parks and wider access to the countryside, and so on. After death, a Death Grant was introduced by the Atlee government to cover the cost of a basic funeral.

Some of this changed dying and bereavement. The NHS, providing health care for all, paid for through taxation and therefore experienced as free at the time of need, included medical and nursing care for the dying as well as the sick, and not just for those who could afford it. Over time, increasing numbers of deaths therefore occurred in hospital. For many, this was a blessing. For others, as pharmaceutical and surgical techniques developed, anyone finding themselves in hospital – not just those who could afford private medicine – risked enduring heroic but futile medical treatment in their final weeks and months.

As decades of peace and affluence came to succeed the years of wartime hardship and common purpose, so the sense of solidarity among citizens waned. By the 1980s, this made more plausible Margaret Thatcher's free market ideology that began to trim back the state and to promote the idea that citizens are responsible not for each other but primarily for themselves and their families. In this context, industries such as coal, gas, electricity, water, telecoms, and railways have become privatized, and privatization is entering the NHS. The Death Grant has been abolished, its replacement covering only part of the cost of a funeral and only for low-income families.

The other thing that happened after 1945 was the collapse of the cult of the fallen soldier that had so dominated the 1920s (Gillis, 2000: 12–13). Was this because in Germany, Japan, and the UK there had been more civilian than military deaths? Or because this *Blitzkrieg* war left cities, railways, ports, factories in many countries needing to be rebuilt, which therefore became top priority? Or because the nationalism that underlay the cult of the dead was waning? Whatever the reason or reasons, people in many combatant countries wanted to leave the dead behind and build a new society, in which everyone had access to jobs, schooling, and housing, a reasonable standard of living and guaranteed health care.

If state expansion, necessitated by engagement in total war, continued into peacetime and affected, among many other things, dying and mourning, in the American Civil War it was in a sense the other way around. It was the number of deaths that necessitated federal programmes 'of a scale and reach unimaginable before the war' (Faust, 2008: xiv). The federal government inaugurated national cemeteries for the fallen, records to preserve the names of all those who died, and a civil war pension for the families of the dead. It was having to manage death at scale that caused Americans to accept a federal government with expanded powers.

Coping

If the sense of solidarity induced by war can continue for a generation afterwards, this is also true of coping styles. I have argued elsewhere (Walter, 1999b) that coping strategies learned in childhood and youth often become lifelong strategies. Those who came to maturity within the years 1914 to 1945, in their formative years experiencing war and/or economic depression, learned to contain their emotions; there was a war to be fought, children to be fed on precious little money, and no time to explore the inner emotional life. After 1945 it took another generation – the baby boomers – and their very different experience of growing up in peace and affluence to challenge wartime stoicism with a counter culture that valued informality and emotional expressiveness, expressed not least in palliative care and bereavement counselling.

Baby boomers are also, arguably, notorious for prioritizing self-development over personal sacrifice, possibly induced by the shift from a producer to a consumer society. If industrialization required a Protestant ethic or something like it, valuing saving, hard work, and duty (Weber, 1930), then post-industrialism's problem is not how to get people to work, but how to get them to consume when they already have life's basic necessities. A consumer ethic is therefore required, emphasizing personal expression and fulfilment, devotion to family, and pleasure seeking. It is not hard to see how industrialism's producer ethic fits what is needed in war, while the consumer ethic is more suited to the development of advanced peacetime economies. As discussed in Chapter 3, the two ethics have very different implications for the management of grief.

In *Death in War and Peace: A history of loss and grief in England, 1914–1970*, Pat Jalland (2010) argues for a somewhat different process. Rather than seeing stoicism and solidarity as a *natural* response to being under fire or being bombed, she shows how Churchill ensured that newspapers and cinema newsreels – which were monitored by the enemy as well as a major source of information at home – portrayed a stiff upper lip among Brits whose homes and streets had been bombed. He needed to bolster British morale, and convince Hitler that he could not bomb Britain into submission. In so far as many Britons believed the image they were shown and acted in accordance with it, this must count as one of modern history's most successful media campaigns to manipulate public attitudes and behaviour. This requirement to present stoic courage in the face of trauma is not, for Jalland, natural; for her, its repression of pain and grief did not serve people psychologically in the years to come. That did not, of course, prevent this stoical response to loss remaining after the war. This story illustrates how coping styles in bereavement can be intimately tied up not only with war but also with perceptions of 'national character', however manipulated.

Arguably (Gorer, 1965), post-war Britain did not face mortality – it was too busy rebuilding its shattered economy and looking to a better future, expressed not least in the NHS's promise of curative medicine for all. But did Germany and Austria – in addition to economic and political reconstruction – suffer from complicated guilt that made it doubly hard to address loss and suffering? I have already mentioned the thesis of post-war Germany's 'inability to mourn'. Did this inability, if such it was, affect not only mourning the intimates and the ideals destroyed by the war, but post-war peacetime deaths too? Is this why palliative care took a generation longer to establish itself in German-speaking countries than in Britain? Or can this be more readily explained in other ways, such as hospice founder Cicely Saunders relying on English-language internships to spread her concepts and techniques?

Afterlife beliefs

Afterlife beliefs can induce anxiety or comfort in the face of one's own or a loved one's death. It is clear that some of those who witnessed appalling deaths on the front line or among bombed civilians, with people dying in flames and bodies dismembered, came to question what they had been taught in childhood about life after death. An unpublished doctoral thesis on afterlife beliefs reported interviews with 100 English people in the late 1990s (Jones, 2000). Those who had experienced being under fire in battle, typically in the Second World War, stood out; this experience had in several instances changed what they believed. For some, it challenged their previous sense that when you die there is nothing more to come – after such appalling experiences, there had to be some kind of afterlife belief. Merridale (2000) reports something similar in the USSR when in 1941–45 loyal communist soldiers returned to religion. For others in Jones' study, wartime experiences made their childhood acceptance of an afterlife impossible. The same has been noted of the First World War: a physical resurrection that might have been plausible for Victorians witnessing peaceful death at home came to seem impossible for some who witnessed dismembered dying and dead bodies in Flanders and Gallipoli (Knight, 2018). At the same time, battle-field padres backpedalled on preaching hell for those who did not believe or who led less than pure lives; many such soldiers had endured hell on earth for their country, and no padre could even hint that they had not gone to heaven (Wilkinson, 1978). It is not only Muslims who believe that those who die for their country go straight to heaven.

Whether at the cultural or biographical level, any history of afterlife beliefs has to consider the effects of war.

Biography

I have illustrated how wartime practices can shape social institutions that deal with the dying and dead (e.g. the NHS, embalming) and cultures of grief and coping. It is also clear that war shapes different individuals and their families in different ways, according to their wartime experiences. Western Europeans growing up within the 1914–50 period, experiencing war and/or economic depression first hand and learning stoicism and probably a degree of fatalism, came to view life and death very differently from baby boomers growing up 1950–70 who directly experienced affluence and economic growth yet against a background of possible nuclear annihilation. For the latter cohort, any background anxiety the theoretical possibility of annihilation may have induced was very different from their parents' very practical struggles with loss and deprivation. And different individuals can have very different wars, one person witnessing traumatic events or participating in atrocities on the battlefield or losing close family, while others are spared such difficulties and may even benefit from war – as did young Americans who grew up in poverty in the 1930s recession but whose Second World War military duty entitled them post-war to federal programmes enabling veterans to attend college. Some witness death all too directly in war, others see it only in movies; this cannot but affect personal feelings about mortality.

Those growing up in Russia, characterized by fear and brutalization from 1917 right through to 1989 and even beyond, developed different values, coping strategies, and philosophies of life again (Merridale, 2000). In the eastern part of Germany, ordinary people who had been loyal members of the Hitler youth in the 1930s, fought in the 1940s for the fatherland and then went on to become dutiful citizens of communism, may have wondered as they aged and died in the newly democratic 1990s and 2000s what their lives had been lived for.[3] What Malcolm Johnson (2016) calls 'biographical pain' at the end of life can be caused by the intersection of national and personal history, by the fortunes and misfortunes of when and where you were born – as Glen Elder demonstrated in his classic study *Children of the Great Depression* (1998). Komaromy and Hockey (2018) show how personal experience of war can filter down through the generations within a family. They prompt us to look at our own family's experience of war, taking note of who in the family was born when, how that shaped their experiences of loss and trauma, their opportunities or lack of opportunity, and how that subsequently impacted on their, their children's and their grandchildren's lives.

CONCLUSION

This chapter has sketched some ways that death and loss in war can shape the lives of individuals, families, and whole nations. I have focused on how wartime death lies at the foundation of many nation states and of national identity; how globalization's challenge to nationalism has reconstructed collective memory of war and wartime death, a reconstruction that continues to be contentious in many countries, especially after civil war; and finally how innovations brought about by war can shape the peacetime management of death and dying, cultural norms about how to cope with loss, and afterlife beliefs. Because international wars are waged between nations, won by some and lost by others, the consequences can be quite specific to a particular nation or nations.

FURTHER READING

- Bull, A.C. and Hansen, H.L. (2016) 'On agonistic memory', *Memory Studies*, 9: 390–404.

- Faust, D.W. (2008) *This Republic of Suffering: Death and the American Civil War.* New York: Vintage.

- Holst-Warhaft, G. (2000) *The Cue for Passion: Grief and its political uses.* Cambridge, MA: Harvard University Press.

- Jalland, P. (2010) *Death in War and Peace: A history of loss and grief in England, 1914–1970.* Oxford: Oxford University Press.

- King, A. (2010) 'The Afghan war and "postmodern" memory: commemoration and the dead of Helmand', *British Journal of Sociology*, 61: 1–25.

- Komaromy, C. and Hockey, J. (2018) *Family Life, Trauma and Loss in the Twentieth Century: The legacy of war.* Basingstoke: Palgrave Macmillan.

- Marvin, C. and D. Ingle (1999) *Blood Sacrifice and the Nation: Totem rituals and the American flag.* Cambridge: Cambridge University Press.

- Schwartz, B. (1991) 'Mourning and the making of a sacred symbol: Durkheim and the Lincoln assassination', *Social Forces*, 70: 343–64.

Questions to discuss

- How does your nation remember and/or forget, include and/or exclude, its war dead?

- How have wars shaped your country's peacetime death system and/or grief culture?

- Are your own thoughts about death and loss influenced by wartime experiences – whether your own or those of earlier generations in your family? If so how?

- More generally, how does when and where you were born shape your feelings about and understanding of mortality?

Notes

1. Chris Reynolds, Nottingham Trent University. Contribution to UNREST seminar, University of Bath, 9 January 2018.

2. Contribution to UNREST seminar, University of Bath, 9 January 2018.

3. Personal communication from an East German psychotherapist about many of her clients, early 1990s.

13

POLICY AND POLITICS

Countries such as France and Singapore are highly centralized, while Switzerland is decentralized, as are to a lesser extent federal nations such as the USA, Canada, Australia, and Germany. But however much a nation is decentralized, many laws, institutions, policies, and (in certain countries) a powerful ideology remain at the national level, shaping what individuals, families, businesses, communities, and local governments are expected to do, in death as in the rest of life. Ideology, law, institutions, and policy are inter-related, so this chapter's division into these categories is a bit arbitrary, but I hope helpful nonetheless.

IDEOLOGY

The USA, the first 'invented' or 'new' nation, has a uniquely strong national ideology, linked to the idea of American exceptionalism – the idea that the USA is different. This ideology centres on America being the birthplace of modern democracy, the land of liberty and opportunity where anything is possible, a nation with a unique destiny (Lipset, 1955). Without going into all the nuances of this ultimately political ideology, I will sketch some implications for America's death system.

Whereas in some countries, such as France or Norway, existential angst is more fashionable in some circles than being happy, in some other countries – most famously the USA – a national culture expects people to be upbeat, optimistic about the future, and happy. Both approaches could be seen as a cultural response to the mortal human condition, and it would be surprising if such differences did not affect how individuals deal with, or at least speak about, death and loss. American cultural historian Lawrence Samuel (2013: xvii) considers that 'death and dying run counter to virtually all of the nation's defining values – youth, beauty, progress, achievement, winning, optimism, independence, and persistence.' He cites approvingly British historian Arnold Toynbee's (1968: 131) suggestion that 'death is un-American'. It is important to consider this claim if we are to sort out whether it is modernity in general, or the USA in particular, that sequesters death and dying; or whether the USA embraces an extreme version of triumphant modernism, in which case modernity in general sequesters death and the USA especially so.

It certainly seems the case that, on balance, Americans display consistently more optimism, vitality and faith in progress, in technology (including high tech medicine), and in the ability of humans to control nature for their own ends, none of which prepares Americans for progressive frailty, incurable illness and the body's ultimate decay in death. Faith in technology encourages Americans to accept medical interventions near the end of life that in many other countries would be deemed futile. And it is not surprising that cryogenic preservation has been developed and most actively marketed in the USA; for a hefty sum, a deceased person's head or entire body can be super-cooled and preserved until such time, the customer hopes, that science finds a cure for whatever killed him or her; the frozen deceased can then be unfrozen and cured!

There is also a religious factor in the USA where the many Christian funda-mentalists see human rule over nature as mandated by God. As we saw in Chapter 10, this encourages them to approve of heroic medical efforts to save life over the 'letting die' approach of hospice and euthanasia.

And yet it is not that simple. Despite widespread American antipathy to socialized medicine (such as the UK's NHS), federally funded Medicare has, since the 1980s, paid for hospice care with greater generosity than is the case in the UK and most other countries. Over half of Americans have now written living wills specifying what kind of heroic life-saving medicine they would reject if near death, and of course many Americans vehemently defend the death penalty. None of this looks like a death-denying society.

Of course, American optimism and faith in technology and progress face challenges. On the one hand, de-industrialization and globalization have wreaked havoc on many once-prosperous agricultural and manufacturing communities, and optimism may not be so evident there. Once unimaginable, American progress has gone into reverse. On the other hand, many baby boomers who prospered and embraced post-material values (Chapter 6) have rejected 1950s materialism, not least Cadillac hearses, mahogany caskets and public viewing of the dead, opting instead for simple cremation and scattering the ashes over the Pacific (Prothero, 2000; Sloane, 2018). Even more radically, some are now opting for natural burial, the mourners themselves lowering the shrouded body into the cold, black soil (Kelly, 2015). Now that is a revolution for Americans – even if it was how many pioneers and slaves had to bury their dead well into the nineteenth century.

The baroque mid-twentieth century 'American way of death', acceptable at the time to most Americans and taking two English outsiders – satirist Evelyn Waugh (1948) and critic Jessica Mitford (1963) – to expose, demonstrates the possibility of a uniquely national way to manage the dead. It is also likely that twenty-first century reactions against it are uniquely American too. Thus in the USA, cremation means simple, cheap, with little or no ceremony, a rejection of post-death material display; cremation in other countries can mean very different things.

In this section, I have sketched some aspects of a specifically American ideology and considered their implications for the American death system. This ideology is closely linked to politics and to culture. It provides a sensibility, a hope, a faith, from which American norms and habits – the heart of culture – derive.

LAW

One has only to consider that laws regarding burial, organ donation, euthanasia, abortion, suicide, and capital punishment vary from country to country to appreciate the significance of law in a country's death system. There are also clusters of nations that embrace particular legal frameworks for death-related matters.

One such cluster comprises those countries which in 1804 belonged to Napoleon Bonaparte's European empire. Wanting to erode the Church's power, revolutionary France had some years earlier tried to replace the Catholic cult of the dead with a new state-centred cult, but by the late 1790s it became clear this was a step too far for most French citizens. With commercial operators entering the scene, the state realized it needed to rationalize funerals and burials; it did this through the Imperial Decree of 12 June 1804 which came into force across France's by then extensive empire. The decree ended churchyard burial by requiring municipalities to establish, administer, and regulate secular cemeteries in which each grave could be rented for five to ten years, after which it would be re-used. Families who wished to pay for longer or for permanent occupancy could do so. Elements of this system may still be found not only in France, but also in territories held (in part or in whole) by Napoleon at that time – Italy, Germany, Austria, Greece, Spain, and Portugal (Kselman, 1993; Goody and Poppi, 1994).

The citizen's duty to the state

Countries vary as to the degree to which citizens are considered to have a duty to the state rather than to themselves as autonomous individuals, in other words the balance between personal liberty and loyalty to the national community. This affects national laws about organ donation. Some countries have an opt-in (informed consent) system, where donors choose to be donors; others have an opt-out (presumed consent) system, where the donor's consent is presumed unless they or their family specifically state otherwise. Within Europe, predominantly

Catholic countries typically have presumed consent laws, while historically Protestant countries tend to require informed consent. This may possibly be related to Catholic countries' traditionally stronger emphasis on the citizen's duty to the state, while Protestant theology has long emphasized personal freedom and individual rights (Kjaersgaard Markussen, 2013). That said, Catholics' loyalty to the Vatican relativizes their loyalty to their own nation (leading in the 1930s to greater resistance to Nazism by German Catholics), so the Catholic duty to the state has limits.

I have yet to find any theory accounting for why some countries and not others have legalized euthanasia and assisted suicide. It is clear, however, that certain distinctive legal aspects of the American death system follow from that country's aversion to the state, especially the federal government, organizing or controlling any more than it has to. Hence the ideological hostility to socialized health care, and the widespread – though by no means universal – advocacy of the right to own guns. With the spread of neo-liberalism (see Chapter 8) in which citizens have a duty to be consumers and autonomous decision makers until the very end, American ideas are becoming more widespread, influencing policy (e.g. advance decisions) if not law in many countries.

There is another kind of duty, the duty of the citizen not to self or state, but to the local community. Personal charity is consistent with free market ideology (which prefers charity rather than the state to make up for market failings), as the USA clearly demonstrates (Esping-Andersen, 1990). In the Indian state of Kerala, where the compassionate community approach to end-of-life care has been pioneered through using huge numbers of volunteers, duty to the community seems rooted more in socialism and Christianity (Santhosh, 2016).

The state's duty to its citizens

Today, the concepts of 'human' and 'human rights' extend in theory to all humans regardless of nationality, ethnicity, gender, and abilities. Part of being human is to be granted appropriate death rites by other members of your community, other creatures rarely being granted such rites.[1] Appropriate care is offered to humans at the end of life, the state records each death and ascertains a cause, a funeral is held and a place made available to deposit the remains. Withholding such things is a powerful way of saying that the deceased is 'not one of us' and symbolizing exclusion from the community.

But not everyone receives the right to such things, for democratic states protect their own citizens, not those of other countries, and laws are made and enforced primarily by nation states for those resident in the country, rather than for humans in general (Králová, 2019). Those lacking national citizenship or full citizenship, therefore, may struggle to have their human rights respected. The stateless and/or those lacking full citizen rights includes – in some of the world's most violent and unstable countries – those finding themselves on the wrong side in civil wars, the disappeared, and victims of genocide. The Nazis, for example, denied Jews the right to burial in municipal cemeteries, and later destroyed Jewish burial grounds in many parts of the country. German soil was for 'Aryans' (Black, 2012). But even peaceful democratic societies may deny full rights to refugees, asylum seekers, undocumented migrants, prisoners, those without an address (gypsies, other travellers, the homeless), foetuses, and those deemed to lack mental capacity: their deaths may be counted and respected, but they may also be ignored, stigmatized, or manipulated by state or media, their deaths rendered ungrievable (Butler, 2004).

Prisoners, for example, lose many citizen rights, not least access to the highest standards of palliative care or the right to attend family funerals; the USA has many more prisoners than other western democracies, followed by the UK where imprisonment of historic child abuse perpetrators has markedly increased the numbers of older men dying in prison of natural causes (Turner and Peacock, 2017). Undocumented immigrants in the USA who leave their children there for a few days in order to visit a parent dying over the border in Latin America risk not being able to re-enter the USA (Bravo, 2017); they must choose between the needs of a dying parent and the ongoing upbringing of their own children. The rights of those without mental capacity, not least the comatose and those with dementia, are governed by law in each country, as are the rights of foetuses. Death and citizenship are intimately connected; laws and policies concerning death practices implicitly define – and at the same time are shaped by – who is, and who is not, afforded de facto citizenship.

INSTITUTIONS

How health care is funded – through taxation, insurance (compulsory or voluntary), or charity – affects the management and experience of dying. Most obviously, some funding regimes implicitly encourage expensive aggressive treatment, while others do the opposite, leading to very different levels of treatment for the same condition in different countries. For patients with a life-threatening disease, there may come a time when doctors need to ascertain whether curative treatment is no longer worthwhile; medicine is often more of a craft than an exact science, and at this moment professional judgement needs to be exercised. It would be surprising if funding regimes and other organizational constraints, such as waiting times and the availability of hospital beds and operating theatres, did not affect such judgements, consciously or subconsciously (Kaufman, 2005).

Funding

Dying

In 1982, America's Medicare was extended – with remarkably little opposition – to fund hospice, which in the USA generally means care at home. Consequently, one-third of all dying Americans now benefit from hospice care.[2] Questions have been raised, however, about whether Medicare has undermined hospice's original holistic goals. Medicare pays per patient per day, regardless of services rendered, which provides an economic incentive to hospice services to take on more patients and provide each with less care (Abel, 1986; Livne, 2014). And hospice is only Medicare-fundable where prognosis indicates death within six months; so some hospice referrals are based on a predictable prognosis rather than clinical need. To be eligible the terminally ill person must forgo any other Medicare-covered benefits such as assisted living or hospital treatment for their terminal disease; this serves to separate hospice not only from other medical care but also from palliative care which can be provided alongside curative treatment. This means that hospice and palliative care, deemed equivalent in some countries, are separated in the USA. This makes cross-national comparison tricky when the same words mean different things in different countries – simply because of different funding regimes.

In 1983, Medicare Diagnostic Related Groups (DRGs) became law. This aimed to reduce Medicare expenditure by paying specific amounts for specific diseases, meaning that hospital care could only be reimbursed if the patient was being treated *for* something. Anthropologist Sharon Kaufman (2005: 91) notes that this excludes the kind of hospital dying that had previously been common – the patient lingered, and family and hospital waited. As several young doctors told her, 'Dying is not billable'. Active treatment and palliative care are billable, but waiting is not.

Meanwhile, though schools and social care in the USA are organized and co-ordinated locally, this is not true of health: any provider can enter the market. This means that there may be almost as many providers as terminally ill patients in a neighbourhood, making home visits very inefficient. Efforts to plan at the local level are, however, being trialled (Lynn, 2016).

Grieving

The American Psychiatric Association's *Diagnostic and Statistical Manual of Mental Disorders* (DSM) has international standing, but each new edition has been criticized for labelling more and more human experiences and behaviours as psychiatric disorders. Ever since Freud's 1917 article distinguishing mourning from melancholia (Freud, 1984), there has been debate about how to distinguish normal grief (which need not require professional psychological help) from major depression (which does). Those revising each new edition of the DSM struggle with the question whether recently bereaved people should be excluded from a diagnosis of clinical depression, since the depression may simply be a temporary and normal manifestation of grief; and whether certain manifestations of grief should be classified as a mental disorder, and, if so, how this should be defined in terms of duration and severity of symptoms. Advocates on the one side do not want to medicalize normal grief; advocates on the other side do not want mentally ill people who happen to be bereaved, and people whose bereavement produces abnormal reactions, to be denied professional help. This is a significant issue in the USA where psychological therapy can only be reimbursed by a patient's insurance company if it is for a defined mental disorder. We may also note that depression is the most common cause of referral to American psychiatrists – they would stand to lose business were depressed bereaved people ineligible for professional help. This is not an issue in all countries; it depends on the funding regime. Meanwhile, similar debates rage in the revision of the *International Classification of Diseases* (ICD), whose eleventh edition now includes a diagnosis of 'prolonged grief disorder' (Killikelly and Maercker, 2017).

Every country has its own health care system, producing its own constraints and unintended consequences. What is and is not funded, and how health or social care markets operate, influence who is eligible for care, levels of care, and what aspects of dying and grieving are medicalized and with what consequences.

Religious institutions

We could similarly analyse how religion is funded. Churches in the USA are membership organizations, funded by their members, so have little interest in providing funerals for non-members. This is increasingly also true of the established Church of England, for increasing numbers of its clergy are theologically evangelical and have a membership model of church (Woodhead and Brown, 2016). In the Nordic countries, by contrast, most citizens support the Lutheran church through payments organized through the state tax system, even though regular church attendance is among the lowest in the western world; this creates well-funded churches whose ministers are available at all reasonable hours and who feel a duty to provide good-quality funeral care to everyone, which in turn motivates citizens not to opt out of the church tax.

Closed organizations

Zaman et al. (2018) are troubled that the organization of modern health care creates barriers to everyday compassion being exercised by people not within the health care organization. First, the more 'developed' a country, the more professionalized its health care (Chapter 2), so that care by non-professionals is considered to be second best. Challenging this requires a new mindset. Second, professional ethics requires patient confidentiality, limiting the information that can be disseminated to those other than the patient and possibly his or her family. Health care professionals share knowledge about patients with other professionals within their organization's firewalled IT system; it is not always easy sharing information with other health care organizations; and sharing information online with the patient's friends and neighbours is taboo. In any case, their informal care is increasingly likely to be co-ordinated using social media, operating with little regard to confidentiality. In these and other ways, professionalized health care organizations are closed systems.

Third, professionals who are highly trained and heavily insured can be nervous about informal care by an untrained and uninsured non-professional; professionals, and even more so their managers, may be anxious about litigation on health and safety grounds. Levels of anxiety vary from country to country, depending on how readily people will sue and how seriously health and safety legislation is taken. Some societies are more risk-averse than others, but as a general rule, the more post-industrial, the more risk-averse, leading for example to an obsession with patient confidentiality that does more harm than good (Chapter 6).

Path dependency

An institution's early years can shape its subsequent scope and development. Hospice care was first developed in the late 1950s with British cancer patients, and as a result its practices – now disseminated globally – are shaped by two things: Anglo-Saxon values, and the dying trajectory typical of cancer patients.

First, the major Anglophone countries (Chapter 8) tend to be highly individualistic, valuing personal autonomy. This is reflected in hospice and palliative care's aim to enable a fully-informed patient to live as he or she wants in his or her final weeks and months. Palliative care doctors strongly recommend giving the diagnosis or prognosis to the patient rather than to the family – as had been traditional until 50 or so years ago and is still common practice in more collective and family-oriented cultures. Second, the disease. The last stages of cancer, unlike heart disease or elderly frailty, are relatively easy to identify, and follow a relatively predictable timeframe (Figure 1.3). (This may be one reason that Medicare defines eligibility for hospice care in terms of time.) Further, most people with cancer are conscious and have full cognitive capacity until the last few days or even hours, so care decisions can be made with rather than for them – in line with the cultural value of personal autonomy.

Proponents of palliative care have been passionate about spreading its message and its practices to other countries, and to patients with diseases other than cancer. With minor modifications to take account of different cultures, different health care funding arrangements, or different disease trajectories, proponents assume the British model will work anywhere. This is questionable (Zaman et al., 2017b).

It is worth considering what might have happened had palliative care first been developed elsewhere. In the Netherlands, I first came across palliative care in the early 1990s in the context of nursing homes for the elderly. Had palliative care originated in the Netherlands, it might well have been shaped not only by Dutch values but also by the specifics of elder care; as it is, its stance on euthanasia differs from that of the British hospice movement. Palliative care in Switzerland has a slightly different ethos again; it was introduced in the 1980s when the major end-of-life challenge was people dying with AIDS; even though their numbers have declined, certain practices have endured since those early days.

Palliative care therefore displays a recurring theme in this book: path dependency. The first path taken influences where you get to later, even though that may not be where you would wish to be had you started out afresh.

POLICY

Late modern rationality requires that organizations be, in appearance if not reality, goal-driven, with the means to achieving those goals governed by clear standards. Financial accountability drives much of this (Power, 1997). Governments and organizations – from manufacturing companies to universities to hospitals – are therefore replete with policies. As with laws and institutions, policies relevant to the end of life – for example, bereavement leave (Cann, 2014: 10) – can vary considerably from country to country.

Some death policies aim simply to ease citizens' suffering at a difficult time. In many cases, however, a policy may use bereavement leave, palliative care, or disposal of the body as a means to another goal – whether that be reducing public expenditure, inducing loyalty to the state, or controlling the power of the medical profession or of organized religion. Death rites in Singapore, for example, have changed radically in the past generation: funerals have become simpler, traditional mourning dress is no longer worn, cremation has replaced burial and ancestral altars removed from homes. Why? Anthropologist Ruth Toulson (2015) argues that these changes are not an automatic result of modernization but 'part of a larger, politically orchestrated shift to mutate the form taken by religious belief itself, transforming a Daoist-infused obsession with ancestors, into a sterile, more easily controlled, "Protestant" Buddhism.'

Promote/oppose

State policies, like religion (Chapter 10), may aim to promote particular death practices, or to oppose, undermine, limit, or control them. We have already seen how Medicare has given a real boost to hospice in the USA, how Napoleon's civil code reformed burial practice across much of Europe, and how governments in 1870s Japan and 1990s South Korea successfully promoted cremation. In the UK, cremation was quietly but successfully promoted from the 1940s to the 1960s by local rather than national government; saddled with the cost of maintaining perpetual graves (unlike Napoleonic Europe), British local authorities chose to build crematoria as a financially viable alternative (Jupp, 2006).

Because, I suspect, of the conservatism of mourners who want as much of their world as possible to stay the same when death has torn it apart (Marris, 1974; Winter, 1995), radical new burial and memorial policies promoted by revolutionary governments have not always been entirely successful. This and previous chapters have provided examples in respect of revolutionary governments in France, Russia, and Vietnam.

Promoting a policy often means undermining existing practice. We have seen how, because China's Maoist government wished to induce loyalty to socialism, state, and workplace above family, it attempted to undermine ancestor veneration, not least in socialist funerals. More recently, China has promoted digital commemoration in order to control the traffic jams caused by millions of people travelling to visit family graves at Qingming (tomb-sweeping day) (Cann, 2013: 106). Another East-Asian government, Taiwan, has tried to restrict burning paper offerings to the ancestors for ecological reasons.

POLITICS

Though institutions can develop out of all manner of curious and one-off circumstances, policy and law may more often be more directly related to political interests and to lobbying by pressure groups.

Despite only about one-third of people dying of cancer today, since the middle of the twentieth century in western countries cancer has become synonymous with dying. Palliative care is oriented toward cancer patients; in some countries these patients receive better resourced care than do people dying of other causes, especially those dying in late old age; a significant number of cancer deaths occur in middle age, leaving youthful dependants, and so are considered premature and tragic; cancer is perceived not as the body naturally wearing out through age but as invasion from within by unnatural cell growth; people dying of cancer usually know they are dying and can speak for themselves. Autobiographical books and blogs by dying people are overwhelmingly written by people with cancer (Hawkins, 1990). It is hardly surprising if governments devote more resources to cancer cure and care than to other life-threatening conditions. Even within cancer, there can be hierarchies. Breast cancer, which may kill a mother in her forties leaving dependent children, seems to be taken more seriously – both in public awareness and in health care resources – than rarer cancers and cancers more likely to develop in older life.

By the twenty-first century, however, many cancers can be treated successfully, and longevity continues to rise. Several advanced industrial societies have therefore witnessed greater public and official awareness that many or even most of their citizens will die in their eighties or even nineties, after a time (averaging two years) of dependency. Many articulate baby boomers have witnessed their parents die not of cancer, but in frail old age after some years of dementia. For some baby boomers, especially those who have valued control over their lives, fear of developing dementia now seems to outweigh fear of cancer. Further, as baby boomers age, the number of old people grows. On the one hand, there are more of them to vote for pro-age policies; on the other hand, the reduced number of working-age taxpayers and insurance contributors reduces the funds potentially available for elder care – which in effect means end-of-life care. The power of a country's 'grey lobby', especially as it comes to be populated with baby boomers, is therefore crucial; also crucial is the extent to which this lobby focuses on promoting healthy active 'young' old age, or on funding care in frail life-threatening 'old' old age.

The USA's federal system, with many powers devolved from the federal government to state legislatures, has enabled successful death-related lobbying at the state level. This was noted by Jessica Mitford (1963), who observed how local funeral directors and cemetery owners were able to persuade state-level politicians that managing dead bodies should be restricted to professionals, that is, themselves; this led to laws in various states restricting what can be done with human remains and where. In the UK, by contrast, where the funeral industry lobby is poorly organized and Westminster creates higher hurdles for lobbyists to jump, there are very few such restrictions. If they wish, British families can legally do almost anything with their dead, though few families know this.

The open-ness of state legislatures in the USA to lobbying has also led to within-nation variation in other death-related fields. The death penalty remains legal in 31 states and is illegal in 19. As of 2018, doctor-assisted suicide is allowed in the states of California, Colorado, District of Columbia, Hawaii, Montana, Oregon, Vermont, and Washington. While reflecting the values and interests of dominant groups in each state, this diversity also allows monitoring of how assisted suicide legislation works in practice in America, which can then inform debate whether to introduce it into other states. Likewise in federal Australia, assisted dying was legalized, briefly, in the Northern Territories, while health-promoting palliative care became state policy in Victoria. Law-making in federal countries can therefore be more evidence-based than in centralized states that lack such opportunities for experimentation – how assisted suicide works in other countries provides much poorer evidence than how it works in other parts of one's own country.

Principles vs pragmatism

Nations differ in the degree to which parliamentary debate appeals to popularly understood principles, and the degree to which it highlights undesirable consequences of existing legislation. Both principles and consequences can be dramatically displayed in matters of life and death. The USA is a nation founded on principle rather than tradition, and this is reflected in both its legal system and its terms of political debate. American politicians and pressure groups readily debate issues such as euthanasia, abortion, and capital punishment in terms of principles and rights. With abortion, the contrast with some European countries is very stark. In the USA, anti-abortionists claim the foetus's 'right to life', while those in favour of legalizing abortion claim 'a woman's right to choose'. In Britain, by contrast, the 1967 act that made abortion legal came about through supporters pointing not to fundamental rights but to the life-threatening consequences of botched back-street abortions; objectors pointed to a 'slippery slope' on which justifiable abortions might over time lead to abortion on demand (C. Davies, 1991).

In twenty-first century Britain, though press coverage of assisted dying – highlighting tragic cases that demand a right to die – is overwhelmingly positive and principled (Hausmann, 2004), parliamentary debates are more pragmatic, pointing for example to the difficulties legislation might pose for some doctors and (again) to a possible slippery slope. With religious leaders and Christian doctors in the House of Lords, such arguments are sometimes a front for religious principles which in pragmatic and increasingly secular Britain it may be counterproductive to appeal to. Whereas in the USA political self-interest may sometimes need to be dressed up as principle, in Britain principles sometimes need to be dressed up as pragmatism.

CHANCE

Some practices and policies come into being because of coincidences of timing, which political party is in power when policy is formed, peculiarities of existing practice, lack of information, historical events, and so on. In other words, chance and contingency. I will give just a few examples, from the eighteenth, twentieth, and twenty-first centuries.

The long-standing power of the Danish Lutheran church is not the only factor shaping the form of Danish burial grounds. In 1772, King Christian VII invited the Moravian sect to Denmark where they founded Christiansfeld, a planned settlement representing the Moravians' understanding of the Protestant urban ideal (and now a UNESCO World Heritage Site); the town's burial ground influenced subsequent churchyard policy throughout Denmark. Thus a particular historical event – the invitation to the Moravians which could just as easily not have happened – has shaped the form of Danish graveyards to this day (Kjaersgaard, 2017, Ch. 4).

In Taiwan, the first hospice home care programme was established 'to facilitate dying at home as the majority of Taiwanese terminally ill cancer patients prefer the strong cultural practice of "the fallen leaves can return to their roots"', connected to the Confucian doctrine of filial duty'.[3] But in Hong Kong where notions of filial duty are equally strong, very few people die at home. Why? In Hong Kong, doctors do not go to the home to inspect the body and determine cause of death; so the body is transferred to hospital where, if the medical staff have not previously treated the patient, there will have to be a post-mortem, which families do not favour. Better therefore that the dying, not the dead, person go to hospital and avoid any need for a post-mortem. In Singapore, by contrast, doctors go to the home to issue death certificates for a home death, so more people die at home. This shows how a local practice about one thing (certifying death) can have major consequences for another (where people spend their dying hours).[4]

Another example concerns the introduction of hospice and palliative care to Japan and Singapore, two highly urban, ultra-modern East-Asian nations. The introduction in Japan was slow because hospice advocates – following Anglophone practice – insisted on open disclosure, which was not part of Japanese culture. In Singapore, by contrast, hospice advocates recognized that some patients and some families want to know if the disease is terminal, and some do not.[5]

Each of the UK's four constituent countries (England, Wales, Scotland, Northern Ireland) have similar end-of-life care policies, but there are subtle differences, for example between England and Scotland. Though both English and Scottish policies – unlike America's Medicare – consider clinical need more important than estimated imminence of death, the English policy identifies a dying phase in which end-of-life care is appropriate, while the Scottish envisages the possibility of palliative care alongside curative treatment. This has implications for when and how in each country professionals might initiate conversations about end-of-life planning (Teggi, 2018). Palliative care professionals in the two countries are similar in their understanding of palliative care, yet this has not translated into identical policy.

CONCLUSION

Once a mythology, a law, an institutional practice, or a policy has been brought into existence, the path is set for future generations, at the end as in the rest of life. This chapter has explored this 'path dependency', giving examples of national mythology, law, institutions, and policy and how they have shaped citizens' experience of the end of life. Of course, policies, laws, and institutional practices are never static, national mythologies can be undermined, and some policies (such as the Northern Territories' short flirtation with assisted suicide) get reversed. Also, the less bureaucratically efficient a country, the less official policies and practices affect individual life. In both the Soviet Union and in post-Soviet society, people find their own ways of getting by in the face of official systems that are often not fit for purpose (Mokhov and Sokolova, in press).

FURTHER READING

- Abel, E.K. (1986) 'The hospice movement: institutionalizing innovation', *International Journal of Health Services*, 16: 71–85.

- Davies, C. (1991) 'How people argue about abortion and capital punishment', in P. Badham (ed.), *Ethics on the Frontier of Human Existence*. New York: Paragon, pp. 103–37.

- Hawkins, A.H. (1990) 'Constructing death: three pathographies about dying', *Omega*, 22: 301–17.

- Parsons, T. and Lidz, V. (1963) 'Death in American society', in E. Shneidman (ed.), *Essays in Self-Destruction*. New York: Science House, pp. 133–70.

- Zaman, S., Whitelaw, A, Richards, N., Inbadas, H. and Clark, D. (2018) 'A moment for compassion: emerging rhetorics in end-of-life care', *Medical Humanities*, 44: 140–3.

Questions to discuss

- What ideologies, if any, in your country shape attitudes to old age, dying, and death?

- What politics, institutions, or state actions shape how people in your country die?

- In your country, how does the funding of health care or other organizations affect care/practice at the end of life?

- How is citizenship in your country expressed today through ungrieved deaths?

Notes

1. This is not true of animist societies. An unusual example of a highly modern society that still venerates the natural world is Japan, where rites are offered not only for deceased non-human creatures but also for discarded inanimate objects (Kretchmer, 2000).

2. NHPCO Facts and Figures 2018 www.nhpco.org/sites/default/files/public/Statistics_
    Research/2017_Facts_Figures.pdf (accessed 18/6/19).

3. International Palliative Care Family Carer Research Collaboration (IPCFRC)
    Newsletter, September 2016, p.1.

4. Information from Cynthia Goh, 2015.

5. Information from Cynthia Goh, 2015.

PART V

GLOBALIZATION

Many features of the modern world pay little respect to national or cultural boundaries – infections, global warming, plastics in the ocean, and nuclear fallout, to name but a few. Unless such life-and-death issues can be controlled, all humans may face a common extinction of their species. Controlling them requires both a global perspective and co-operation between nation states. Environmental concerns are an important but not the only reason to lead some to argue that global processes are eroding the relatively short-lived dominance of the nation state. Multinational companies set up shop wherever labour is cheapest; containerization makes sea transport around the globe unprecedentedly cheap and efficient; communication and information technology enable ideas, news, and music to be disseminated globally in an instant; high birth rates and lack of employment in the global South drive labour migration to the global North where, despite automation, there are labour shortages; cheap air fares enable economic migrants to travel home for weddings and funerals, and have turned tourism from a day trip to the local seaside into a fortnight on another continent. In other words, goods, services, people, ideas, germs, and pollution flow around the world as never before (Ritzer and Dean, 2015).

That said, the newness of globalization can be overstated. For at least three millennia empires have brought races and cultures together, and religions have spread ideas and practices across and between continents; overland and maritime 'silk roads' have linked the economies of East Asia and Europe for over two millennia (Frankopan, 2015); slaves have been traded across continents for centuries; and the biggest single leap toward the instantaneous global transmission of information was the invention in 1844 of the telegraph. What is new is the scale and rapidity of globalization, together with its challenge to the nation state that many had taken for granted as the modern world's core political unit.

Part V looks at how all this impacts death, dying, and bereavement.

14

GLOBAL FLOWS

This chapter looks at global flows of death-related goods and services, of people, information, and practices. Of particular interest are the directions of flow, and to what extent modern western deathways are becoming globalized or getting undermined by globalization.

GOODS AND SERVICES

Funerals

Recently I phoned an acquaintance who is a funeral director in my country, England, assuming him to be in his office, only to hear him reply from Ghana in West Africa where he has set up a funeral home. The Internet has made customized Ghanaian coffins world famous, but he told me there is also a demand for prestigious imported caskets. Chinese manufacturers are now producing American-style caskets and so can undercut American manufacturers, one of which has therefore now outsourced its manufacturing base to Mexico; this company had asked my friend to help market their Mexican-made American caskets in Ghana. So, an American company is using an Englishman to help them compete with the Chinese in Africa – one product, four continents.

Is this the shape of things to come, even in an industry as traditionally conservative as the funeral industry? Not necessarily. In 1993 Service Corporation International (SCI), North America's largest provider of funeral and cemetery services, 'acquired major death care companies in Australia, the United Kingdom and France, plus smaller holdings in other European countries and South America. At the end of 1999, the Company's global network numbered more than 4,500 funeral service locations, cemeteries and crematories in 20 countries.'[1] Yet the following decade, SCI divested all its overseas holdings; its website cites various economic reasons – there may also have been cultural sensitivities.

Health care

The health sector is more globalized than the funeral industry, with health care companies winning contracts across multiple countries and pharmaceuticals marketed globally. End-of-life care, however, seems something of an exception. There has been some success in transferring the British/American *idea* of palliative care to many other countries around the world, not least through cross-national medical internships, but I am not aware of a global *market* in palliative care services. This may be because it is comparatively low-tech and therefore relatively unprofitable; and end-of-life care is clearly shaped by what is culturally acceptable (Zaman et al., 2017b).

Many countries continue to limit morphine in end-of-life care, to the frustration of western-trained experts in palliative medicine who rely on morphine for pain control. High-income countries comprise only 17 per cent of the world's population but consume 92 per cent of medical morphine production; the remaining 83 per cent of the world's population accounts for only 8 per cent of total morphine consumption. The considerable increase in medical morphine consumption in the 2000s is almost entirely due to increased use in North America, Western and Central Europe, and Oceania. Reported impediments to morphine use are issues in sourcing, onerous regulations, fear of addiction, restricted financial resources, lack of awareness by professionals, and lack of training (Berterame et al., 2016). There is also fear that prescription opioids may be diverted into illicit uses, though this seems to be a significant problem only in high use countries like the USA. Thus the one area of palliative care – namely pharmaceuticals – that one might expect to be driven by global market forces is severely limited by culture and by organizational issues.

Organs

Organs, whether obtained from living or deceased donors, are another matter. Even if freely donated by the deceased and/or their survivors, they then enter an increasingly global market. McManus (2013) argues that medicine no longer sees death as a failure but as a managed process for procuring organs through a global market:

> Death is understood as a condition to be managed in multiple and potentially lucrative ways rather than an irreversible biological process … Raw materials flow consistently from poorer countries to highly technologized, Western nations … contain[ing] a proportionately higher percentage of wealthy older people with degenerative medical conditions. (p. 56)

With organs 'becoming more valuable than the people from whom they are harvested' (p. 59), McManus concludes that there is 'a fresh paradigm of death for advanced modernity – one driven by a commodification and commercialization of death rather than a denial of it' (p. 61). She does not say what percentage of deaths are affected by this new paradigm, though it seems likely the deaths of poor young people with 'healthy' organs are the most likely candidates. That said, body parts from 95-year-old journalist Alastair Cooke who died in 2004 were extracted without permission by rogue morticians in Brooklyn and sold for transplant. Criminal markets in body parts are centuries old (Richardson, 1989); what is new is these markets' global spread.

Whole bodies and body parts are also used in medical education and for display in museums and exhibitions. Here there are two opposing trends. On the one hand, the nineteenth-century practice of collectors from colonial powers taking bodies and body parts from indigenous people for display in western museums has been challenged, both by indigenous peoples themselves (Fforde, 2004) and by western museum professionals (Jenkins, 2010), resulting in the repatriation of many such parts. On the other hand, German anatomist Gunther von Hagens' development from the 1980s of the process of plastination has spawned a number of exhibitions that display plastinated bodies whose supply chains are global. Von Hagens' Body Worlds organization, for example, is based in Germany but uses donated bodies from around the world.[2] He set up a factory in Dalian, China, where the highly-skilled process of plastination could be performed by skilled Chinese doctors who earn more than they would by practising medicine; Dalian now hosts factories producing plastinates for several organizations that exhibit globally. There has been controversy whether all plastinated bodies have been donated or whether some have come from executed Chinese prisoners; it can be difficult to ascertain whether such allegations are based on fact or on popular mistrust of organizations that use dead bodies for profit.

In sum, with the possible exception of indigenous remains of anthropological interest, bodies and body parts circulate the globe as never before. Even donated bodies quickly become commodified in global markets, whether these be legal or illegal, ethical or unethical.

Disaster response

A disaster is often quite local in its direct effects and the national government is usually expected to provide resources to assist immediate rescue of survivors, recovery of bodies, and long-term reconstruction; after Hurricane Katrina's 2005 devastation of New Orleans, the federal US government in Washington was criticized for its lack of response. But McManus (2013: Ch. 7) observes that the immediate response to major disasters is almost always also global, or at least multinational, even when the afflicted belong to a rich nation. Naomi Klein (2008) goes further in her 'disaster capitalism' thesis (see Chapter 7), arguing that multinational corporations are quick to seize the investment opportunities provided by disaster's (or war's) destruction of infrastructure; the result is often not only physical destruction, but a reconstruction that destroys traditional cultures, communities, and economies. Beachfront cafés destroyed by the 2004 Boxing Day tsunami were replaced by hotels owned by multinational corporations, the cafés' self-employed owners and their families (who may have lost not only their livelihood but also loved ones) forced to become employees of the new hotels. Both bereaved survivors and national governments struggling to cope are ripe for exploitation by a 'saviour' bearing know-how and investment. All this then shows up positively in indicators of 'development'.

Rebecca Solnit (2009), however, is as optimistic as Klein is pessimistic. In her book *A Paradise Built in Hell: The extraordinary communities that arise in disaster*, Solnit shows how disaster survivors may rise to the occasion with a joy that reveals an ordinarily unmet yearning for community, purposefulness, and meaningful work that disaster often provides. For her, this embodies a new vision of what society could become – less authoritarian and fearful, more collaborative and local. Anne Allison (2013) argues that the 2011 Fukushima nuclear disaster reinvigorated a Japan that, following the 1990s erosion of the 'salaryman' economic order, had lost a sense of direction. Because of Fukushima, many protested against nuclear power, and within a year or so all Japan's nuclear power stations shut down; the country reduced its power consumption by 15 per cent. Many, including hitherto isolated and disillusioned young people, went to the affected area to volunteer; working together, they felt alive. People talked of hope.

If Klein is right, disaster creates a vacuum into which global capitalism can expand, further commodifying both life and death. If Solnit is right, it can enable de-commodification and a revival of community. Or perhaps the picture is more mixed (Gill, Steger and Slater, 2013).

To conclude this section, there clearly are global markets in goods (e.g. drugs) and to a lesser extent services for the dying, and in goods (such as caskets) for the dead and in body parts extracted from the dead; and global economic actors are quick to muscle in on local disasters, though not always with total success. Several of these markets are controversial, some downright illegal. But we should not overstate globalization; many economic markets relating to death and dying remain primarily national and even local; and culture profoundly shapes and limits the practices – and hence the goods and services – that are acceptable at the end of life, as we shall see in this chapter's later discussion of the flow of ideas. Colonial assumptions of western superiority continue to drive the global dissemination of palliative care, while post-colonial politics have reversed the Victorian global trade in indigenous bodies for display in museums.

PEOPLE

Migration

Migration is not new – it is inherent in empire, urbanization and industrialization. Ancient Rome's one million population attracted labour, both free and slave, from much of Europe and North Africa. Industrialization transforms rural workers into industrial workers, which usually means they have to move, and increasingly they move internationally. The 'New World' of nineteenth- and twentieth-century North America and Australia needed to import labour from the old world of Europe and then, increasingly, from Asia. In the twenty-first century, labour mobility is truly global with almost every country exporting or importing labour in considerable quantities. China's labour supply, however, is relatively self-contained; its population is so large that it can fuel its remarkable economic expansion with domestic labour, and there are enough new jobs that Chinese do not need to emigrate; migration within China from country to city is massive, deeply affecting family relationships and care of the elderly and dying.

If most migrants from poorer countries move to find work, many migrants from richer countries do so when they retire from work, usually to a place that is cheaper and has a better climate – whether in their own country or elsewhere. If they migrate abroad as a couple, sooner or later one partner is very likely to become widowed and must decide whether to continue in the adopted country or return home (King, Warnes and Williams, 2000). With adult children back in the home country, the survivor may feel very alone and unprepared for frailty in the adopted country; dementia may erode newly (and perhaps poorly) acquired language skills, reducing the ability to cope in the adopted country. Yet returning to the home country is also fraught with problems, such as no longer being able to afford a nice home, feeling a stranger there and not really feeling at home anywhere.

Some of those who migrate in order to work may eventually go home on retirement. A Greek cab driver in his early sixties in Toronto told me how he had moved to Canada over thirty years earlier and had raised a family there, all of whom were now settled in Canada – a family and a life of which he was proud. And the culmination of this North American success story? To retire back to Greece where he would tend his orange grove – sunnier, cheaper and, in his eyes, home. There are also migrants who go home not to retire, but to die – of which more anon.

Privileged readers of this book, whether students used to global backpacking or university teachers accustomed to attending international conferences, can easily over-estimate the fluidity of the global movement of people and under-estimate the reality of borders. Less privileged members of rich countries, resentful of immigrant labour and worried about a perceived 'flood of immigrants', also over-estimate the ease with which borders may be crossed. People from poorer countries attempting to migrate to the richer West are all too aware of borders and the difficulties and dangers of crossing them (Gunaratnam, 2013).

How migrants care

One form of labour that technology struggles to automate is personal service, especially caring for other people's bodies, whether in yuppie coffee shops or in elder care. This is a growth area for many post-industrial nations that have automated manufacturing or outsourced it to East Asia. These nations are rapidly ageing, with fewer young people to look after many more old people, so there is demand for paid labour to care for those old people who are frail and/or dying. My own mother, living on her own at home after a fall at the age of 90, depended in her last months on a care agency that supplied a rotating team of three live-in carers, two of whom came from Zimbabwe. They remitted what they earned as carers in the UK back to Zimbabwe to pay boarding school fees for their own children who could therefore be safely looked after in an increasingly precarious Zimbabwe and have some chance of bettering themselves. The carers returned home once a year to see their families. This is a classic chain of commodified care in which people are paid to care for other people's children and for other people's parents, framing the beginning and the end of life.[3]

In her book *Death and the Migrant* (2013), Yasmin Gunaratnam outlines the pluses and minuses of these global care chains from which she considers there to be no escape. It has been estimated that there are more Malawian doctors in Manchester than in the whole of Malawi, a drain of professional expertise leading to excess deaths in Malawi. For over forty years, a quarter to one-third of NHS doctors have qualified outside the UK, and the NHS employs more workers from other countries than any other organization in Europe. When Britons require end-of-life care, it is provided 'in some part by migrant and minoritized workers. These caregivers deliver our children, tend to our parents and grandparents, cook our food, clean our hospitals and bear witness to our naked emotional distress' (p. 14).

If migrants often provide paid care to members of the host country, they also want or need to care for their own family members when they near the end of life. Vanessa Bravo (2017) talked to 12 undocumented migrants from Latin America who live in the USA but who have had to cope with dying and death in their family of origin back home. They cannot go home, as they may not then be able to get back into the USA where they have husband and children; back in Latin America, they could not earn enough to support either their American family or the dying parent back home. (Some legal migrants to the USA who have been granted political asylum face a similar situation; they cannot go home to care for a dying parent as they would be arrested.) To create the next best thing to 'being there', these migrants are avid users of digital media; Facebook, WhatsApp and – especially when the person is dying – Skype create a kind of virtual presence. Yet this is not like actually being there, being able to touch and hold, still less to help feed and toilet. So digital media are a godsend, yet one that induces sadness and guilt.

Dying in the right place

When the dying person is himself or herself a migrant, he or she may want to go home to die or to be buried. Many brought up in the global South have a strong sense of belonging – to family, to land, to village, to country – that trumps the autonomy that is so important to many brought up in the global North. Going home to die, or being buried back home, may therefore be a cherished dream. Transporting a terminally ill person thousands of miles by plane (often two or three planes, which may not conveniently connect), let alone getting to and from the airport, is not straightforward, especially if against medical advice. Airfares for the dead are up to ten times those for the living, however sick, which adds to the pressure to get the person back home before they die. Some families have chosen to hide this kind of end-of-life care plan from even the most flexible hospice and themselves made all the arrangements to get the person home before they die (Gunaratnam, 2013).

Dying in the right place can also be an issue when a migrant falls mortally ill or dies while visiting the family of origin. In this circumstance, not all family members may agree on what counts as 'home'. Ethnographer Yvon van der Pijl (2016) was living with a family in Suriname, South America, when Lando, a male member of the extended family who had emigrated to Toronto several decades ago and had just arrived for a long-awaited visit, dropped dead of a heart attack. Van der Pijl's reading of the anthropological literature informs her of a near-universal notion of the good death – after a long and successful life, without pain or violence, at home, surrounded by family with the opportunity to say farewell, and buried in one's own land. But in Lando's case, where was home? Suriname where he grew up, where 'the family home' was, and where he unexpectedly died? Or Toronto, where he had lived most of his adult life and where he and his new wife, now widow, had set up their marital home? Some family members construed Lando's sudden death to be without pain or violence and taking place 'at home', and therefore a good death. Others, not least his widow in Toronto, saw it as bad and tragic, far from home. Van der Pijl observed 'multiple, crisscrossing scripts and tellings' (p. 162). But in every script, home and place, however construed, were important.

Burying in the right place

Lando's death raises the question of where the migrant should be buried. Hunter (2016) interviewed 67 Christians of Middle-Eastern origin currently living in

Britain, Denmark, and Sweden about their preferred places of burial. He found that migrants face various considerations – practical, family, territorial, and sacred – which question the simple hypothesis that the longer a migrant has lived in the new country the more likely he or she is to be buried there. Certainly some migrants become the 'new first ancestor', the first in the family to be buried in the new land, providing a magnet for later generations to be buried nearby. For others Hunter spoke to, what encouraged burial in the country of residence was 'preponderant presence' – the overall number of their ethnic group, living and dead, residing nearby. For yet others, the cost and complexity of transporting the body home might be offset by a cheaper and less bureaucratic funeral.

Serbian economic emigrants generally expect to return home, so do not plan to die in, for example, France or the USA, but may well do so. As the funeral oration for an American Serb eloquently stated, his soul 'goes to the Serbian heaven, while his body lies in this hospitable American land' (Pavicevic, 2009: 239). Elsewhere, I have written of the symbolism for Americans, especially for first- and second-generation Americans, of burial in 'American soil', in 'the land of the free', 'the land of opportunity' (Walter, 1993a). They have truly made it, even if their soul goes to the Serbian, Italian, or Vietnamese heaven. Maurice Bloch's (1971) study of death rites in Madagascar showed how Malagasy people live in two worlds – an everyday world of global capitalism, and the symbolic world of the ancestors. We may extend this notion beyond Bloch's original context, for migrants also typically live in two worlds – the place to which they have moved, which provides practical economic and educational opportunities, and the place from which they have moved, which symbolizes family and roots, as my Greek Canadian cab driver expressed to me so eloquently.

For migrant families who accept cremation as a possibility, cremation followed by division of the ashes provides a solution where hearts are attached to more than one place, or where survivors live on different continents and each wants a special place for the deceased. Grandma's ashes may be divided into three, with one-third buried in the family grave in Scotland, one-third scattered in the ocean by a daughter living in Perth, Australia, and one-third kept on the mantelpiece 3,000 miles further east in Auckland, New Zealand, by a grandson who has yet to decide what to do with them. In countries where disposal of ashes is more regulated than in the UK, there may be restrictions; in Norway, for example, ashes are not permitted to be divided.

Limits to mobility

Migrants are typically young adults in vigorous health, yet like all humans are mortal. They may survive their migrant journey and succeed in their hope of a new life of personal and economic security for themselves and their children, but sooner or later the skills they have developed in order to live in two worlds will be challenged by their own, or others', frailty, dying, and death. The body that once could easily take a cheap flight home to see the family may eventually to be in no fit state to undertake any journey, let alone across continents. Those wanting to care for, or say goodbye to, a suddenly deteriorating parent on another continent may be impeded by borders, visa irregularities, money, the sheer complexity and exhaustion of the journey, or other caring responsibilities, not to mention several false alarms before the parent finally dies. So yes, migration is part of an increasingly globalized economy, but borders and barriers – economic, political, administrative, bodily – limit migrants' subsequent mobility, especially at the end of life (Gunaratnam, 2013; Hunter and Ammann, 2016).

As well as such practicalities and complex family dynamics, there can be questions of both individual and collective identity. The mode of dying, the kind of funeral, the place of burial, all demonstrate the person's identity as coming from their original country, their residence in and membership of the new country, or a fusion of the two (Reimers, 1999). And then when the last of the immigrant generation dies, their children – growing up in the new country – cannot rely, like their parents, on first-hand knowledge of their culture of origin; inevitably, they have different personal agendas and different sources of cultural knowledge with which to construct their identity.

Dangerous journeys

So far, I have considered migration in relation to paid employment – either to find employment, or to retire from employment. Refugees, however, flee for political reasons – to find sanctuary from persecution, to escape the violence of war and civil war. Their departure, journey, and arrival are all likely to be fraught, possibly costing a highly inflated sum, and also dangerous. Many are refugees seeking safety and asylum, but some economic migrants face similar risks. At the time of writing, Europeans are all too aware of media reports of economic migrants from Africa and refugees from the Middle East drowning as they attempt to cross the Mediterranean, while Americans have some awareness of the risks faced by those trying to enter the country via the land border with Mexico. Death may therefore come not decades after a successful life as an immigrant to the new country, but in the very process of attempting to migrate. If bodies are never found, as may happen with trans-Mediterranean drownings, survivors are left indefinitely not knowing whether their relatives and friends are alive or not (Perl, 2016). When bodies are found, local people sometimes make extraordinary efforts to ensure decent burial (Stierl, 2016).

Perl and Strasser (2018: 507) argue that the risks faced by refugees from violence and persecution result from 'organised irresponsibility' in which foreign policy, including the waging of war, is engaged in with no plan for managing the ensuing chaos or providing for those fleeing from it. National and local authorities may provide refugee camps and transit camps for those who survive and pick up (some of) the bodies of those who do not survive, but this entails retrospective, not prospective, responsibility. The deaths are the predictable consequence of irresponsible national and international policies.

Tourism

In the eighteenth century, young English gentlemen and a few ladies embarked on the Grand Tour to Italy in order to complete their education, but the birth of modern tourism is usually dated from 1841 when Thomas Cook organized a one-day rail excursion at a shilling a head from Leicester to Loughborough, a distance of just 11 miles. By the twenty-first century, millions fly from one country to another for short city breaks, or for week or fortnight holidays, seeking sun and exotic places; and year-long global backpacking trips have become the modern equivalent of the Grand Tour. Tourism is truly global.

But what has all this travel and tourism to do with death? Well, a clue is provided by the first-ever conversion of a plane to take passengers, which was also the first-ever tourist flight. In 1919, armchairs were placed in a converted bomber and flights were advertised from Paris to view from the air the battle-fields of the recently ended Great War. Like sound recording (Chapter 4), modern tourism began with a desire to connect with the dead, or at least to view where people had fought and died and were buried. And so it continues. One of the world's most famous tourist sites, India's Taj Mahal, is a mausoleum, built to house the tomb of a Mughal emperor's favourite wife. Some 'death tourism', therefore, far from being macabre or voyeuristic, is about experiencing sheer beauty – not to mention providing a photo-op to share immediately on social media with friends and family on other continents.

Memorial tourism

Amongst all the sun-seeking and consumption of 'heritage', an identifiable part of today's global tourism concerns death and memory of the dead, often broadly termed 'dark tourism' within British academic tourism studies (Lennon and Foley, 2000) and 'memorial tourism' in the Francophone and Hispanic tourist industries (Vázquez, 2018). Examples include war grave pilgrimages and battlefield tourism, more often on the ground than from the air, whether that be Gettysburg, the Normandy beaches or the Viet Cong's tunnel network; memorials to genocide, such as Auschwitz and Holocaust museums; places of death and disaster, such as Hiroshima and Ground Zero; war memorials, such as Washington, D.C.'s Vietnam Veterans Memorial; and the many archaeological sites that display human remains and items buried with the dead (which comprise perhaps a half of all archaeo-logical artefacts). Sometimes visiting such sites is the prime purpose of travel, as in pilgrimages to war graves overseas. More often, the visit is an item within a holiday whose main purpose is not death-oriented – the backpacking trip that includes the Taj Mahal, the city break to New York that takes in Ground Zero, the stroll in Amsterdam that chances by the Anne Frank house, the trek in the French Alps that passes a memorial to resistance fighters. The light-hearted tourist unexpectedly finds himself or herself reflecting on life and death, on what it means to be Jewish or Armenian or African, on the human condition (Walter, 1993b).

Gillis (2000) argues that from the nineteenth century to around 1970 such commemorative sites were primarily national, but have subsequently become increasingly global on the one hand, and local on the other. Events and places with international meaning, such as Hiroshima, Chernobyl, Auschwitz, and Nanjing capture the world's attention even when the nations responsible may wish to forget them. What Williams (2007) calls 'memorial museums', 'reconstruct a version of the past that makes sense in a world where national boundaries are superseded by transnational institutions, corporations and personal identities as people migrate and communicate across borders as never before' (McManus, 2013: 171). At the same time, people now prefer to devote more time to local, ethnic, and family memory; local history, family genealogy, local folklore, ethnic traditions, are all booming (Gillis, 2000: 14).

The trends Gillis and McManus identify are certainly evident, but I suggest that the nation remains an essential ingredient in memorial museums and memorial tourism. Even if a significant proportion (sometimes a majority) of visitors to major memorial sites are international (e.g. Mantei, 2012), the sites themselves are often erected and maintained by national governments or by nationally organized voluntary organizations such as veterans associations. Major memorials and memorial museums are typically framed within a national perspective. Thus the Vietnam Veterans Memorial, though evoking in some visitors the tragedy of all war, lists only deceased American service personnel – not Vietnamese or Australian. Hiroshima, though evoking the universal horror of nuclear devastation, depicts a unique tragedy that changed the course not just of Hiroshima but of Japan. Holocaust museums, implicitly or explicitly, provide a rationale for the founding of the state of Israel. An ongoing multinational research project on museums to the First and Second World Wars in France, Slovenia, Germany, and Poland is discovering very different frames in which the same war is depicted in different countries. These frames reflect different experiences of conflict, differently contested national boundaries, different ethnic population mixes within countries then and now, specific experiences of victory, defeat, and occupation, not to mention different national traditions of museum display.[4]

When I recently put 'memorial museum' into Google's search engine, the first site to come up was *Culture Trip*, a website of ideas for global travellers and tourists. Its list of 'The World's Ten Most Important Memorial Museums' is as follows:

- Japan: Hiroshima Peace Memorial Museum

- Chile: Museum of Memory and Human Rights

- Poland: Auschwitz-Birkenau

- Cambodia: Tuol Sleng Genocide Museum

- Armenia: The Armenian Genocide Museum

- Israel: Yad Vashem

- China: Nanjing Massacre Memorial Museum

- South Africa: Apartheid Museum

- USA: September 11 Memorial Museum

- Senegal: La Maison des Esclaves (The House of Slaves)

Starting each entry by identifying the country in which the museum is located not only helps would-be travellers but also suggests the intensely national character of each atrocity – perpetrated either against the nation and its people (Israel, China, USA, Senegal) or by the nation's one-time government (Cambodia, Chile, South Africa). Tourists from some countries may struggle to gain a visa to visit the relevant destination, so national boundaries are still significant. At the same time, these top ten memorial museums are advertised on a website for global tourists. Each museum's power to evoke reflection and emotion in visitors derives from its unique response to global interest in a nationally driven atrocity or war and what this says about humanity and inhumanity, who may be killed, and who may be grieved (Butler, 2004).

INFORMATION

Traders and empire builders have for millennia been transferring ideas and practices from one part of the globe to another, with those receiving them adapting the ideas and practices to their own needs and circumstances. In recent centuries, cheaper and faster travel, together with the development of printing and literacy, accelerated this process, and now mass media and social media have created a quantum leap in both the amount of information transfer and the speed of transfer.

In the following sections, I look at some global flows of information and practices in relation to death and dying, along with barriers to flow. I also ask whether these flows are leading to an increasingly homogenous 'modern way of death', or to what extent ideas and practices become so modified by the receiving society that they are fundamentally changed. Ideas and practices flow around the world, but get understood in new ways, read in different imagined worlds, so get indigenized differently (Appadurai, 1990). I also examine the direction of flow. Has it all been a matter of 'less developed' societies adopting 'modern' (i.e. western) practices such as medicalized dying? Or has there also been reverse transfer, with modern societies learning from indigenous practices, ex-colonial nations learning from those they once colonized? In other words, are the flows entirely from West to East, from North to South?

I start with flows of ideas and information.

Mass media

Sumiala (2013) examined coverage by Finnish media of that country's nine biggest disasters since the 1950s and found that, as in other western countries, recent media coverage of disaster has become 'more emotional, intimate and sentimental' (p. 110). Grieving Finns are portrayed like everyone else, or at least like other westerners, perhaps reflecting cross-national cultural trends in public mourning, perhaps reflecting trends in a global or semi-global media industry. At the same time, media coverage of these disasters, as in other countries, portrayed the nation playing a key role as 'a cohesive centre, bringing and holding people together with the aid of official institutions such as the church, the police and the political establishment' (p. 12). So Finnish media, in behaving like media in any western country, portray national solidarity and national leadership – not just a globally approved emotional expressiveness – as key to recovery after disaster. This is consistent with Meyer et al.'s thesis (1997) that there is now a world culture in which nations remain the key players but in which most, if not all, nations behave pretty much the same way.

Social media

That said, there are differences in the use of mass media and social media between countries. In a series of research studies, digital anthropologist Daniel Miller and his colleagues have shown that digital and social media are used differently by people from different countries (Miller et al., 2016). As we have already seen, Miller (2017) identifies a specifically English way in which contemporary rural English people use a range of communication media when they are terminally ill. Communication technologies afford all kind of possibilities, but which possibilities are taken up and how they are combined is very much up to the individual user with particular needs, belonging to a particular age and peer group within a particular culture.

Death studies

Another example is the cross-disciplinary academic field of death studies. Starting in the USA in the late 1950s (Feifel, 1959), and re-incarnated in the UK in the 1990s, it is now to be found in several countries around the world. Death studies conferences often attract researchers and practitioners from 20 or more countries and several continents. Is there a process of dissemination over time? Will India, Africa, and the Arab world – currently displaying little or no interest in the field – catch up in time? It is not that simple. Those countries and groups of countries where scholars have shown interest have not done so in the same way. In the USA, the field has been dominated by psychologists who combine clinical practice with academic research, often using standardized questionnaires asking about individuals' attitudes and feelings, not least in relation to death anxiety. In the UK by contrast, the field is dominated by social scientists and historians using ethnographic, historical, and archaeological methods to research what people actually do or have done. Danish, Swedish, Finnish, and Dutch scholars, coming from small language groups, are fluent in English, read British research publications and mix with British scholars at national as well as international English-language conferences. Scholars whose native tongue is French, Spanish, or Italian are less in evidence in Anglophone conferences and journals.

In France, the field has long been dominated by historians; relatively few French studies have been translated into English (Philippe Ariès being the major exception), and little English-language research has been translated into French. Thus death studies in the Francophone and Anglophone worlds proceed in some isolation from each other, with the two language groups reading little of each other's literature and going to different conferences – though Romanian and Québécois academics and students are often bilingual in French and English, and some Hispanic and Italian death studies scholars are familiar with English as well as French literature. Possibly the one discipline which brings these traditions together is anthropology where American, British, and French anthropologists studying death practices and rites around the world are more aware of each other's work. Nascent interest in death studies elsewhere in the world is likely to follow colonial histories and contemporary economic links, with French-speaking areas following French intellectual traditions, Australia and New Zealand following British traditions, and the Far East sending its bright students to the USA to gain their doctorates.

So yes, modern media and cheap travel enable widespread and fast transfer of ideas in the academy as elsewhere, but there are barriers as well as flows, and ideas can flow along different channels. This results in – often language-based – clusters of scholars thinking and researching in ways that differ from other clusters. I now move on to practices and their direction of flow.

PRACTICES
From West to East
Medicine and diet

The most obvious flow of death-related practices from West to East, North to South, concerns life-saving and life-threatening practices. In 1900, the main killers in Western Europe and North America were infectious diseases such as pneumonia, tuberculosis, and diarrhoeal disease. Since then, western scientific and medical knowledge has been exported around the world, enabling country after country effectively to fight the age-old battle against infectious disease. Sewerage systems, clean water, scientific knowledge such as germ theory and environmental risk assessment, health and safety procedures, western medicine and drugs have saved and extended billions of lives as the global South becomes more and more influenced by the global North.

Today's main killers – heart disease, cancer, and chronic lung disease – derive substantially from modern lifestyles, and these too have been exported from the West, increasing disease and reducing life-expectancy in many countries. The traditional fish- and plant-based Japanese diet is probably the chief cause of Japan's famous longevity, but heart disease and various cancers have increased among those many Japanese who in recent decades have westernized their diets. The shift from consuming locally caught fish to poor quality meat high in saturated fats imported from New Zealand and the USA has dramatically increased obesity and premature death in Pacific islands such as Tonga. A very thorough review of the integration of immigrants to the USA found that first-generation immigrants, both now and in past decades and from all parts of the world, have better health and longer life-expectancy than native-born Americans, but within a generation or two health and life-expectancy worsen to match the native-born population (National Academies, 2015).

In terms of health and longevity, the world is becoming more and more like the West – for better and for worse.

Hospice and palliative care

The West has profoundly influenced the world by transforming dying from a human event at home into a medical event in hospital (Chapter 2). But western innovators have also challenged this transformation. In the 1950s, English physician Cicely Saunders developed the idea of humane, de-institutionalized palliative care of the whole person and shortly after built the first hospice, St Christopher's, in London. Her lifelong mission was to spread the hospice idea across the globe, and in this she was remarkably successful. Few people have a 50-year life-plan to change the world, still fewer achieve it. The spread of Saunders' concept of hospice, however, was uneven. Her strategy focused on foreign doctors serving internships at St Christopher's and taking their newly acquired skills back home. This meant that countries where health care professionals were not fluent in English were slow to adopt hospice, if at all. Other factors such as cultural expectations (Chapter 8), legal restrictions on morphine availability (see above), and funding regimes (Chapter 13) have limited or modified hospice practices in various countries.

The other female doctor who almost single-handedly changed modern people's attitudes to dying and who, like Saunders, placed care of the dying in a broader frame than the simply physical, was Swiss-American psychiatrist Elisabeth Kübler-Ross. She influenced people not through demonstrating an alternative organizational model of care (hospice) but through her books, notably *On Death and Dying* (1969) which has sold millions of copies and been translated into many languages. Whereas Saunders trained doctors from countries where English is taught, the many translations of Kübler-Ross's books were more widely influential among the many who cared to read.

Saunders, a deeply religious woman unafraid to read difficult works of theology and philosophy and who trained in social work and nursing before qualifying in medicine, had a truly holistic view of the human being; she therefore taught palliative care both as a philosophy and in very practical terms. By contrast, Kübler-Ross's specialty of psychiatry was reflected in her model of five emotional stages which portray dying and grieving as essentially psychological processes – simple to grasp, the model has profoundly influenced both professional care and lay attitudes around the world.

Largely through the initiative of these two exceptional women and their many disciples, hospice and palliative care have spread from the UK and USA to many countries around the world. Kübler-Ross and especially Saunders were like religious missionaries from colonial countries in their impassioned belief that their approach to humane end-of-life care was universally applicable, needing only minor adjustment as each new country implemented it. Zaman et al. (2017b), writing from a subaltern and post-colonial perspective, rightly challenge this belief, pointing to 'the plurality of past and present local problems and issues relating to end of life care, as well as the plural possibilities of how they might be overcome… Instead of homogenising end of life interventions, we seek to be open to multiple futures for the care of the dying' (p. 72).

A recent survey (Economist Intelligence Unit, 2015) ranks nations on a 'quality of death' index, with the UK leading the table – delighting British palliative care physicians yet perplexing others as the UK has experienced numerous high-profile end-of-life care scandals leading to widespread media and public concern about the quality of end-of-life care (Borgstrom and Walter, 2015). Zaman et al. (2017b) observe that the Economist Intelligence Unit's index values specialist and highly professionalized palliative care services over the quality of general medical and nursing care for the dying or empowering local communities to care. The index does not therefore measure quality of dying, but the resources a country has put into a very particular model of care which may not be appropriate in the global South.

In sum, western palliative care practices have spread around the world, benefitting millions. To maximize their benefit, however, the practices may need modification to such an extent that they become an entirely different species of care. And the West needs to be open to learning from the East.

From East to West

As yet, flows of death practices the other way, from East to West, have been modest.

Compassionate community

A potentially significant example of transfer from East to West, from global South to global North, is the grassroots volunteer-based palliative care movement pioneered on a mass scale in the Indian state of Kerala (Kumar, 2007) which is inspiring projects not only in poor countries such as Bangladesh (Zaman et al., 2017a), but also in affluent countries with highly developed health care systems such as the UK. However, as noted in the previous chapter, there are socio-political structural barriers limiting successful transfer to post-industrial societies – barriers such as a strong sense of privacy and individualism, highly professionalized health care systems, anxiety about being sued on health and safety grounds, and a general political context of mistrust (Zaman et al., 2018). In social democratic post-industrial countries such as Sweden, high levels of employment may reduce the pool of volunteers who, it may be feared in a society that has traditionally used taxation to fund paid care, will put paid carers out of work. Zaman et al. conclude (2018: 142) by wondering whether the global South, despite its many barriers to health care access, has more potential for compassion to flow freely among community members? And if so, how might 'reverse learning' occur in which the North, for once, learns from the South?

Buddhism

Buddhist approaches to dying have filtered into the West (e.g. Rinpoche, 1992). Despite immense variation in its practices, Buddhism at heart teaches that nothing is permanent and that suffering is at the core of existence. So dying and loss – rather than being an affront to western values of growth, happiness and prosperity– take one to the heart of reality. Various western individuals and groups have therefore looked to Buddhism both for an underlying philosophy of death and for specific practices in end-of-life care (e.g. Levine, 1988; Ostaseski, 1990).

Two studies of the transfer of Buddhist death practices to the USA reveal how they become Americanized. One group, Nāropā, has a profoundly Tibetan sense of grief, but sees continuing bonds between the living and the dead always to be positive, contrasting with many eastern cultures where the dead are potential trouble-makers who need appeasing (Goss and Klass, 2005). The other study, *Mourning the Unborn Dead: A Buddhist ritual comes to America* (Wilson, 2009), examines Mizuko kuyō, a ceremony for aborted foetuses performed by millions of Japanese mothers. (The statuettes of deceased foetuses that line the entrance to Japanese temples are highly visible to western tourists.) Wilson shows how over the past 40 years, Mizuko kuyō has gradually been adopted by North Americans not of Japanese descent, who have reconfigured the ritual's meaning and purpose. In Japan, Mizuko kuyō is performed to placate the potentially dangerous spirit of the angry foetus. In North America, it has become a way for the mother to mourn and receive solace for her loss. The Japanese concern with the foetus as a spiritual agent is replaced by American concern for the mother's psychological adjustment – consonant with Kübler-Ross's psychologization of grief. An ancient concern with the dead as a soul in transit, possibly causing trouble on the way, becomes a secular western and especially American concern with the psychological health of the living.

Cultural theft?

Eastern Buddhists and Kerala project members might prefer the East-to-West transfer to be easier than it is. However, not all whose forebears were colonized by the West approve of their traditions being appropriated by those whose forebears had been their colonial masters. Allegations of cultural theft have complicated the ready transfer of, for example, Māori tattooing and the Mexican *Dia de los Muertos* (Day of the Dead).

Though ice-preserved mummies with elaborate tattoos have been discovered in Siberia from 2,500 years ago and simple tattoos have been found on European remains from over 35,000 years ago, tattooing is generally acknowledged to have been brought to Europe a few centuries ago by sailors visiting the Pacific islands. The word 'tattoo' is derived from the Polynesian *tatau*. In New Zealand, the post–1980s Māori cultural revival has revived the practice of tattooing to inscribe graphically on a person's body their *whakapapa* (genealogy, ancestral identity). 'When you wear a *moko*, you are the face of your ancestors' (Te Awekotuku and Nikora, 2007: 180). Each tattoo is therefore a unique representation of the wearer's *whakapapa*. When Māori tattooists inscribe traditional designs on European bodies, or these designs are used by western tattoo artists, there can be controversy: is this a good way for indigenous tattooists to make a living, or a post-colonial appropriation that diminishes the design's *mana* (power)? This issue is relevant to death because *moko* represent the wearer's deceased ancestors.

Westerners also often use tattoos to commemorate a deceased loved one (Davidson, 2017), though these usually represent the wearer's personal feelings for, or memory of, the deceased and are rarely Māori designs.

Dia de los Muertos is a Mexican religious and family festival deriving from the Catholic All Souls' Day in which the family dead are remembered and prayed for. Reminding the living that life is short, the festival highlights the vanity of human endeavour and traditionally satirizes political leaders. When transformed into American pop culture as The Mexican Day of the Dead, however, it can raise similar issues as the appropriation of Māori tattoos (Cann, 2016). In England and the Netherlands, initiatives to create a more vibrant way to commemorate the dead and reflect on mortality have drawn on *Dia de los Muertos* in a non-commercial way.

Imagination

Whether and how ideas and practices flow around the globe depends in part on the receiver's imagination (Appadurai, 1990). Does the receiver believe modernity (if so, whose modernity?) to be worth emulating? Or does the receiver, disillusioned with western modernity, consider indigenous cultures and their practices to be purer and more healthy? Or does the receiver consider there to be multiple modernities, so each country is responsible for its own unique development, drawing ideas potentially from anywhere (Eisenstadt, 2000)? How does the receiver imagine modernity or indigeneity? My concepts of 'imagined modernity' and 'imagined indigeneity' draw on Benedict Anderson's (1991) concept of 'imagined communities' and Appadurai's (1990) 'imagined worlds'.

Imagined modernity

Here, the classic case is Meiji Japan's adoption of cremation, discussed in Chapter 11. Attempting to fast-track modernization in the 1870s, Japan looked to copy modern technologies and practices from Europe and the USA and, mistakenly, identified cremation as a typically modern and therefore widespread practice engaged in by Italy, Germany, England, and the USA. Actually, at that time these western countries were only talking about cremation. So Japan became the first modern nation to develop cremation on a large scale, because of how it had *imagined* modernity (Bernstein, 2000). This case illustrates the power of imagined modernity.

To drive reform, however, imagination need not be mistaken. After the collapse of communism in 1989, eastern European countries had their own ideas of what capitalist modernity looked like and pursued it vigorously. Singapore looks to both East and West for ideas to drive its own unique hyper-modernization, while New Zealand looks both to Britain and to North

America. I recall talking in 1987 to a New Zealand funeral director who was planning to develop a crematorium; aware of the very different cremation practices in the USA and the UK, he had to decide which to follow. Whether well or ill informed, imagining what counts as progress is crucial to how ideas and practices flow.

Imagined indigeneity

In the USA, Britain, and some other European countries, ideas of a 'natural' death and 'natural' burial have gained traction. Those embracing such ideas typically romanticize pre-industrial and non-western deathways, especially those that predate the world religions; 'the noble savage' and his (in today's imagination, more often *her*) ways are idealized (Walter, 1995; Hockey, 1996). How we humans did things before patriarchy, religion, industry, cities, and modern medicine divorced us from our supposed natural state can carry quite an appeal to those disillusioned with modern life and with modern ways of death and dying.

The basic idea here is that death is, or can be, a natural process. But as we saw in Chapter 2, the idea of death as a natural process is not traditional but modern. Among 47 traditional cultures reviewed by Simmons (1945), 17 regarded death as unnatural – the result of hexes, witchcraft, supernatural interventions, and so on – and 26 others only partially accepted the idea that death was a natural event. Mbiti (1970: 203–4) notes that Africans consider the commonest cause of death to be not natural processes but 'magic, sorcery, and witchcraft'. Nevertheless, the *idea* of natural death and burial as traditional and healthy continues to drive the natural death movement in various western societies. Imagination shapes and becomes reality, just as it did in Meiji Japan.

CONCLUSION

Flows of goods, services, and people are greatly facilitated by contemporary globalization, yet at the same time face barriers – migrants face literal barriers at national borders, multinational corporations face cultural barriers and consumer resistance in countries into which they seek to expand, ideas face language barriers. Flows of practices, ideas, and people are driven by imagination – of a better future elsewhere, of descendants who will care for my grave, of a practice as 'modern', 'natural', or 'healthy'. In the following final brief chapter, I seek to identify global trends in the experience and management of death and loss, and therefore what 'the future of death' may hold.

FURTHER READING

- Appadurai, A. (1990) 'Disjuncture and difference in the global cultural economy', in M. Featherstone (ed.), *Global Culture*. London: Sage, pp. 295–310.

- Bravo, V. (2017) 'Coping with dying and deaths at home: how undocumented migrants in the United States experience the process of transnational grieving', *Mortality*, 22: 33–44.

- Gunaratnam, Y. (2013) *Death and the Migrant: Bodies, borders and care*. London: Bloomsbury.

- Hunter, A. (2016) 'Staking a claim to land, faith and family: burial location preferences of Middle Eastern Christian migrants', *Journal of Intercultural Studies*, 37: 179–94.

- Lennon, J. and Foley, M. (2000) *Dark Tourism: The attraction of death and disaster*. London: Continuum.

- McManus, R. (2013) *Death in a Global Age*. Basingstoke: Palgrave Macmillan.

- Ritzer, G. and Dean, P. (2015) *Globalization: A basic text* (2nd edn). Oxford: Wiley-Blackwell.

Questions to discuss

- What issues do immigrant families in your country face in dying, funerals, and mourning?

- Where has your country looked for ideas about how best to manage death and loss? Where might it look?

- Do you feel indigenous peoples have a healthier approach to death, dying, and loss?

Notes

1. www.sci-corp.com/en-us/about-sci/our-business-history.page (accessed 18/6/19).

2. https://bodyworlds.com/about/faq/ (accessed 18/6/19).

3. There is also a new and as yet small reverse trend. Some families in Germany and Switzerland now arrange for a frail elderly parent to migrate hundreds or thousands of miles to Poland or Thailand where they spend the rest of their lives cared for by strangers at much reduced expense to their families (Schwiter, Brütsch and Pratt, in press).

4. www.unrest.eu/work-packages/wp-4/7/ (accessed 18/6/19).

15

DEATH'S FUTURES

Part I of this book identified how responses to death and dying change as countries modernize. At the same time, Parts II, III, and IV identify how and why these responses differ between nations, social classes, and ethnic groups within the modern world. This fits what we know about health care systems in general, namely that shared demographic challenges and copying lead to convergence between modern nations, while institutional path dependence creates separate lines of development (Beckfield, Olafsdottir and Sosnaud, 2013). This concluding chapter asks whether this mix of similarity and difference points toward an overall convergence over time in how different nations and cultures manage death, loss, and grief (Ritzer and Dean, 2015)? Or does each culture and nation create its own hybrid with modernity, otherwise known as 'glocalization' (Robertson, 1995)? Or do different modernities run on separate tracks, or to use another metaphor, cluster into a few groupings (Eisenstadt, 2000)? Any answer requires a survey of current trends and possible futures.

CURRENT TRENDS

The rise and rise of the individual

As societies become more affluent, people need each other – and perhaps God – less and less in order to survive and thrive. Private cars, washing machines, televisions, and tablets replace publicly provided transport, laundries, theatres, and libraries. Does this mean that a sense of belonging to a local community, traditionally kin-based and bound together by religion, is giving way across the world to individual self-sufficiency – or at least to a self-sufficient nuclear family purchasing goods and services to meet its needs instead of having to rely on kin, neighbours, and God? This at any rate is how Hofstede (2001) and Inglehart and Welzel (2005) read the findings of research projects comparing national cultural values.

Medical writer Atul Gawande, whom I mentioned in Chapter 8, teases out some implications for death and dying in his best-seller *Being Mortal* (2014). Gawande, who grew up in the USA after his parents migrated there from India, is very aware of social trends in ageing and dying across the world. He is particularly concerned about what he sees as a global trend toward cultivating personal independence, at all ages – for it raises the question how independence can be sustained when, toward the end of life, infirmity or frailty strike. Professional care in hospital may not be the answer, for people who have cultivated independence throughout life are unlikely to want to be institutionalized at the end of life. Gawande (p. 192) cites Gu et al.'s (2007) three historical stages of where people die, deriving from three levels of economic development:

- When communities are in extreme poverty, there are no medical facilities, so death occurs at home.

- Then as the economy develops, personal and/or national resources enable the sick to turn to medicine and die in hospital.

- Finally, as development turns into affluence, 'people have the means to become concerned about the quality of their lives, even in sickness, and deaths at home actually rise again.'

In Chapter 6 I termed this affluent humanized, non-institutional dying 'post-material'. Wherever the person breathes their final breath, much of the preceding period of frailty and illness is spent at home. To sustain this, however, local communities will have to become practically compassionate. In my own quite affluent street I have witnessed frailty and serious illness drive a revival of neighbourly support for the dying and their family carers (Walter, 1999a), but as the previous chapter argued, in post-industrial societies this may be the exception rather than the rule. There is a contradiction here: the compassionate communities that are required in post-industrial societies if independently-minded people are to die in their own homes may work much better in developing societies such as Kerala where people may value independence less. The future of death in post-industrial societies will depend in large part on if and how this contradiction is resolved, on whether compassionate communities at end of life can be developed in such societies, against the odds (Zaman et al., 2018).

Clustering

If one scenario is global convergence toward societies of individuals, another points to regional clusters of nations. This is Inglehart and Baker's conclusion (2000: 49): 'Economic development tends to push societies in a common direction, but rather than converging, they seem to move on parallel trajectories shaped by their cultural heritage.' These clusters comprise adjacent nations sharing a religious history, an individualistic or collectivist culture, a similar physical environment, and similar levels of gross national product (GNP) and therefore of disease patterns. Examples include Latin America, Central and Eastern Europe, sub-Saharan Africa, East Asia.[1] Some argue that GNP trumps everything else, but my assessment is that the jury is still out on this.

To take just one example. Santa Muerte is a skeleton saint who over the past decade has attracted devotion from millions of Latin Americans and immigrants in the USA. This folk saint's supernatural powers, condemned by mainstream churches, cause her statuettes and paraphernalia to outsell those of more traditional popular saints. Most notable among her many devotees are drug traffickers; she has become their patron saint, protecting both them and their trade. Her altars are often found in the safe houses of drug smugglers (Chesnut, 2017). Santa Muerte is not traditional but modern; she is linked to a highly profitable, if illegal, industry; she clearly comes from the Latin-American Catholic/indigenous cultural cluster and would find few if any devotees among drug runners in, for example, Confucian East Asia or the Arab world. Each 'cluster' of death cultures, even as it is eroded by global economic development, is also constantly renewed by a wide variety of forces.

Glocalization

Another possibility is what Roland Robertson (1995) has termed 'glocalization'. He sees both global homogeneity and local heterogeneity, of which I have given many examples in this book. Modernity changes the contours of death (Chapter 1), and this leads to a global medicalization, rationalization, and commodification of death, dying, and grief (Part I), but quite how death is medicalized or what aspects of death are commodified and to what extent displays wide variation, depending on culture (Part III), national histories, laws, and institutions (Part IV), and local circumstances and actors. It does not seem to me that in death the nation has collapsed into the local on the one hand, and the global on the other. Culture – not least of ethnic and religious groups within and across nations – continues to affect the experience and organization of dying and grieving. And the more people migrate from one country to another, the more diversity there is within nations.

This is shown in funerals. Migrants from the global South to the global North rarely change the host country's funeral practices. The ethnic restaurants immigrants often set up typically lead to a diversification of the host country's culinary tastes and habits; and native-born children may learn about immigrants' religious practices at school. But even those native-born citizens who have attended an immigrant funeral are unlikely to change their own funeral practices. The result within the host country is increasing diversity in funeral rites.

When migrants arrived as colonizers, however, things were very different. Even if colonization was driven largely by each European country's desire to grab land overseas before another country did, colonizers throughout history typically have displayed arrogance about the superiority of their own culture, which they then have some power to impose on those they colonize. Often this has included religion and its rituals, which of course includes funerals. Colonization thus led to funerals becoming more homogenous, to a modest extent. Reverse migration in a post-colonial era does the opposite.

FUTURE SCENARIOS

The future of death

In sum, the experience and social organization of death and dying show both similarities and differences across countries:

- Similarities – not least the movement of dying into old age – are driven by economic and technological development. Countries also copy from one another.

- Differences between countries with similar GNPs are driven by different cultures, national histories and institutions, physical environments, and levels of inequality.

- Similarities and differences interact.

- As a result, there is a degree of global convergence, there is some regional clustering, and there is glocalization.

In other words, modernity's consequences for how death and dying are managed and experienced (medicalization, rationalization, commodification) are largely predictable. But how societies – their cultures, laws, and institutions – respond to these consequences and how they operationalize them is not predictable. As Eisenstadt (2000) argued, modernities are multiple.

This book has shown how specific historical events or legal arrangements, along with accidents of timing, create particular path dependencies that provide particular cultural or institutional tramlines that govern the organization of death and loss within any one country for decades to come. Thus the UK's particular experience of the Second World War culturally sustained stoicism as Britons' normative response to loss for at least another generation, and institutionally led to the formation of a welfare state that included socialized medicine – a National Health Service under whose auspices the medicalization and institutionalization of death takes a very particular form in the UK.

What cannot be predicted is what future historical events will set up new path dependencies. We know there will be global warming, and we know this will likely lead to political collapse in some countries, to new wars and to increased human migration, not least from low-lying areas near the sea. We know that current use of insecticides and antibiotics, if not reduced, may increase disease in humans. But we cannot predict which of the countries or health systems at risk will collapse, precisely where the wars will be and when, or which countries will be most affected, positively or negatively, by increased immigration. Nor can we predict how societies will respond or how initial responses may set up new path dependencies in the management of death. Nor can we predict if one global mega-disaster will change everything. In other words, however much we understand contemporary trends, death's future is not predictable. But it is likely to be multiple − death's future*s*.

What can be predicted with some certainty (Clark et al., 2017) is that global annual deaths, currently around 56 million, will reach an all-time high of around 90 million by the middle of the twenty-first century before going down later in the century − reflecting declining fertility rates since the 1970s throughout the world outside sub-Saharan Africa. More and more of these 90 million will be very old, many of them experiencing a degree of dementia. Both the sheer numbers of those nearing death and their evolving age profile mean we can predict with some certainty that in the coming half century managing dying, dead bodies, and grief will face new challenges, likely to prompt new responses.

The future of grief

Loss of ideals

Humans feel grief not only for the loss through death of those they care for, but also for the loss of hopes and ideals. This latter kind of grief can afflict an entire society or an entire generation and can form the socio-political context for more intimate griefs. I think of two friends who were both born in the 1920s and who, seeing the evils of fascism in the 1930s and 1940s, embraced socialism and as young adults joined the Communist Party of Great Britain − as did many of their generation. As the years rolled by and the problems with Soviet society became better known in the West, each became disillusioned with the Party and eventually left. One turned his idealism into a successful career that helped improve health outcomes in the UK, cheerfully embracing social democracy and always remaining buoyant and optimistic about what could be achieved. The other became bitter about the state both of the world and of her own life, her lifelong grief for the loss of communist ideals impacting, and being impacted by, losses in her personal life. In psychological terms, he worked through the loss and grew in stature; she got stuck in lifelong rumination (Eisma and Stroebe, 2017).

If some mourn the loss of socialism, others (not least in Spain) mourn the loss of fascism, the loss of empire, and (for those many Britons who voted to remain in the European Union) the loss of their European citizenship. Others lose any expectation of lifelong employment as jobs become increasingly precarious; in Japan, where lifelong employment within the same company had been the norm since the 1950s, its loss in the 1990s was acutely felt (Allison, 2013). Others mourn the loss of respect for their profession or their class. It is likely that more and more people will come to grieve the loss of the planet we once knew.

Loss of being valued

In 1963, Jeremy Seabrook began a successful career writing about poverty and the insults of social class. In his article 'The living dead of capitalism' (Seabrook, 2008), he argues that being thrown on the scrap heap is endemic in capitalism and will continue to be the experience of millions. The article is a eulogy/elegy for the death of each class and occupational group that capitalism throws up and then sooner or later (often sooner) discards. In its ascendancy, each class or group feels it is the future, shaping its own destiny, yet each is in turn discarded – each is both born and killed by forces beyond the individual's control. Seabrook writes as a working-class boy who did well at grammar school and went into journalism – others went into social work, teaching, or town planning – to create a better world. In the 1960s, capitalism needed this new meritocracy of welfare professionals to manage the working class, just as from the 1980s it discarded them. Capitalism once needed Seabrook to tell its elite how the working class felt, but after the Miners strike in 1984–85 and the fall of communism in 1989, the working class no longer posed any threat to capital, which now needs journalists to report instead on the subterranean world of radical Islam. The magazine for which Seabrook first wrote, *New Society*, closed down in 1988 and he increasingly struggled to find work.

Yet Seabrook knows that the hedonistic values of the new dominant consumer class of celebrities, media stars, and multi-millionaires will itself be discarded, perhaps in the face of the need to moderate our lifestyles in order to survive ecologically. Seabrook also charts the rise and fall of other classes – the self-taught man, destroyed by the UK's 1944 Education Act and the meritocracy it created; the small shopkeeper, destroyed by the chain store. This enduring sense of loss, though endemic in capitalism, is disenfranchised by each ascendant class, for whom 'to dwell on the costs of change is to call into question the belief that "we" are going somewhere.' (Seabrook, 2008: 31).

Seabrook writes from England. I wonder, though, what a Portugese writer on this theme might say? In the fifteenth and sixteenth centuries, Portugal established the first global empire and became a major power, but declined from the eighteenth century so that it is now one of the poorest countries in Western Europe. Portugese *fado* music, dating at least from the 1820s and popular today, is famous for its melancholy, its expression of *saudade* – 'a feeling of longing, melancholy, or nostalgia that is supposedly characteristic of the Portuguese tem-perament'.[2] Portugese song and poetry are suffused with longing for a lost past, whether that be economic or romantic, or both. Portugese popular culture embraces nostalgia and mourning, just as Buddhism accepts suffering and loss. Both are utterly different from American optimism. If capitalism continues to give birth to and then kill one skill, one profession, after another, then how people will cope with chronic loss will depend in part on whether their culture, art, and religion ride roughshod over loss or articulate it. How the overall social or national context of hope and loss, optimism and pessimism, shapes personal grief over the death of a loved one has yet to be researched. What we do know is that a sense of a life unfulfilled makes it harder to face old age and mortality (Johnson, 2016).

Social acceleration

In his theory of social acceleration, Rosa (2015) draws on Gronemeyer's (1996) observation that the biblical concept of time, running from Creation to Final Judgement, has been replaced in people's imagination by secular time, running from birth to death. This causes a chronic lack of time. If the well-lived life was once one lived according to the Ten Commandments and faithful to God, now the well-lived life is the fulfilled life. The godly life could be lived by a child and was not threatened by child mortality; the full life is enabled by contemporary longevity (you need to live a fair number of years in order to fulfil your poten-tial), and threatened by premature death (Walter, 1985). So, Rosa argues, con-temporary people indulge in an accelerated enjoyment of worldly options, that is, a faster life in the hope of fitting everything into one's allotted time: 'The good life is the full life … savouring as much of what the world has to offer as possible' (p. 182). Unfortunately, capitalism operates by ensuring that once an experience or good has been supplied, the consumer is tempted by several more; rather than satiation, the experience-seeking consumer falls ever further behind what is possible. The result? Whereas the pre-modern peasant who reached old age could die 'old and sated with life, the modern person never reaches this point' (p. 185). The modern person reaches old age and then faces death mourn-ing what they have not achieved.

The evidence for Rosa's thesis is dubious. It is disconfirmed by several studies of those entering old age in the final third of the twentieth century, especially in North America, who were found typically to look back on their lives with some contentment, enabling them to enter old age and to die without major regrets (Butler, 1963; Marshall, 1981). Unprecedented numbers of this generation had experienced upward social mobility as white-collar work expanded with the decline of factory work, and the middle class came to replace the working class as the numerically largest social class – an experience of upward mobility on a scale that can never be repeated within these now post-industrial countries (though it is currently occurring in China). No wonder this generation entered old age feeling good about their life. This leaves Rosa's thesis as a hypothesis to be tested for the following generation – the post-war baby boomer generation, the first mass-consumer generation, the first generation to experience capitalism's ratcheting up of consumer needs way beyond basic needs. Will baby boomers die unfulfilled, unlike the generation that preceded them? And what about Generation X who followed the baby boomers and who grew up in more economically uncertain times, or the Millennials whose economic future is even more precarious? Maybe they too will die in mourning, or perhaps regret, for a life in which achievement fell way behind aspiration.

The future of death studies

Like any academic field, death studies – or 'thanatology' as it is often called in the USA – is influenced by the social and political context of the time. I sketch a couple of time periods.

1950s to 1970s

Two features of the post-war 1950s and 1960s that motivated scholars may be mentioned here. Nazism and the Holocaust prompted questions about human existence: how can ordinary humans become so evil? How do humans survive evil? Time in a concentration camp underlay Austrian psychiatrist Viktor Frankl's cult 1960s book *Man's Search for Meaning* (1987) which influenced hospice founder Cicely Saunders' conviction that meaning can be found in even the most difficult of circumstances. Authoritarianism and evil also preoccupied Ernest Becker, a maverick Jewish American anthropologist who as a young GI had helped liberate a Nazi concentration camp and whose book *The Denial of Death* (1973) has probably had more global influence than any other single thanatology book apart from Kübler-Ross's *On Death and Dying* (1969).[3] Becker argued that humans have a need to act heroically if their lives are to have meaning, and this is driven by a universal but unconscious fear of death. Directing and containing this need is crucial for civilization, for acting it out can be highly dangerous; Nazis saw themselves, and certainly their Führer, as heroes.

The other feature of the post-war period was the curious mix of the 'affluent society' and the Cold War between the USA and the Soviet Union. This created a paradox. On the one hand, westerners in general, and Americans in particular, were living longer and healthier lives of unprecedented comfort, convenience and safety, so thoughts of death could rather easily be put off. Yet in the background was fear of The Bomb, the possibility of nuclear annihilation, erupting into near reality in the 1962 Cuban missile crisis. This is the context in which

American psychologists invented scale after scale to measure 'death anxiety', and the notion of 'death denial' came to have currency.

2000s and 2010s

Today all humans experience a similar contradiction. With ever increasing knowledge of global warming and other human-induced environmental risks, there is increasing awareness that civilization and perhaps even the human species is at risk of extinction. What is the point of culture, of civilization, of bringing children into the world if humanity's foothold on the planet is doomed? Like the bomb in the 1950s, this fear of mass extinction is abstract, but it has consequences. Try this thought experiment: what would be the meaning of my life if humans were about to become extinct and no-one would survive me (Scheffler and Kolodny, 2013)? Many people answer that there would be no meaning. Scheffler therefore argues that the entire edifice of human civilization and culture is predicated on our having descendants. The prospect of extinction of our species would lead to a crisis of meaning different from that prompted by the concentration camp where, for Frankl at least, there was hope that some of his family would survive.

In the meantime, the everyday experience of the populations of the more unequal western countries such as the UK and USA is split. On the one hand are the economically secure post-materialists who can indulge in liberal attitudes and humanistic endeavours, on the other hand are the economically insecure who value strong – often right-wing and nationalistic – government (Chapter 6). In this context, euthanasia, assisted dying, advance directives, and so forth become issues of political, media, and popular debate, and the subject of thanatological research.

Post-materialists lurch between diffuse environmental anxiety and more immediate projects of personal fulfilment, while the economically insecure lurch between hope in authoritarian government and immediate experience of under-employment and foodbanks. The post-materialists bury their heads in the sand, trying not to notice that their security, healthy lifestyle, and environmental enlightenment come at the expense of others' insecurity; the economically insecure bury their heads in the sand, trying not to notice the health and environmental consequences of their everyday actions.

In the meantime, China is becoming the world's dominant country, with millions of its citizens continuing to migrate from country to city. Will filial piety survive this mass movement of the young? What is the future for ancestor veneration? Who will care for dying Chinese? When China moves from industrial to post-industrial, will it too witness a flourishing of post-material values that challenge modern ways of dying as has happened in the West (Gu et al., 2007)? Will China develop its own academic study of ageing and dying in order to support the new challenges its citizens face as they and their loved ones age and die? Will China replace North America and Europe as the epicentre of death studies?

How all this will work out over coming decades, no-one knows. What is certain is that the context for death studies – global, national, and local – will continue to change and evolve.

FURTHER READING

- Eisenstadt, S.N. (2000) 'Multiple modernities', *Daedalus*, 129: 1–29.

- Gawande, A. (2014) *Being Mortal: Illness, medicine, and what matters in the end.* London: Profile.

- Robertson, R. (1995) 'Glocalization: time-space and homogeneity-heterogeneity', in M. Featherstone, S. Lash and R. Robertson (eds), *Global Modernities*. London: Sage, pp. 25–44.

- Zaman, S., Inbadas, H., Whitelaw, A. and Clark, D. (2017) 'Common or multiple futures for end of life care around the world?', *Social Science and Medicine*, 172: 72–9.

Questions to discuss

- What convergence, if any, do you see in how modern societies respond to death, dying, and bereavement? What do you see as the main enduring differences?

- How do you expect patterns of mortality to change in the next century?

Notes

1. These clusters are pictured in the Inglehart-Welzel World Values Survey map www.worldvaluessurvey.org/WVSContents.jsp?CMSID=Findings (accessed 26/6/19).

2. https://en.oxforddictionaries.com/definition/saudade (accessed 26/6/19).

3. https://ernestbecker.org/about-becker/biography/ (accessed 26/6/19).

REFERENCES

Abel, E.K. (1986) 'The hospice movement: institutionalizing innovation', *International Journal of Health Services*, *16*: 71–85.

Agamben, G. (1998) *Homo Sacer: Sovereign power and bare life*. Stanford, CA: Stanford University Press.

Aldrich, D.P. (2012) *Building Resilience: Social capital in post-disaster recovery*. Chicago, IL: University of Chicago Press.

Allison, A. (2013) *Precarious Japan*. Durham, NC: Duke University Press.

Anderson, B. (1991) *Imagined Communities: Reflections on the origin and spread of nationalism*. London: Verso.

Appadurai, A. (1990) 'Disjuncture and difference in the global cultural economy', in M. Featherstone (ed.), *Global Culture*. London: Sage, pp. 295–310.

Ariès, P. (1962) *Centuries of Childhood*. London: Cape.

Ariès, P. (1981) *The Hour of Our Death*. London: Allen Lane.

Árnason, A. and Hafsteinsson, S.B. (2018) *Death and Governmentality in Iceland: Neo-liberalism, grief and the nation-form*. Reykjavik: University of Iceland Press.

Arney, W.R. and Bergen, B.J. (1984) *Medicine and the Management of Living*. Chicago, IL: University of Chicago Press.

Aveline-Dubach, N. (2012) *Invisible Population: The place of the dead in East Asian megacities*. Lanham, MD: Lexington Books.

Avineri, S. (1972) *Hegel's Theory of the Modern State*. Cambridge: Cambridge University Press.

Badone, E. (1989) *The Appointed Hour: Death, worldview and social change in Brittany*. Berkeley, CA: University of California Press.

Baeke, G., Wils, J.P. and Broeckaert, B. (2011) 'We are (not) the master of our body: elderly Jewish women's attitudes towards euthanasia and assisted suicide', *Ethnicity and Health*, *16*: 259–78.

Bailey, E. (1997) *Implicit Religion in Contemporary Society*. Kampen: Kok Pharos.

Bailey, T. (2010) 'When commerce meets care: emotional management in UK funeral directing', *Mortality*, *15*: 205–22.

Barford, V. (2010) '"Secretive world" of suicide websites', *BBC News*. Available at www.bbc.co.uk/news/uk-11387910 (accessed 5/6/19).

Barthes, R. (1993) *Camera Lucida*. London: Vintage.

Basu, M. (2014) 'Hotel Death', *CNN International Edition+*. Available at http://edition.cnn.com/interactive/2014/04/world/india-hotel-death/index.html?hpt=hp_c4 (accessed 5/6/19).

Baudrillard, J. (1993) *Symbolic Exchange and Death*. London: Sage.

Baugher, J.E. (2008) 'Facing death: Buddhist and western hospice approaches', *Symbolic Interaction*, *31*: 259–84.

Bauman, Z. (1989) *Modernity and the Holocaust*. Oxford: Polity.

Bauman, Z. (1992) *Mortality, Immortality and Other Life Strategies*. Cambridge: Polity.

Bauman, Z. (2000) *Liquid Modernity*. Cambridge: Polity.

Bayatrizi, Z. and Tehrani, R.T. (2017) 'The objective life of death in Tehran: a vanishing presence', *Mortality*, *22*: 15–32.

Beck, U. (1992) *Risk Society: Towards a new modernity*. London: Sage.

Beck, U. and Beck-Gernsheim, E. (2002) *Individualization*. London: Sage.

Becker, E. (1973) *The Denial of Death*. New York: Free Press.

Beckfield, J., Olafsdottir, S. and Sosnaud, B. (2013) 'Healthcare systems in comparative perspective: classification, convergence, institutions, inequalities, and five missed turns', *Annual Review of Sociology*, *39*: 7.1–7.20.

Behringer, W. (2018) *Tambora and the Year Without a Summer: How a volcano plunged the world into crisis*. Cambridge: Polity.

Bellah, R., Madsen, R., Sullivan., W.M., Swidler, A. and Tipton, S.M. (1985) *Habits of the Heart: Individualism and commitment in American life*. Berkeley, CA: University of California Press.

Ben-Ari, E. (2005) 'Epilogue: a "good" military death', *Armed Forces & Society*, 31.

Berger, P. (1969) *The Social Reality of Religion*. London: Faber.

Berger, P. (2012) 'Further thoughts on religion and modernity', *Society*, *49*: 313–16.

Berger, P. (2014) *The Many Altars of Modernity*. Boston, MA: de Gruyter.

Berggren, H. and Trägårdh, L. (2010) 'Pippi Longstocking: the autonomous child and the moral logic of the Swedish welfare state', in H. Mattsson and S-O. Wallenstein (eds), *Swedish Modernism*. London: Black Dog, pp. 11–22.

Berns, N. (2011) *Closure: The rush to end grief and what it costs us*. Philadelphia, PA: Temple University Press.

Bernstein, A. (2000) 'Fire and earth: the forging of modern cremation in Meiji Japan', *Japanese Journal of Religion Studies*, *27*: 297–334.

Berterame, S., Erthal, L., Thomas, J., Fellner, S., Vosse, B., Claire, P., Hao, W., Johnson, D.T., Mohar, A., Pavadia, J., Samak, A.K., Sipp, W., Sumyai, V., Suryawati, S., Tougiq, J., Yans, R. and Mattick, R.P. (2016) 'Use of and barriers to access to opioid analgesics: a worldwide, regional, and national study', *Lancet*, *387*: 10028.

Beyer, P. (2013) 'Questioning the secular/religious divide in a post-Westphalian world', *International Sociology*, *28*: 663–79.

Black, M. (2012) *Death in Berlin: From Weimar to divided Germany*. Cambridge: Cambridge University Press.

Blauner, R. (1966) 'Death and social structure', *Psychiatry*, *29*: 378–94.

Bloch, M. (1971) *Placing the Dead: Tombs, ancestral villages and kinship organisation in Madagascar*. New York: Seminar Press.

Bolton, S.C. and Wibberley, G. (2014) 'Domiciliary care: the formal and informal labour process', *Sociology*, *48*: 682–97.

Bonsu, S.K. and Belk, R.W. (2003) 'Do not go cheaply into that good night: death-ritual consumption in Asante, Ghana', *Journal of Consumer Research*, *30*: 41–55.

Boret, S.P. (2014) *Japanese Tree Burial: Ecology, kinship and the culture of death*. London: Routledge.

Borgstrom, E. and Walter, T. (2015) 'Choice and compassion at the end of life: a critical analysis of recent English policy discourse', *Social Science & Medicine*, 136–7: 99–105.

Boserup, E. (1965) *The Conditions of Agricultural Growth: The economics of agrarian change under population pressure*. Chicago, IL: Aldine.

Bowker, J. (1991) *The Meanings of Death*. Cambridge: Cambridge University Press.

Bowlby, J. (1980) *Attachment and Loss, Vol. 3: Loss, Sadness & Depression*. London: Hogarth Press.

Bowman, M. and Valk, U. (2012) *Vernacular Religion in Everyday Life*. Sheffield: Equinox.

Bramadat, P., Coward, H. and Stajduhar, K. (2013) *Spirituality in Hospice Palliative Care*. Albany, NY: SUNY Press.

Bramley, L., Seymour, J. and Cox, K. (2015) 'Living with frailty: implications for the conceptualisation of ACP', *BMJ Supportive & Palliative Care*, 5: A19.

Bravo, V. (2017) 'Coping with dying and deaths at home: how undocumented migrants in the United States experience the process of transnational grieving', *Mortality*, 22: 33–44.

Brinkmann, S. (2019) 'A society of sorrow: the constitution of society through grief', *Distinktion: Journal of Social Theory, 20*: 207–21.

Brown, K. and Korczynski, M. (2017) 'The caring self within a context of increasing rationalisation', *Sociology*, 51: 833–49.

Brubaker, J.R. and Callison-Burch, V. (2016) '*Legacy Contact: designing and implementing post-mortem stewardship at Facebook*', CHI Conference, San Jose, CA.

Brubaker, J.R. and Hayes, G.R. (2011) ' *"We will never forget you [online]": an empirical investigation of post-mortem MySpace comments*', CSCW Conference, Hangzhou.

Brubaker, J.R., Hayes, G.R. and Dourish, P. (2013) 'Beyond the grave: Facebook as a site for the expansion of death and mourning', *The Information Society*, 29: 152–63.

Bruce, S. (2002) *God is Dead*. Oxford: Blackwell.

Bull, A.C. and Hansen, H.L. (2016) 'On agonistic memory', *Memory Studies, 9*: 390–404.

Burns, S.B. (1990) *Sleeping Beauty: Memorial photography in America*. Altadena, CA: Twelvetrees Press.

Butler, J. (2000) *Antigone's Claim: Kinship between life and death*. New York: Columbia University Press.

Butler, J. (2004) *Precarious Life: The powers of mourning and violence*. London: Verso.

Butler, J. (2009) *Frames of War: When is life grievable?* London: Verso.

Butler, R.N. (1963) 'The life review: an interpretation of reminiscence in the aged', *Psychiatry, 26*: 65–76.

Bynum, C.W. (1991) *Fragmentation and Redemption: Essays on gender and the human body in medieval religion*. New York: Zone Books.

Campbell, C. (1987) *The Romantic Ethic and the Spirit of Modern Consumerism*. Oxford: Blackwell.

Cann, C.K. (2013) 'Tombstone technology: deathscapes in Asia, the UK and the US', in C. Maciel and V.C. Pereira (eds), *Digital Legacy and Interaction*. Santa Barbara, CA: Praeger, pp. 101–13.

Cann, C.K. (2014) *Virtual Afterlives: Grieving the dead in the twenty-first century*. Lexington, KY: University Press of Kentucky.

Cann, C.K. (2016) 'Contemporary death practices in the Catholic Latina/o community', *Thanatos, 5*: 63–74.

Cave, S. (2012) *Immortality: The quest to live forever and how it drives civilisation*. London: Biteback.

Chakrabarty, D. (2007) *Provincializing Europe: Postcolonial thought and historical difference*. Princeton, NJ: Princeton University Press.

Chesnut, A. (2017) *Devoted to Death: Santa Muerte, the skeleton saint*. New York: Oxford University Press.

Childe, V.G. (1945) 'Directional changes in funerary practice during 50,000 years', *Man*, 45: 13–19.

Christakis, N.A. (1999) *Death Foretold: Prophecy and prognosis in medical care*. Chicago, IL: University of Chicago Press.

Clark, D. (1999) '"Total pain", disciplinary power and the body in the work of Cicely Saunders, 1958–1967', *Social Science & Medicine*, 49: 727–36.

Clark, D. (2018) 'End-of-life care: can it be everyone's business?', *Royal College of Physicians*. Available at www.rcplondon.ac.uk/news/end-life-care-can-it-be-every-ones-business (accessed 5/6/19).

Clark, D., Inbadas, H., Colburn, D., Forrest, C., Richards, N., Whitelaw, S. and Zaman, S. (2017) 'Interventions at the end of life: a taxonomy for "overlapping consensus"', *Wellcome Open Research*, 2.

Clark, N. (2014) 'Geo-politics and the disaster of the Anthropocene', *Sociological Review*, 62: 19–37.

Clarke, D. (2019) *Constructions of Victimhood: Remembering the victims of state socialism in Germany*. New York: Palgrave Macmillan.

Cohen, J., Marcoux, I., Bilsen, J., Deboosere, P., van der Wal, G. and Deliens, L. (2006) 'European public acceptance of euthanasia: socio-demographic and cultural factors associated with the acceptance of euthanasia in 33 European countries', *Social Science and Medicine*, 63: 743–56.

Coleman, P.G. (2016) 'Ritual and memories of ritual in older people's lives: contrasts between Eastern and Western Europe', in M. Johnson and J. Walker (eds), *Spiritual Dimensions of Ageing*. Cambridge: Cambridge University Press.

Cook, G. and Walter, T. (2005) 'Rewritten rites: language and social relations in traditional and contemporary funerals', *Discourse and Society*, 16: 365–91.

Curran, J., Fenton, N. and Freedman, D. (2012) *Misunderstanding the Internet*. London: Routledge.

Davidson, D. (2017) 'Art embodied: tattoos as memorials', *Bereavement Care*, 36: 33–40.

Davie, G. (2001) 'The persistance of institutional religion in modern Europe', in L. Woodhead (ed.), *Peter Berger and the Study of Religion*. London: Routledge, pp. 101–11.

Davies, C. (1991) 'How people argue about abortion and capital punishment', in P. Badham (ed.), *Ethics on the Frontier of Human Existence*. New York: Paragon, pp. 103–37.

Davies, C. (1996) 'Dirt, death, decay and dissolution: American denial and British avoidance', in G. Howarth and P. Jupp (eds), *Contemporary Issues in the Sociology of Death, Dying and Disposal*. Basingstoke: Macmillan.

Davies, D. (1990) *Cremation Today and Tomorrow*. Bramcote: Grove Books.

Davies, D. (2015) *Mors Britannica: Lifestyle and death-style in Britain today*. Oxford: Oxford University Press.

Davies, D. and Mates, L. (2005) *Encyclopaedia of Cremation*. Aldershot: Ashgate.

Davis, K.G. (2006) 'Dead reckoning or reckoning with the dead: Hispanic Catholic funeral customs', *Liturgy*, *21*: 21–7.

Day, A. (2017) *The Religious Lives of Older Laywomen: The last active Anglican generation*. Oxford: Oxford University Press.

Day, A., Vincett, G. and Cotter, C.R. (2013) *Social Identities Between the Sacred and the Secular*. Farnham: Ashgate.

Day, P., Pearce, J. and Dorling, D. (2008) 'Twelve worlds: a geo-demographic comparison of global inequalities in mortality', *Journal of Epidemiology and Community Health*, *62*: 1002–10.

de Tocqueville, A. (1988 [1835]) *Democracy in America*. New York: HarperPerennial.

de Vries, B. and Rutherford, J. (2004) 'Memorializing loved ones on the World Wide Web', *Omega*, *49*: 5–26.

Déchaux, J-H. (2002) 'Paradoxes of affiliation in the contemporary family', *Current Sociology*, *50*: 229–42.

Derrida, J. (2001) *On Cosmopolitanism and Forgiveness*. London: Routledge.

Diamond, H. and Gorrara, C. (2003) 'Facing the past: French wartime memories at the millennium', in S. Milner and N. Parsons (eds), *Reinventing France*. Basingstoke: Palgrave Macmillan, pp. 173–85.

Dias, K. (2003) 'The ana sanctuary: women's pro-anorexia narratives in cyberspace', *Journal of International Women's Studies*, *4*: 31–45.

Doi, T. (1981) *The Anatomy of Dependence*. Tokyo: Kodansha International.

Doka, K.J. (2002) *Disenfranchised Grief*. Champaign, IL: Research Press.

Doka, K.J. and Martin, T.L. (2010) *Grieving Beyond Gender: Understanding the ways men and women mourn*. New York: Routledge.

Doss, E. (2010) *Memorial Mania: Public feeling in America*. Chicago, IL: Chicago University Press.

Douglas, M. (1966) *Purity and Danger: An analysis of concepts of pollution and taboo*. London: Routledge & Kegan Paul.

Douglas, M. (2004) *Jacob's Tears*. Oxford: Oxford University Press.

Dowd, Q.L. (1921) *Funeral Management and Costs: A world-survey of burial and cremation*. Chicago, IL: Chicago University Press.

Draper, J.W. (1967) *The Funeral Elegy and the Rise of English Romanticism*. London: Frank Cass.

du Boulay, S. (1984) *Cicely Saunders*. London Hodder.

Dumont, R.G. and Foss, D.C. (1972) *The American View of Death: Acceptance or denial?* Cambridge, MA: Schenkman.

Durkheim, E. (1915) *The Elementary Forms of the Religious Life*. London: Unwin.

Durkheim, E. (2002 [1897]) *Suicide*. London: Routledge.

Dye, N. and Smith, D. (1986) 'Mother love and infant death, 1750–1920', *Journal of American History*, *73*: 329–53.

Economist Intelligence Unit (2015) *The 2015 Quality of Death Index: Ranking palliative care across the world*. London: The Economist.

Edwards, R., Ribbens McCarthy, J. and Gillies, V. (2012) 'The politics of concepts: family and its (putative) replacements', *British Journal of Sociology*, *53*: 730–46.

Ehrenreich, B. (2018) *Natural Causes*. London: Granta.

Eisenstadt, S.N. (2000) 'Multiple modernities', *Daedalus*, *129*: 1–29.

Eisma, M.C. and Stroebe, M.S. (2017) 'Rumination following bereavement: an overview', *Bereavement Care*, *36*: 58–64.

Elder, G. (1998) *Children of the Great Depression*. Boulder, CO: Westview Press.

Elias, N. (1978) *The Civilizing Process: Vol. 1, The History of Manners*. New York: Urizen.

Elias, N. (1985) *The Loneliness of the Dying*. Oxford: Blackwell.

Endres, K.W. and Lauser, A. (2011) *Engaging the Spirit World: Popular beliefs and practices in modern Southeast Asia*. Oxford: Berghahn.

Esping-Andersen, G. (1990) *The Three World of Welfare Capitalism*. Oxford: Polity.

Fang, C. (2018) 'Bereavement and motivation in three contrasting cultures: Britain, Japan and China'. Doctoral thesis, University of Bath.

Farrell, J.J. (1980) *Inventing the American Way of Death, 1830–1920*. Philadelphia, PA: Temple University Press.

Faust, D.W. (2008) *This Republic of Suffering: Death and the American Civil War*. New York: Vintage.

Feifel, H. (1959) *The Meaning of Death*. New York: McGraw Hill.

Feldman, J. (2008) *Above the Death Pits, Beneath the Flag: Youth voyages to Poland and the performance of Israeli national identity*. New York: Berghahn.

Ferguson, R.B. (1997) 'Violence and war in prehistory', in D.L. Martin and D.W. Frayer (eds), *Troubled Times: Violence and warfare in the past*. Amsterdam: Gordon & Breach, pp. 321–55.

Ferrándiz, F. (2013) 'Exhuming the defeated: Civil War mass graves in 21st-century Spain', *American Ethnologist*, *40*: 38–54.

Ferrándiz, F. and Robben, A.C.G.M. (2015) *Necropolitics: Mass graves and exhumations in the age of human rights*. Philadelphia, PA: University of Pennsylvania Press.

Fforde, C. (2004) *Collecting the Dead: Archaeology and the reburial issue*. London: Duckworth.

Finch, J. (2007) 'Displaying families', *Sociology*, *41*: 65–81.

Finch, J. and Mason, J. (2000) *Passing On: Kinship and inheritance in England*. London: Routledge.

Firth, S. (1997) *Dying, Death and Bereavement in a British Hindu Community*. Leuven: Peeters.

Fitzpatrick, D. (1994) *Oceans of Consolation: Personal accounts of Irish migration to Australia*. Cork: Cork University Press.

Fong, J. (2017) *The Death Café Movement: Exploring the horizons of mortality*. New York: Palgrave Macmillan.

Foster, L. and Woodthorpe, K. (2013) 'What cost the price of a good send off? The challenges for British state funeral policy', *Journal of Poverty and Social Justice*, *21*: 77–89.

Foucault, M. (1973) *The Birth of the Clinic: An archaeology of medical perception*. London: Tavistock.

Foucault, M. (2003) *Society Must Be Defended: Lectures at the College de France 1975–6*. New York: Picador.

Francis, A. (2019) *Epilogue to Lynn Lofland, The Craft of Dying*. Cambridge, MA: MIT Press.

Frankl, V. (1987) *Man's Search for Meaning*. London: Hodder & Stoughton.

Frankopan, P. (2015) *The Silk Roads: A new history of the world*. London: Bloomsbury.

Frayling, C. (2017) *Frankenstein: The first two hundred years*. London: Reel Art Press.

Freud, S. (1984) 'Mourning and melancholia', in S. Freud (ed.), *On Metapsychology*. London: Pelican, pp. 251–67.

Furedi, F. (2002) *Culture of Fear: Risk-taking and the morality of low expectation*. London: Continuum.

Garces-Foley, K. (2006a) *Death and Religion in a Changing World*. Armonk, NY: M.E. Sharpe.

Garces-Foley, K. (2006b) 'Hospice and the politics of spirituality', *Omega*, *53*: 117–36.

Garces-Foley, K. and Holcomb, J.S. (2005) 'Contemporary American funerals: personalizing tradition', in K. Garces-Foley (ed.), *Death and Religion in a Changing World*. Armonk, NY: M.E. Sharpe, 207–27.

Gauthier, F. (2019) *Religion, Modernity, Globalisation: From nation state to market*. London: Routledge.

Gauthier, F. and Martikainen, T. (2016) *Religion in Consumer Society*. Abingdon: Routledge.

Gawande, A. (2014) *Being Mortal: Illness, medicine, and what matters in the end*. London: Profile.

Giddens, A. (1991) *Modernity and Self-Identity: Self and society in the late modern age*. Cambridge: Polity.

Giddens, A. (1994) 'Living in a post-traditional society', in U. Beck, A. Giddens and S. Lash (eds), *Reflexive Modernisation*. Cambridge: Polity, pp. 56–109.

Gilding, M. (2010) 'Reflexivity over and above convention: the new orthodoxy in the sociology of personal life, formerly sociology of the family', *British Journal of Sociology*, *61*: 757–77.

Gill, T., Steger, B. and Slater, D.H. (2013) *Japan Copes with Calamity: Ethnographies of the earthquake, tsunami and nuclear disasters of March 2011*. Oxford: Peter Lang.

Gillis, J.R. (ed.) (2000) *Commemorations: The politics of national identity*. Princeton, NJ: Princeton University Press.

Gittings, C. (1984) *Death, Burial and the Individual in Early Modern England*. London: Croom Helm.

Gittings, C. and Walter, T. (2010) 'Rest in peace? Burial on private land', in A. Maddrell and J. Sidaway (eds), *Deathscapes: Spaces for death, dying, mourning and remembrance*. Farnham: Ashgate, pp. 95–118.

Glaser, B. and Strauss A. (1965) *Awareness of Dying*. London Penguin.

Goffman, E. (1959) *The Presentation of Self in Everyday Life*. London: Doubleday.

Goffman, E. (1961) *Asylum*. Garden City, NY: Anchor.

Goldscheider, C. (1971) 'The mortality revolution', in C. Goldscheider (ed.), *Population, Modernization and Social Structure*. Boston, MA: Little Brown, pp. 102–3, 124–34.

Goodhart, D. (2017) *The Road to Somewhere: The populist revolt and the future of politics*. London: Hurst.

Goody, J. and Poppi, C. (1994) 'Flowers and bones: approaches to the dead in Anglo and Italian cemeteries', *Comparative Studies in Society & History*, *36*: 146–75.

Gordon, D.R. and Paci, E. (1997) 'Disclosure practices and cultural narratives: understanding concealment and silence around cancer in Tuscany, Italy', *Social Science & Medicine*, *44*: 1433–52.

Gorer, G. (1965) *Death, Grief and Mourning in Contemporary Britain*. London: Cresset.

Goss, R.E. and Klass, D. (2005) *Dead but Not Lost: Grief narratives in religious traditions*. Walnut Creek, CA: AltaMira.

Gott, M., Wiles, J., Moeke-Maxwell, T., Black, S., Williams, L., Kearse, N. and Trussardi, G. (2017) 'What is the role of community at the end of life for people dying in advanced age? A qualitative study with bereaved family carers', *Palliative Medicine*, *32*: 268–75.

Gould, H., Kohn, T. and Gibbs, M. (2019) 'Uploading the ancestors: experiments with digital Buddhist altars in contemporary Japan', *Death Studies*, 1–10.

Graham, B. (1987) *Facing Death and the Life After*. Milton Keynes: Word.

Graham, J. (2018) 'Funeral food as resurrection in the American south', in C.K. Cann (ed.), *Dying to Eat: Cross-cultural perspectives on food, death, and the afterlife*. Lexington, KY: University Press of Kentucky.

Gronemeyer, M. (1996) *Das Leben als letzte Gelegenheit: Sicherheitsbedürfnisse und Zeitknappheit [Life as a last opportunity: security needs and time constraints]*. Darmstadt: Wissenschaftliche Buchgesellschaft.

Gu, D., Liu, G., Vlosky, D.A. and Yi, Z. (2007) 'Factors associated with place of death among the Chinese oldest old', *Journal of Applied Gerontology*, *26*: 34–57.

Gunaratnam, Y. (2013) *Death and the Migrant: Bodies, borders and care*. London: Bloomsbury.

Gurven, M. and Kaplan, H. (2007) 'Longevity among hunter-gatherers', *Population and Development Review*, *33*: 321–65.

Gustavsson, A. (2015) 'Death, dying and bereavement in Norway and Sweden in recent times', *Humanities 4*: 224–35.

Hacking, I. (1975) *The Emergence of Probability*. Cambridge: Cambridge University Press.

Hamdy, S. (2016) 'All eyes on Egypt: Islam and the medical use of dead bodies amidst Cairo's political unrest', *Medical Anthropology*, *35*: 220–35.

Hanusch, F. (2010) *Representing Death in the News*. Basingstoke: Palgrave Macmillan.

Harari, Y.N. (2015) *Sapiens: A brief history of humankind*. London: Vintage.

Harper, S. (2010) 'Behind closed doors? Corpses and mourners in American and English funeral premises', in J. Hockey, C. Komaromy and K. Woodthorpe (eds), *The Matter of Death*. Basingstoke: Palgrave Macmillan, pp. 100–16.

Hass, J.K. (2015) 'War, fields, and competing economies of death: lessons from the Blockade of Leningrad', *Poetics*, *48*: 55–68.

Hausmann, E. (2004) 'How press discourse justified euthanasia', *Mortality*, *9*(3): 206–22.

Hawkins, A.H. (1990) 'Constructing death: three pathographies about dying', *Omega*, *22*: 301–17.

Hayes, J.W. and Lipset, S.M. (1993–94) 'Individualism: a double-edged sword', *The Responsive Community*, *4*: 69–80.

Hazelgrove, J. (2000) *Spiritualism and British Society Between the Wars*. Manchester: Manchester University Press.

Heelas, P. (2002) 'The spiritual revolution: from religion to spirituality', in L. Woodhead (ed.), *Religions in the Modern World: Traditions and transformations*. London: Routledge.

Heelas, P. and Woodhead, L. (2004) *The Spiritual Revolution: Why religion is giving way to spirituality*. Oxford: Blackwell.

Herlihy, D. (1997) *The Black Death and the Transformation of the West*. Cambridge, MA: Harvard University Press.

Hertz, R. (1960 [1907]) 'A contribution to the study of the collective representation of death', *Death and the Right Hand*. London: Cohen & West, pp. 27–86.

Herzfeld, M. (2014) *Cultural Intimacy*. London: Routedge.

Hockey, J. (1996) 'The view from the West', in G. Howarth and P. Jupp (eds), *Contemporary Issues in the Sociology of Death, Dying and Disposal*. Basingstoke: Macmillan.

Høeg, I.M. (2019) 'Religious practices in the framework of ash scattering and contact with the dead', in P. Repstad (ed.), *Political Religion, Everyday Religion*. Leiden: Brill, pp. 67–83.

Hofstede, G. (2001) *Culture's Consequences: Comparing values, behaviours, institutions and organizations across nations*. Thousand Oaks, CA: Sage.

Hoggart, R. (1957) *The Uses of Literacy*. Harmondsworth: Penguin.

Holloway, M., Adamson, S., Argyrou, V., Draper, P. and Mariau, D. (2013) '"Funerals aren't nice but it couldn't have been nicer": the makings of a good funeral', *Mortality*, *18*: 30–53.

Holmes, S. (2008) 'Free-Marketeering', *London Review of Books*, 30.

Holst-Warhaft, G. (2000) *The Cue for Passion: Grief and its political uses*. Cambridge, MA: Harvard University Press.

Honeybun, J., Johnston, M. and Tookman, A. (1992) 'The impact of a death on fellow hospice patients', *British Journal of Medical Psychology*, *65*: 67–72.

Hooykaas, R. (1972) *Religion and the Rise of Modern Science*. London: Chatto & Windus.

Horsfall, D., Noonan, K. and Leonard, R. (2011) *Bringing Our Dying Home: Creating community at the end of life*. Sydney: University of Western Sydney.

Horsfield, P. (2015) *From Jesus to the Internet: A history of Christianity and media*. Chichester: Wiley Blackwell.

Howarth, G. (1996) *Last Rites: The work of the modern funeral director*. Amityville, NY: Baywood.

Hui, T.B. and Yeoh, B.S.A. (2002) 'The "remains of the dead": spatial politics of nation-building in post-war Singapore', *Human Ecology Review*, *9*: 1–13.

Hunter, A. (2016) 'Staking a claim to land, faith and family: burial location preferences of Middle Eastern Christian migrants', *Journal of Intercultural Studies*, *37*: 179–94.

Hunter, A. and Ammann, E.S. (2016) 'End-of-life care and rituals in contexts of post-migration diversity in Europe: an introduction', *Journal of Intercultural Studies*, *37*: 95–102.

Huntington, S.P. (1993) 'The clash of civilisations', *Foreign Affairs*, *72*: 22–49.

Hutchings, T. (2012) 'Wiring death: dying, grieving and remembering on the internet', in D. Davies and C-W. Park (eds), *Emotion, Identity and Death*. Aldershot: Ashgate, pp. 43–58.

Illich, I. (1976) *Limits to Medicine*. London: Marion Boyars.

Inglehart, R. (1981) 'Post-materialism in an environment of insecurity', *American Political Science Review*, *75*: 880–900.

Inglehart, R. and Baker, W.E. (2000) 'Modernization, cultural change, and the persistence of traditional values', *American Sociological Review*, *65*: 19–52.

Inglehart, R. and Welzel, C. (2005) *Modernization, Cultural Change and Democracy*. New York: Cambridge University Press.

Inglehart, R., Basanez, M. and Moreno, A. (1998) *Human Values and Beliefs: A cross-cultural sourcebook: political, religious, sexual and economic norms in 43 societies: findings from the 1990–1993 World Values Survey*. Ann Arbor, MI: University of Michigan Press.

Inglehart, R., Foa, R., Peterson, C. and Welzel, C. (2008) 'Development, freedom, and rising happiness: a global perspective (1981–2007)', *Perspectives on Psychological Science*, *3*: 264–85.

Inglis, T. (1998) *Moral Monopoly: The rise and fall of the Catholic Church in Ireland*. Dublin: University College Dublin Press.

Inglis, T. (2014) *Meanings of Life in Contemporary Ireland*. New York: Palgrave.

Jacobsen, M.H. (2016) '"Spectacular death": proposing a new fifth phase to Philippe Ariès's admirable history of death', *Humanities*, 5: 19.

Jakoby, N.R. (2012) 'Grief as a social emotion', *Death Studies*, 36: 679–711.

Jakoby, N.R. and Reiser, S. (2013) 'Grief 2.0: exploring virtual cemeteries', in T. Benski and E. Fisher (eds), *Internet and Emotions*. London: Routledge, pp. 65–79.

Jalland, P. (2010) *Death in War and Peace: A history of loss and grief in England, 1914–1970*. Oxford: Oxford University Press.

James, D. (2009) 'Burial sites, informal rights and lost kingdoms: contesting land claims in Mpumalanga, South Africa', *Africa*, 79: 228–51.

Jenkins, T. (2010) *Contesting Human Remains in Museum Collections: The crisis of cultural authority*. London: Routledge.

Jindra, M. and Noret, J. (2011) *Funerals in Africa: Explorations of a social phenomenon*. Oxford: Berghahn.

Johnson, M. (2016) 'Spirituality, biographical review and biographical pain at the end of life in old age', in M. Johnson and J. Walker (eds), *Spiritual Dimensions of Ageing*. Cambridge: Cambridge University Press, pp. 198–214.

Jolly, H. (1976) 'Family reactions to child bereavement', *Proceedings of the Royal Society of Medicine*, 69: 835–7.

Jones, B. (2000) 'Afterlife beliefs in a secular society'. Unpublished doctoral thesis, University of Reading.

Jones, G. (2018) *The Shock Doctrine of the Left*. Cambridge: Polity.

Jupp, P.C. (2006) *From Dust to Ashes: Cremation and the British way of death*. Basingstoke: Palgrave.

Jupp, P.C. and Gittings, C. (1999) *Death in England: An illustrated history*. Manchester: Manchester University Press.

Kabayama, K. (2012) 'The death and rebirth of society: the consequences of the Black Death and the Lisbon earthquake', in T. Ohtoshi and S. Shimazono (eds), *Commemorating the Dead in a Time of Global Crisis*. Tokyo: University of Tokyo.

Kalish, R. and Reynolds, D. (1981) *Death and Ethnicity: A psychocultural study*. Farmingdale, NY: Baywood.

Kang, J-M. (2014) 'Ask a North Korean: is religion allowed?', *Guardian*, 2 July.

Karapliagou, A. and Kellehear, A. (n.d.) *Public Health Approaches to End of Life Care: A toolkit*. London: Public Health England/National Council for Palliative Care.

Kasket, E. (2012) 'Continuing bonds in the age of social networking: Facebook as a modern-day medium', *Bereavement Care*, 31: 62–9.

Kasket, E. (2019) *All the Ghosts in the Machine: Illusions of immortality in the digital age*. London: Little, Brown.

Kastenbaum, R. (2007) *Death, Society and Human Experience* (9th edn). Boston, MA: Pearson.

Kaufman, S. (2005) *… and a Time to Die: How American hospitals shape the end of life*. Chicago, IL: University of Chicago University Press.

Kearl, M.C. (2010) 'The proliferation of postselves in American civic and popular cultures', *Mortality*, 15: 47–63.

Kellehear, A. (1984) 'Are we a death-denying society? A sociological review', *Social Science & Medicine*, *18*: 713–23.

Kellehear, A. (1990) *Dying of Cancer: The final years of life*. Chur: Harwood Academic.

Kellehear, A. (2005) *Compassionate Cities*. London: Routledge.

Kellehear, A. (2007) *A Social History of Dying*. Cambridge: Cambridge University Press.

Kellehear, A. (2014) *The Inner Life of the Dying Person*. New York: Columbia University Press.

Kellehear, A. (2016) 'Current social trends and challenges for the dying person', in N.R. Jakoby and M. Thönnes (eds), *Zur Soziologie des Sterbens*. Berlin: Springer, pp. 11–26.

Kelly S. (2015) *Greening Death: Reclaiming burial practices and restoring our tie to the earth*. Lanham, MD: Rowman & Littlefield.

Kelner, M. (1995) 'Activists and delegators: elderly patients' preferences about control at the end of life', *Social Science and Medicine*, *41*: 537–45.

Kerr, C., Dunlop, J.T., Harbison, F.H. and Myers, C.A. (1973) *Industrialism and Industrial Man*. Harmondsworth: Penguin.

Killikelly, C. and Maercker A. (2017) 'Prolonged grief disorder for ICD-11', *European Journal of Psychotraumatology*, 8.

King, A. (2010) 'The Afghan war and "postmodern" memory: commemoration and the dead of Helmand', *British Journal of Sociology*, *61*: 1–25.

King, R., Warnes, T. and Williams, A. (2000) *Sunset Lives: British retirement migration to the Mediterranean*. Oxford Berg.

Kjaersgaard Markussen, A. (2013) 'Death and the state of Denmark', in E. Venbrux, T. Quartier, C. Venhorst, and B. Mathijssen (eds) *Changing European Death Ways*. LIT Verlag: Münster, pp. 165–87.

Kjaersgaard, A. (2017) *Funerary Culture and the Limits of Secularization in Denmark*. Zurich: LIT Verlag.

Klass, D., Silverman, P.R. and Nickman, S.L. (1996) *Continuing Bonds: New understandings of grief*. Bristol, PA: Taylor & Francis.

Klein, N. (2008) *The Shock Doctrine: The rise of disaster capitalism*. London: Penguin.

Knight, F. (2018) 'Cremation and Christianity: English Anglican and Roman Catholic attitudes to cremation since 1885', *Mortality*, *23*: 301–19.

Knoeff, R. and Zwijnenberg, R. (2015) *The Fate of Anatomical Collections*. London: Routledge.

Komaromy, C. and Hockey, J. (2018) *Family Life, Trauma and Loss in the Twentieth Century: The legacy of war*. Basingstoke: Palgrave Macmillan.

Koslofsky, C. (2002) 'From presence to remembrance: the transformation of memory in the German Reformation', in A. Confino and P. Fritzche (eds), *The Work of Memory: New directions in the study of German society and culture*. Urbana, IL: University of Illinois Press.

Králová, J. (2019) 'Social death'. Doctoral thesis, University of Bath.

Kretchmer, A. (2000) 'Mortuary rites for inanimate objects', *Japanese Journal of Religious Studies*, *27*: 379–404.

Kselman, T. (1993) *Death and the Afterlife in Modern France*. Princeton, NJ: Princeton University Press.

Kübler-Ross, E. (1969) *On Death and Dying*. New York: Macmillan.

Kumar, S. (2007) 'Kerala, India: a regional community-based palliative care model', *Journal of Pain & Symptom Management, 33*: 623–7.

Kwon, H. (2008) 'The ghosts of war and the spirit of cosmopolitanism', *History of Religions, 48*: 22–42.

Lagerkvist, A. (2017) 'Existential media: toward a theorization of digital thrownness', *New Media & Society, 19*: 96–110.

Lagerkvist, A. and Andersson, Y. (2017) 'The grand interruption: death online and mediated lifelines of shared vulnerability', *Feminist Media Studies, 17*: 550–64.

Lane, C. (1981) *The Rites of Rulers: Ritual in industrial society – the Soviet case*. Cambridge: Cambridge University Press.

Latour, B. (2003) 'Is re-modernization occurring – and if so, how to prove it? A commentary on Ulrich Beck', *Theory, Culture & Society, 20*: 35–48.

Lennon, J. and Foley, M. (2000) *Dark Tourism: The attraction of death and disaster*. London: Continuum.

Leong, C. (2018) '"Too busy, too much pressure": an ageing China and the erosion of filial piety', *Hong Kong Free Press*, 15 April.

Leslie, J. (1991) 'Suttee or Sati: victim or victor?', in J. Leslie (ed.), *Roles and Rituals for Hindu Women*. London: Pinter, pp. 175–91.

Levine, S. (1988) *Who Dies? An investigation of conscious living and conscious dying*. Bath: Gateway.

Lim, C. (2018) 'Death spaces and death practice in the Klang Valley, Malaysia'. Doctoral thesis, Monash University, Malaysia.

Lin, M. (2000) 'Grounds for remembering: monuments, memorials, texts'. Berkeley, CA: Occasional Papers of the Doreen B. Townsend Center for the Humanities, no. 3, pp. 8–14.

Linnenthal, E.T. (2001) *The Unfinished Bombing: Oklahoma City in American memory*. New York: Oxford University Press.

Lipset, S.M. (1955) *The First New Nation*. New York: Basic Books.

Liu, H.L. (2015) 'Dying socialist in capitalist Shanghai'. Doctoral thesis, Boston University.

Livne, R. (2014) 'Economies of dying: the moralization of economic scarcity in U.S. hospice care', *American Sociological Review, 79*: 888–911.

Lofland, L. (1978) *The Craft of Dying: The modern face of death*. Beverly Hills, CA: Sage.

Lofland, L. (1985) 'The social shaping of emotion: the case of grief', *Symbolic Interaction, 8*: 171–90.

Long, S.O. (2004) 'Cultural scripts for the good death in Japan and the United States: similarities and differences', *Social Science and Medicine, 58*: 913–28.

Long, S.O. (2005) *Final Days: Japanese culture and choice at the end of life*. Honolulu, HI: University of Hawaii Press.

Loudon, J.C. (1981 [1843]) *On the Laying Out, Planting, and Managing of Cemeteries and on the Improvement of Churchyards*. Redhill: Ivelet Books.

Lukhele, A. (2013) 'Stokvels, Death and Society'. Unpublished manuscript, South Africa.

Lynn, J. (2016) *MediCaring Communities: Getting what we want and need in frail old age at an affordable price*. Scotts Valley, CA: CreateSpace.

Lynn, J. and Adamson, D.M. (2003) *Living Well at the End of Life: Adapting health care to serious chronic illness in old age*. Santa Monica, CA: Rand.

Macfarlane, A. (1978) *The Origins of English Individualism*. Oxford: Blackwell.

Macpherson, C.B. (1962) *The Political Theory of Possessive Individualism*. Oxford: Clarendon.

Makary, M. and Daniel, M. (2016) 'Medical error – the third leading cause of death in the US', *British Medical Journal*, 353.

Małecka, K. (2012) '*Medical, spiritual, and cultural aspects of grief and mourning in modern bereavement memoirs*'. Paper presented at the 12th International Conference on the Social Context of Death, Dying and Disposal, Alba Iulia, Romania.

Malinowski, B. (1925) *Magic, Science and Religion*. London: Macmillan.

Mantei, C. (2012) *Le Tourisme de Mémoire en France*. Paris: Atout France.

Marris, P. (1958) *Widows and Their Families*. London: Routledge.

Marris, P. (1974) *Loss and Change*. London: Routledge.

Marshall, M. (1981) *Last Chapters: A sociology of ageing and dying*. Monterey, CA: Books/Cole.

Martin, B. (1981) *A Sociology of Contemporary Cultural Change*. Oxford: Blackwell.

Martin, D. (1978) *A General Theory of Secularization*. Oxford: Blackwell.

Martin, D. (1990) *Tongues of Fire: The explosion of Protestantism in Latin America*. Oxford: Blackwell.

Maruyama, T.C. (1997) 'The Japanese pilgrimage: not begun', *International Journal of Palliative Nursing*, 3: 87–91.

Marvin, C. and Ingle, D. (1999) *Blood Sacrifice and the Nation: Totem rituals and the American flag*. Cambridge: Cambridge University Press.

Marzano, M. (2009) 'Lies and pain: patients and caregivers in the "conspiracy of silence"', *Journal of Loss and Trauma*, 14: 57–81.

Maslow, A. (1954) *Motivation and Personality*. New York: Harper.

Masuzawa, T. (2005) *The Invention of World Religions*. Chicago, IL: University of Chicago Press.

Mathews, G. (2013) 'Death and "the pursuit of a life worth living" in Japan', in H. Suzuki (ed.), *Death and Dying in Contemporary Japan*. London: Routledge, pp. 33–48.

Maxwell, D. (1998) '"Delivered from the spirit of poverty"? Pentecostalism, prosperity and modernity in Zimbabwe', *Journal of Religion in Africa*, 28: 350–73.

Mbiti, J.S. (1970) *African Religions and Philosophies*. Garden City, NY: Doubleday.

McCormick, L. (2015) 'The agency of dead musicians', *Contemporary Social Science*, 10: 323–35.

McGuire, M. (2008) *Lived Religion: Faith and practice in everyday life*. Oxford: Oxford University Press.

McIlwain, C.D. (2005) *When Death Goes Pop: Death media and the remaking of community*. New York: Peter Lang.

McManus, R. (2013) *Death in a Global Age*. Basingstoke: Palgrave Macmillan.

Mellor, P. and Shilling, C. (1993) 'Modernity, self-identity and the sequestration of death', *Sociology* 27: 411–31.

Menzfeld, M. (2017) 'When the dying do not feel tabooed: perspectives of the terminally ill in Western Germany', *Mortality*, 22: 308–23.

Merridale, C. (2000) *Night of Stone: Death and memory in Russia*. London: Granta.

Meyer, J.W., Boli, J., Thomas, G.M. and Ramirez, F.O. (1997) 'World society and the nation-state', *American Journal of Sociology*, 103: 144–81.

Miah, A. and Rich, E. (2008) *The Medicalization of Cyberspace*. London: Routledge.

Miller, D. (2017) *The Comfort of People*. Cambridge: Polity.

Miller, D., Haynes, N., McDonald, T., Nicolescu, R., Sinanan, J., Spyer, J., Venkatraman, S. and Xinyuan Wang (2016) *How the World Changed Social Media*. London: UCL Press.

Miner, H. (1956) 'Body ritual among the Nacirema', *The American Anthropologist*, *58*: 503–7.

Mishra, A., Ghate, R., Maharjan, A., Gurung, J., Pathak, G. and Upraity, A.N. (2017) 'Building ex ante resilience of disaster-exposed mountain communities: drawing insights from the Nepal earthquake recovery', *International Journal of Disaster Risk Reduction, 22*: 167–78.

Mitford, J. (1963) *The American Way of Death*. London: Hutchinson.

Mitscherlich, A. and Mitscherlich, M. (1975 [1967]) *The Inability to Mourn*. New York: Grove Press.

Mokhov, S. and Sokolova, A. (in press) 'Broken infrastructure and soviet modernity: the funeral market in Russia', *Mortality*.

Moore, J. (1980) 'The death culture of Mexico and Mexican Americans', in R. Kalish (ed.), *Death and Dying: Views from many cultures*. Farmingdale, NY: Baywood, 72–91.

Moreman, C. (2018) *Beyond the Threshold: Afterlife beliefs and experiences in world religions* (2nd edn). Lanham MD: Rowman and Littlefield.

Morgan, D. (2011) *Rethinking Family Practices*. Basingstoke: Palgrave Macmillan.

Morris, Z.A. (2017) 'Review of Schrecker & Bambra "How politics makes us sick"', *People, Place and Policy, 11*: 125–7.

Mouffe, C. (2005) *On the Political*. London: Routledge.

Mount, F. (1982) *The Subversive Family*. London: Cape.

Mouzelis, N. (2012) 'Modernity and the secularization debate', *Sociology, 46*: 207–23.

Murray, S.A. and McLoughlin, P. (2012) 'Illness trajectories and palliative care', in L. Sallnow, S. Kumar and A. Kellehear (eds), *International Perspectives on Public Health and Palliative Care*. London: Routledge, pp. 30–51.

Nash, D. (2013) *Christian Ideals in British Culture: Stories of belief in the twentieth century*. Basingstoke: Palgrave Macmillan.

Natali, C. (2008) 'Building cemeteries, constructing identities: funerary practices and nationalist discourse among the Tamil Tigers of Sri Lanka', *Contemporary South Asia, 16*: 287–301.

National Academies of Sciences, Engineering and Medicine (2015) *The Integration of Immigrants into American Society*. Washington, DC: National Academies Press.

Neimeyer, R., Klass, D. and Dennis, M.R. (2014) 'A social constructionist account of grief: loss and the narration of meaning', *Death Studies, 38*: 485–98.

Nelson, G.K. (1969) *Spiritualism and Society*. London: Routledge & Kegan Paul.

Northcott, H.C. and Wilson, D.M. (2008) *Dying and Death in Canada*. Toronto: University of Toronto Press.

Norwood, F. (2007) 'Nothing more to do: euthanasia, general practice, and end-of-life discourse in the Netherlands', *Medical Anthropology, 26*: 139–74.

Norwood, F. (2009) *The Maintenance of Life: Preventing social death through euthanasia talk and end-of-life care – lessons from the Netherlands*. Durham, NC: Carolina Academic Press.

Noys, B. (2005) *The Culture of Death*. Oxford: Berg.

Ong, W.J. (2012) *Orality and Literacy: The technologizing of the word*. London: Routledge.

Ostaseski, F. (1990) 'Living with the dying', *Inquiring Mind*, *6*: 8–11.

Pajari, I. (2015) 'Soldier's death and the logic of sacrifice', *Collegium*, *19*: 179–201.

Park, C-W. (2010) 'Between God and ancestors: ancestral practice in Korean Protestantism', *International Journal for the Study of the Christian Church*, *10*: 257–73.

Parker Pearson, M. (1999) *The Archaeology of Death and Burial*. Stroud: Sutton Publishing.

Parkes, C.M. (1988) 'Bereavement as a psychosocial transition', *Journal of Social Issues*, *44*: 53–65.

Parkes, C.M. (2008) *Love and Loss: The roots of grief and its complications*. London: Routledge.

Parkes, C.M., Laungani, P. and Young, B. (2015) *Death and Bereavement Across Cultures* (2nd edn). London: Routledge.

Parsons, T. (1966) *Societies: Evolutionary and comparative perspectives*. Englewood Cliffs, NJ: Prentice-Hall.

Parsons, T. and Lidz, V. (1963) 'Death in American society', in E. Shneidman (ed.), *Essays in Self-Destruction*. New York: Science House, pp. 133–70.

Patterson, O. (1982) *Slavery and Social Death*. Cambridge, MA: Harvard University Press.

Pavicevic, A. (2009) 'Death in a foreign land: entering and exiting the Serbian emigrant's world', in U. Brunnbauer (ed.), *Transnational Societies, Transterritorial Politics, and Migrations in the (Post)Yugoslav Area 19th–21st Century*. Munich: Oldenbourg Verlag, pp. 235–48.

Pavicevic, A. (2015) *From Mystery to Spectacle: Essays on death in Serbia from the 19th–21st century*. Belgrade: Serbian Academy of Sciences & Arts, Institute of Ethnography.

Pennington, N. (2013) 'You don't de-friend the dead: an analysis of grief communication by college students through Facebook profiles', *Death Studies*, *37*: 617–35.

Pentaris, P. (2018) 'The marginalization of religion in end of life care', *International Journal of Human Rights in Healthcare*, 11.

Perl, G. (2016) 'Uncertain belongings: absent mourning, burial, and post-mortem repatriations at the external border of the EU in Spain', *Journal of Intercultural Studies*, *37*: 195–209.

Perl, G. and Strasser, S. (2018) 'Transnational moralities: the politics of ir/responsibility of and against the EU border regime', *Identities*, *25*: 507–23.

Peters, J. (1999) *Speaking into the Air: A history of the idea of communication*. Chicago, IL: Chicago University Press.

Phillips, M.M. (2006) 'In Madagascar, digging up the dead divides families', *Wall Street Journal*, 10 October.

Phillips, W. (2011) 'LOLing at tragedy: Facebook trolls, memorial pages and resistance to grief online', *First Monday*, 16.

Pickett, K. and Wilkinson, R. (2015) 'Income inequality and health: a causal review', *Social Science and Medicine*, *128*: 316–26.

Pinchevski, A. (2016) 'Screen trauma: visual media and post-traumatic stress disorder', *Theory, Culture & Society*, *33*: 51–75.

Pine, V.R. (1975) *Caretaker of the Dead: The American funeral director*. New York: Irvington.

Pinker, S. (2012) *The Better Angels of Our Nature: Why violence has declined*. London: Penguin.

Plokhy, S. (2018) *Chernobyl: History of a tragedy*. London: Allen Lane.

Pollock, K. and Seymour, J. (2018) 'Reappraising "the good death" for populations in the age of ageing', *Age & Ageing*, *47*(3): 328–30.

Power, M. (1997) *The Audit Society*. Oxford: Oxford University Press.

Prior, L. (1997) 'Actuarial visions of death: life, death and chance in the modern world', in P.C. Jupp and G. Howarth (eds), *The Changing Face of Death*. Basingstoke: Macmillan.

Prior, L. and Bloor, M. (1992) 'Why people die: social representations of death and its causes', *Science as Culture*, 3: 346–74.

Prothero, S. (2000) *Purified by Fire: A history of cremation in America*. Berkeley, CA: University of California Press.

Quereshi, H. and Walker, A. (1989) *The Caring Relationship: Elderly people and their families*. London: Macmillan.

Raun, T. (2017) '*Vulnerability and emotional self-management in relation to mourning online.*' Paper presented at Digital Existence II Conference, Sigtuna, Sweden.

Reader, I. (2012) 'Secularisation, R.I.P.? Nonsense! The "rush hour away from the gods" and the decline of religion in contemporary Japan', *Journal of Religion in Japan*, 1: 7–36.

Reimers, E. (1999) 'Death and identity: graves and funerals as cultural communication', *Mortality*, 4: 147–66.

Ribbens McCarthy, J., Evans, R., Bowlby, S. and Wouango, J. (2018) 'Making sense of family deaths in urban Senegal', *OMEGA – Journal of Death and Dying*, 25 October.

Richardson, R. (1989) *Death, Dissection and the Destitute*. London: Penguin.

Riches, G. and Dawson, P. (1998) 'Lost children, living memories: the role of photographs in processes of grief and adjustment amongst bereaved parents', *Death Studies*, 22: 121–40.

Riches, G. and Dawson, P. (2000) *An Intimate Loneliness: Supporting bereaved parents and siblings*. Buckingham: Open University Press.

Riesman, D. (1950) *The Lonely Crowd*. New Haven, CT: Yale University Press.

Riley, J. (2001) *Rising Life Expectancy: a global history*. Cambridge: Cambridge University Press.

Rinpoche, S. (1992) *The Tibetan Book of Living and Dying*. London: Rider.

Ritzer, G. (2018) *The McDonaldization of Society* (9th edn). Thousand Oaks, CA: Sage.

Ritzer, G. and Dean, P. (2015) *Globalization: A basic text* (2nd edn). Oxford: Wiley-Blackwell.

Roberts, P. (2004) 'The living and the dead: community in the virtual cemetery', *Omega*, 49: 57–76.

Robertson, R. (1995) 'Glocalization: time-space and homogeneity-heterogeneity', in M. Featherstone, S. Lash and R. Robertson (eds), *Global Modernities*. London: Sage, pp. 25–44.

Robson, P. and Walter, T. (2012–13) 'Hierarchies of loss: a critique of disenfranchised grief', *Omega*, 66: 97–119.

Romo, R.D., Allison, T.A., Smith, A.K. and Wallhagen, M.I. (2017) 'Sense of control in end-of-life decision-making', *Journal of the American Geriatrics Society*, 65: e70–e75.

Rosa, H. (2015) *Social Acceleration: A new theory of modernity*. New York: Columbia University Press.

Rosenblatt, P. (1983) *Bitter, Bitter Tears: Nineteenth-century diarists and twentieth-century grief theories*. Minneapolis, MN: University of Minnesota Press.

Rosenblatt, P., Walsh, P. and Jackson, D. (1976) *Grief and Mourning in Cross-Cultural Perspective*. Washington, DC: Human Relations Area Files Press.

Rotar, M. (2015) 'Attitudes towards cremation in contemporary Romania', *Mortality*, 20: 145–62.

Rowe, M. (2007) 'The Buddhist dead', in B.J. Cuevas and J.I. Stone (eds), *Grave Changes: Scattering ashes in contemporary Japan*. Honolulu, HI: University of Hawai'i Press, pp. 405–37.

Royal College of Physicians (2018) 'Talking about dying: how to begin honest conversations about what lies ahead', 19 October. Available at www.rcplondon.ac.uk/projects/outputs/talking-about-dying-how-begin-honest-conversations-about-what-lies-ahead (accessed 5/6/19).

Rugg, J. (1997) 'The emergence of cemetery companies in Britain', in P. Jupp and G. Howarth (eds), *The Changing Face of Death*. Basingstoke: Macmillan, pp. 105–19.

Ryan, S. (2016) *Death and the Irish: A miscellany*. Dublin: Wordwell.

Sahlins, M. (1974) 'The original affluent society', *Ecologist*, 4: 181–90.

Samuel, L.R. (2013) *Death, American Style: A cultural history of dying in America*. Lanham, MD: Rowman & Littlefield.

Santhosh, R. (2016) 'Voluntarism and civil society in the neoliberal era: a study on the palliative care movement in Kerala', *Journal of Social and Economic Development*, 18: 1–16.

Santino, J. (2006) *Spontaneous Shrines and the Public Memorialization of Death*. Basingstoke: Palgrave Macmillan.

Scheffler, S. and Kolodny, N. (2013) *Death and the Afterlife*. New York: Oxford University Press.

Scheper-Hughes, N. (1990) 'Mother love and child death in northeast Brazil', in J. Stigler, A. Shweder, and G. Herdt (eds), *Cultural Psychology*. Cambridge: Cambridge University Press.

Schrecker, T. and Bambra, C. (2015) *How Politics Makes Us Sick: Neoliberal epidemics*. Basingstoke: Palgrave Macmillan.

Schwartz, B. (1991) 'Mourning and the making of a sacred symbol: Durkheim and the Lincoln assassination', *Social Forces*, 70: 343–64.

Schwartz, S.H. (2006) 'A theory of cultural value orientations', *Comparative Sociology*, 5: 137–82.

Schwiter, K., Brütsch, J. and Pratt, G. (in press) 'Sending granny to Chiang Mai: debating global outsourcing of care for the elderly', *Global Networks*.

Seabrook, J. (2008) 'The living dead of capitalism', *Race & Class*, 49: 19–32.

Seale, C. (1998) *Constructing Death: The sociology of dying and bereavement*. Cambridge: Cambridge University Press.

Seale, C. (2000) 'Changing patterns of death and dying', *Social Science & Medicine*, 49: 917–30.

Shalamov, V. (1994) 'Dry Rations' in *Kolyma Tales*. London: Penguin, pp. 31-47.

Sharma, B.K. (2011) 'Funerary rites in Nepal: cremation, burial and Christian identity'. Doctoral thesis, University of Wales / Oxford Centre for Mission Studies.

Shelley, M. (2010 [1818]) *Frankenstein*. London: Collins.

Simmons, L.W. (1945) *The Role of the Aged in Primitive Society*. New Haven, CT: Yale University Press.

Sloane, D.C. (2018) *Is the Cemetery Dead?* Chicago, IL: University of Chicago Press.

Smart, C. (2007) *Personal Life*. Cambridge: Polity.

Smith, H. (2005) 'What costs will democracies bear? A review of popular theories of casualty aversion', *Armed Forces & Society*, 31: 487–512.

Smyth, C. (2018) 'Life expectancy falls by a year in some regions of England', *The Times*, 17 January.

Socialstyrelsen (2017) 'Vård och omsorg om äldre: Lägesrapport' [Care of the elderly: progress report]. Available at www.socialstyrelsen.se/Lists/Artikelkatalog/Attachments/20469/2017-2-2.pdf (accessed 9/3/19).

Solnit, R. (2009) *A Paradise Built in Hell: The extraordinary communities that arise in disaster.* New York: Viking.

Solomon, S., Greenberg, J. and Pyszczynski, T. (2015) *The Worm at the Core: On the role of death in life.* London: Penguin.

Standing, G. (2011) *The Precariat: The new dangerous class.* London: Bloomsbury.

Steadman, L.B., Palmer, C.T. and Tilley, C.F. (1996) 'The universality of ancestor worship', *Ethnology, 35*: 63–76.

Steffen, E.M. and Klass, D. (2018) 'Culture, contexts and connections: a conversation with Dennis Klass about his life and work as a bereavement scholar', *Mortality, 23*: 203–14.

Steffen, W., Broadgate, W., Deutsch, L., Gaffney, O. and Ludwig, C. (2015) 'The trajectory of the Anthropocene: the great acceleration', *The Anthropocene Review, 2.*

Sterne, J. (2003) *The Audible Past: Cultural origins of sound reproduction.* Durham, NC: Duke University Press.

Stierl, M. (2016) 'Contestations in death: the role of grief in migration struggles', *Citizenship Studies, 20*: 173–91.

Strathern, M. (1992) *After Nature: English kinship in the late twentieth century.* Cambridge: Cambridge University Press.

Stringer, M.D. (2008) 'Chatting with gran at her grave', in P. Cruchley-Jones (ed.), *God at Ground Level.* Oxford: Peter Lang, pp. 23–39.

Stroebe, M. and Schut, H. (1999) 'The dual process model of coping with bereavement', *Death Studies, 23*: 197–224.

Stroebe, M., Gergen, M.M., Gergen, K.J. and Stroebe, W. (1992) 'Broken hearts or broken bonds: love and death in historical perspective', *American Psychologist, 47*: 1205–12.

Stroebe, M. and Schut, H. (2008) 'The dual process model of coping with bereavement: overview and update', *Grief Matters, 11* (1): 4–10.

Stuckler, D. and Basu, S. (2013) *The Body Economic: Why austerity kills.* London: Allen Lane.

Sudnow, D. (1967) *Passing On: The social organization of dying.* Englewood Cliffs, NJ: Prentice Hall.

Sumiala, J. (2013) *Media and Ritual: Death, community and everyday life.* London: Routledge.

Taylor, L. (1983) *Mourning Dress: A costume and social history.* London: Allen & Unwin.

Te Awekotuku, N. and Nikora, L.W. (2007) *Mau Moko: The world of Māori tattoo.* Rosedale, NZ: Penguin.

Teggi, D. (2018) 'Unexpected death in ill old age: an analysis of disadvantaged dying in the English old population', *Social Science and Medicine, 217*: 112–20.

Thaxton, R. (2008) *Catastrophe and Contention in Rural China: Mao's Great Leap Forward, famine and the origins of righteous resistance in Da Fo Village.* New York: Cambridge University Press.

Therborn, G. (2013) *The Killing Fields of Inequality.* Oxford: Polity.

Timm, H. (2018) 'It seems people don't fear death, as much as they fear the process of dying', *Discover Society, 53.*

Tinker, B. (2017) 'US life expectancy drops for second year in a row', *CNN,* 22 December.

Titmuss, R.M. (1970) *The Gift Relationship: From human blood to social policy.* London: Allen & Unwin.

Todd, E. (2019) *Lineages of Modernity: A history of humanity from the Stone Age to Homo Americanus.* Cambridge: Polity.

Tong, C-K. (2004) *Chinese Death Rituals in Singapore*. London: Routledge.

Tori (2014) 'How much do you know about Nepali Christian traditions?', *Field Notes*, 28 January. Available at http://tori-fieldnotes.blogspot.co.uk/2014/01/how-much-do-you-know-about-nepali.html (accessed 5/6/19).

Torrie, M. (1987) *My Years with CRUSE*. Richmond: CRUSE.

Toulson, R. (2015) 'Being a corpse the Buddhist way: scenes from a Singaporean Chinese mortuary', USC US-China Institute, 21 April. Available at https://china.usc.edu/calendar/being-corpse-buddhist-way-scenes-singaporean-chinese-mortuary (accessed 5/6/19).

Townsend, P. (1964) *The Last Refuge*. London: Routledge.

Toynbee, A. (1968) *Man's Concern with Death*. London: Hodder.

Trabsky, M. (2017) '*The dead records office*'. Paper presented at CDAS conference Death at the Margins of the State, University of Bath, 9–10 June.

Tsintjilonis, D. (2007) 'The death-bearing senses in Tana Toraja', *Ethnos*, 72: 173–94.

Tsuji, Y. (2002) 'Death policies in Japan: the state, the family, and the individual', in R. Goodman (ed.), *Family and Social Policy in Japan*. Cambridge: Cambridge University Press, pp. 177–99.

Tuan, Y-F. (1974) *Tophophilia: A study of environmental perception, attitudes and values*. New York: Columbia University Press.

Turner, B.S. (1990) 'The two faces of sociology: global or national?', in M. Featherstone (ed.), *Global Culture*. London: Sage, pp. 343–58.

Turner, M. and Peacock, M. (2017) 'Palliative care in UK prisons', *Journal of Correctional Health*, 23: 56–65.

Turner, V. (1974) *The Ritual Process*. London: Penguin.

Ulmanen, P. (2015) 'Kvinnors och mäns hjälp till sina gamla föräldrar [Women's and men's filial care]', *Socialvetenskaplig Tidskrift*, 2: 111–32.

United Nations (2017) *World Mortality 2017*. New York: United Nations Population Division.

Valentine, C. (2018) *Families Bereaved by Alcohol or Drugs*. London: Routledge.

Valentine, C. and Woodthorpe, K. (2014) 'From the cradle to the grave: funeral welfare from an international perspective', *Social Policy & Administration*, 48: 515–36.

van der Geest, S. (2000) 'Funerals for the living: conversations with elderly people in Kwahu, Ghana', *African Studies Review*, 43: 103–29.

van der Loo, H. and Willem, V.R. (1997) *Modernisierung: Projekt und paradox*. Munich: DTV.

van der Pijl, Y. (2016) 'Death in the family revisited: ritual expression and controversy in a Creole transnational mortuary sphere', *Ethnography*, 17: 147–67.

van Heijst, A. (2011) *Professional Loving Care: An ethical view of the health care sector*. Leuven: Peeters.

Vázquez, D.G. (2018) 'Dark tourism and memorial tourism', *European Journal of Tourism Research*, 20: 46–58.

Verdery, K. (1999) *The Political Lives of Dead Bodies: Reburial and postsocialist change*. New York: Columbia University Press.

Vijay, D. (2018) 'Being mortal', *Discover Society*, 53.

Vitebsky, P. (2008) 'Loving and forgetting: moments of inarticulacy in tribal India', *Journal of the Royal Anthropological Institute (N.S.)*, 14: 243–61.

Wagner-Pacifici, R. and Schwartz, B. (1991) 'The Vietnam Veterans Memorial: commemorating a difficult past', *American Journal of Sociology*, 97: 376–420.

Walklate, S., Mythen, G. and McGarry, R. (2011) 'Witnessing Wootton Bassett', *Crime Media Culture*, 7: 149–65.

Walter, T. (1985) *All You Love is Need*. London: SPCK.

Walter, T. (1990) *Funerals and How to Improve Them*. Sevenoaks: Hodder & Stoughton.

Walter, T. (1993a) 'Dust not ashes: the American preference for burial', *Landscape*, 32: 42–8.

Walter, T. (1993b) 'War grave pilgrimage', in I. Reader and T. Walter (eds), *Pilgrimage in Popular Culture*. Basingstoke: Macmillan, pp. 63–91.

Walter, T. (1995) 'Natural death and the noble savage', *Omega*, 30: 237–48.

Walter, T. (1996) *The Eclipse of Eternity: A sociology of the afterlife*. Basingstoke: Macmillan.

Walter, T. (1999a) 'A death in our street', *Health and Place*, 5: 119–24.

Walter, T. (1999b) *On Bereavement: The culture of grief*. Buckingham: Open University Press.

Walter, T. (2005) 'Three ways to arrange a funeral: mortuary variation in the modern West', *Mortality*, 10: 173–92.

Walter, T. (2010) 'Grief and culture', *Bereavement Care*, 29: 5–9.

Walter, T. (2015a) 'Communication media and the dead: from the Stone Age to Facebook', *Mortality*, 20: 215–32.

Walter, T. (2015b) 'New mourners, old mourners: online memorial culture as a chapter in the history of mourning', *New Review of Hypermedia & Multimedia* 21.

Walter, T. (2016) 'The dead who become angels: bereavement and vernacular religion', *Omega*, 73: 3–28.

Walter, T. (2017a) 'How the dead survive: ancestor, immortality, memory', in M.H. Jacobsen (ed.), *Postmortal Society*. Farnham: Ashgate, pp. 19–39.

Walter, T. (2017b) *What Death Means Now: Thinking critically about dying and grieving*. Bristol: Policy Press.

Walter, T. (2018) 'The pervasive dead', *Mortality*. Available at www.tandfonline.com/doi/full/10.1080/13576275.2017.1415317 (accessed 5/6/19).

Walter, T. and Bailey, T. (in press) 'How funerals accomplish family: findings from a Mass-Observation study', *Omega*.

Walter, T. and Waterhouse, H. (1999) 'A very private belief: reincarnation in contemporary England', *Sociology of Religion*, 60: 187–97.

Walter, T., Hourizi, R., Moncur, W. and Pitsillides, S. (2011–12) 'Does the internet change how we die and mourn?', *Omega*, 64: 275–302.

Wambach, J.A. (1985) 'The grief process as a social construct', *Omega*, 16: 201–11.

Warner, W.L. (1959) *The Living and the Dead: A study of the symbolic life of Americans*. New Haven, CT: Yale University Press.

Watson, J.L. (1982) 'Of flesh and bones: the management of death pollution in Cantonese society', in M. Bloch and J. Parry (eds), *Death and the Regeneration of Life*. Cambridge: Cambridge University Press, pp. 155–86.

Watson, J.L. and Rawski, E.S. (1988) *Death Ritual in Late Imperial and Modern China*. Berkeley, CA: University of California Press.

Waugh, E. (1948) *The Loved One: An Anglo-American tragedy*. New York: Little, Brown.

Weber, M. (1930) *The Protestant Ethic and the Spirit of Capitalism*. London: Allen & Unwin.

Whitley, J. (2002) 'Too many ancestors?', *Antiquity*, 76: 119–26.

Whoriskey, P. and Keating, D. (2014) 'Dying and profits: the evolution of hospice', *Washington Post*, 26 December.

Whyte, M.K. (1988) 'Death in the People's Republic of China', in J.L. Watson and E.S. Rawski (eds), *Death Ritual in Late Imperial and Modern China*. Berkeley, CA: University of California Press, pp. 289–316.

Wikan, U. (1988) 'Bereavement and loss in two Muslim communities: Egypt and Bali compared', *Social Science & Medicine*, 27: 451–60.

Wilkinson, A. (1978) *The Church of England and the First World War*. London: SPCK.

Wilkinson, R. and Pickett, K. (2009) *The Spirit Level: Why equality is better for everyone*. London: Allen Lane.

Williams, P. (2007) *Memorial Museums: The global rush to commemorate atrocities*. Oxford: Berg.

Wilson, J. (2009) *Mourning the Unborn Dead: A Buddhist ritual comes to America*. New York: Oxford University Press.

Wilson, J. (2017) 'A mixed method, psychosocial analysis of how senior health care professionals recognise dying and engage patients and families in the negotiation of key decisions'. Doctoral thesis, University of Bath.

Winter, J. (1995) *Sites of Memory, Sites of Mourning: The Great War in European cultural history*. Cambridge: Cambridge University Press.

Witte, J. (2013) '"God is hidden in the earthly kingdom": the Lutheran two-kingdoms theory as foundation of Scandinavian secularity', in J. Casanova, T. Wyller and R. van den Breemer (eds), *Secular and Sacred? The Nordic case of religion in human rights, law and public space*. Göttingen: Vandenhoeck & Ruprecht, pp. 56–84.

Woodhead, L. (2012) 'Mind, body and spirit: it's the de-reformation of religion', *Guardian*, 7 May.

Woodhead, L. and Brown, A. (2016) *That Was the Church That Was: How the Church of England lost the English people*. London: Bloomsbury.

Woodthorpe, K. and Rumble, H. (2016) 'Funerals and families', *British Journal of Sociology*, 67: 242–59.

Worden, J.W. (2003) *Grief Counselling and Grief Therapy*. Philadelphia, PA: Brunner-Routledge.

World Bank (2013) *Risk and Opportunity: Managing risk for development* (World Development Report 2014). Washington, DC: World Bank.

World Health Organization (2019) *International Classification of Diseases* (11th edn). Geneva: WHO.

Wortman, C.B. and Silver, R.C. (1989) 'The myths of coping with loss', *Journal of Consulting & Clinical Psychology*, 57: 349–57.

Yamazaki, H. (2008) '*Rethinking good death: insights from a case analysis of a Japanese medical comic*'. Paper presented at University of Oxford: Uehiro-Carnegie-Oxford Conference on Medical Ethics, 11–12 December.

Yeoh, B.S.A. and Kong, L. (2003) 'Making space for the dead in the body of the living nation', in L. Kong and B.S.A. Yeoh (eds), *The Politics of Landscapes in Singapore*. New York: Syracuse University Press, pp. 51–74.

Young, L. (1997) *Rational Choice Theory of Religion*. London: Routledge.

Zaman, S., Ahmed, N., Ur Rashid, M. and Jahan, F. (2017a) 'Palliative care for slum populations: a case from Bangladesh', *European Journal of Palliative Care*, *24* (4): 156–60.

Zaman, S., Inbadas, H., Whitelaw, A. and Clark, D. (2017b) 'Common or multiple futures for end of life care around the world?', *Social Science and Medicine*, *172*: 72–9.

Zaman, S., Whitelaw, A., Richards, N., Inbadas, H. and Clark, D. (2018) 'A moment for compassion: emerging rhetorics in end-of-life care', *Medical Humanities*, *44*: 140–3.

Zivkovic, T. (2017) '*The magical thinking in advance care plans*'. Paper presented at the 13th International Conference on the Social Context of Death, Dying and Disposal, Preston, Lancashire.

Zivkovic, T. (2018) 'Forecasting and foreclosing futures: the temporal dissonance of advance care directives', *Social Science and Medicine*, 215.

Zuckerman, P. (2008) *Society without God: What the least religious nations can tell us about contentment*. New York: New York University Press.

INDEX

Page numbers in **bold** indicate tables and in *italic* indicate figures.